Public Relations Cases

Public Relations Cases

NINTH EDITION

DARRELL C. HAYES
American University

JERRY A. HENDRIX
American University

PALLAVI D. KUMAR
American University

WADSWORTH
CENGAGE Learning·

Australia • Brazil • Japan • Korea • Mexico • Singapore • Spain • United Kingdom • United States

WADSWORTH
CENGAGE Learning·

Public Relations Cases, Ninth Edition, International Edition

Darrell C. Hayes, Jerry A. Hendrix and Pallavi D. Kumar

Senior Publisher: Lyn Uhl

Publisher: Michael Rosenberg

Assistant Editor: Erin Bosco

Editorial Assistant: Rebecca Donahue

Media Editor: Jessica Badiner

Marketing Program Manager: Gurpreet Saran

Production Management and Composition: PreMediaGlobal

Manufacturing Planner: Doug Bertke

Rights Acquisition Specialist: Mandy Groszko

Cover Image: George Doyle

International Edition:

ISBN-13: 978-1-111-83682-5

ISBN-10: 1-111-83682-5

Cengage Learning International Offices

Asia
www.cengageasia.com
tel: (65) 6410 1200

Brazil
www.cengage.com.br
tel: (55) 11 3665 9900

Latin America
www.cengage.com.mx
tel: (52) 55 1500 6000

Australia/New Zealand
www.cengage.com.au
tel: (61) 3 9685 4111

India
www.cengage.co.in
tel: (91) 11 4364 1111

UK/Europe/Middle East/Africa
www.cengage.co.uk
tel: (44) 0 1264 332 424

Represented in Canada by Nelson Education, Ltd.
www.nelson.com
tel: (416) 752 9100 / (800) 668 0671

Cengage Learning is a leading provider of customized learning solutions with office locations around the globe, including Singapore, the United Kingdom, Australia, Mexico, Brazil, and Japan. Locate your local office at: **www.cengage.com/global**

For product information: **www.cengage.com/international**
Visit your local office: **www.cengage.com/global**
Visit our corporate website: **www.cengage.com**

Printed in the United States of America
1 2 3 4 5 6 7 15 14 13 12 11

Brief Contents

Contents

Preface

We continue to believe that readers of a public relations textbook should be provided with a clear set of guiding public relations principles accompanied by cases that generally illustrate those principles in a positive light and thus serve as models of effective management and practice. In order to give students the most current examples of award-winning communication campaigns, all but two of the 33 cases are new to this edition. Most of the cases were winners of the Public Relations Society of America's prestigious Silver Anvil Award contest, and therefore constitute some of the finest examples of public relations practices available.

NEW TO THIS EDITION

Besides the largely new public relations case studies for each chapter, this edition includes a new chapter on social media. Today's public relations practitioner often uses a variety of strategies and tactics around digital, mobile and Internet-based social media, therefore, the book reflects this new elevation of social media on public relations campaigns. Also, many of the lists of audiences and approaches in the chapters have been updated to reflect current practices and technologies.

ORGANIZATION AND LAYOUT

The book is divided into four sections: Solving Public Relations Problems, Reaching Major Audiences, Crisis Public Relations, and Integrated Marketing Communications.

In Part 1, the introductory chapter begins with a philosophy we have held for a long time—that the best public relations is characterized by interaction, or better still, interactive participation among sources and receivers of communication. This philosophy is based on the underlying premise that public relations is most persuasive through informed and trustworthy "engagement with publics."

Chapter 1 continues to focus on the impact emerging technologies have on the field of public relations and the importance of ethics to practitioners. As in previous editions, we have included the PRSA Member Code of Ethics in Appendix II.

In Chapter 2, you will encounter the "Hendrix process model," which involves initial research, the setting of objectives, programming, and evaluation. (The elements of this process model form a convenient mnemonic device, the acronym ROPE.) This model focuses special attention on the significance of objectives and their arrangement in a hierarchical order of output and impact functions. Another feature of this process model is special emphasis on the role of interpersonal communication, including speeches, speakers bureaus, small-group and one-on-one formats, and nonverbal aspects of communication. The same approach is appropriate for today's social media. In a word, the ROPE process model is interactive. We caution against oversimplifying the model and not including an in-depth analysis of messaging strategies and an understanding of persuasive techniques with different audiences.

Part 2 consists of audience-centered applications of the process, with accompanying illustrative cases. The audience-centered forms of public relations included are media relations, social media (new to this edition), employee and member relations, community relations, public affairs and government relations, investor relations, international public relations, and relations with special publics. The cases often follow the Silver Anvil entry format, which is somewhat different from the format of the ROPE model but still constitutes an emphasis on strategic management of a campaign. The major difference is that the ROPE model sets objectives apart as a separate category, and the Silver Anvil format does not. The ROPE programming phase includes planning and communication (execution), and both Silver Anvil and ROPE models begin and end with research and evaluation. Thus, the two models have a difference mainly in format, not substance.

Part 3 includes both theory and illustrative cases for crisis public relations. This field of PR is not oriented to a particular audience, so we have distinguished this area in a separate section of the book.

Also set apart is the section on integrated marketing communications (IMC) because of the breadth of this area of public relations. IMC is a combination of public relations and marketing techniques. Though some practitioners, scholars, and the PRSA itself omit the word "marketing" and call it "integrated communications," our preference is to use the widely accepted term "integrated marketing communications."

Finally, the appendixes contain questions for class discussion and the PRSA Member Code of Ethics 2000, which contains guidelines for the ethical practice of public relations.

ADDITIONAL RESOURCES

Resources for Students

Student Companion Website. The website for *Public Relations Cases*, Ninth Edition includes chapter summaries and PR Cases, available for download.

Resources for Instructors

Instructor's Edition (IE).   Examination and desk copies of the Instructor's Edition of *Public Relations Cases*, Ninth Edition are available upon request.

DVD for Public Relations Cases.   This DVD is available to instructors upon request and includes public relations campaigns hand selected by author Darrell Hayes. These brief videos, such as one on the Red Dress Campaign, show how public relations agencies use TV as well as digital media to tell their campaign's story. Videos are organized by chapter and case number for easy presentation in the classroom.

Instructor Companion Website.   This password-protected website includes the Instructor's Resource Manual, available for download.

Instructor's Resource Manual.   The Instructor's Manual contains resources designed to streamline and maximize the effectiveness of your course preparation. This helpful manual includes suggestions for developing a course syllabus, case study resources, final exam questions, class-tested activities and exercises, test items, and assessment tests. Each chapter includes teaching topics and desired learning objectives, as well as test items. The activities provide innovative ways to present relevant concepts in each chapter. Some chapters also provide additional cases.

ACKNOWLEDGMENTS

Many public relations practitioners have helped by granting permission to use their cases. We hope they will accept our sincere gratitude and understand that space does not permit a list of all their names.

As with previous editions, we are indebted to the students and administrators in the American University School of Communication for their encouragement and support. We would particularly like to acknowledge graduate assistants Susannah Kopp, Cara Kelly and Rosemari Ochoa for helping us with the ninth edition.

Many professionals at Cengage Learning contributed to the publication and success of our book. We'd like to thank Editor Rebecca Donahue and Publisher Michael Rosenberg for their leadership, guidance, and patience on this edition. Authors work closely with their production editors, and it is a pleasure to thank Content Project Manager Divya Divakaran for her outstanding work on this edition. We thank Assistant Editor Erin Bosco and Media Editor Jessica Badiner for working with us on the Instructor's Manual and DVD, and Assistant Editor Jillian D'Urso for conducting the peer review that helped inform the plan for the new edition.

Finally, we gratefully acknowledge the following reviewers, whose constructive comments helped in the development of this ninth edition: Tamara L. Gillis, Elizabethtown College; Jan W. Kelly, PhD, The University of Scranton; and Suzanne FitzGerald, Rowan University.

About the Authors

Darrell C. Hayes is an adjunct associate professor at American University's School of Communications in Washington, D.C. In addition to nine years of full-time teaching experience, he has more than 15 years of work experience with technology firms, nonprofit associations, and as a government communication manager. He is an accredited member of the Public Relations Society of America.

Jerry A. Hendrix, Ph.D., is professor emeritus of communication at American University, Washington, D.C., where he taught for 37 years. He is an accredited member of the Public Relations Society of America.

Pallavi D. Kumar is an assistant professor and associate division director for the Public Communication Division in the School of Communication at American University. Besides teaching many of the public relations courses at the university, she has more than 15 years experience in the public relations industry having worked as a vice president in Fleishman Hillard social marketing practice, a vice president/account supervisor in Ketchum's healthcare practice as well as associate director of international public relations at Wyeth Pharmaceuticals.

Solving Public Relations Problems

1

Public Relations in Action

O ne of the best ways to learn about public relations is through the study of contemporary examples of its practice. Such case studies can bring public relations to life in a way that theoretical textbooks and classroom lectures cannot. Here we will first examine the nature of public relations through its definition and a process model. Then, we will look at various forms of public relations along with several cases to illustrate each form.

One way of defining public relations has been simply to invert the term, so it becomes "relations with publics." An improved modification of this definition is "*interrelationships* with publics." This better reflects the nature of contemporary public relations as an *interactive* form of communication in which the targeted audiences yield information to the organization through its research efforts and often *participate* in the public relations programming itself. This interactive or mutual dimension of public relations is seen in the comprehensive description adopted by the Public Relations Society of America (PRSA) in 1982 (see Exhibit 1-a).

In helping to define and implement policy and to achieve strategic goals for an organization, the public relations practitioner utilizes a variety of professional communication skills and plays an integrative role both within the organization and between the organization and the external environment.

PROCESS

In fact, the public relations process can be seen as a method for solving problems. It has four phases: research, objectives, programming, and evaluation. Each element may be modified to better match the communication campaign with different audiences or publics, including employees, members, customers, local and online communities, shareholders, and, frequently, the news media.

E X H I B I T 1-a PRSA's Official Statement on Public Relations*

Public relations helps our complex, pluralistic society to reach decisions and function more effectively by contributing to mutual understanding among groups and institutions. It serves to bring private and public policies into harmony.

Public relations serves a wide variety of institutions in society such as businesses, trade unions, government agencies, voluntary associations, foundations, hospitals, and educational and religious institutions. To achieve their goals, these institutions must develop effective relationships with many different audiences or publics such as employees, members, customers, local communities, shareholders, and other institutions, and with society at large.

The managements of institutions need to understand the attitudes and values of their publics in order to achieve institutional goals. The goals themselves are shaped by the external environment. The public relations practitioner acts as a counselor to management, and as a mediator, helping to translate private goals into reasonable, publicly acceptable policy and action.

As a management function, public relations encompasses the following:

- Anticipating, analyzing, and interpreting public opinion, attitudes, and issues that may have an impact, for good or ill, the operations and plans of the organization.
- Counseling management at all levels in the organization with regard to policy decisions, courses of action and communication, taking into account their public ramifications and the organization's social or citizenship responsibilities.
- Researching, conducting, and evaluating, on a continuing basis, programs of action and communication to achieve informed public understanding necessary to the success of an organization's aims. These may include marketing, financial, fund-raising, employee, community, or government relations, and other programs.
- Planning and implementing the organization's efforts to influence or change public policy.
- Setting objectives, planning, budgeting, recruiting and training staff, developing facilities—in short, *managing* the resources needed to perform all of the above.
- Examples of the knowledge that may be required in the professional practice of public relations include communication arts, psychology, social psychology, sociology, political science, economics, and the principles of management and ethics. Technical knowledge and skills are required for opinion research, public issues analysis, media relations, direct mail, institutional advertising, social media implementation, publications, film/video productions, special events, speeches, and presentations.

---

*Formally adopted by the PRSA Assembly on November 6, 1982. Reprinted courtesy of PRSA.

The *research* phase of the process involves identifying and learning about three key elements: (1) a *client* or organization that has (2) a *problem* or potential problem to be solved that involves (3) one or more of its *audiences*, or publics. Conversely, the client or organization may also have an opportunity to capitalize on with their audiences or publics.

The second phase of the public relations process involves the setting of *objectives* for a program to solve the problem. These objectives may include the kind of influence the client hopes to exert with the audiences, such as informing them or modifying their attitudes or behaviors. The objectives may also include statements about the program itself, such as its composition or how it will operate.

The third phase of the process consists of planning and executing a *program* to accomplish the objectives. The program comprises a central theme, messages, and various forms of communication aimed at reaching the audiences.

Finally, *evaluation,* as defined in this process, consists of two parts. First, it includes an ongoing procedure of program monitoring and adjustment. Second, evaluation refers back specifically to the objectives that were set in the second phase of the process and examines the practitioner's degree of success in achieving them.

CASES

The illustrations of this process in action—the cases—are grouped in this text according to the various audiences that public relations practitioners reach. Each audience calls for some modifications in the overall four-step process, and the cases illustrate the modified process in action.

Cases are presented to illustrate relations with the media, with internal audiences, with the local community, with online communities, with the government, with investors, with consumers, with international audiences, and with special groups.

Effective public relations cases serve as models for students and practitioners alike. They enhance public relations theory, making it come alive with illustrations and examples of the PR process in action. Moreover, audience-centered cases exemplify the constraints involved in conducting research, setting objectives, designing and executing a program with effective and persuasive messages, and evaluating what has been done. In sum, cases, especially audience-centered cases, effectively illustrate public relations principles and management and test theoretical applications in real situations and environments.

NEW TECHNOLOGY

The most striking aspect of the cases included here is the pervasiveness of digital technology in campaigns, most notably the use of the Internet and mobile digital delivery systems.

First-generation "brochure-ware" websites have evolved into more interactive forums for conversations with publics. Conversations on social media sites have even replaced much email for some people. Emerging communication systems create new venues to conduct relations with a variety of publics. Organizations keep their media kits on a website in the form of news releases, background information, photographs, videos, executive speeches, quarterly and annual reports to shareholders, position papers, interviews as podcasts, and so forth. The sites provide means for email feedback, online customer responses to blogs and articles, discussion boards and even online collaboration through wikis where individuals can meet at a website and provide content, coordinate ideas, and update the contributions of others. The most famous is "Wikipedia," an online encyclopedia with millions of users able to update and correct an entry.

Discussions about Web 2.0 suggest the new technology has not only brought new channels of communication but also changed the fabric of interaction and even the very culture of society. Web 2.0 involves an interconnectedness of communities with people engaged in mutually beneficial conversations at sites such as Facebook and a multitude of other social media sites, health discussion boards, or even on eBay to sell their stuff. Social media is an expression of this trend where everyone has the ability to publish and share information on the Web. Instead of passive recipients of the traditional "mass media," such as newspapers, books, and movies, individuals may post information on blogs; maintain Facebook accounts where they link to "friends" to update each other on their lives; establish social news sites such as Gawker, Digg, and Mixx; post video narratives on YouTube; or show their photos on Flickr and Zooomr. In essence, a few media gatekeepers no longer filter information for public consumption, but each individual can select trusted news sources from many different online sites, even posts from other digital citizens. *The New York Times* columnist Thomas L. Friedman suggested the convergence of new technologies has made this a "horizontal world" where global collaboration has become the skill that differentiates the best in their businesses.

E-mail became a dominant form of communication both internally and externally, and along with new social media and mobile platforms, largely replaced internal print materials, such as newsletters, written memos, and some face-to-face communication. Externally, email posts evolved into status updates on social media sites and Twitter feeds have become the major means of communicating news releases, media alerts, and other forms of media relations. Email and social media sites also provide instant communication with consumers, investors, and a variety of other targeted publics. Shorter communication bursts via text messaging and Twitter feeds further migrated communication to the mobile phone and tablets. Mobile devices have become the standard for communicating quickly with friends and family and are the system of choice for emergency notifications on college campuses. The ability to deliver messages, video, and news via the cell phone has become the next technological frontier for communication campaigns.

Many organizations created *intranets*—internal Internets—to handle large volumes of internal communication with employees and members. Some organizations also created *extranets*—selective external Internets—to reach targeted external groups, such as investors, journalists, consumers, and others. DVDs and digital audio and video files also have become a major public relations tool, with vast storage and the potential for interaction with targeted groups. Instant messaging and social media interactions have made online collaboration immediate, speeding both the flow of information and decision-making loops in organizations. Smart phones made computer email and website searches portable and even led to the rapid mobilization of street protests in many countries. Viral messaging uses the natural propensity of people to share information with others to spread organizational information. Many newspapers have dropped their film critics because text messages and online postings became the preferred recommendations on whether or not young people view a film.

Web logs, or blogs, allow anyone to become a publisher and to share personal opinions or their own "news." Microblogs and Twitter with a 140 character limitation, allow millions more to post information online. This has further blurred the distinction between traditional journalism and other information sources. Some senior managers in organizations have established their own blogs and Twitter identities to make sure the organization's positions are posted on this wider tableau of public opinion. At the same time, many blogs solicit viewer comments, which enhance public discussions and provide ready access to public opinion about an issue. Podcasting and video posts emerged as tools for reaching audiences. With the popularity of "personal on-demand" players, podcasts and video casts became other ways to share news, special events, or personal opinions via the Internet. The rapid exchange of information and messages in this digital universe not only affects the way organizations must more quickly respond to an emergency but has also had an impact the practice of public relations in a major, ever-expanding way. It has both cluttered the message channels and yet opened new avenues for connecting with publics.

The emphasis on technology comes with a caveat. Even as PR agencies and corporations rush to incorporate emerging digital practices and social media specialties, this trend often assumes new technology that provides all communication to all publics. All audiences are not equally technologically engaged. A Pew Internet & American Life Project study found 41 percent of Americans rarely used tech assets or were completely off the network.[1] Solid strategic communication, no matter the technology or channel used to communicate, still stands as the foundation principle of this book.

ETHICS

The PRSA Member Code of Ethics (see Appendix II), adopted by the PRSA Assembly in 2000, provides a way that each member "can daily reaffirm a commitment to ethical professional activities and decisions." The code of ethics first presents a set of core professional values that should guide all ethical practitioners of public relations. These values include responsible advocacy; honesty; expertise; independence (objective and responsible counsel to clients);

loyalty to clients while serving the public interest; and fairness in dealing with clients, employers, competitors, the media, and the general public.

The second part of the code consists of such ethical principles of conduct as "protecting and advancing the free flow of accurate and truthful information," "promoting healthy and fair competition" among professional public relations practitioners, disclosing honest and accurate information in all communications, protecting "the privacy of clients, organizations, and individuals by safeguarding confidential information," "avoiding real, potential, or perceived conflicts of interest," and working constantly to "strengthen the public's trust in the profession." All students of public relations, as well as long-time practitioners, should read the entire code.

This commitment to ethical practices on the part of the PRSA is intended to counter the image of public relations practitioners as "hired guns" who will say or do whatever it takes to accomplish the goals of their clients. There is some basis for this negative public perception of the profession. The following is a discussion of some of the practices that have earned public relations a sometimes-less-than-savory reputation.

On a continuum going from bad to worse, we might begin with the relatively innocuous practice of *lowballing*. This consists of downplaying expectations for a program or project that may not be especially successful in its outcome. The mass media frequently accuse the White House of "lowballing" a presidential visit abroad, a peace initiative in some part of the world, or some other effort that may not yield tangible results.

Closely related to lowballing is the ubiquitous *spin* that is used by governmental and corporate public relations practitioners to make their programs look good. The "spin" actually consists of the one-sided use of facts or data to create a desired impression. These practitioners are often referred to by the mass media as *spin doctors*. By selectively using only positive aspects of a program or a political campaign, practitioners can portray their clients' activities in a favorable light. Conversely, the endeavors of an opponent may be selectively portrayed only in the negative.

Next we might examine six types of *distortion* sometimes found in the practice of public relations. The first of these is commonly called *hype*. Hype is the use of hyperbole or magnification, sometimes referred to as the "blowing out of proportion" of the attributes of a person, event, or product. The mass media are fond of portraying various criminal acts as "the crime of the century." Advertising constantly uses hype in its exaggerated claims for products and services, and public relations practitioners have been known to "stretch the truth" about clients and their programs.

A second type of distortion is *minimizing,* the exact opposite of hype. Sometimes practitioners will play down the seriousness of a failure or the negative aspects of a product or other problems experienced by a client.

A third type of frequently used distortion is *overgeneralization,* or drawing sweeping conclusions based on one isolated case or example. If a candidate for the presidential nomination of a political party loses the New Hampshire primary, for example, the mass media, along with the candidate's opposition, usually conclude that the nomination is lost, based on the results of that one primary election. Similarly, singular successes have been used to draw sweeping positive conclusions. One case study should never be the sole basis for such generalizations.

Categorization is a fourth type of distortion sometimes found in the practice of public relations. An example of categorization may involve the portrayal of a person, event, or product as "good" or "bad" with no middle ground or shades of gray. Other frequently used categories include "successful," "unsuccessful," "useful," "useless," and the like.

Closely related to categorization is the practice of *labeling*. An individual or program may be labeled either a "winner" or a "loser," often on the basis of sketchy or nonexistent evidence. History is replete with the use of such labels as "witch," "communist," "limousine liberal," and "right-wing conservative." The list could go on endlessly.

A final form of distortion may be called *image transfer*. This involves the deliberate shifting of image from one person, event, or product to another, but dissimilar, person, event, or product. Such advertising techniques as the identification of a product with an attractive or sexy model are perhaps the most frequent use of image transfer. Public relations practitioners also seek to transfer the high-credibility images of popular paid spokespersons to low-credibility or unknown programs, causes, or events.

In addition to lowballing, spinning, and a variety of distortions, we should consider the even more offensive practices of using outright *lies* and *coverups*. One example of these practices is the manufacturer that knows its product is defective and potentially dangerous. Instead of making this information public, the company blames accidents on improper consumer use and handles the resulting litigation on a case-by-case basis. These case-by-case settlements are usually substantially less expensive than staging a product recall. Meanwhile, the company's public relations office is busy denying product fault, issuing statements blaming the consumer. In regard to coverups, the defining event *that has become generic* in its field was the Watergate affair, a major turning point in American political history and the coverup by which all subsequent coverups have been measured.

This is by no means an exhaustive list of unethical public relations practices. The PRSA Member Code of Ethics cites other activities such as corruption of communication channels and other deceptive practices. For an understanding of the ethical practice of public relations, the student of public relations should carefully study the Member Code of Ethics in Appendix II, along with the unethical practices discussed here.

In the public relations workplace, the best argument for ethical practices is that they are "good business." The positive side is that the company or organization can point with pride to its ethical practices. The negative side is that, if an organization or client is caught by the ubiquitous mass media in an unethical practice, this will become a headline news story and perhaps blot out all previous positive accomplishments. This study of applied ethics should therefore become an overriding concern in the education of public relations practitioners.

THE OVERALL PLAN OF THIS BOOK

Part I introduces you to public relations, with special emphasis on the process outlined previously. The elements of this process are eclectic, but the arrangement of those elements forms the acronym ROPE (research, objectives, programming, and evaluation). A major feature is an emphasis on public relations objectives. Objectives are viewed as the central and guiding element in the process, and they are arranged in a hierarchical order. It keeps the focus of a campaign on the strategic big picture.

Another feature of this public relations process, consistent with its interactive nature, is a heightened emphasis on interpersonal interaction as a form of controlled communication. The importance of traditional interaction such as speeches and speakers' bureaus as methods of public relations communication is recognized, but this book also advocates the extensive use of small-group and dyadic (one-on-one) interpersonal formats, and engaging online communities through personal dialogue. A recurring theme is that in truly effective communication there can be no substitute for direct interaction.

Part II explores how public relations reaches major audiences. It looks at media relations; internal communication, including employee and member relations; social media community relations; public affairs, or government relations; investor and financial relations; consumer relations; international public relations; and relations with special publics. Following a conceptual treatment of each form of relations are several example cases. Most of these illustrative cases have won Silver Anvil Awards from the PRSA. As such, they represent the very best among models of public relations.

Part III concentrates on emergency or crisis public relations, an important area in contemporary practice. Both students and professionals quickly understand the need to study crisis PR procedures and the special challenges inherent in responding quickly and effectively to protect the reputation of an organization. Crisis PR still requires a strategic communication mindset but also requires special skills.

Part IV focuses on Integrated Marketing Communications, the combination of both public relations and advertising to accomplish essentially marketing objectives.

Finally, the appendixes include the PRSA Member Code of Ethics.

ENDNOTE

1. Horrigan, John B. "A Typology of Information and Communication Technology Users," Pew Internet & American Life Project (May 2007) www.pewinternet.org, accessed March 24, 2008.

GENERAL PUBLIC RELATIONS READINGS

Austin, Erica Weintraub, and Bruce E. Pinkleton. *Strategic Public Relations Management*. Mahwah, NJ: Erlbaum, 2001.

Botan, Carl H., and Maureen Taylor. "Public Relations: State of the Field," *Journal of Communication* 54 (December 1, 2004): 645–661.

Bruning, Stephen D., Melissa Dials, and Amanda Shirka. "Using Dialogue to Build Organization-Public Relationships, Engage Publics, and Positively Affect Organizational Outcomes," *Public Relations Review* 34 (March 2008): 25–31.

Center, Allen H., Patrick Jackson, Stacey Smith, and Frank Stansberry. *Public Relations Practice: Managerial Case Studies and Practice*, 7th ed. Englewood Cliffs, NJ: Prentice-Hall, 2007.

Cutlip, Scott M., Allen H. Center, and Glen M. Broom. *Effective Public Relations*, 10th ed. Englewood Cliffs, NJ: Prentice-Hall, 2009.

Diggs-Brown, Barbara. *Strategic Public Relations: Audience-Focused Practice*. Boston: Wadsworth. 2011.

Gower, Karla A. *Legal and Ethical Considerations for Public Relations*, 2d ed. Long Grove, IL: Waveland Press, 2008.

Grunig, Larissa A., James E. Grunig, and David M. Dozier. *Excellent Public Relations and Effective Organizations*. Mahwah, NJ: Erlbaum, 2002.

Guth, David W., and Charles Marsh. *Public Relations: A Values-Driven Approach*, 5th ed. Boston: Allyn & Bacon, 2011.

Heath, Robert L. *Sage Handbook of Public Relations*, 2nd ed. Thousand Oaks, CA: Sage Publications, 2010.

Lamb, Lawrence F., and Kathy Brittain McKee. *Applied Public Relations*. Mahwah, NJ: Erlbaum, 2005.

Ledingham, John A., and Stephen D. Bruning. *Public Relations as Relationship Management*. Mahwah, NJ: Erlbaum, 2001.

Lesly, Philip, ed. *Lesly's Handbook of Public Relations and Communications*, 5th ed. New York: AMACOM, 1998.

Marken, G.A. "Social Media … The Hunted Can Become the Hunter," *Public Relations Quarterly* 52(4) (2009): 9–12.

Newsom, Doug, Judy VanSlyke Turk, and Dean Kruckeberg. *This Is PR: The Realities of Public Relations*, 10th ed. Belmont, CA: Wadsworth, 2009.

Seitel, Fraser P. *The Practice of Public Relations*, 11th ed. Englewood Cliffs, NJ: Prentice-Hall, 2009.

Smith, Ronald D. *Strategic Planning for Public Relations*, 2d ed. Mahwah, NJ: Erlbaum, 2005.

Wilcox, Dennis L. *Public Relations Writing and Media Techniques*, 6th ed. Boston: Allyn & Bacon, 2009.

Wilcox, Dennis L., Glen T. Cameron, Phillip H. Ault, and Warren K. Agee. *Public Relations: Strategies and Tactics*, 9th ed. Boston: Allyn & Bacon, 2008.

2

A Public Relations Process

As we saw in Chapter 1, the public relations problem-solving process involves four procedures. First, initial research is performed to establish the basic elements of the communication transaction. Second, objectives for the transaction are established. Third, programming, including all the methods of communication used, is planned and executed to carry out the objectives. Finally, ongoing and follow-up evaluation is conducted both to monitor and to measure how well the program accomplished its objectives.

Now for a detailed look at each of the elements in this process.

RESEARCH

Research consists of investigating three aspects of the overall public relations procedure: the client or organization for whom the program is being prepared, the opportunity or problem that accounts for the program at this time, and all audiences to be targeted or publics to be engaged for communication in the PR program.

Client Research

First, public relations practitioners must be thoroughly familiar with their clients. If the practitioner is working in an in-house PR department, the client will be the organization housing the department. An employee of a PR firm will obviously be independent of the client. In either case, background data about the client or organization—its financial status, reputation, past and present public relations practices, and public relations strengths, weaknesses, and opportunities—are an essential starting point for any program. A communication audit, whether formal or informal, can reveal much about an organization's distinctive style of culture, communication practices, and relationships with its publics. Business leaders are familiar with the process of accessing "internal" strengths and weaknesses and "external" threats and opportunities so applying these principles to the communications process will make sense to them.

If the organization is a business, the practitioner needs to be familiar with its products and services as well as the overall competitive environment. The practitioner should also know about the marketing, legal, and financial functions of the organization in order to coordinate them with the public relations efforts. Interviews with key management personnel and documents such as annual and quarterly reports can provide this information. The location of the organization, whether in a single city or in multiple branches, the delivery system for the products or services (such as the use of a dealer network), the organization's major suppliers or vendors, and, of course, the identity and demographics, values and culture of the customers and clientele are all necessary to understand the client.

If the organization is nonprofit, the practitioner must become acquainted with the services provided and the organization's clientele, including major donors, partners and supporters.

Other important background information includes the precise mission of the organization, its management's goals, priorities, and problems, and how this proposed public relations program might help accomplish these overall objectives.

Along with this background information, the practitioner needs a good working knowledge of the organization's personnel—its total workforce, both management and general workforce. Special attention must be given to key management people, not just the director of public relations, if there is one. How does top management view the role of public relations? Are PR people regarded as problem solvers and decision makers, just as technicians to implement details of a campaign or are they simply "hired guns"?

The financial status of a publicly owned corporation is easy to determine. Financial data for such organizations must be reported to the U.S. Securities and Exchange Commission (SEC), and this information is available in the company's annual report or other financial publications.

Finally, the practitioner needs to raise questions that directly relate to public relations. What is the client's reputation in its field and with its customers or clientele? In marketing, this often refers to brand identity and brand equity. The answers to these questions constitute the organization's public image, an area of primary concern to PR practitioners. What image liabilities or assets does the organization possess? What are its present and past public relations practices? Does the organization have particular PR strengths, that is, practices or programs that would enhance its public image? What are its PR weaknesses, the practices or programs that might create an unfavorable image or negative public opinion? What opportunities exist for promoting favorable public opinion or behavior toward the organization?

Thus, the first requisite for effective research in the public relations process is an in-depth understanding of the client for whom the program is prepared.

Opportunity or Problem Research

The second aspect of research, a logical outgrowth of knowledge of the client, consists of clearly determining why the organization should conduct a particular PR program at a particular time. Is it because of a unique opportunity to favorably influence public opinion or behavior toward the client, or is it in response to the development of unfavorable opinion or behavior toward the client? If it is the latter, extensive research must be done on the source of the issue or problem, whether it is an individual or an organization.

Public relations programs that arise out of opportunities are called proactive programs. In the short run, effective proactive programming may seem extravagantly expensive to management, but these programs often head off the need to respond to problems with even more expensive reactive programs. The proactive program is like preventive medicine, or the concept of "wellness" now being widely promoted by health maintenance organizations. Preventive medicine is far more desirable than surgery in response to a severe illness. Similarly, an organization should keep close tabs on its ongoing relations with its constituent audiences to avoid PR problems.

This is not to argue that proactive programs are good and reactive programs are bad. In spite of all efforts to avert them, problems may develop. The reactive program then becomes necessary and perhaps beneficial. When a fire breaks out, we must call the fire department. Public relations practitioners must be ready to extinguish "fires," but they should also be skilled in "fire prevention."

Proactive programs are generally long range and strategic in nature. The organization cannot afford to let its guard down in maintaining good relations with important audiences. The best PR practitioners are continually looking for ways to contribute to the strategic goals of an organization and to be issue managers. Reactive programs, on the other hand, are usually short range, often ending as soon as the immediate problem is cleared up. But a good, ongoing, proactive program with the same audience may prevent the recurrence of similar problems.

Thus, an investigation of why a public relations program is necessary, whether it should be proactive or reactive, and whether it should be ongoing or short range is the second aspect of research in the public relations process.

Audience Research

The third aspect of research in the public relations process involves investigating the target audiences, or "publics." This part of the research process includes identifying the particular groups that should be targeted, determining appropriate research data that will be useful in communicating with these publics, and compiling or processing the data using appropriate research procedures.

Audience Identification.   All organizations have long-range, and sometimes short-term, "relations" or communications, with certain "standard" publics. The publics of principal concern to most organizations include the media, internal employees or members, the organization's home community and online community, and the national, state, and local governments. A business that provides a product or service for customers is concerned with consumers as an important public. A publicly owned business has the additional, significant audience of its shareowners and the financial community. Finally, all organizations have unique groups of constituent audiences, or special publics. Nonprofit organizations are concerned with donors as a special public. Schools are interested in maintaining communications with parents and the community. Large corporations may need to communicate regularly with their dealers and suppliers as well as shareholders if they are a public company.

To address publics most effectively, we should segment each public into its diverse components, so each component may become a separate public to be targeted for special messages and through appropriate communication channels. The media, for example, can be segmented into mass and specialized groups. Of the two internal publics, employees can be segmented into management and nonmanagement, and members should be divided into organization employees, officers, members, prospective members, state or local chapters, and related or allied organizations (see Chapter 4). The organization's home community should be segmented into community media, community leaders, and community organizations. Government publics should be subdivided into federal, state, county, and city levels; then each of these levels should be further segmented into legislative and executive branches. Consumer publics can be subdivided into groupings that include company employees, customers, activist consumer groups, consumer publications, community media, and community leaders and organizations (see Chapter 8). Investor publics for financial relations should be segmented into shareowners and potential shareowners, security analysts and investment counselors, the financial press, and even government regulators such as the SEC. (See Exhibit 2-a for suggested segmentation of these major publics.) For example, instead of marketing a thriller movie to a broad audience, it would be valuable to know that test viewings produced an audience that was 78 percent female and almost half were under the age of 18.

Targeting. Once the publics have been identified and segmented into their components, the practitioner is ready for the more difficult task of targeting the most important publics on a priority basis. This prioritizing calls for a situational assessment of the significance to the client or organization of each potential public. The importance of a potential public is determined by its degree of influence, prestige, power, or perhaps need, and by its level of involvement with the client or organization. Four key questions to consider in targeting and prioritizing publics are:

- Who is this public (demographics, psychographics, technographics and so on)?
- Why is it important to us?
- How active or involved is this public, relative to our interests?
- Which publics are most important to us, in priority rank order?

E X H I B I T 2-a   Major Publics

Media Publics

Mass media

    Local
        Print and online publications
            Newspapers
            Magazines
        TV stations
        Radio stations
    National
        Print and online publications
        Broadcast, online and cable networks
        Wire services

Specialized media

    Local
        Trade, industry, and association publications
        Organizational house and membership publications
        Ethnic and community publications
        Publications of special interest groups
        Specialized broadcast programs and stations
    National/International
        General business publications
        Trade, industry, and association publications
        Organizational house and membership publications
        Ethnic publications
        Publications of national special subject groups
        Specialized broadcast programs and networks

Employee Publics

Management

    Upper-level administrators
    Mid-level administrators
    Lower-level administrators

Nonmanagement (staff)

    Specialists
    Administrative support personnel
    Operational workforce

Equipment operators
Transportation specialists
Security personnel
Production team membersUnion representatives
Other personnel

Member Publics

Organization employees

Headquarters management
Headquarters nonmanagement (staff)
Field operations staff
Other headquarters personnel

Organization officers

Elected officers
Appointed officers
Legislative groups
Boards, committees

Organization members

Regular members
Members in special categories—sustaining, emeritus, student members
Honorary members or groups

Prospective organization members

State or local chapters
Organization employees
Organization officers
Organization members
Prospective organization members

Related or other allied organizations

Community Publics

Community media

Mass
Specialized

Community leaders

Public officials
Educators

Religious leaders
Professionals
Executives
Bankers/Financial leaders
Union leaders
Ethnic leaders
Neighborhood leaders

Community organizations

Civic
Service
Social
Business
Cultural
Religious
Youth
Political
Special interest groups
Online interest groups
Other

Government Publics

Federal

Legislative branch
   Representatives, staff, committee personnel
   Senators, staff, committee personnel
Executive branch
   President
   White House staff, advisers, committees
   Cabinet officers, departments, agencies, commissions

State

Legislative branch
   Representatives, delegates, staff, committee personnel
   Senators, staff, committee personnel
Executive branch
   Governor
   Governor's staff, advisers, committees
   Cabinet officers, departments, agencies, commissions

County

County executive
Other county officials, commissions, departments

City

Mayor or city manager
City council
Other city officials, commissions, departments

International

Official delegations
Nongovernmental organizations

Investor Publics

Shareowners and potential shareowners

Security analysts and investment counselors

Financial press

Major wire services: Dow Jones & Co., Thomson Reuters, AP, UPI, Bloomberg
Major business magazines: *Business Week, Fortune, Forbes,* and the like—mass circulation and specialized
Major newspapers: *The New York Times, Wall Street Journal, USA Today*
Statistical services: Standard & Poor's Corp., Moody's Investor Service, Hoover's and the like
Private wire services: PR Newswire, Business Wire, PR Web
Securities and Exchange Commission (SEC), for publicly owned companies

Consumer Publics

Company employees

Customers

Professionals
Segment by lifestyle interest group
Segment by socio-economic status
Segment by geographic area
Gender and sexual orientation
Minorities
Other

Activist consumer groups

Consumer publications

Community media, mass, and specialized

Community leaders and organizations

International Publics

International media

Host country media

    Mass
    Specialized

Host country leaders

    Public officials
    Educators
    Social leaders
    Cultural leaders
    Religious leaders
    Political leaders
    Professionals
    Executives

Host country organizations

    Business
    Service
    Social
    Cultural
    Religious
    Political
    Special interests
    Other

Special Publics

Media consumed by this public

    Mass
    Specialized

Leaders of this public

    Public officials
    Professional leaders
    Ethnic leaders
    Neighborhood leaders

Organizations composing this public

    Civic
    Political
    Service

Business
Cultural
Religious
Youth
Other

Integrated Marketing Communications

Customers

New customers
Old customers
Potential customers

Employees

Management
General workforce

Media

Mass
Specialized

Investors

Shareowners and potential shareowners
Financial analysts
Financial press

Suppliers

Competitors

Government Regulators

Desired Data. Once target publics have been segmented into their key components, the practitioner is ready to assess communication needs for each public. Typically, the practitioner will want to know each targeted public's level of information about the organization; the image and other relevant attitudes held about the organization and its product or service; and past and present audience behaviors relevant to the client or organization. Researching the demographics, media habits, and levels of media use (both offline and online) of each targeted audience will tell the practitioner how best to reach it. All these data are used to formulate objectives for the public relations program. During this process, a central concern involves the messages that would be most appropriate to attain the objectives and how the messages are framed to best resonate with the public.

Research Methods

With this general framework of informational needs in mind, the practitioner must next decide which research procedures will yield the necessary data.

Public relations people use two general methods of research: nonquantitative and quantitative.

Nonquantitative Research. One source of nonquantitative data is organization or client records (business reports, statistics, financial reports, and past public relations records) and communications (speeches and personal blogs by executives, newsletters, news releases, memorandums, pamphlets, and brochures).

A second source of nonquantitative data is published materials. These include news articles from mass media and trade publications, published surveys or polls, library references, government documents, directories, Internet discussion groups, social media dialogues, and published trade association data. For example, social media sites have people tag an item as "like" or "recommend," which may influence an audience.

Third, nonquantitative research can be conducted through interviews or conversations with key members of targeted publics. Important civic leaders, elected officials, business leaders, religious leaders, educators, influential editors, reporters, and other key individuals in the community can provide invaluable background information for a public relations program.

Fourth, feedback from the client's customers or clientele can be helpful as a means of nonquantitative research. Customer responses may come via telephone, mail, email, comments posted on interactive forums, or face-to-face interactions.

Fifth, talking with organized groups with an interest in the client can be useful. These groups may include the organization's formal advisory boards, committees, commissions, or panels from inside or outside the organization.

Finally, groups created especially for research purposes can provide valuable insight. The most popular form of this procedure is the focus group, usually consisting of eight to 12 people who are representative of the audience the client wishes to reach. A moderator who is skilled in interviewing and group-process management encourages the participants of the focus group to consider the client's image, products, services, and communication proposals, or other issues affecting the client. The focus-group meetings are usually videotaped and carefully studied to identify and analyze participants' reactions and comments.

Throughout this process, the Internet has become an essential source of information for public relations practitioners. Whether using popular search sites such as Google or Yahoo!, specialized meta-search engines or news aggregators, there seems to be an ever-evolving source of data mining sites.

It should be emphasized that although these six methods of nonquantitative research may yield useful data regarding all areas of concern in the research process, the data will not be scientifically reliable. For a scientific level of reliability, statistical research methods must be used.

Quantitative Research.   Three methods of quantitative research are widely used in public relations: sample surveys, experiments, and content analysis. The key to each is the use of statistical methods.

The sample survey is the most frequently used quantitative research method in the public relations process. It is most useful in determining audience information levels, attitudes, behaviors, and media habits. Surveys can be conducted by mail, by telephone, via online responses or in person, with cost increasing in that order.

Questionnaires conducted via mail or online email) are the least expensive survey method because of lower staffing requirements. They can yield more data because length is no problem and respondents can give thorough answers. The major problem with such questionnaires is the low response rate. Unless the intended respondents have a high level of interest in the subject, mail questionnaires can be a big waste of the researcher's time and money.

Telephone interviews have become the most popular means of conducting surveys. Sampling can be done using the random digit dialing technique and an ordinary telephone directory. Although more expensive than mail question-naires, telephone interviews provide a more economical use of staff time. The limitations of communicating by voice alone may hamper the rapport between interviewer and respondent since the interviewer cannot make judgments about accuracy and sincerity based on nonverbal cues. Nonetheless, telephone interviewing has become the first choice in the conduct of sample surveys. With many people relying strictly on wireless cell phones, there are concerns about the ability to reach an appropriate cross section of the public when using phone interviews.

Personal interviews remain an important, though expensive and time-consuming, survey method. The interviewer can make judgments based on the respondent's nonverbal as well as verbal cues, so no survey method is more accurate. Getting a good sample, however, is much more difficult than with the random digit dialing technique used for telephone interviews. Many people are reluctant to consent to a personal interview because of the time and inconvenience involved. As with mail questionnaires, personal interviews are most effective with respondents who are truly interested in the subject and willing to sacrifice their time.

With all their limitations, and with the onus of being considered "quick and dirty" by most social and behavioral scientists, surveys remain the most popular of quantitative research methods used in public relations.

Controlled experiments have been gaining in popularity. Conducted either in laboratory settings or in the field, experiments are the most accurate indicator of causality in the behavioral sciences. Experiments are often used in advertising or public relations to determine which forms of communication or messages may be most effective with selected audiences. In the experimental method, two groups of subjects are randomly chosen. One group is exposed to the communication media, and the other is not. Both groups are tested before and after the communication exposure. If the responses of the exposed group change significantly after the communication, then these responses can be attributed causally to the messages.

A third quantitative method of research often used in public relations is content analysis. This systematic procedure is used in analyzing themes or trends in the message content of selected media. Content analysis can be used to learn how the media are treating clients—their public image as reflected in the media, negative or positive coverage, and the like. This research procedure is also useful in issues management, in which practitioners identify and analyze the impact of public issues on a client's corporate or organizational interests. Thus, content analysis can be helpful in the evaluation of media treatment in the publicity process and in tracking social, economic, or political trends or issues that may affect clients.

For best results, quantitative research should be conducted by professional firms with good reputations and experience in their field or by staff members who are trained and experienced researchers.

With the public relations program's informational needs satisfied through nonquantitative or quantitative research methods, the practitioner is ready to attend to the second phase of the process—that of formulating objectives.

OBJECTIVES

Objectives are the single most important element in this public relations process. They represent the practitioner's desired outcomes in communicating with the targeted publics. They are the *raison d'etre* for PR programs. Some writers draw a distinction between "goals" as more general outcomes and "objectives" as specific, immediate results. Here avoid that confusion by consistently using one term to signify desired program outcomes, and that term is objectives. Whether they are to be broad or narrow, long-range or short-range, they should be stipulated in the statement of the objective itself. Before discuss the types of objectives used in public relations, we should examine the method used in formulating such objectives.

Many organizations use a strategic planning process to align general organizational objectives with those for individual work units, such as the public relations department. To best support the needs of the organization, the PR operation should devise strategically focused short-term and long-range objectives and evaluation procedures for the work unit and for its particular programs.

To be most effective, two criteria apply to all program objectives.

First, objectives should be stated in the form of infinitive phrases, each containing one infinitive and each being a specific and separately measurable desired outcome. An infinitive phrase consists of a verb plus the complement, or receiver of the verb's action. For example, a practitioner may hope that, after the PR program is executed, the audience will be informed that a special event is taking place and will attend the event. The phrasing of the objectives in infinitive form could be:

- To publicize special event X
- To stimulate attendance at special event X
- To obtain social media endorsements for issue X

These objectives could be combined—to publicize and stimulate attendance at special event X—but this compound phrasing would complicate the measurement or evaluation of both objectives.

Second, public relations objectives should be verifiable. To be verifiable, the desired outcome should be stated in quantified, measurable terms, and a time frame or target date should be set for its accomplishment. Although the objectives just stated meet our infinitive test, they are not stated specifically in quantitative or chronological terms. Thus, they can be reworded as:

- To publicize special event X through the community's daily newspaper, its TV station, and its three radio stations during the month of October
- To stimulate an attendance of at least 1,500 persons at special event X on May 15

We can measure the first objective by using a clipping service and a broadcast media monitoring service to determine how many media outlets actually used the announcement of the special event. We can measure the second objective by checking actual attendance figures or ticket sales at the event itself.

Two basic types of objectives are used in public relations programs: impact objectives and output objectives. Together, they can be viewed as a hierarchy in ascending order of importance (see Exhibit 2-b). Within each category, however, there is no performance hierarchy or order of importance. For example, informational objectives need not be completed before attitudinal or behavioral objectives, and the importance of each of these subsets of impact objectives is purely situational.

Output Objectives

Output objectives, the lower category in the hierarchy, represent the work to be produced, that is, the distribution or execution of program materials. Some writers refer to these activities as "process objectives," "support objectives," or "program effort." Whatever the terminology, these activities should not be confused with desired program impacts. Output objectives, as discussed here, refer to stated intentions regarding program production and effort (or output). They are classified as a form of objective because they describe a type of desired outcome often stated in public relations programs. In the best of all possible worlds, PR directors would use primarily impact objectives. But here it seems appropriate to deal with PR objectives as they

---

E X H I B I T 2-b   A Hierarchy of Public Relations Objectives

Impact Objectives

Informational objectives

    Message exposure
    Message comprehension
    Message retention

Attitudinal objectives

    Attitude creation
    Attitude reinforcement
    Attitude change

Behavioral objectives

    Behavior creation
    Behavior reinforcement
    Behavior change

Output Objectives

Distribution of uncontrolled media

Distribution or execution of controlled media

---

actually exist in the real world. Such objectives can easily be made specific and quantitative. For example:

- To send one news release to each of the community's major media outlets: its daily newspaper, its TV station, and its three radio stations by May 10
- To make an oral presentation to an important conference of security analysts in each of the following five cities: New York, Los Angeles, Chicago, Houston, and Denver, before December 15
- To send five Twitter updates each day to followers aimed at creating a conversation

These objectives can then be measured easily by counting the number of news releases actually sent to the media outlets and the number of oral presentations actually made to security analysts. Time frames can be added if desired.

Some practitioners use only output objectives in their public relations programs. The advantage of such usage is that output objectives set definite, specific, and attainable goals, which can be measured quantitatively. Once these goals have been met, the practitioner can claim success. Unfortunately, output objectives are unrelated to the actual impact the program may have on its intended audiences, and for this we must move to the top, and more significant, category in our hierarchy of public relations objectives.

Impact Objectives

There are three kinds of impact objectives: informational, attitudinal, and behavioral. These are called impact objectives because they represent specific intended effects of public relations programs on their audiences.

Informational Objectives. Informational objectives include message exposure to, message comprehension by, and/or message retention by the target public. Such objectives are appropriate when the practitioner wishes to publicize an action or event; seeks to communicate instructions, operating procedures, or other forms of information; or wants to educate an audience about a noncontroversial subject. Three examples of informational objectives are:

- To increase awareness of the company's open house (by 10 percent) among all segments of the community (during the month of May)
- To increase employee awareness of new plant safety procedures (by 50 percent during our three-month safety campaign)
- To increase awareness of distracted driving hazards (by 20 percent during the summer months)

Attitudinal Objectives. Attitudinal objectives aim at modifying the way an audience feels about the client or organization and its work, products, or services. Attitude modification may consist of forming new attitudes where none exists, reinforcing existing attitudes, or changing existing attitudes.

There will probably be no public attitudes toward a completely new organization. The task of public relations, then, will be the creation of favorable attitudes toward the organization. Two examples of such objectives are:

- To create favorable public attitudes toward a new restaurant (among 25 percent of local neighbors during the grand opening celebration)
- To promote favorable attitudes toward new food nutrition labels (among 80 percent of current shoppers during the current fiscal year)

It should be stressed that this type of attitudinal objective (forming new attitudes) usually applies only to organizations and actions that have not generated prior audience attitudes. Some new organizations or actions immediately create strong reactions among affected groups. In these cases, objectives that seek to reinforce or change existing attitudes are more appropriate.

The second form of attitudinal objective has as its goal the reinforcement, enhancement, or intensification of existing attitudes. A given audience may have moderately favorable, but weak, attitudes toward an organization. In this case, public relations may seek to strengthen these attitudes through a variety of actions, events, or communications. An example of this might be:

- To reinforce favorable public opinion toward a nonprofit organization (among 80 percent of its past donors during March and April)

The final form of attitudinal objective is the changing, or reversing, of (usually negative) existing attitudes. In this case, the practitioner must be careful not to take on a "Mission Impossible." The reversal of negative attitudes is, of course, the most difficult of all tasks in public relations, so first assess the importance of tackling the issue. Is it worth the cost? Attitude or behavior reversal takes time and, as a rule, it cannot be accomplished with one short-range PR campaign. When Ivy Lee attempted to reverse the public image of John D. Rockefeller, Sr., the task took years. Little by little, Lee was successful in converting Rockefeller's image from that of corporate villain to the image of a beloved philanthropist. Many practitioners would rightly have regarded such an enormous task as a "losing battle," given the resources of most individuals or organizations. But with unlimited Rockefeller money and a concerted public relations effort, the image repair was finally accomplished.

Sometimes the practitioner will seek to reverse existing positive attitudes. For example, some Republicans in Congress (and in the White House) have attempted to portray many of the government's social programs in a negative light, although most of these programs have enjoyed great popularity since their inception during U.S. President Franklin D. Roosevelt's New Deal era.

Two examples of objectives that seek attitude change are:

- To reverse (within a period of one year) the negative attitudes and ill will now being expressed toward the manufacturer of a defective product (among 20 percent of the manufacturer's former and current customers)
- To change the favorable attitudes that exist regarding the proposed program (among 10 percent of the members of the U.S. Congress before the vote on the bill)

Attitudinal objectives, then, may involve any of three goals: formation of new attitudes where none exist, reinforcement of existing attitudes, or change in existing attitudes.

Behavioral Objectives. Behavioral objectives involve the modification of behavior or action for the client or organization. Like attitude modification, behavior modification may consist of the creation or stimulation of new behavior, the enhancement or intensification of existing favorable behavior, or the reversal of negative behavior on the part of an audience for the practitioner's client or organization.

Examples of the creation of new behavior might include:

- To accomplish adoption of new safety procedures (among 75 percent of the organization's employees by September 15)
- To persuade (60 percent of) persons over the age of 50 to regularly take a colon cancer test (during the next two years)

- To stimulate new diet procedures (among 70 percent) of children in the city school system (during the current school year)

Enhancement or intensification of existing positive behaviors might involve such objectives as:

- To encourage (30 percent) greater usage of seat belts in automobiles (this year)
- To stimulate (50 percent) higher attendance at meetings by association members (during the next national convention)
- The reversal of negative behaviors could include:
- To discourage defacement of public monuments (by 20 percent) in a city park (over a period of eight months)
- To discourage smoking (by 25 percent) in the parking lot of the school (during the next three months)

Objectives, as presented here, result from and are shaped by the findings revealed in the research phase. As mentioned earlier, research data should be sought in the area of audience information levels, attitudes, behaviors, and media habits. If information levels about the client or related matters are low, then informational objectives are called for in the public relations program. If audience attitudes toward the client are nonexistent, weak, or negative, then the practitioner will know the kinds of attitudinal objectives to formulate. Finally, if desired audience behaviors are nonexistent, weak, or negative, the practitioner will have a framework for developing appropriate behavioral objectives and likely a complementary phase of awareness and attitude objectives to support the change in actions. Data regarding audience media habits may not contribute directly to the formulation of program objectives, but these findings are useful in determining appropriate media usage in the programming phase of the process.

In addition to impact objectives, the practitioner may devise output objectives for each PR program. These objectives should be connected to achieving the impact objectives but actually represent outcomes that are secondary to program effects on target audiences.

In the public relations process, objectives precede and govern programming decisions. The degree of influence these objectives exert can best be seen in the programming phase itself.

PROGRAMMING

Public relations programming, as presented in this process, includes the following elements of planning and execution:

1. Stating a theme, if applicable, and the messages to be communicated to the audiences

2. Planning the action or special event(s) sponsored by the client
3. Planning the use of the media, either uncontrolled or controlled
4. Effectively communicating the program

Theme and Messages

The first element of a program, its theme and messages, should encompass the program's entire scope and must be carefully planned in conjunction with the action or special event central to the program.

The program theme should be catchy and memorable. The best themes are in the form of short slogans consisting of no more than five words. Not all programs require themes or slogans, but a brief, creative theme can become the most memorable part of the entire public relations effort. Often, extensive research is conducted to evaluate the effectiveness of different potential messages. "Framing" a message involves crafting appropriate language that influences perceptions and subsequent judgments about a campaign. For example, a campaign to influence distracted driving could focus on "watching out for the safety of friends" rather than "don't text and drive." The language affects the tone and focus of the communication.

Most PR programs will have one central message epitomized in such a slogan or theme. In some cases, programs may have several messages, possibly one for each separate audience. The practitioner should work out as concisely as possible just what is to be communicated to each audience during the entire program.

Action(s) or Special Event(s)

A central action or a special event to be sponsored by the client should be considered along with the program's theme and message. The client's actions or events will usually be the focal point of the theme and messages, although some PR programs omit this element and concentrate on theme and messages alone. However, it is highly recommended that programs be action oriented. A central action or event can make most programs more newsworthy, interesting, and effective. To best advance the public image of the client, this action or event should be substantive and in the public interest. It will be most effective if the event involves large numbers of people and includes the presence of at least one celebrity who connects with the targeted public. Shallow "pseudoevents" should be avoided; they sometimes do more harm than good by damaging the client's credibility. Sometimes gimmicks and stunts and similar activities can raise funds for worthy causes, but be cautious to avoid damaging the reputation of the organization. In the same way, humor may work but not with all publics. If these events can be seen as serving the public interest, they may enhance the client's credibility. Typical public relations actions and special events are included in Exhibit 2-c.

EXHIBIT 2-c   Actions and Special Events

Special days, nights, weeks, months

Displays and exhibits

Trade shows and exhibitions

Fairs, festivals, expositions

Meetings, conferences, conventions, symposia, rallies

Anniversaries, memorial events

Special awards, retirements, salutes

Open houses, plant tours

Town meetings, public debates, parties

Coffee hours, teas

Contests

Parades, pageants, beauty contests, fashion shows

Sponsoring community events

Sponsoring organizations (community youth organizations. Little League, Junior Achievement Organization)

Sponsoring scholarships, contributions

Creating charitable and educational foundations

Receptions

Concert tours, theatrical tours

Performing and graphic arts tours

Visits, pleasure tours for selected publics and groups

Picnics, outings, cookouts, barbecues

Nature trails, flower shows

Groundbreaking ceremonies, cornerstone layings, safety programs

Product demonstrations

Traveling demonstrations, home demonstrations

Visits by dignitaries, celebrities

Guest lectures, kickoffs, farewells, going-aways, welcome-backs, welcoming ceremonies

Elections of officers

Issuing reports or statistics

Announcing results of polls or surveys

Grand openings

Announcing an appointment

Announcing a new policy or policy change

Announcing a new program, product, or service

Announcing important news about the client or organization

Public relations personalities (Miss America, celebrity spokespersons/ ambassadors)

Dedications

School commencements, assemblies, events, convocations

Fetes, galas, proms, dances, balls, parties

Banquets, luncheons, breakfasts, dinners, buffets

Art shows, openings, exhibits

Concerts, plays, ballets

Film festivals, fashion shows

Animal shows

Sporting events, ski trips, ocean cruises, pack trips, hikes, marathons, bike-a-thons, swim-a-thons, miscellaneous-a-thons, races

Celebrity sporting events, cruises

Museum tours, home tours

Embassy tours

Celebrity appearances, autograph-signing ceremonies

Neighborhood cleanups, services for the elderly

Environmental awareness day

Health screening tests

Committee hearings

Training programs

Opinion-leader meetings and conferences

Special education programs: thrift education, health education, conservation education

Leadership programs

Participation in community events

Celebrations of national holidays

Theme events and celebrations: "Roaring Twenties," "Old New Orleans," "Colonial New England," "Ancient Greece"

Events honoring other nations or cultures

Uncontrolled and Controlled Media

The two forms of communication used in public relations are usually classified as uncontrolled and controlled media.

The use of uncontrolled media involves the communication of news about the client or organization to the mass media and to specialized media outlets. Specifically, the decision-making editors of these outlets become the target audiences for uncontrolled media. The objective of this form of communication is favorable news coverage of the client's actions, initiatives and events. The standard formats used to communicate client news to the media include news releases, feature stories, captioned photographs or photo opportunities, and news conferences. A more complete listing of these formats can be found in Exhibit 2-d. They are called uncontrolled media because the practitioner loses control of these materials at the media outlet itself. An editor may choose to use the practitioner's release or feature story in its entirety, partially, or not at all; or editors may send reporters who will write or videotape their own stories about the client, ignoring the practitioner's efforts. Because the client or practitioner does not pay the media outlet to use the story as advertising, the use of the material is at the discretion of the media outlet. Similarly, conversations about

E X H I B I T 2-d   Uncontrolled and Controlled Media

Uncontrolled Media

News releases—print and video news releases (VNRs)

Feature stories

Photographs with cutlines (captions) or photo opportunities

News conferences

Media kits—paper or digital (DVD or CD-ROM, or thumbdrive)) or online format

Radio/TV public service announcements (PSAs) (nonprofit organizations only)

Interviews

>   Print media and online publications
>   Broadcast and cable media
>   Alternative online media

Teleconferences

Personal appearances on broadcast media

News audio files for radio

News images and video for TV and YouTube

Special programs for radio and TV radio, TV and YouTube

Recorded telephone news capsules and updates from an institution

Informing and influencing editors, broadcast news and public service directors, columnists, and reporters (phone calls, email, tip sheets, newsletters with story leads, media advisories)

Business feature articles

Financial publicity

Product publicity

Pictorial publicity

Background editorial material (backgrounders and fact sheets)

Letters to the editor

Op-ed pieces

Controlled Media

Print communication methods

>   House publications
>   Brochures, information pieces
>   Handbooks, manuals, books
>   Letters, bulletins, memos
>   Podcasts and online videos

Bulletin boards, posters, flyers

Information racks

E-mail

External periodicals: opinion-leader periodicals, corporate general public periodicals, distributor-dealer periodicals, stockholder periodicals, supplier periodicals, periodicals for special publics

Annual reports

Commemorative stamps

Exhibits and displays

Mobile libraries, bookmobiles

Mobile displays

Attitude or information surveys

Suggestion boxes, systems

Instructions and orders

Pay inserts

Written reports

Billing inserts

Financial statement inserts

Training kits, aids, manuals

Consumer information kits

Legislative information kits

Teacher kits, student games

Teacher aids

Print window displays

Audiovisual communication methods

Institutional videos

Easel pad presentations

Telephone calls, phone banks,
recorded messages

Multimedia exhibits and displays

Audio files, MP3s, CD-ROMs, DVDs

Video DVDs

Visual and multimedia window displays

Oral presentations with visuals

Multimedia training aids

    Slide shows using computer presentation software)

    Teacher aids, student games

Specially equipped vans, trains, buses, boats, airplanes, blimps

Interpersonal communication methods

Formal speeches, lectures, seminars

Online discussion forums

Teleconferences

Roundtable conferences

Panel discussions

Question-and-answer discussions

Oral testimony

Employee town hall meetings

Legal, health, miscellaneous counseling

Committee meetings

Staff meetings

Informal conversations

Demonstrations

Speakers bureaus: recruiting and training speakers, speech preparation, clearance of materials with management, list of subjects, speakers' guide, engagements and bookings, visual aids, follow-up correspondence

Training programs

Interviews

Personal instructions

Social affairs/events

Face-to-face reports

Public relations advertising (not designed to stimulate product sales)

Print and broadcast advertising

Institutional advertising—image building

Public affairs (advocacy) advertising: institutional or organizational statements on controversial issues

Direct mail institutional advertising

Outdoor advertising: billboards, signs

Yellow Pages institutional advertising

Transit advertising, skywriting, fly-by advertising

Specialty items: calendars, ashtrays, pens, matchbooks, emery boards, memo pads

Online banner ads

Websites

organizations and campaigns on social media sites, such as Facebook, are easily influenced by factors and people outside the influence of the organization.

The use of controlled media, on the other hand, involves communication about the client that is governed by the client. The wording of the material, its format, and its placement in the media are all at the discretion of the client. The formats for controlled media include print materials such as brochures, newsletters, and reports; audiovisual materials such as videos, flash animations, and computer slide shows; and interpersonal communication such as speeches, meetings, and interviews. Also included in controlled media are institutional advertising aimed at enhancing the client's image, advocacy advertising that communicates the client's stand on a controversial issue, and other forms of nonproduct advertising. Blogs sponsored by the organization and Twitter feeds could also be considered a form of controlled media. Websites are indispensable in communicating large amounts of information about the client. Exhibit 2-d includes a more detailed listing of the forms of controlled media.

Effective Communication

The final aspect of programming is the effective communication of the program. Thus, the factors of source, message, channel, receivers, and feedback will be useful in our examination of communication principles. That is, effective communication depends on:

1. Source credibility
2. Salient information (message)
3. Effective verbal cues (message)
4. Effective nonverbal cues (message)
5. Two-way communication (channel and feedback)
6. Opinion leaders (receivers)
7. Group influence (receivers)
8. Selective exposure (receivers)
9. Audience participation (feedback)

Source Credibility. The success or failure of the entire public relations campaign can hinge on how the source of communication, the voice for the client or organization, is perceived by the intended audience. Credibility involves a set of perceptions about sources held by receivers or audiences. The personal characteristics of believable sources that continually appear in communication research are trustworthiness, expertise, dynamism, physical attractiveness, and perceived similarities between the source and receivers.[1] These characteristics should serve the PR practitioner as guidelines for selecting individuals to represent the client or organization. Communication coming from high-credibility sources will clearly be in the best interests of the PR program.

Salient Information. A second principle of effective communication involves the use of salient information in the client's messages addressed to target audiences. Members of audiences can be viewed as information processors whose attitudes and behaviors are influenced by their integration of significant new information into their preexisting beliefs.[2] This is another way of saying that the message content must be motivational for the intended audiences—it must strike responsive chords in their minds and provide benefits that resonate with the public's value system.

Nonverbal Cues. A third principle of effective communication involves the use of appropriate nonverbal cues in the PR program's messages. Countless volumes have been published on a variety of aspects of nonverbal communication. But for purposes of effective programming, the PR practitioner should closely examine the nature of the client's actions or special events that are to serve as a basis for the overall effort. Choosing appropriate symbols to represent the client or the cause can be the most important aspect of nonverbal communication. Questions involving the mood, or atmosphere, desired at the event, the personnel to be used, the guests to be invited, the setting, the forms of interpersonal interaction, and the scheduling should be raised. For example, the people seated behind a speaker and banners at events are chosen to augment the messages of the speaker. These are essential details that can make the difference between success and failure for the client. Exhibit 2-e provides more details useful in planning effective nonverbal communication for the client.

Verbal Cues. The use of effective verbal message cues, or the actual wording of the client's messages, is the fourth principle of communication considered

---

E X H I B I T 2-e   Nonverbal Communication

Appropriate symbols
    Mood or atmosphere desired: excitement, quiet dignity
    Organizational personnel involved, including spokesperson(s) to be used
        Demographics and appearance of the audience
        Appearance, dress, actions/interactions expected
    Guests: appearance and dress
        Setting, buildings, rooms, or exterior environment desired
        Colors
        Background: banner, logo
        Lighting
        Sound system
        Nature and use of space
        Types and arrangement of furniture, seating arrangements
        Other artifacts to be used: paintings, wall tapestries, sports banners, colored balloons
        Nature of central presentation appropriate for setting (vice versa)
        Music: type, volume
        Entertainment (if any)
        Food, beverages, refreshments (if any)
    Forms of interpersonal interaction: sit-down dinner, stand-up cocktail party, reception
    Use of time: where will emphasis be placed; will activity build to climax?

here. The two most important characteristics of effective language usage are clarity and appropriateness.

To be clear, language must be accurate. The forms of communication used in a PR program should use words precisely, so the practitioner may need to consult a dictionary or thesaurus. Messages should be tested with a small audience to eliminate ambiguity before their actual use in a PR program. Ensure the meaning associated with your messages. In addition to accuracy, simplicity of word choice contributes to language clarity. Why use big words when simple ones will do? Audiences will relate to such words as try better than endeavor, help better than facilitate, explain better than explicate, tell better than indicate, and learn better than ascertain. Finally, coherence is an important factor in clear language. The words in a message should be logically connected—they should hang together well. The use of simple sentences rather than compound or complex ones contributes to coherence. Clear transitions and summaries in messages also aid coherence. Accuracy, simplicity, and coherence, then, are the major factors in constructing clear messages.

Messages should also be appropriate to the client, the audience, and the occasion. If the client is the city's leading bank, some levels of language may be inappropriate. Language used by a fast-food chain is different from that used in the messages of a funeral home. Similarly, language must be appropriate to the demographic level of the audience. Young people will obviously respond to a different use of language than senior citizens. The occasion for the use of the message also influences the level and type of language to be used. A diplomatic function held in a Washington embassy requires a different level of language from that used at a locker room gathering of an athletic team. Thus, appropriateness and clarity are the two major requisites for effectiveness in the use of verbal message cues.

Two-Way Communication.   The fifth principle of effective communication involves two-way interaction. Communication was once considered a linear process involving the transmission of a message from a source through a channel to a receiver. On receipt of the message at its destination, the communication transaction was considered complete. Today, however, the PR practitioner must program two-way communication activities that permit audience response—or feedback—in brief, the interactive aspects discussed earlier. For example, comments and ratings of an organization's video posted on YouTube.com constitute a form of two-way interaction. Facebook and blog comments allow the voice of your public to be heard. Expect social media and groups interested in your campaign to carry on conversations about your issues.

Traditionally, a variety of print-oriented response mechanisms are available, such as the suggestion box for employee communication, response cards to be returned to the source of communication, and letters to the editors of publications. The most effective means of two-way interaction, however, is interpersonal communication activities: speeches with question-and-answer sessions, small-group meetings, and one-on-one communication. It is usually possible to divide target audiences into small groups that provide excellent opportunities for interpersonal communication. This is the most effective form of persuasion because of the high level of source-receiver engagement.

Opinion Leaders. The sixth principle of effective communication involves the identification and targeting of opinion leaders as receivers of communication. Sometimes communication operates efficiently in a direct, one-step flow from source to receiver. On many occasions, however, communication is more effective when staged in a two-step or multiple-step flow. In these cases, the practitioner should seek opinion leaders, or "influentials," who in turn will communicate with their followers or cohorts. One simple way to identify opinion leaders is to catalog the leadership of all important groups in a given community or institution. These may include elected political leaders and others who hold formal positions in the community. In some cases, opinion leaders may hold no formal positions, but their advice is nonetheless sought and respected within given groups, institutions, or communities. Practitioners should create a list of opinion-leader contacts, much like their media contacts list, including all relevant data about the leaders, their positions, their availability, and their influence on other audiences. Certain social media "friends" are more influential than others.

Group Influence. A seventh effective communication principle involves the use of group influence. People belong to a variety of formal and informal groups, whether through personal face-to-face interaction or via online affinity groups. The most valued groups, which exert the greatest influence on their members, are known as reference groups. Members feel a sense of cohesiveness, of belonging together; have mutual, face-to-face interactions and influence each other; and share a set of norms and roles that structure and enforce a degree of conformity by each member. When newspapers list the most popular or most emailed stories of the day, they attract additional viewers due to group influence.

The practitioner's task is to identify and target for communication key groups that can be most useful to the client or organization. Special effort should go into the preparation of a group contacts list, similar to the media and opinion-leader lists. Groups should be reached through interpersonal communication (speeches or presentations) as well as other appropriate methods such as online forums. Traditionally, it is especially important to contact a formal group's program chairperson to schedule a speech or other presentation on behalf of the client. Acceptance of the client's message or position by key group leaders will then effectively engage the essential nature of group influence: acceptance by all members because of the group's operative cohesiveness and conformity.

Selective Exposure. An eighth principle of effective communication that should be observed by the public relations practitioner is selective exposure. Because the objectives of public relations include attitude and behavior modification, the temptation is always present to take on the most difficult all tasks: changing existing attitudes or behaviors. Why is this the toughest

The principle of selective exposure holds that people will accept and even seek out communication supporting their beliefs. However, communication researchers have also found that people will not necessarily avoid information incompatible with their views, as was once thought to be the case.[3] Moreover, other communication research indicates that when a persuasive message falls within the region (latitude) of personal acceptance, opinion or attitude will change in the direction of the advocated position. But when it falls within the region of rejection, attitudes will not change.[4] These communication research findings send a clear message to the PR practitioner—the easiest task in persuasion is reinforcement of existing attitudes or behaviors.

Clearly, trying to change attitudes or behavior is difficult and counter-productive, particularly in the face of strong resistance. Avoid fighting a losing battle. When controversial messages are necessary, audiences or individual receivers should always be categorized on the basis of their agreement or disagreement with the message in question. Using terms that coincide with the Likert scale often used in attitude surveys, audiences can be categorized as "positive" (those who strongly agree with the message); "somewhat positive" (those who agree with the message); "undecided"; "somewhat negative" (those who disagree with the message); and "negative" (those who strongly disagree with the message).

The principle of selective exposure dictates that the practitioner first target the "positives," then the "somewhat positives," next the "undecideds," and last, if at all, the "somewhat negatives." The pure "negatives," those strongly opposed or in disagreement with the program's message, should usually be written off. If their attitudes are hardened, and especially if they have publicly expressed their disagreement, they are highly unlikely to change their minds. Given a long period of time, along with perhaps unlimited funds, the hard-core negatives may be slowly changed; but for most practical and immediate situations requiring persuasion, conversion of the negatives is not worth the time, effort, or money. If those individuals with negative views of an issue are rather influential, then your campaign faces special challenges.

Audience Participation. A final principle of effective communication, observed whenever possible, is the use of audience participation. This is the only means of communication that encourages audience self-persuasion through direct experience or involvement with the client's services or products. Communication researchers have found that self-persuasion is more effective, by far, than many other means of influence.[5] Therefore, the practitioner should constantly seek opportunities to include audience participation in PR programs. Many online games are used to engage an audience through digital participation. Letting audiences construct digital stories and virtual worlds is the same as traditional community participation.

In summary, public relations programming consists of planning, including attention to theme and message, the use of an action or special event, the use of ncontrolled and controlled media, and program execution following the ciples of effective communication.

EVALUATION

Evaluation as discussed here is an ongoing process of monitoring and, when appropriate, final assessment of the stated objectives of the PR program. It is usually inadvisable to wait until the execution of the program has been completed to begin the evaluation process. Instead, the practices described here should be engaged in at stipulated intervals during the execution, with program adjustments made as deemed appropriate.

Evaluating Informational Objectives

The measurement of informational objectives includes three dimensions: message exposure, message comprehension, and message retention.

Message exposure is most commonly determined by publicity placement through national or local clipping and media monitoring services. It can also be measured through the circulation figures and audience-size data readily available for publications, websites and broadcast media. Twitter followers and attendance figures for events or meetings also provide an index of message exposure. Finally, exposure is measured by computerized tracking systems that have been developed by some public relations firms for monitoring their effectiveness in delivering messages to audiences.

Message comprehension, or at least the potential for comprehension, is most frequently determined by the application of readability formulas to the messages used in PR programs. The most often used are the Flesch Reading Ease Formula, the Gunning Fog Index, and the Dale-Chall Formula.[6] These predict ease of comprehension based on measuring the difficulty of the words and the length of the sentences used in messages, but surveys must be used to measure actual message comprehension.

Message retention is usually tested by asking appropriate questions designed to check target audiences' knowledge of the client's message. Although message retention can be measured by the nonquantitative research methods discussed earlier, retention questions are usually administered in the form of sample surveys.

Thus, the key to determining the effectiveness of informational objectives lies in the assessment of message exposure, comprehension, and retention. The more of these measurements used, the more accurate the evaluation of effectiveness is likely to be.

Evaluating Attitudinal Objectives

Attitudinal objectives can be measured by several well-established survey research instruments, the most frequently used being Likert scales and the Semantic Differential.[7] Both of these instruments measure attitude intensity and direction; thus, they are useful in assessing whether new attitudes have been formed or whether existing attitudes have been reinforced or changed. These measurements require both pretesting and posttesting of target audiences to determine the degree of influence on attitudes attributable to the PR program. To be of any value at all, attitude measurement must be done by competent professionals, well-schooled and experienced in quantitative research methods.

Evaluating Behavioral Objectives

Finally, behavioral objectives can be measured in two ways. First, target audiences can be asked what their behaviors have been since exposure to the PR program. Like attitude measurement, assessment of audience behaviors requires testing before and after program exposure. However, the questions used will be different from those used in attitude research. Closed-end multiple-choice questions or checklists designed to determine audience behaviors are commonly used for this measurement.

A second means of assessing audience behavior is simply observing the behaviors of target audiences. In some cases, these can be counted, as in attendance at special events, numbers of telephone calls received, website "hits," or Facebook "likes". And in many situations, audiences may be small enough to observe before, during, and after exposure to the PR program.

Nonquantitative research methods can provide useful information both in asking audiences about their behaviors and in observing these behaviors. To obtain the most reliable evaluations of all three types of impact, however, competent professionals with established reputations in research should be retained.

Evaluating Output Objectives

In addition to measuring impact objectives, the PR practitioner must be concerned with assessing the effectiveness of output objectives, which involves the distribution of uncontrolled and controlled media. This effectiveness can be evaluated by keeping records of the number of news releases sent to publications and television stations, the number of contacts made with journalists, the number of speeches given to targeted audiences, the number of publications distributed to each public, and the number of meetings held with key audiences. In the realm of output objectives, practitioners accomplish their goals by distributing appropriate quantities of media according to their original plans. Although these are easily achievable objectives, it should be reiterated that they may have little bearing whatever on the PR program's priority goal—audience impact.

Throughout the campaign, the campaign process may be evaluated for efficiency and best use of resources in the communication effort. At the same time, mid-course corrections to campaigns can make messages more effective, refine target audiences and alter communication tactics.

Evaluation of the two general forms of program objectives—impact and output—constitutes an ongoing dimension of this public relations process model. The process will not be completed, however, when the program objectives are evaluated. These evaluative data are recycled as part of a continuing procedure. They are useful in adjusting ongoing relations with various audiences, and they can be helpful when planning the client's next short-term PR program with similar audiences.

SUMMARY

The public relations problem-solving process includes four parts: research, determination of objectives, programming, and evaluation. The following outline provides a useful summary and review of the whole process.

Outline of the Public Relations Process

I.   Research
    A.   Client/organization: background data about your client or organization—its personnel, financial status, reputation, past and present PR practices, PR strengths and weaknesses, opportunities
    B.   Opportunity/problem: proactive or reactive PR program; long-range or short-range campaign
    C.   Publics and audiences: identification of key groups to be targeted for communication
        1.   Desired research data: each targeted audience's level of information about your client/organization; image and other relevant attitudes held about your client/organization and its products or services; audience behaviors relevant to your client/organization; demographics, media habits, and media-use levels of each targeted audience
        2.   Research procedures: nonquantitative and quantitative

II. Objectives
    A.   Impact objectives
        1.   Informational objectives: message exposure, comprehension, retention
        2.   Attitudinal objectives: formation of new attitudes, reinforcement of existing attitudes, change in existing attitudes
        3.   Behavioral objectives: creation of new behavior, reinforcement of existing behavior, change in existing behavior
    B.   Output objectives: distribution or execution of uncontrolled and controlled media

III. Programming—planning and execution of:
    A.   Theme (if applicable) and message(s)
    B.   Action or special event(s)
    C.   Appropriate media and channels of communication: 1) uncontrolled media: news releases, feature stories, photos and social media sites; 2) controlled media: print, audiovisual, interpersonal communication, PR advertising
    D.   Effective communication using principles of: source credibility, salient information, effective nonverbal and verbal cues, two-way communication, opinion leaders, group influence, selective exposure, and audience participation

IV. Evaluation—ongoing monitoring and final assessment of:
    A.   Impact objectives
        1.   Informational objectives: measured by publicity placement, surveys

    2. Attitudinal objectives: measured by attitude surveys

    3. Behavioral objectives: measured by surveys and observation of behaviors

  B. Output objectives: measured quantitatively by simply counting the actual output

ENDNOTES

1. For a summary of this research, see Daniel J. O'Keefe, *Persuasion: Theory and Research*, 2d ed. (Thousand Oaks, CA: Sage Publications, 2002), and Mary John Smith, *Persuasion and Human Action* (Belmont, CA: Wadsworth, 1982): 219ff, the latter a classic in its field.

2. For a detailed discussion of the information integration approach to persuasion, see Smith, *Persuasion and Human Action*, pp. 243–261.

3. The best discussion of selective exposure is David O. Sears and Jonathan L. Freedman, "Selective Exposure to Information: A Critical Review," *Public Opinion Quarterly* 31 (summer 1967): 194–213. Also a classic in the field.

4. For a good explanation of this research, called social judgment theory, see Nan Lin, *The Study of Human Communication* (Indianapolis, IN: Bobbs-Merrill, 1977), pp. 118–122. Also see Smith, *Persuasion and Human Action*, pp. 264–274.

5. For a review of this research, see Smith, *Persuasion and Human Action*, pp. 191–207.

6. For the Flesch Formula, see Rudolf Flesch, *How to Test Readability* (New York: Harper & Row, 1951); Gunning's Fog Index is found in Robert Gunning, *The Technique of Clear Writing*, rev. ed. (New York: McGraw-Hill, 1968); for the Dale-Chall Formula, see Edgar Dale and Jeanne Chall, "A Formula for Predicting Readability," *Educational Research Bulletin* 27 (January and February 1948).

7. For a discussion of these and other research instruments used in attitude measurement, see O'Keefe, *Persuasion: Theory and Research*.

HEADINGS ON THE PUBLIC RELATIONS PROCESS

Research

Alreck, Pamela L., and Robert B. Settle. *The Survey Research Handbook*, 3d ed. Burr Ridge, IL: Irwin, 2003.

Asher, Herbert. *Polling and the Public: What Every Citizen Should Know*, 7th ed. Washington: CQ Press, 2007.

Buddenbaum, Judith M., and Katherine B. Novak. *Applied Communication Research*. Ames: Iowa State University Press, 2001.

Clary, Sandy. "You Are What You Know: Research for Campaign Success," *Public Relations Tactics* 15 (January 2008): 10.

Damon, Christine and Immy Holloway. *Qualitative Research Methods in Public Relations and Marketing Communications*, 2nd ed. New York: Routledge, 2011.

Greely, Andrew. "In Defense of Surveys," *Transaction Social Science and Modern Society* 33 (May–June 1996): 26ff.

Hocking, John E., Don W. Stacks, and Steven T. McDermott. *Communication Research*, 3d ed. Boston: Allyn & Bacon, 2003.

Karlberg, Michael. "Remembering the Public in Public Relations Research: From Theoretical to Operational Symmetry," *Journal of Public Relations Research* 8 (fall 1996): 263–278.

Keyton, Joann. *Communication Research: Asking Questions, Finding Answers.* New York: McGraw-Hill, 2010.

Moore, David W. *The Opinion Makers: An Insider Exposes the Truth Behind the Polls.* Boston: Beacon Press, 2008.

Paine, Katie Delahaye. *Measure What Matters: Online Tools For Understanding Customers, Social Media, Engagement, and Key Relationships.* Oxford, UK: Wiley, 2011.

Rubin, Rebecca B., Alan M. Rubin, and Paul M. Haridakis. *Communication Research: Strategies and Sources.* Boston: Wadsworth, 2010.

Shao, Alan T., and Kevin Zheng Zhou. *Marketing Research, An Aid to Decision Making*, 3d ed. Boston: Atomic Dog, 2007.

Stacks, Don W. *Primer of Public Relations Research*, 2d ed. New York: Guilford Publications, 2011.

van Ruler, Betteke (ed), Ana Tkalac Vercic (ed), and Dejan Vercic (ed) *Public Relations Metrics: Research and Evaluation.* New York: Routledge, 2008.

Objectives

Benoit, William, and Pamela Benoit. *Persuasive Messages: The Process of Influence.* Malden, MA: Blackwell, 2008.

Brock, Timothy C., and Melanie C. Green, eds. *Persuasion: Psychological Insights and Perspectives*, 2d ed. Thousand Oaks, CA: Sage Publications, 2005.

Broom, Glen M., and David M. Dozier. "Writing Program Goals and Objectives." In Using *Research in Public Relations: Applications to Program Management.* Englewood Cliffs, NJ: Prentice-Hall, 1996, pp. 39–44.

Cutlip, Scott M., Allen H. Center, and Glen M. Broom. *Effective Public Relations*, 10th ed. Englewood Cliffs, NJ: Prentice-Hall, 2009.

Hauss, Deborah. "Setting Benchmarks Leads to Effective Programs," *Public Relations Journal* 49 (February 1993): 16–17.

Jaques, Tony. "Systematic Objective Setting for Effective Issue Management," *Journal of Public Affairs* 5 (February 2005): 33–42.

Smith, Ronald D. "Establishing Goals and Objectives," *Strategic Planning for Public Relations*, 3d ed. Mahwah, NJ: Erlbaum, 2009, 79–92.

Programming

Cutlip, Scott M., Allen H. Center, and Glen M. Broom. *Effective Public Relations*, 10th ed. Englewood Cliffs, NJ: Prentice-Hall, 2009.

Grunig, James E., ed. *Excellence in Public Relations and Communication Management.* Hillsdale, NJ: Erlbaum, 1992.

Guth, David, and Charles Marsh. *Public Relations: A Values-Driven Approach*, 4th ed. Boston: Allyn & Bacon, 2009.

Newsom, Doug, Judy VanSlyke Turk, and Dean Kruckeberg. *This Is PR: The Realities of Public Relations*, 10th ed. Belmont, CA: Wadsworth, 2009.

Okigbo, Charles, and Sonya Nelson. "Precision Public Relations: Facing the Demographic Challenge," *Public Relations Quarterly* 48 (summer 2003): 29–35.

Pratt, Cornelius B. "Crafting Key Messages and Talking Points—or Grounding Them in What Research Tells Us," *Public Relations Quarterly* 49 (fall 2004): 15–21.

Seitel, Fraser P. *The Practice of Public Relations*, 9th ed. Englewood Cliffs, NJ: Prentice-Hall, 2006.

Smith, Ronald D. *Strategic Planning for Public Relations*, 3d ed. Mahwah, NJ: Erlbaum, 2009.

Wilcox, Dennis L., Glen T. Cameron, Philip H. Ault, and Warren K. Agee. *Public Relations: Strategies and Tactics*, 10th ed. Boston: Allyn & Bacon, 2011.

Evaluation

Broom, Glen M., and David M. Dozier. "Using Research to Evaluate Programs." In *Using Research in Public Relations: Applications to Program Management*. Englewood Cliffs, NJ: Prentice-Hall, 1996, pp. 71–88.

Charland, Bernie. "The Mantra of Metrics: A Realistic and Relevant Approach to Measuring the Impact of Employee Communications," *Public Relations Strategist* 10 (fall 2004): 30–32.

Cutlip, Scott M., Allen H. Center, and Glen M. Broom. "Step Four: Evaluating the Program." In *Effective Public Relations*, 10th ed. Englewood Cliffs, NJ: Prentice-Hall, 2009.

Coffman, Julia. Public Communication Campaign Evaluation: an Environmental Scan of Challenges, Criticisms, Practice, and Opportunities. Communications Consortium Media Center, Harvard Family Research Project (May 2002).

Freitag, Alan R. "How to Measure What We Do," *Public Relations Quarterly* 43 (summer 1998): 42–47.

González, Ana Rita. "Grassroots Approaches to Reach the Hispanic Audience: Non-traditional Approaches to Measure ROI," *Public Relations Tactics* 12 (July 2005): 24.

Lindemann, Walter K. "An 'Effectiveness Yardstick' to Measure Public Relations Success," *Public Relations Quarterly* 38 (spring 1993): 7–9.

Paine, Katie Delahaye. How to Measure Social Media Relations: The More Things Change, the More They Remain the Same. Institute for Public Relations (April 2007).

_____ *Measure What Matters: Online Tools For Understanding Customers, Social Media, Engagement, and Key Relationships*. Oxford, UK: Wiley, 2011.

Pilmer, John. "Small Business? Small Budget? How to Measure for Success," *Public Relations Tactics* 12 (July 2005): 23.

Pratt, Cornelius B., and George Lennon. "What's wrong with outcomes Evaluation?" *Public Relations Quarterly* 46 (winter 2001): 40–44.

Rossi, Peter H., and Howard E. Freeman. *Evaluation: A Systematic Approach*, 7th ed. Beverly Hills, CA: Russell Sage Foundation, 2003.

Stacks, Don W. *Primer of Public Relations Research*. 2nd ed. New York: Guilford Publications, 2011.

PART II

Reaching Major Audiences

3

Media Relations

ournalists representing the mass and specialized media usually make up a priority external audience for public relations practitioners. Media relations consists essentially of obtaining appropriate publicity, or news coverage, for the activities of the practitioner's client or organization. The field of public relations began as publicity and for many years was called that. Despite the emerging importance of using social media to engage publics, the news media remains a powerful message multiplier for the public relations practitioner. A single news story in one media outlet can reach vast audiences and cause ripples among other media that also builds exposure via word-of-mouth and social media chatter. Also, mediated communication via the news media is seen as a highly credible source of information by publics.[1] Just appearing in print, online, or in a television program suggests the information is credible. Indeed, this process remains the basis for the burgeoning disciplines of public relations, public affairs, and corporate communications.

Media relations involves targeting the "gatekeepers" of the mass and specialized media for communication about the client or organization. However, the media are actually intermediate audiences. The ultimate targeted audiences in media relations are the consumers of the media.

RESEARCH

The research process for media relations includes investigation of the practitioner's client or organization, of the opportunity or problem that accounts for communication with the media, and of the various audiences themselves to be targeted for the PR effort.

Client Research

First, the practitioner should be familiar with background data about the client or organization, including its personnel, financial status, and reputation. Special attention must be given to past and present relations with media representatives. Has the client had negative or positive news coverage in the past? Has there been little or no coverage? Does the client have any particular media coverage strengths, such as unusual or glamorous products or a newsworthy chief executive officer? On the other hand, what are the client's publicity "negatives"? In what areas is the client vulnerable? Finally, the practitioner should assess the client's publicity opportunities. What special events can be most profitably staged for the client? What can be done to tie the client in with ongoing community or national special events? With information of this kind, the practitioner will be better prepared to serve the client's publicity or media relations needs.

Opportunity or Problem Research

The second aspect of research in preparation for media relations involves determining the reason for the program. Is it because an opportunity has presented itself for good news coverage, or has some problem arisen that will bring media representatives to the client's doorstep? This chapter is concerned more with the former situation, the publicity *opportunity*. For information on managing the media when a problem or crisis develops, see Chapter 12, "Emergency Public Relations."

Audience Research

The final aspect of research for media relations is thought by most practitioners to be the most important—identifying the appropriate media and *their* audiences to target for communication. These media fall into two broad categories, mass and specialized, each of which can be further subdivided (see Exhibit 3-a).

With these media categories, the practitioner's task is to prepare a comprehensive list of media contacts. Appropriate *media directories*, such as those listed in the suggested readings in this chapter, should be consulted in preparing such a list. Practitioners may find that much of their work has already been done for them by these directories. The national, regional, state, and city directories are thorough, but in some cases more information must be gathered. To be of optimal use, the media contact list should include:

1. The type and size of the audience reached by each media outlet
2. The type of material used by the media outlet—spot news, feature material, interviews, or photos
3. The name and title of the appropriate editor, director, producer, reporter, or staff writer who handles news of organizations such as the client's
4. The deadlines for that media contact—monthly, weekly, daily, morning, afternoon, evening, date, day, or hour

The best advice for the practitioner in media relations is simply to *know the media outlet*. Each outlet has its own unique set of departments and editorial staffing,

---

EXHIBIT 3-a Media Publics

Mass media

Local

> Print publications
> Newspapers
> Magazines
> TV stations
> Radio stations
> Other online and digital information sources (bloggers)

National

> Print publications
> Broadcast networks
> Wire services

Specialized media

Local

> Trade, industry, and association publications
> Organizational house and membership publications
> Ethnic publications
> Publications of special groups
> Specialized broadcast programs and stations
> Other online and digital information sources (bloggers and local news sources)

National

> General business publications
> National trade, industry, and association publications
> National organizational house and membership publications
> National ethnic publications
> Publications of national special groups
> National specialized broadcast programs and networks
> Other online and digital information sources (bloggers)

---

with particular requirements for submitting material. If in doubt, call the media outlet to obtain the necessary guidelines, along with the name and address of the person who holds the editorial position. It is usually best not to ask to speak with journalists themselves. They may be very busy and resent intrusions for routine information. As a rule, news releases for newspapers should be addressed to the city editor if they are general in nature or to the appropriate section editor or reporter if they are of special interest. For broadcast outlets, news releases should usually be addressed to the news director or, in some cases, to the public service director.

Practitioners should never feel that their media contact lists are complete when they have compiled necessary information about the mass media alone. Each client or organization will be operating in a special field. Automobile manufacturers, fashion designers, dentists, and music groupshave their own organizations or associations, and are served by their own specialized publications. Public relations practitioners must be aware of all such publications that serve their client's field. The process of compiling a list of specialized media contacts begins with consulting a media directory. For comprehensive listings in a great variety of fields, look at publications or online services such are Cision, Vocus' and Burrelles *Luce* media directories. Later in this chapter, other directories and services are listed for medical, scientific, military, and minority media contacts.

Among the finished products of the practitioner's audience research, then, will be two media contact lists: one for mass media and the other for specialized media, which are relevant to the campaign and client. News releases, photos, and feature stories directed to and published in specialized publications can often be of greater value to the client than similar exposure in the mass media. It should be emphasized that the purpose of compiling these *two* media contact lists is communication with the consumers of both the mass and specialized media— the client's ultimate intended audiences.

In the cases included later in this chapter, these audiences are sometimes specialized and sometimes mass in character.

Thus, the research process in media relations involves a thorough under-standing of the practitioner's client or organization; the reason—opportunity or problem—for communicating with the media; and, most important, knowledge of the targeted media themselves—the nature of the media outlets, audiences reached, types of material used, specific names and titles of staff contacts, and their deadlines.

OBJECTIVES

Media relations uses both impact and output objectives. Some typical examples of both types are examined here, along with a sampling of the objectives used in the media relations cases included in this chapter.

Impact Objectives

Impact objectives represent the desired outcomes of modifying the attitudes and behaviors of target audiences. In media relations, they usually include such statements as:

1. To increase knowledge of news about the client among community media representatives
2. To enhance the client's credibility among media people

3. To reinforce favorable attitudes toward the client on the part of media representatives

4. To increase favorable client news coverage

Note that in each of these statements, percentages and time frames can be added as desired. The first statement could be rephrased to read: to increase knowledge of news about the client by 30 percent among community media representatives during the period from June 1 to December 1. However, a majority of the award-winning cases in this book do *not* quantify their objectives or set time frames.

Almost invariably the objectives used in our sample cases targeted the client's ultimate audiences, rather than the media audiences, for desired impact. It is understood in each case, however, that the media must be the intermediate target audience. Perhaps the objectives would have been clearer and easier to measure if they had targeted *both* the desired media and the ultimate audiences.

Output Objectives

Output objectives in media relations refer to the efforts made by the practitioner on behalf of the client. These statements suggest activities intended to support the client's desired influence on audiences. Output objectives may include:

1. To be of service to the media—both proactively and reactively
   a. Proactively, to provide *newsworthy* stories about the client or organization
   b. Reactively, to be available for responses to media inquiries
2. To coordinate media interviews with client or organizational officers and personnel
3. To distribute feature story ideas to three trade publications

PROGRAMMING

Programming for media relations includes the same planning and execution elements used in other forms of public relations: (1) theme and messages, (2) action or special event(s), (3) uncontrolled or controlled media, and (4) principles of effective communication.

Theme and Messages

Program themes, especially in connection with special events, should be included in the messages sent to media outlets. In media relations, the messages themselves should be governed by the requirements for newsworthiness applicable to the targeted media outlets. Since media relations essentially involves the communication of client news to media outlets or the stimulation of news coverage of the client, the practitioner must understand the nature of news and the criteria for newsworthiness.

Some practitioners believe there are two kinds of news: "hard" and "soft." It is more accurate, however, to think of *spot news* and *feature material* as the two kinds of news.

Spot news is temporal, or time-bound, in nature. Within the rubric of spot news are two subcategories: hard and soft. *Hard spot news* is normally found on prominent pages of major metropolitan dailies. It affects large numbers of people and is of great and immediate interest to the audiences of most mass media outlets. Unfortunately, most hard spot news handled by PR practitioners is *bad news* about the client, such as disasters, plant closings, or layoffs. *Good news* about clients may involve hard news about new initiatives or new product launches, but many news items are usually classified as *soft spot news*. If it doesn't contain much newsworthy value, don't expect the material to generate much interest outside the organization itself, in which case it should be printed in a house publication and not sent to a mass media outlet. A major challenge to the practitioner is to create special events or *make* good news about the client that will receive favorable coverage in the media.

Feature material, on the other hand, is not time-bound but may be used as "filler" for print and broadcast media. Feature stories for both kinds of media usually focus on human interest topics. Types of feature stories include "a day in the life of …"; profiles of personalities; interviews; descriptions of events that emphasize human interest factors and the personalities involved; and sidebars, or feature stories designed to accompany spot news stories in news outlets.

Keeping in mind the differences between spot news and feature material, the practitioner should also be sensitive to the general criteria used by journalists to determine what is newsworthy. The usual characteristics of news include what is new or novel, involves famous persons, is important to large numbers of people, involves conflict or mystery, may be considered confidential, will have significant consequences, is funny, is romantic, or involves sex.

News has also been defined as anything a media outlet chooses to print, broadcast, or film as "news." Since the selection is always the outlet's choice, the public relations practitioner must become familiar with the criteria used by that particular group of editors. This is simply another way of saying *Know the media outlet.*

Like other aspects of programming, theme and messages should be governed by the practitioner's understanding of what is news and both the general and particular newsworthiness criteria in use at individual media outlets.

Action(s) or Special Event(s)

The use of actions on the part of the client and the staging of special events assume special importance in media relations. They provide the basis for news coverage. They *are* the news about the client. Thus, the PR practitioner should review the list of actions and special events included in Exhibit 2-c. These can serve as methods of *making* news for the client. Each action or special event should be carefully planned and orchestrated for its maximum news value. Celebrities may often help focus additional interest in the campaign, and as many other news criteria should be incorporated as is feasible.

Uncontrolled Media

Uncontrolled media are the major vehicles for reporting client news to media representatives. The most commonly used forms are:

1. News releases—print/online and video
2. Photographs and photo opportunities
3. News conferences
4. Media interviews

News Releases—Print/Online and Video. Of these four frequently used formats, news releases are the most popular with public relations practitioners. News releases provide a quick, economical means of communicating client spot news or feature material to appropriate media outlets. *Print news releases* are delivered by hand courier, mailed, faxed, or emailed. Twitter feeds may include a URL to direct media attention to your campaign's website. Corporations and other organizations often place current news releases on their websites or use online distribution services to reach audiences.

Online and emailed releases may be customized to include links to additional sources of information and even links to social media sites. Through the online links, the journalist may quickly retrieve other background information about an organization or see what the CEO is saying in a personal blog.

Search engine optimization further customizes the language in a news release through the use of key words that are relevant to current news issues. The news release may then gain higher exposure and rankings on search engines such as Google and Yahoo! Unfortunately, print news releases have become overused in major markets throughout the United States. Each morning, editors may be confronted with a stack of 70 or more releases from practitioners seeking news coverage for their clients or organizations. A prominent Washington bureau chief confided to one of our classes that, faced with his daily pile of news releases, he simply pulls a large, desktop-high wastebasket over to the edge of the desk and "files" most of the morning mail.

How, then, can practitioners expect to break through the blizzard of print news releases to call attention to their own client's news? The "secret" of successful news releases lies in the first word of the term itself—*news*. A really newsworthy story about a client can easily be telephoned or emailed to a city editor. The editor, if interested in the story, will assign a reporter to cover it. Major metropolitan editors or broadcast news directors rarely use news releases verbatim or even partially. If a story is there, the news release may alert them to it; but they invariably prefer to assign their own staff to do the actual news gathering and writing. A news release should be accompanied by appropriate contact with the media outlet whether by email, phone calls, personal contact at public events, Twitter feeds, or on social media sites. Be prepared to provide additional information and interviews to flesh out the story. Expect the reporter to contact both your friends and your critics.

The news release may be used to initiate a relationship with a journalist, but the relationship must be cultivated through personal contacts such as phone calls and email. Your goal is to become a credible and valued source of information about your organization for the journalist. Successful variations on the basic news release include *media alerts, media advisories,* and *fact sheets.* All media outlets, in markets large or small, depend on PR practitioners for *information* about news events in their market areas. Print news releases and their shorter variations, despite their overuse, remain the major method of transmitting information from the client to the journalist.

The *video news release* (VNR) became a popular form of client news in the past, but its popularity has waned because of the stigma broadcast journalists have attached to "fake news" used wholesale by a news outlet without attributing the real source of the story. Like its print counterpart, the successful VNR must focus on *news* rather than on promotional pap about the client. VNRs are most frequently used in medium or small markets rather than major metropolitan markets. They should be produced by a reputable firm specializing in VNRs, and, ideally, the firm should be equipped to handle the entire task, including scripting, production, and satellite distribution. Most VNRs today, if produced at all, include accompanying B-roll and sound bites that might better be interspersed in television newscasts than the complete VNR. The video clips and background material allow interested editors to customize the story for local use.[2]

Photograph and Video Opportunities.   Photographs and videos are another widely used form of uncontrolled media. As with news releases, public relations photographs and videos are seldom used directly by major newspapers. But, like news releases, they may serve to attract the attention of major editors to client news that might otherwise be overlooked. Public relations photographs and videos have a better chance of being used by smaller publications in smaller markets. They are important enough to warrant attention to the details of their proper composition and preparation for PR purposes.

Good public relations photographs should be creative and imaginative in composition, avoiding the clichés a client may request, such as a speaker standing at a podium, one person handing something to another, a group shot of 10 or more people, or one person sitting at a desk. Photographs of this kind usually find their way into house publications. A good public relations photograph depicts something a newspaper photographer cannot duplicate or restage. Unique and interesting photographs may be used because of their creativity and news value.

A frequently used contemporary technique is the staging of a "photo opportunity," especially in markets where the major dailies or magazines are likely to assign their own photographers to a story. The photo opportunity should be carefully planned in advance and staged in a natural—not theatrical—way, so that it becomes an integral or necessary part of the news story and not something that can be missed by the assigned journalists and photographers. Similarly, video opportunities must offer compelling visuals that tell a real story and accent key themes for a client.

News Conferences.   A third frequently used form of uncontrolled media is the news conference. News conferences should be used sparingly since they are usually inconvenient for journalists. If staged, the conference must live up to its descriptive adjective, *news*. Even on their very best days, metropolitan journalists are easily annoyed if their time is wasted. They can resent being summoned to a news conference to hear a routine announcement that could have been emailed to the city desk or reported in a written release.

Many organizations use news conferences for significant announcements, such as major corporate changes, takeovers, mergers, introductions of new product lines, or responses to false accusations of wrongdoing. Other than for major government agencies, news conferences should never be routine. They should be reserved for truly newsworthy occasions that call for a personal presentation by the organization's CEO or by a visiting celebrity or dignitary. Video and audio recordings of the news conference may be posted on your website to increase exposure to your news. Don't forget to invite alternative media/bloggers to a news conference or teleconference as they may also generate coverage of the event. Journalists may also desire time to interact privately with the spokesperson to customize a story.

News conferences can be conducted profitably, but the practitioner should always keep the preceding reservations in mind and usually resist the urge to hold one.

Media Interviews.   Media interviews are a fourth frequently used form of un-controlled media. Whether given to print or broadcast journalists, interviews provide the most direct contact between the client and the media. The practitioner's role in this situation is that of a link, or coordinator, and sometimes also that of a trainer or coach for the client. The interview is not just to answer the reporter's questions, but to accent the themes and messages as outlined in the campaign.

In the case of print interviews, clients may have the option of declaring beforehand that their comments will be for background, not for attribution, or completely off the record. In these cases the client's name cannot be used; and in off-the-record interviews the content of the interview cannot be used in the media. Aside from interviews with high government officials in sensitive positions, however, most clients want to be both quoted and identified in the media as a means of promoting their organizations' interests.

Broadcast interviews do not permit the luxury of being off the record. If clients consent to broadcast interviews, they do so with the knowledge that while on camera (or microphone), they may be asked hard, grilling questions by an enterprising journalist. Moreover, the client loses control of the editing function. For this reason, many organizations insist on bringing their own videotaping equipment and crew in order to have an independent record of the interview. To best prepare spokespersons for these encounters with the media, organizations are paying specialized consultants for "media training" that helps keep the focus on key campaign messages.

Print and broadcast interviews, then, are one of the four most frequently used forms of uncontrolled media in the client's communication with journalists. In addition to news releases, photographs, news conferences, and interviews, the practitioner should consider the other communication vehicles listed in Exhibit 2-d.

Controlled Media

A variety of forms of controlled media can be used to provide journalists with background information. For example, practitioners usually prepare a media kit for news conferences. These kits include the opening statement made at the conference, a basic news release, backgrounder, fact sheet, photos with cutlines (captions), and such printed materials as brochures, folders, annual reports, speeches, and other information pieces. Increasingly, paper media kits are being supplemented or replaced by online interactive releases that contain links to much broader background information, quotes from executives and graphics, video, and audio files. Additionally, media kit materials are usually made available on corporate and organizational websites. In the true sense of the term, however, controlled media are not used in media relations. When journalists are given controlled communications, they make their own uses (or nonuses) of them. Thus, the client or practitioner has no control over how such materials will be used by journalists. Many publics actively search for an organization's media relations material via online sources, so the material offers another venue for messaging dissemination directly to key audiences.

A case can be made that public relations advertising constitutes the use of controlled communications in media relations. The practitioner *does* deal with media outlets in such cases, but not with journalists. Advertising is purchased directly from the media outlet's advertising department.

The exhibits included with the cases in this chapter demonstrate the scope of both uncontrolled and controlled communications used in media relations.

Effective Communication

In media relations, the communication process can be aptly described as a two-step flow. The traditional two-stage model depicts a stream of messages from a mass media source to opinion leaders and then to the colleagues of the opinion leaders. In media relations, this process is partially reversed. Communication flows from the practitioner's client to the media and then in turn to the media audience.

Because of the special nature of media relations, not all of the nine principles of effective communication discussed in Chapter 2 apply.

Source credibility clearly is applicable in the case of media relations. Media representatives must perceive the client or organization and its spokesperson as trustworthy and reliable. Additionally, just placing a story in a media outlet enhances receptiveness of the message as the media is often perceived as more credible than the client.

Salient information, on the other hand, must be redefined for media relations. Information that meets the criteria of newsworthiness constitutes the salience for journalists. Both nonverbal and verbal cues contribute to communication effectiveness in media relations, just as they do in other forms of public relations. The use of two-way communication, however, plays a less important role in media relations than in other forms unless a journalist is wishing to check the accuracy of information used in a story. Journalists generally resent inquiries from practitioners asking to change the content of a story. The feedback that practitioners really want in media relations is the use of their materials in the media.

The use of opinion leaders in the usual sense is not a part of media relations. In media relations, practitioners communicate directly with journalists. In some instances, journalists are regarded as community opinion leaders, but this principle applies more directly to community relations. The selective exposure principle may apply in some cases to media relations but, in general, journalists look for "balance" on issues and seek comment from sources contrary to their own opinion. However, much has been written about the subtle way bias creeps into stories through word choice and the selection of quotes. Finally, the audience participation principle is valid and useful in media relations. When introducing new product lines, for example, many companies invite journalists to use the product on an introductory basis. Journalist participation at news conferences and other meetings arranged by PR practitioners provides other instances of effective audience participation in media relations.

Thus, most of the principles of effective communication apply to media relations to some degree. However, the group-influence principle is rarely used in media relations since journalists pride themselves on their independence of thought and action. On the other hand, journalists may face some peer pressure if other media outlets are covering a story and they aren't. But, on the whole, principles of effective communication should be a priority concern of the public relations practitioner in media relations.

EVALUATION

The evaluation process in all forms of public relations always refers to the program's stated objectives. In media relations, as in all of public relations, impact objectives are of the highest priority.

Evaluating Impact Objectives

The impact objective of informing the media about the client is generally measured by assessing the exposure of the message in the media, or publicity placement. National or local clipping and media monitoring services are usually retained to take this measure of effectiveness. Message exposure can also be measured by the circulation figures and audience-size data available from the publications and broadcast media themselves. Additionally, some public relations firms use sophisticated computerized tracking systems to evaluate effectiveness in delivering messages to audiences. Publicity placement, however, remains the predominant method for evaluating the success of message exposure.

Attitude objectives in most forms of public relations are measured by conducting sample surveys of the target audiences, but this may not be feasible with journalists targeted for communication. Some might react negatively to such an intrusion from a PR practitioner. Content analyses of media placement, however, can yield the desired measurements. A scientific assessment of attitudes is therefore possible and relatively easily obtained.

This same procedure is also useful in measuring favorable client news coverage. This objective is the ultimate goal of all media relations.

Evaluating Output Objectives

Along with the measurement of impact objectives, practitioners want to determine the effectiveness of their media relations output objectives. These consist essentially of distributing uncontrolled media to outlets, being responsive to media inquiries, and coordinating media interviews. They can be evaluated by keeping records of all such transactions. Although these objectives are easily accomplished, the practitioner should be reminded that these goals may have little bearing on media relations impact.

Evaluation of media relations, then, is heavily concentrated on successful and favorable placement of the practitioner's uncontrolled media. Other objectives are useful, but successful media relations ultimately boils down to the matter of placement. This is clearly visible in the priority given to placement in the evaluations of the cases in this chapter.

SUMMARY

With some modifications, the four-stage process is as useful in media relations as it is in other forms of public relations. Essentially, media relations involves establishing a favorable working relationship between PR practitioners and journalists representing appropriate mass and specialized media.

The most important aspect of research for media relations is the preparation of up-to-date lists of media contacts for both mass and specialized outlets. Objectives in media relations usually emphasize the desired behavioral impact of obtaining favorable news coverage for the client. An absolute essential for media relations programming is an understanding of the particular media outlets' audiences and the media's definitions of news for those audiences. This information should provide criteria for the development of newsworthy, client-centered special events, news releases, photographs, news conferences, interviews, and/or other forms of uncontrolled media used in reaching journalists.

Evaluation of media relations always refers back to the program's stated objectives Impact objectives are generally measured through publicity placement, circulation and audience data, computer tracking of messages, or content analysis The accomplishment of output objectives can be simply determined by counting or otherwise observing the desired outputs as they are set in motion In essence, however, the effectiveness of media relations always comes down to media placement, that is, obtaining the desired publicity for the client.

ENDNOTES

1. Page, Benjamin I., Robert Y. Shapiro and Glenn R.Dempsey. "What Moves Public Opinion?" *The American Political Science Review* 81 (March 1987): 23-44. Schultza, Friederike. Sonja Utz, and Anja Göritz. "Is the medium the message? Perceptions of and reactions to crisis communication via twitter, blogs and traditional media," Public Relations Review 37 (March 2011): 20-27.

2. The VNR itself is "A-roll." Most news directors prefer the unedited "B-roll" and sound bites to create their own news stones.

READINGS ON MEDIA RELATIONS

Anderson, Rebecca B. "Thinning Out Your Target List: When Less Is More in Media Relations," *Public Relations Tactics* 13 (May 2006): 21-22.

Barbaro, Michael. "Wal-Mart Begins Quest for Generals in P.R. War," *New York Times* (March 30, 2006): C3.

Barstow, David, and Robin Stein. "Under Bush, a New Age of Prepackaged TV News," *New York Times* (March 13, 2005): A1.

Beasley, David. "Traditional Media Relations Finesse: The Power of the Phone Pitch in the Age of Click to Open," *Public Relations Tactics* 15 (May 2008): 21.

Beckman, Carol. "Nine Things to Remember When Talking to a Reporter," *Public Relations Tactics* 3 (September 1996): 13ff.

Bergman, Eric. "The Ethics of Not Answering," *Communication World* 22 (September–October 2005): 16–142.

Bressers, Bonnie and Joye Gordon. "Increasing Publicity and Thematic News Coverage: The Impact of Localizing News Releases in a State-Wide Experimental Field Study," *Public Relations Journal* 4.4 (fall 2010).

Bush, Lee. "Focusing on Strategy: Moving Beyond Media Relations and Getting to the New Brand Marketing Table," *Public Relations Strategist* 13 (Spring 2007): 30-33.

Chermak, Steven, and Alexander Weiss. "Maintaining Legitimacy Using External Communication Strategies for Police-Media Relations," *Journal of Criminal Justice* 33 (September 2005): 501-512.

Davis, Ellen. "Push Your Luck: Successful Media Relations Often a Function of Chance, Timing," *Public Relations Tactics* 15 (May 2008): 23.

Deigh, Robert. "Be Part of the Media Mix: Tips for Becoming a News Source Journalists Seek," *Public Relations Tactics* 15 (May 2008): 22.

Erjavec, Karmen. "Hybrid Public Relations News Discourse," *European Journal of Communication* 20 (June 2005): 155-179.

Eveland, William P., and Douglas M. McLeod. "The Effect of Social Desirability on Perceived Media Impact: Implications for Third-Person Perceptions," *International Journal of Public Opinion Research* 11 (winter 1999): 315-333.

Geary, David L. "The Decline of Media Credibility and its Impact on Public Relations," *Public Relations Quarterly* 50.3 (Fall 2005): 8-12.

Goldberg, Betsy. "That Other Broadcast Medium: Tuning in to the Power of Radio," *Public Relations Tactics* 12 (July 2005): 13-15.

Greve, Frank. "Journalism in the Age of Pseudoreporting," *Nieman Reports* 69 (summer 2005): 11-13.

Guiniven, John. "PR Professional, Not Telemarketer: The Do's and Don'ts of Pitching," *Public Relations Tactics* 12 (July 2005): 6.

Hallett, Josh. "In Through the Back Door: Using Blogs to Reach Traditional Media," Public Relations Tactics 15 (May 2008): 25.

Howard, Carole M., and Wilma K. Mathews. *On Deadline: Managing Media Relations*, 4th ed. Prospect Heights, IL: Waveland, 2006.

"How to Manage Media Relations When the Journalist Is a Blogger," *PR News* 63 (January 2007): 1.

"How to Optimize a Press Release for Search," *PR News* 63 (September 25, 2006): 36.

"How to Sell the Media," *PR News* 63 (November 2007).

Macaluso, Susan. "The Media World in Transition: What Is the VNR's Role in This New Landscape?" *Public Relations Tactics* 12 (June 2005): 21.

"Mapping Your Message: The Key to Telling a Media Relations Success Story," *PR News* 63 (June 2007).

O'Brien, Tim. "Professional courtship: The rise of social media and the death of the cover letter," *Public Relations Tactics* 17.11 (Nov 2010): 16.

Reese, Stephen D., Oscar H Gandy, Jr., and August E. Grant, *Framing Public Life Perspectives on Media and Our Understanding of the Social World*. Mahwah, NJ, Erlbaum, 2001.

Robe, Karl. "Get Smart Steps To Develop On-Strategy, On-Message, Value-Producing Media Pitches," *Public Relations Tactics* 15 (May 2008): 20.

Sallot, Lynne M., Thomas M. Stemfatt, and Michael B. Salwen. "Journalists' and Public Relations Practitioners' News Values Perceptions and Cross Perceptions," *Journalism and Mass Communication Quarterly* 75 (summer 1998): 366ff.

Sommer, Robert and John R. Maycroft. "How to Influence Editorials: A Case Study," *Public Relations Journal* 4.3 (summer 2010).

Spaeth, Merne. "Presidential Politics and Public Relations in 2004," *Journalism Studies* 6 (May 2005): 237–240.

Stoff, Rick. "Taking Back the Message," *St Louis Journalism Review* 35 (April 2005): 6–7.

Sweeney, Katie. "Fuzzy Picture for VNRs, SMTs—Both Vehicles Come Under Scrutiny, and Congress Gets into the Act," *Public Relations Tactics* 12 (June 2005): 18.

Thompson, Mike. "Step into a Reporter's Shoes to Fine-Tune Your Media Relations," *Public Management* 89 (September 2007): 25–29.

Trufelman, Lloyd P. "Consumer-Generated Media—Challenges and Opportunities for Public Relations," *Public Relations Tactics* 12 (May 2005): 17-19.

Wallack, Lawrence M., Katie Woodruff, Lon E. Dorfman, and Iris Diaz. *News for a Change An Advocate's Guide to Working with the Media*. Thousand Oaks, CA: Sage Publications, 1999.

Warneke, Kevin. "Keeping Tabs at the Ronald McDonald House in Omaha How a Nonprofit Garnered Press Attention," *Public Relations Tactics* 12 (August 2005): 19.

Ziegler, Todd. "Eight Ways for Organizations to Employ New Media," *Public Relations Tactics* 13 (December 2006): 20–21.

Media Directories

Bacon's Media Directories. Chicago: Cision'

Broadcasting/Cablecasting Yearbook Washington, DC: Broadcasting Publications

Burrelle's Media Directories. Livingston, NJ: Burrelle*Luce*'

Burrelle's Special Directories: Black Media /Hispanic Media/Women's Media. Livingston, NJ: Burrelle*Luce*'

Editor and Publisher International Yearbook. New York: Editor and Publisher

Gale Directory of Publications. Boston: Cengage

All-In-One Media Directory. New Paltz, NY: Gebbie Press

Media Services

Burrelles*Luce*, Livingston, NJ

Cision', Chicago

Business Wire, San Francisco

MarketWire, Toronto

Media Distribution Services, New York

Medialink, New York

PRIMEZONE Media Network, Los Angeles

PR Newswire, New York

Vocus, Lanham, MD

Media Relations Cases

Case 3-1

Generating "buzz" defines many campaigns. Given the widespread media focus on climate change, this campaign focused on developing a stratosphere level of buzz through a special event designed to generate massive media exposure and audience engagement. Each year the initiative sparks new levels of awareness of climate change issues. Exhibit 3-1A is a fact sheet on Earth Hour and Exhibit 3-1B is a news release.

EARTH HOUR 2008—
A Global Statement on
Climate Change

World Wildlife Fund, Creaxion, Jasculca Terman and Associates, Moses Anshell, Glodow Nead Communications, and Sullivan Birney Communications

OVERVIEW

Those who see the light ... turn it off! Turning off lights was the simple, yet powerful idea behind Earth Hour 2008—an international event in which an estimated 50 million people in more than 400 cities made a highly visible statement of concern about the need for the world to take action on climate change. Under the leadership of World Wildlife Fund (WWF), the simple act of having cities, businesses, and individuals switch off their lights for one hour turned into a bold, symbolic message with global impact on Saturday, March 29, 2008 at 8 pm local time.

To help launch this monumental, multi-faceted initiative in the United States, members of the WWF-U.S. communications team, along with leading PR agencies in four flagships cities (Creaxion in Atlanta, Jasculca Terman in Chicago, Moses Anshell in Phoenix, and Glodow Nead in San Francisco), developed and implemented an innovative, non-traditional strategic communications campaign to support the objectives of the program on both a local and national level, and helped turn the historic evening into a worldwide phenomenon.

RESEARCH

While the topic of climate change is often heavily covered by U.S. media, the event organizers wanted to get a better sense of the importance of this issue by demographic, and if the U.S. population was aware of an upcoming opportunity to participate in a global event on climate change. A pre-event national survey conducted by Zogby International indicated that while 73 percent of those surveyed had interest in environmental issues, only 22 percent had heard of Earth Hour, and only 18 percent were planning on participating. The research also indicated that women and African Americans had the strongest interest in these types of issues. Our secondary research examined what had worked the year before, when Sydney, Australia hosted the first Earth Hour event. The research confirmed our belief that there was a high level of interest in environmental issues, but low awareness about specific activities that could put those beliefs into action.

After reviewing our findings, we geared our messaging, activities and communication vehicles toward presenting a simple, accessible, and inclusive "call to action" which would resonate with our audience. We also began to create a "wish-list" of well-known personalities, iconic landmarks, and cultural symbols in each U.S. time zone which could be used as news hooks, and would help inspire audiences to act.

PLANNING

Specific **objectives** were identified to maximize opportunities with Earth Hour:

- Highlight solutions and encourage involvement across all levels of society—from government to business to individuals—to address the issue of climate change in an engaging and accessible manner.

- Increase WWF's overall visibility and influence around the issue of climate change on a local, national, and global scale within a wide variety of key audiences.

- Create a platform to further WWF's programmatic, financial, and legislative goals around climate change.

- Have significant, wide-spread, measurable participation in key flagship cities by individuals, businesses, and governments by creating dramatic skyline views and active participation on a personal level.

- The organizers made a strategic decision to not set specific energy-saving goals (since we wanted the event's focus on the power of symbolism and sustainability), but, nevertheless, were hoping to have a "measurable" drop in energy usage to report post-event.

Specific **strategies** were utilized, including:

- Develop consistent branding and messaging—used locally, nationally, and globally—to communicate with a collaborative, engaging, and non-political tone.

- Maximize the reach of the messaging to national audiences through media, corporate communications teams, and broader community groups.

- Overcome early skepticism by national media that the event was actually going to occur by involving influential, credible third-party partners, such as local utilities and mayors in flagship cities All local/national promotions (including VIP viewing events and agency fees in the flagship cities) were "revenue neutral" by utilizing a budget valued at $600,000 composed of funds raised from corporate sponsors and in-kind marketing donations spread throughout the markets.

EXECUTION

A project of this complexity and scope required the implementation of several tactics to maximize the impact, including:

- Frequent media announcements, providing updates on the progress of the campaign by highlighting the growing momentum and addition of iconic landmarks, supporting organizations and partners.

- Utilizing a combination of traditional and non-traditional PR tactics (such as media "clutter busters" mailings, employee rallies, city proclamations, and op-eds to generate early interest).

- An aggressive communications outreach campaign involving civic leaders, local governments, property managers, retail/hospitality/tourism attractions, sport venues, cultural icons, community associations, and schools (i.e., distributed 20,000 "I'm not afraid of the dark" stickers to students in Georgia).

- Provided hundreds of businesses' internal communication teams with tools to engage employees and customers utilizing their own communication channels.

- Utilized a number of key spokespeople to serve as main voices for the event, including WWF officials, local officials such as Atlanta Mayor Shirley Franklin, and corporate/logistical partners in media interviews.

- Holding weekly "steering committees" meetings led by supporting agencies, comprised of corporate and civic leaders to ensure widespread participation, community acceptance and public safety.

- Developed comprehensive media and sponsorship kits including videos, press releases, bios, and city images from the initial Earth Hour event held the previous year in Sydney, Australia.

- Developed a bank of themes/stories to provide direction for the media (such as Coke's digital Time Square billboard going dark, logistics of turning off a city's lights and major icons, and theme/trivia nights at local restaurants, etc.) to give print/broadcast media a wide range of ways to cover the story.

- Engaged senior journalists' at large, national media outlets to ensure "ownership" of the event.

- Heavily promoted the main website, earthhour.org, to encourage sign-ups, through extensive coverage in PR/ marketing collateral, leveraging environmental influencers, and online promotional partners.

- Developed media partnerships with Cox Enterprises, National Geographic, and The Weather Channel. The team also had to overcome serious logistical issues after a freak tornado hit Atlanta's downtown core two weeks prior to the event by working with individual property managers to ascertain their participation.

EVALUATION

The successful execution of this high-profile activity captured the imagination of the general public as it cascaded throughout the world and gained prominence in the United States:

- Thousands of buildings and landmarks went dark in the United States, including cultural icons such as: the Golden Gate Bridge, Ghirardelli Square, Alcatraz, Sears Tower, Wrigley Field, Georgia Aquarium, Bank of America Tower, and US Airways Center; in Atlanta alone, more than 400 buildings participated, and more than 97 percent of the city's symbolic skyline.

- These landmarks were joined by dozens more around the world from Dubai to Dublin, including the Sydney Opera House, Rome's Coliseum, Scott Base in Antarctica, and Niagara Falls.

- Major digital/electronic landmarks also went dark, including Google's main homepage, Coca Cola's digital billboard in Times Square, and hundreds of McDonald's Golden Arches.

- The events were covered in all major U.S. media outlets, including Associated Press, ABC, AFP, Bloomberg, CBS, CNN, NBC, NPR, FOX, *The New York Times*, Reuters, *USA Today*, *Time Magazine*, *Wall Street Journal*, and *The Washington Post*, with full features on NBC Nightly News, Good Morning America, CNN, The Today Show, and on Oprah (who said "wow" when she described the event); coverage on more than 2,000 local U.S. TV stations, and hundreds of newspaper and radio stations placements, with media impressions exceeding several hundred million.

- An extensive online presence fueled by prominent features on top sites including Google.com, MSNBC.com, The Drudge Report, Yahoo!, iVillage.com, Time.com, Daily Candy, Ideal Bite, and TreeHugger.com; the global event website had more than 7 million unique visitors within a six day-period.

- In the United States, a post-event national poll by Zogby International showed a 56 percent increase of awareness of the event, with 29.8 percent of the general population (up from 18.4 percent who said they would) participating, and a 4 percent increase in interest in environmental issues on a national level by a sampling of U.S. adults.

- While there were no specific energy savings goals for the event, Georgia Power measured a 4 percent drop in energy usage in Atlanta, despite evening rain, and in Chicago, ComEd reported savings of 7 percent. The 818 megawatt hours saved in Chicago had the carbon emissions equivalent of 1.3 million pounds of CO^2; 1 million cars off the road for one hour; 72,000 gallons of gas consumed, and 158 acres of trees planted.

WWF considered the event overwhelmingly successful, and one that drew unprecedented attention to their organization and causes. The activities created an engaging platform to discuss broader climate issues with media and sparked discussions about actions needed to solve Earth's environmental challenges. WWF also felt it extended their reach and brand in a new way with new consumer audiences and groups of civic and business leaders, as well as influencers around the world. WWF also benefited from new and strengthened connections with local governments and legislators, and new revenue generation from new and existing partners.

EXHIBIT 3-1A   Earth Hour Fact Sheet

ABOUT EARTH HOUR

Earth Hour started in 2007 in Sydney, Australia when 2.2 million individuals and more than 2,000 businesses turned their lights off for one hour to take a stand against climate change. Only a year later and Earth Hour had become a global sustainability movement with more than 50 million people across 35 countries/territories participating. Global landmarks such as the Sydney Harbour Bridge, CN Tower in Toronto, Golden Gate Bridge in San Francisco, and Rome's Collosseum, all stood in darkness, as symbols of hope for a cause that grows more urgent by the hour.

In March 2009, hundreds of millions of people took part in the third Earth Hour. Over 4,000 cities in 88 countries/territories officially switched off to pledge their support for the planet, making Earth Hour 2009 the world's largest global climate change initiative.

On Saturday March 27, Earth Hour 2010 broke new records for participation with 128 countries and territories joining the global display of climate action. Iconic buildings and landmarks from Asia Pacific to Europe and Africa to the Americas switched off. People across the world from all walks of life turned off their lights and came together in celebration and contemplation of the one thing we all have in common—our planet.

And Earth Hour just keeps growing. On Saturday March 26th, Earth Hour 2011 became the biggest Earth Hour ever. 135 countries took part, many for the first time including Lebanon, Jamaica, Iran, Uganda, Swaziland, Tajikistan, Chad, Azerbaijan, Gibraltar, Palestine, Suriname, Uzbekistan, Trinidad & Tobago, and Lesotho.

Earth Hour 2011 marks the beginning of a new era, with individuals, organizations, and governments asked to go beyond the hour by committing to ongoing action for the planet. Visit our Beyond the Hour platform to share your stories and to get inspiration from the actions our supporters have shared with us already.

This year's event has illustrated without question what can be achieved when people unite with a common purpose and rally to action. Earth Hour 2012 will take place on Saturday 31st March at 8:30 pm—so save the date and keep coming back to earthhour.org to find out what's in store and how you can get involved.

Earth Hour by WWF

Earth Hour is organized by WWF. With almost 5 million supporters and a global network in over 100 countries/territories, it's one of the world's largest and most respected independent conservation organizations. WWF's mission is to stop the degradation of the Earth's natural environment and build a future where people live in harmony with nature.

Earth Hour timeline

Turn back the clock on Earth Hour and discover why, how, where, and when it all started.

Why get involved?

Put simply, because our future depends on it! Earth Hour has done a lot to raise awareness of sustainability issues. But there's more to it than switching off lights for one hour once a year. It's all about giving people a voice and working together to create a better future for our planet.

Courtesy World Wildlife Fund

E X H I B I T 3-1B   Press Release

Press Release

America Ready to Turn Out and Take Action for WWF's Earth Hour

From Coast to Coast, Hundreds of Major U.S. Cities, Iconic Landmarks and Millions of Citizens to Vote for Change on Saturday, March 28 at 8:30 p.m.

For Release: Mar 27, 2009

WASHINGTON—March 27, 2009—As Earth Hour cascades through time zones around the world on Saturday, March 28 at 8:30 p.m., millions of Americans across the country will be showing their support for action on climate change by voting with their light switch on this historic night.

From intimate candlelit dinners to the darkening of the Las Vegas Strip, Americans from all walks of life will be turning out for Earth Hour, and taking action by making a global statement of concern about climate change and a renewed commitment to finding solutions to the escalating climate crisis.

Organized by World Wildlife Fund, the world's largest multinational conservation organization, participation in Earth Hour continues to grow dramatically in the United States by the hour as iconic landmarks, major cities, corporations, and organizations of all sizes, schools, towns, and villages unite in this global effort.

Earth Hour organizers have commitments from nearly 300 U.S. cities and towns, with some of the nation's most famous skylines darkening on Saturday night, including Atlanta, Baltimore, Boston, Chicago, Dallas, Houston, Las Vegas, Los Angeles, Miami, Nashville, New York, Salt Lake City, St. Louis, Tucson, and Washington, D.C. In each of these cities, individuals, businesses, and organizations are participating in activities to engage, enlighten, and spread the message that together, each one of us can make a difference on this global issue. Flagship states include Arkansas, California, Michigan, New Mexico, and Pennsylvania.

Earth Hour activities involve many of America's most iconic landmarks and attractions, including a broad array of people, places and things, including the following highlights:

Atlanta

On the night the lights go out in Georgia, some of Atlanta's most well-known landmarks and buildings, such as the Bank of America Plaza, Philips Arena, and The Varsity restaurant will join more than 500 buildings throughout the metro area as they darken against the southern sky.

Chicago

As Earth Hour blows through the Windy City, Chicago's soaring skyscrapers, including the Sears Tower and John Hancock Center, will join popular attractions such as Navy Pier and Wrigley Field for an hour of darkness in America's heartland.

Las Vegas

What happens in Vegas, normally stays there. But when the infamous Strip goes dark for a full hour for the first time in history, it's worth talking about. City visitors and residents will be in luck as the "Welcome to Fabulous Las Vegas" sign, Stratosphere, Fremont Street Experience (largest digital screen in the world) and Luxor's shining beam turn out for an extraordinary, historic event.

Los Angeles

As one of the last cities to celebrate Earth Hour, the City of Angels knows how to create a big ending, with landmarks from the Santa Monica Pier to Hollywood's biggest studios helping pull down the curtain on the largest climate change event in history. They will celebrate together at an event at L.A. Live with celebrities, performers, and politicians joining to cast their votes in unison.

Miami

Local officials, businesses, and citizens throughout the area will be celebrating Earth Hour in style as Miami's downtown core powers down for its inaugural Earth Hour.

Nashville

The neon lights of Music City's famous honkytonks will join a chorus of support turning out from the local country music scene, including singer Jo Dee Messina, who will be performing a free acoustic concert under a star-lit sky.

New York

From the top of the Empire State Building to the darkened marquees of Broadway's theaters, the Big Apple will be participating in Earth Hour in a big way. New Yorkers will see Coca-Cola's, Reuters and other digital billboards in Times Square go dark, as well as the U.N. headquarters building, the Chrysler Building, Rockefeller Center, the Brooklyn Bridge, and dozens more buildings throughout the famously-busy city as it pauses for one hour to reflect on ways to increase sustainability practices.

San Francisco

As the lights go out on the Golden Gate Bridge, Coit Tower, and the TransAmerica Building, the City by the Bay will enjoy an hour without power as a returning Earth Hour flagship city.

Washington, D.C.

The nation's capitol will set a shining example by turning off some of the city's most recognizable landmarks in the District, such as the National Cathedral, World Bank, Chinatown Arch, and Smithsonian Castle.

Joining these cities will be sites of significance throughout the country, including: Thomas Edison's laboratory in West Orange, NJ (birthplace of the incandescent light bulb), the Gateway Arch in St. Louis, and the Space Needle in Seattle.

Many TV show are symbolically joining in Earth Hour as "American Idol," "Dancing with the Stars," "Family Guy," "CSI," "Bones," "Entertainment Tonight," "Access Hollywood," "The Price is Right," and others dim the lights on their set to cast their vote for action on climate change.

Americans are also actively chatting up their involvement with Earth Hour with online communities numbering in the tens of thousands, ushering in a new era of eco-awareness on social networking sites such as Flickr, Facebook, MySpace, Twitter, Experience Project, and YouTube.

Earth Hour's open-source nature has been the driving force behind the campaign:

- Earth Hour has 1.1 million online social network friends
- Earth Hour videos are being viewed online every 0.8 seconds
- Earth Hour is regularly trending amongst the most tweeted topics on Twitter
- The term "Earth Hour" has appeared online close to 1 million times in the past 24 hours

During the largest climate change event in history, the United States will be joined by more than 84 countries and over 3,900 cities, towns, and villages around the world, with widespread participation in 66 national capitals and 9 of the 10 most populated metropolises on the planet have confirmed their participation in this year's event, with some of the world's most prominent cities outside the United States, including:

▪ Athens	▪ Barcelona	▪ Berlin	▪ Cairo
▪ Bangkok	▪ Beijing	▪ Buenos Aires	▪ Cape Town

■ Copenhagen	■ Kuala Lumpur	■ Moscow	■ Rio de Janeiro
■ Dubai	■ London	■ Mumbai	■ Rome
■ Hong Kong	■ Manila	■ Nairobi	■ Singapore
■ Istanbul	■ Mexico City	■ Paris	■ Toronto

The Great Pyramids of Giza, the world's greatest symbol of the power of collective action, heads up a list of more than 800 landmarks around the world switching off their lights for Earth Hour, including:

Acropolis in Athens

- Arc de Triomphe in Paris
- Bird's Nest Stadium in Beijing
- Burj Dubai (world's tallest unfinished building)
- CN Tower in Toronto
- Christ the Redeemer in Rio de Janeiro
- Coliseum in Rome
- Dome of St. Peter in Rome
- Edinburgh Castle
- Eiffel Tower in Paris
- Gaudi Building in Barcelona
- The London Eye
- The Merlion in Singapore
- Millennium Stadium in Cardiff
- Niagara Falls in Canada
- Symphony of Lights in Hong Kong
- Tapei 101 (world's tallest building)
- Tower Bridge in London
- Table Mountain in Cape Town
- Wembley Stadium Arch in London

The event on March 28th is just one step in an ongoing effort to fight climate change. After the lights go out around the world on this evening, WWF hopes that conversations will continue on climate change and that people will take initiatives to make small changes in their lives to be more carbon efficient.

WWF encourages simple but effective energy-saving measures such as installing compact fluorescent light bulbs, which are more efficient and last much longer than traditional incandescent bulbs, choosing energy efficient appliances, making sure their car tires are properly inflated and unplugging electronics when they are not in use.

WWF officials stress the importance of safety during Earth Hour, asking that all lighting related to public safety remain on.

More information about Earth Hour and ways to get involved can be found at www.EarthHourUS.org/.

National partners for WWF's Earth Hour 2009 are Esurance, Cox Enterprises, The Coca-Cola Company, Wells Fargo and Hewlett-Packard.

Note to Editors: B-roll and Earth Hour still images can be found at www. earthhourus.org/broll.php. Participant interviews available upon request.

Courtesy World Wildlife Fund, Creaxion, Jasculca Terman and Associates, Moses Anshell, Glodow Nead Communications, Sullivan Birney Communications

Case 3-2

Connecting a corporate identity with a significant historical cause/event offers ways to demonstrate corporate support for the community and generate publicity at the same time. Exhibit 3-2A is a news release announcing the below program, Exhibit 3-2B is a media alert about the same special event, and Exhibit 3-2C is a fact sheet explaining the overall landmark preservation program discussed below.

"Save-A-Landmark" Refurbishment at the National Civil Rights Museum
Hampton Hotels

SUMMARY

In preparation for the 40th anniversary of Martin Luther King, Jr.'s untimely death, Hampton Hotels kicked off its 2008 "Save-A-Landmark" campaign by giving the illustrious National Civil Rights Museum a monumental makeover.

For the National Civil Rights Museum preservation effort—the largest in the Save-A-Landmark program's nine-year history—Hampton called on more than 100 volunteers from local Hampton hotels, contributed more than 1,000 volunteer hours and dedicated more than $100,000 towards reviving the national landmark. To date, the refurbishment project has generated more than 220 media placements, 394,233,117 gross impressions and an estimated $6,075,122 in advertising equivalency.

BACKGROUND

On April 4, 1968, the legendary civil rights leader Dr. Martin Luther King, Jr. was assassinated in Memphis, Tennessee while standing on the second floor balcony of the Lorraine Motel, now the site of the National Civil Rights Museum. In preparation for the 40th anniversary of Dr. King's untimely death, Hampton Hotels kicked off its 2008 "Save-A-Landmark" campaign by giving this illustrious museum, and infamous setting in American history, a monumental makeover.

Hampton Hotels' Save-A-Landmark 2008 theme—aptly named "Landmark Legends"—was devoted to preserving sites honoring prominent people and moments in American history, such as the National Civil Rights Museum. The list of legendary figures honored by Save-A-Landmark was generated from a nationwide survey to celebrate the accomplishments of those Americans who have inspired change, overcome adversity and made a difference in their country. For the preservation effort—the largest in the Save-A-Landmark program's nine-year history—Hampton called on more than 100 volunteers from local Hampton Hotels, contributed more than 1,000 volunteer hours and dedicated more than $100,000 towards reviving the national landmark.

RESEARCH

Prior to the Save-A-Landmark program's initial launch in 2000, Hampton conducted a survey of more than 1,000 people, which revealed a staggering nine out of ten Americans believe it is important to preserve the country's roadside landmarks. It also showed that 83 percent of respondents feel they share some sort of responsibility for preserving the nation's landmarks. In 2007, Hampton once again surveyed Americans in preparation for its "Landmark Legends" Save-A-Landmark theme for 2008. According to the "Landmark Legends" survey, Dr. Martin Luther King, Jr. is the most legendary figure in modern American history. More respondents (26 percent) chose Dr. King over any other notable person. In addition, the survey revealed that, not only is King the biggest legend in modern history, his famous "I Have a Dream" speech is so well known that more than one third (36 percent) of Americans rank this as the most legendary phrase of all time. Prior to refurbishing the National Civil Rights museum, Hampton Hotels researched landmarks around the country before identifying the museum as a landmark with 1) a connection to Martin Luther King, Jr., 2) a compelling local/national story, 3) significant refurbishment needs and 4) local Hampton properties nearby from which to acquire enough volunteers to help with the preservation project.

PLANNING AND IMPLEMENTATION

Marketing Objectives

- Generate national and regional awareness and media coverage of Hampton Hotels' landmark preservation efforts.
- Make a meaningful impact in the Memphis community and across the nation.
- Increase awareness of the Save-A-Landmark program among travelers.
- Rally community members to support landmark preservation both locally and across the country.

Based on a 2010 survey conducted by the Harris Poll National Quorum on behalf of Hampton Hotels.

Actions and Events

- Worked with local contractors and museum staff to build relationships/ secure project.
- Scheduled the preservation event a few days before the 40th anniversary of Dr. Martin Luther King, Jr.'s assassination to leverage the media's timely interest in the National Civil Rights Museum.
- Encouraged volunteers from local Hampton hotels to participate in the preservation effort.
- Secured and coordinated supplies for the project.
- Facilitated hands-on participation of critically acclaimed actor, Samuel L. Jackson, who was an usher at Dr. King's funeral and, at the time of the refurbishment, in Memphis shooting a film.
- Researched local/regional/national outlets for inclusion in outreach; created corresponding media lists.
- Crafted outlet- and reporter-specific media materials and pitches, such as:
  - Summer—promoting HamptonLandmarks.com as a resource for road-tripping families, which includes information on the National Civil Rights Museum for travelers.
  - Human Interest—focusing on Jackson and his involvement in the refurbishment.
  - American History—expanding upon reporters' prior museum/land-mark coverage.

MESSAGES

Key Message

- Hampton Hotels' Save-A-Landmark program is devoted to the ongoing care of roadside landmarks and has already committed thousands of volunteer hours and more than $2.5 million toward this cause.

Key Differentiators

- A one-of-a-kind community relations program among hotel brands, Save-A-Landmark ties directly to Hampton Hotels' customer base. It works to preserve roadside landmarks, making a difference to many Hampton guests who travel to the hotels by car.
- Hampton became the first hotel chain ever to be recognized by President George W. Bush and First Lady Laura Bush with the "Preserve America" Presidential Award and the first hotel brand to receive the National Preservation Honor Award from the National Trust for Historic Preservation.
- As the city of Memphis prepared for events surrounding the 40th anniversary of Dr. King's untimely passing, more than 100 volunteers from local Hampton hotels and the brand's corporate offices in Memphis, along with critically acclaimed actor Samuel L. Jackson, spent an estimated 1,000 hours on restoration projects all over the museum's grounds.

RESULTS

Examples of the refurbishment efforts included:

- Museum Exterior—painting, pressure washing walls, installing wheelchair-accessible ramp, landscaping surrounding grounds.
- Little Rock Exhibit—reconstructing display, painting.
- Montgomery Bus Boycott Exhibit—cleaning/restoring.
- Sit-In Exhibit—replacing electric wiring, painting, cleaning.
- Selma, Alabama Exhibit—repainting entire Edmund Pettus Bridge structure.

The refurbishment drew the attention of top-tier national media outlets, including "CNN Headline News," the Associated Press, USA Today and "Entertainment Tonight," who flew correspondent Kevin Frazier to Memphis in order to cover the story.

Local coverage included two features in The Commercial Appeal (Memphis' leading print newspaper) and a total 25 segments on the local ABC, NBC, CBS and FOX broadcast affiliates, including LIVE on-site interviews by FOX, ABC and CBS.

To date, the refurbishment project has generated more than 220 media placements, 394,233,117 gross impressions, an estimated $6,075,122 in advertising equivalency and contributed more than $100,000 to ensure the continued preservation of the National Civil Rights Museum.

E X H I B I T 3-2A   News Release on Historic Refurbishment

HAMPTON PREPARES FOR "LEGENDARY" YEAR OF HISTORIC REFURBISHMENTS

Save-A-Landmark®Program Kicks Off Ninth Year with Restoration Event Honoring 40th Anniversary of Dr. Martin Luther King's Death

MEMPHIS, Tenn., January 17, 2008 — Is Dr. Martin Luther King. Jr. the most legendary figure in modern history? Most people think so. According to survey results released today—just in time for Martin Luther King, Jr. Day on January 21—more respondents (26 percent) chose Dr. King than any other notable person. Hampton Hotels (www.hampton.com), which conducted the survey, also announced today that it would honor Dr. King with a massive restoration of the National Civil Rights Museum in Memphis, Tenn.—the site where he was assassinated—as part of its award-winning Save-A-Landmark® program.

The refurbishment of the National Civil Rights Museum will take place in late March and will be the largest effort in the program's history—more than 100 volunteers will help get the museum ready for the 40th anniversary of Dr. King's assassination on April 4, 1968. The event will also serve as a kick-off for the Save-A-Landmark® program's ninth year, which has been dubbed the year of "Landmark Legends." During the next 12 months, Hampton and its employee-volunteers will restore sites that honor some of the most distinguished people in world history—legendary figures that have inspired change, overcome challenge and made a difference.

"As always, we're ready to roll up our sleeves and do whatever is needed—paint, reconstruct, landscape, anything the sites need—to salute these luminaries and assist with the upkeep of landmarks built in their honor," said Judy Christa-Cathey, vice president of brand marketing for Hampton. "Dr. King is just one shining example of someone who inspired positive change. We are helping the Museum prepare for the anniversary events marking his life and accomplishments."

According to Hampton's "Landmark Legends Survey," not only is King the biggest legend in modern history, his famous "I Have a Dream" speech is also so well known that more than a third (36 percent) of Americans rank this as the most legendary phrase of all time.

The public can visit the just-launched "Landmark Legends" page at the Save-A-Landmark site, www.hamptonlandmark.com and click on "submit a landmark," to enter their nomination for a legendary landmark. Also, those looking to stand in the shadow of renowned people and their landmarks can access the site's database for dozens of ideas. Following is just a sampling of "heroic" landmark already included:

- **Dr. Martin Luther King and the National Civil Rights Museum,** Memphis, Tenn.: This former site of the Lorraine Motel is now home to the National Civil Rights Museum and the site of Dr. Martin Luther King's assassination on April 4, 1968. On that fateful day, Dr King was in Memphis to lead a march of sanitation workers protesting against low wages and poor working conditions. To honor the late Dr. King and to observe the 40th anniversary of his death, Hampton volunteers will be scraping and repainting interior exhibit spaces, landscaping the gardens and power-washing exterior sidewalks and walls.

- **Amelia Earhart Birthplace and Museum,** Atchison, Kan.: Quite possibly the most legendary pilot who ever lived, Earhart was born in the small town of Atchison. Perched atop the west bank of the Missouri River, this award-winning home and museum displays a great number of Earhart artifacts and tells the story of her growing interest in flying. The museum is owned by the Ninety-Nines, an organization of licensed female pilots that Earhart and five friends first formed in 1929.

- **Edgar Allan Poe and the Poe Museum,** Richmond, Vir.: called "America's Shakespeare," Edgar Allan Poe's dark genius has invited children and adults to read and live literature for more than 150 years. Richmond's Poe Museum boasts the world's finest collection of Edgar Allan Poe's manuscripts, letters, first editions, memorabilia and personal belongings. Opened in 1922, in The Old Stone House, the museum is only blocks away poe's first Richmond home and his first place of employment, the "Southern Literary Messenger."

Underscoring the discussion of legendary figures in our culture, Hampton's "Landmark Legends Survey" also revealed a host of statistics about Americans' attitude toward the concept of celebrity:

- **Legendary Saturation:** More than three-quarters (78 percent) of respondents think the word "legend" is overused and feel it should only be used to refer to people who have truly made a contribution to society, rather than those who are simply famous.

- **Life of a Legend:** When asked if they could go down in history as a legend, most respondents (74 percent) would want to be honored for helping others in some way, with one-third (30 percent) of them saying they'd want to be remembered as the best spouse or parent. These responses far outweighed the desire to be the greatest athlete (two percent) or the greatest actor/actress (two percent).

- **Legendary Voice:** Elvis Presley may have died 30 years ago, but his music certainly lives on. In fact, nearly half (43 percent) of Americans consider "The King" to be the most legendary recording artist of all time. Coming in behind him are Frank Sinatra (14 percent) and Michael Jackson (12 percent).

- **Legendary Performers:** Americans also have strong opinions about the most meaningful movie stars. More than a third of survey respondents (36 percent) ranked four-time Oscar-winning actress Katharine Hepburn as the greatest female screen legend of all time. She was followed by Audrey Hepburn (16 percent), Bette Davis (11 percent) and Julia Roberts (10 percent). With actors, one in five (20 percent) of Americans consider Oscar-winner Jimmy Stewart as the greatest male screen legend of all time—followed by Humphrey Bogart (15 percent), Cary Grant (13 percent), Marlon Brando (11 percent), and Will Smith (10 percent).

From helping the 80-foot Blue Whale in Catoosa, Okla. to the historic World War II destroyer U.S.S. Laffey in Mount Pleasant, S.C., the Save-A-Landmark program has helped research landmarks in need, promoted landmark sites and their importance, facilitated hundreds of thousands of volunteer hours, donated several tons of supplies and worked with matching grants—all at an investment of more than $2.5 million. Hampton employee-volunteers work hand-in-hand on the landmarks while Hampton provides the dollars to refurbish selected sites.

Landmark nominations have been a key element of the Save-A-Landmark program's success since its inception in 2000, with thousands of nominations provided by the public. Submissions can be made online at www.hamptonlandmarks.com or by mailing recommendations c/o Save-A-Landmark to 8730 Sunset Blvd, 5th Floor, Los Angeles, Ca 90069.

About the "Landmark Legends Survey"

The Hampton "Landmark Legends Survey" was conducted by Kelton Research between January 2–4, 2008 using an email invitation and an online survey. Quotas are set to ensure reliable and accurate representation of the total U.S. population ages 18 and over. Results of any sample are subject to sampling variation. The magnitude of the variation is measurable and is affected by the number of interviews and the level of the percentages expressing the results. In this particular study, the chances are 95 in 100 that a survey result does not vary, plus or minus, by more than 3.1 percentage points from the result that would obtained if interview had been conducted with all persons in the universe represented by the sample.

About Hampton Hotels   *Boiler plate*

Courtesy of Hampton Hotels

EXHIBIT 3-2B   Media Alert *"Save The Date"*

SAMUEL L. JACKSON, VOLUNTEERS HONOR MARTIN LUTHER KING, JR. WITH REFURBISHMENT OF NATIONAL CIVIL RIGHTS MUSEUM

Hampton Hotels Lends Support in Preparation for 40th Anniversary of Dr. King's Death

WHAT: On Tuesday, March 25, a massive team of more than 100 volunteers from Hampton Hotels' Save-A-Landmark® program will work alongside critically-acclaimed actor Samuel L. Jackson to restore the **National Civil Rights Museum** in Memphis, Tenn. The museum was built around the Lorraine Motel—the site where Dr. Martin Luther King, Jr. was assassinated on April 4, 1968—and chronicles key episodes of the American civil rights movement and the legacy of this movement to inspire participation in civil and human rights efforts. Attracting visitors and dignitaries from around the world, the National Civil Rights Museum houses historic collections, exhibitions and artifacts and provides a variety of educational programs.

As the city of Memphis prepares for events surrounding the 40th anniversary of Dr. King's untimely passing, volunteers from local Hampton Hotel properties and the brand's corporate offices in Memphis will spend an estimated **1,000 hours** on restoration projects all over the museum's grounds. Examples of the refurbishment efforts include:

- Museum Exterior—painting, pressure washing walls, installing wheelchair-accessible ramp, landscaping surrounding grounds
- Little Rock Exhibit—reconstructing display, replacing electric wiring, painting, changing wallpaper
- Montgomery Bus Boycott Exhibit—cleaning/restoring
- Sit-In Exhibit—replacing electric wiring, painting, cleaning
- Selma, Alabama Exhibit—Edmund Pettus Bridge repainting entire structure

WHEN: **Tuesday, March 25, 2008**
8 A.M. TO 3 P.M. CST—Official check presentation ceremony at 11:00 A.M. CST

WHO:
- **Beverly Robertson**, *president, National Civil Rights Museum*
- **Samuel L. Jackson**, *acclaimed actor and usher at Dr. King's memorial service*
- **Chris Epting**, *author and pop-culture historian*
- **Phil Cordell**, *senior vice president, Hampton Hotels*
- **Judy Christa-Cathey**, *vice president, Hampton Hotels*
- Approximately 100 volunteers from local Hampton Hotels and Memphis community

WHERE: **National Civil Rights Museum**
450 Mulberry Street
Memphis, Tennessee 38103

VISUALS:
- **National Civil Rights Museum**—more than a dozen restoration projects on the campus
- **Volunteers from Memphis-area Hampton Hotels**—renovating museum structure and exhibits
- **Presentation ceremony** by Hampton Hotels to fund ongoing refurbishment efforts 11 A.M.

ADDITIONAL BACKGROUND:
The National Civil Rights Museum is the **36th landmark** to be refurbished by the Save-A-Landmark program, which bands Hampton Hotels' employees together to restore historical and cultural sites. The museum is also the first "**Landmark Legend**" site to be restored in 2008—a year dedicated toward honoring legendary figures in history, such as Dr. Martin Luther King, Jr., who have inspired positive change. Hampton Hotels always welcomes submissions for consideration. To nominate a landmark, visit www.hamptonlandmarks.com.

E X H I B I T 3-2C   Fact Sheet on Save-A-Landmark

EXPLORE THE HIGHWAY, WITH HAMPTON'S "SAVE-A-LANDMARK"®

Landmark Details

Overview

In April 2000, Hampton Hotels Launched "Save-A-Landmark," a campaign dedicated to refurbishing historical, fun and cultural landmarks that reside along North America's highways. Landmark refurbishments include painting, cleaning, replacing siding and doors, and landscaping, as well as other preservation and beautification efforts Hampton hotel volunteers can support. The program has provided hundreds of hours and more than $2.5 million toward the research, attention and preservation of America's roadside landmarks for future generations. According to a 2003 Travel Industry Association (TIA) study, there is continuing interest in "travelers' desire to experience cultural, arts, historic and heritage activities." More than 80 percent of U.S. adults who traveld in the past year, or 118 milion, are considered historic/cultural travelers.

Award-Winning Program

The Save-A-Landmark program was honored with the 2006 *Preserve America* Presidental Award—the first hotel chain ever recognized by a U.S. President for its preservation efforts. President George W. Bush presented the prestigious award to Hampton executives during a Rose Garden ceremony at the White House on May 1, 2006. Mrs. Laura Bush is Honorary Chair of the *Preservative America* initiative. The *Preserve America* Presidental Awards are given annually to organizations, businesses, government entities, and individuals for: exemplary accomplishments in the sustainable use and preservation of cultural or natural heritage assets; demonstrated commitment to the protection and interpretation of America's cultural or natural heritage assets; and integration of these assets into contemporary community life, combining innovative, creative, and responsible approaches to showcasing historic local resources.

The Save-A-Landmark program was the winner of the 2004 *SMITHSONIAN* Magazine/Travelers Conservation Foundation Sustainable Tourism Award in the preservation category. The award, which highlights a brand's commitment and ability to protect and restore cultural treasures with an innovative and effective approach, distinguishes Hampton as the first hotel brand ever to be nationally recognized for its preservation efforts. As the part of the distinction, Hampton received a cash prize of $20,000, which was used to complete the restoration of the Admiral Twin Drive-in in Tusla, Oklahoma.

With 35 landmarks saved and several more on the horizon, the program continues to generate support and excitement from tourists all over North America.

Selection Criteria

Roadside attraction projects are selected after conducting extensive research. Selection criteria for landmarks include: overall refurbishment costs, community interest and accessibility to local Hampton hotels for volunteer support.

Refurbishment Projects To Date

WORLD'S LARGEST ROCKING CHAIR *(Gulfort, Mississippi)*

History:

This massive chair, standing 35 feet tall and fashioned from Southern pine, was completed in 1995 as an enormous advertisement for the Dedeaux Family Furniture Factory and a sizable attraction for visitors. The roadside recliner is a giant replica of the family's trademark product, the Magnolina State Rocker.

Refurbishment information:

On December 18, 2007, the Save-A-Landmark program gave a giant gift to the city of Gulport by restoring its beloved Rocking Chair. Volunteers from Gulfort area Hampton Hotels dressed as holiday "elves" and spent an estimated 100 hours sanding and painting the colossal chair, replacing its corroded hardware, installing new light fixtures and landscaping the surrounding area. Hampton Hotels contributed nearly $20,000 to the Rocking Chair's ongoing care, ensuring that future generations of visitors will have the chance to take a relaxing ride atop this gigantic landmark.

In addition to the refurbishment, Hampton Hotels partnered with Toys for Tots to help distribute unwrapped toys during the holiday season to local children in the area. The brand also presented U.S. Marine representatives from Toys for Tots with more than $1,000 in unwrapped toys, as well as a monetary contribution of $5,000 towards the organitation's toy drive.

WORLD'S LARGEST PUMPKIN *(Roland, Manitoba)*

History:

A specimen like this can't be found in just any pumpkin patch! The World's Largest Pumpkin is a super-sized squash replica, weighing 1,684 pounds and measuring 12 feet tall by 12 feet wide. Constructed out of steel rods and covered in orange fiberglass, the Pumpkin was created in 1990 during the Roland Centennial in honor of Edgar VanWyck, the "Pumpkin King." The local legend is remembered for successfully landing his name—and the town—in the *Guinness Book of World Records* for growing the largest pumpkin in the world.

Refurbishment Information:

Just in time for Halloween, on October 30, 2007, the Pumpkin was patched by Save-A-Landmark volunteers. During an estimated 50-hour restoration effort, they sanded and painted the supreme structure with anti-graffiti paint, landscaped the surrounding area with trees and shrubbery, laid stone walkways and installed lighting to illuminate the Pumpkin at night. Hampton Hotels contributed more than $15,000 to the

Pumpkin's ongoing care, ensuring that future generations of visitors will have the chance to behold this giant monument to one historical harvest.

Courtesy of Hampton Hotels

Case 3-3

Seasonal events often capture special media coverage, yet even routine events celebrating an anniversary can connect across generations and inspire a special spate of news stories. Here is a creative way to play on the anniversary theme. Exhibit 3-2A is a program fact sheet, Exhibit 3-3B is a news release for pilots, Exhibit 3-3C is a post event news release and Exhibit 3-3D is a promotional poster.

NORAD Tracks Santa

NORAD Public Affairs

My son is 11 years old and at the age where most of his friends no longer believe in Santa.... Tonight you helped an 11-year-old boy believe in the magic of Christmas for yet another year ... and you made another year of Christmas memories for his mom. For as you know, they outgrow childhood all too quickly so Christmas memories like these are so very priceless.

— A grateful Mom in Holly Springs, N.C.

SUMMARY

In 2008 the North American Aerospace Defense Command (NORAD) celebrated its 50-year tradition of presenting children and families of the world its "NORAD Tracks Santa" (NTS) program, as it positioned the program to reach the next generation of "Santa Trackers." Standing on the precipice of the new media age, NORAD expanded its decades-old international community relations initiative in 2008 by partnering with several corporations, to include Google, Booz, Allen Hamilton, and Verizon to leverage advances in communications and Web technology to take our NTS global outreach initiative into the future. Through detailed research and planning, we reevaluated the program's scope for 2008 for the latest generation of techno-savvy kids and their millennial parents. Our execution included incorporating 2D and 3D kid-friendly Google Earth maps, multi-lingual videos, a redesigned web page, interactive games, and a social media component. We were able to significantly expand the program's national and international reach and appeal. The result was a marked increase in the NTS program's ability to respond interactively with children calling or emailing the NTS Operations Center on December 24, increased national broadcast and print media coverage, and continued favorable brand recognition for NORAD-unique technologies and its long-recognized mission of providing for the defense of North America.

Courtesy NORAD Public Affairs

The serendipitous history of NORAD Tracks Santa began December 24, 1955, when an incorrect number was printed in a local newspaper ad and rang into Air Defense Command's Air Operations Center in Colorado Springs, CO. The commander on duty at the time, Colonel Harry Shoup, indulged the young caller, reporting Santa's official location while playing along to keep the child's belief in Santa alive. From that single act of spirited kindness grew a program that is today institutionalized throughout the NORAD command, as well as loved and anticipated each holiday season by families throughout the world. Few organizations whether profit, not-for-profit, or government, have enjoyed the success and brand recognition of such a far-reaching international community relations program. For one special day, millions of faithful Santa Trackers, young and old, came together in their homes huddled around their computers like firesides of the past, to take a "time out" from the realities and hardships of current times to share together in the joy of tracking Santa's journey around the globe. In 2008, the average "Santa Tracker" cut across cultural, religious, and age barriers. The NORAD Tracks Santa program allowed parents from Nepal to New Zealand, from Russia to the United States and Canada to share in one common goal of keeping the dreams and innocence of their children's holiday imagination alive … be it for "yet another year."

I have fond memories of listening to the "Santa Track" on the radio when I was a child, and now, while driving across the country to visit family on Christmas Eve, I'm able to share these same memories with my own children, only high tech. By virtue of my wireless card and laptop, we can do the same, only now we get to see video of Santa flying over the Great Wall of China!—A very happy parent.

RESEARCH AND PLANNING

Immediately following the 2007 NTS, we began preparing for 2008. We reviewed lessons learned, measured, and evaluated our accomplishments and program reach, then began identifying goals for 2008.

The 2008 NTS program goals were as follows:

- Increase number of new and unique visitors to the NTS website over 2007;
- Expand global reach of NTS by expanding the website content from the current six foreign language options into seven foreign language options · tracking Santa's journey across the world;
- Leverage innovations in the new social media (Twitter, iGoogle, Facebook, and YouTube) to draw in a new generation of Santa Trackers and generate interest and chatter between and among participating Santa Trackers;
- Increase national media coverage (print and broadcast) over 2007 by 25 percent;
- Increase the percentage of calls answered by staff/volunteers in the NTS Operations Center by 50 percent;

- Enhance graphic design of animated videos to appeal to both the youngest as well as the older Santa Tracker audience; and

- Design and create animated videos of Santa's journey over internationally renowned landmarks (Santa Cam Videos) that appear on the website Christmas Eve. Narrate the videos in seven languages to make information accessible to the widest international audience possible.

Private/Public Partnering

A significant part of our planning involved engaging private sector partners. By teaming with experts at Google and Booz Allen Hamilton, NORAD event planners focused on creating an entirely new Santa "route" in an effort to cover more towns, cities, and territories visited by Santa on Christmas Eve. To gain public awareness of the website launch on December 1, NORAD Public Affairs put out several news releases, to include one announcing "Santa's Test Flight" which was timed in conjunction with a local holiday festival. News releases were carefully crafted to build interest and anticipation for the launch of the website, and the eventual tracking of Santa around the world on Christmas Eve. Google Earth worked with NORAD public affairs narrators to develop realistic Santa Cam videos, which were imaginary high tech, high speed digital cameras set to capture Santa and his reindeer as they fly over children's hometowns/countries. These Santa Cams were animated by CGI animations and available upon request to media outlets prior to December 24th event for use in local stories.

EXECUTION

For the "live" tracking of Santa on Christmas Eve, a conference center on Peterson AFB, CO, was transformed into a real-world operational call center. More than 1,200 community volunteers worked two-hour shifts over a 24-hour period Christmas Eve, responding to emails and phone calls from children and parents around the world. Santa's route/progress was broadcast on screens in two tracking rooms, providing volunteer "Trackers" manning their stations with real-time information that they could then relay to callers and emailers. Bilingual community volunteers were identified at in-processing to assist in translating in-bound communications in such varied languages as French, Spanish, Chinese, and Japanese. Two distinct branches of the NTS Operations Center were created dedicated to email communications and telephone communications respectively. Over 73,872 calls were logged and answered in a 24-hour period.

EVALUATION

Program Results: From 19-25 December, the NTS website had 13,755,194 visits from 219 countries. This represents a 43 percent increase over 2007 for the same time period. The program jumped 800 percent in its live media coverage on December 24th, attributable to live satellite distribution which allows media to connect to the command from locations throughout the world. Twelve hundred local community volunteers manned the Colorado Springs Operations Center, up from 1,000 in 2007. Additionally, a review of the more than 6,000 emails received overwhelmingly support the program, 99 percent were favorable or were highly complimentary. All volunteers surveyed had comments to the effect that the NTS experience was the highlight of their holiday season due to their experiences talking to or emailing kids around the world.

CONCLUSION

Here's how we achieved our goals:

- Increased number of new and unique visitors to the NTS website over 2007; In a one week period, we had 13,755,194 from 219 countries compared to 9,620,147 from 210 countries in 2007—an increase of 43 percent over 2007.

- Expanded global reach of NTS through creation of multi-lingual translations tracking Santa's journey across the world and increased the number of countries and territories visited by nine. We also added Chinese to our list of translations. Ultimately, we had 219 countries/territories visiting the site (in order, top 9; US, UK, Canada, Japan, Australia, Ireland, Germany, Brazil, and France) up four percent from 2007.

- Leveraged innovations in the social media (Twitter, Facebook, GMobile, Panoramia, and YouTube) to draw in a new generation of Santa Trackers and generating interest and chatter between and among participating Santa Trackers.

- Increased live national media coverage (broadcast) on December 24th over 2007 by 800 percent.

IMPACT

The 2008 NORAD Tracks Santa program, through its design and execution of an interactive website, cutting edge graphics, kid-friendly Santa tracking maps, and a cadre of volunteers presented to the children of the world an interactive, multi-media experience to follow Santa's journey across the continents on Christmas eve. The 2008 NORAD Tracks Santa program entertained and enlightened an entirely new generation to the iconic symbol of Santa and the spirit of the holiday season through a unique and collaborative public-private partnership. NORAD did this as it reinforced its own brand recognition as protector/defender of North America.

E X H I B I T 3-3A   Fact Sheet on NORAD Santa Tracker

Providing comprehensive, integrated aerospace defense of North America

North American Aerospace Defense Command

Deter. Detect. Defend.   NORAD

NORAD Tracks Santa

On Dec. 24, 1955, a call was made to the Continental Air Defense Command (CONAD) Operations Center in Colorado Springs, Colo. However, this call was not from the president or a general. It was from a girl in Colorado Springs who was following the directions in an advertisement printed in the local paper – she wanted to know the whereabouts of Santa Claus.

The ad said "Hey, Kiddies! Call me direct and be sure and dial the correct number." However, the number was printed incorrectly in the advertisement and rang into the CONAD operations center.

On duty that night was Colonel Harry Shoup, who has come to be known as the "Santa Colonel." Colonel Shoup received numerous calls that night and rather than hanging up, he had his operators find the location of Santa Claus and reported it to every child who phoned in that night.

Thus began a tradition carried on by the North American Aerospace Defense Command (NORAD) when it was formed in 1958. Today, through satellite systems, high-powered radars and jet fighters, NORAD tracks Santa Claus as he makes his Yuletide journey around the world.

Every Christmas Eve, thousands of volunteers staff telephones and computers to answer calls and e-mails from children (and adults) from around the world. Live updates are provided through the NORAD Tracks Santa Web site (in seven languages), over telephone lines, and by e-mail to keep curious children and their families informed about Santa's whereabouts and if it's time to get to bed.

Each year, the NORAD Tracks Santa Web Site receives nearly nine million unique visitors from more than 200 countries and territories around the world. Volunteers receive more than 12,000 e-mails and more than 70,000 calls to the NORAD Tracks Santa hotline from children around the globe.

This year, children and the young-at-heart are able to track Santa through Facebook, Twitter, YouTube, Flickr, and TroopTube.tv. To follow us on any of these Web sites, type in @noradsanta into the search engine and start tracking.

NORAD Tracks Santa has become a magical and global phenomenon, delighting generations of families everywhere.

For more information about NORAD Tracks Santa, please visit www.noradsanta.org
For more information about NORAD, please visit www.norad.mil

Deter. Detect. Defend.
NORAD provides comprehensive, integrated aerospace defense of North America.

Current as of December 2009

Courtesy NORAD Public Affairs

NORTH AMERICAN AEROSPACE DEFENSE COMMAND CANADIAN NORAD REGION

News Release

Public Affairs, 1 Canadian Air Division/
Canadian NORAD Region Headquarters,
PO Box 17000 Stn Forces, Winnipeg, Man. R3J 3Y5
Phone (204) 833-2500 ext 2028, CSN 257-2028;
NORAD website: www.norad.mil
News Release 15 Dec, 2009

Canadian NORAD Region Names Santa's Escort Pilots

Winnipeg, Man. – As Christmas gets closer, the Canadian North American Aerospace Defense Command (NORAD) Region has put the finishing touches on this year's plan to welcome and track Santa Claus when he visits Canada, by naming four CF-18 fighter pilots as his official escorts.

Lieutenant-Colonel Sean Penney and Captain David Chamberlin of 4 Wing Cold Lake, Alta., and Captain Yannick Jobin and Captain Dave Patrick of 3 Wing Bagotville, Que., will take on the responsibility of welcoming Santa when he arrives in Canada for his annual Christmas Eve journey.

The pilots will also take photos and video of Santa and his sleigh using special NORAD SantaCams mounted on their aircraft. The SantaCams instantly download the photo and video imagery so that it may be viewed by children worldwide on the NORAD Tracks Santa website, www.noradsanta.org, on December 24. All of this information will be available in English, French, German, Italian, Japanese, Spanish and Chinese.

In coordination with the North Pole, NORAD has been informed that Santa intends to begin his journey at 6 a.m. EST, on Dec. 24. A dedicated crew of radar operators from the Canadian Air Defence Sector Operations Centre at 22 Wing in North Bay, Ont., will alert NORAD when they detect Santa approaching North America off the coast of Newfoundland and Labrador. NORAD will then direct two CF-18 Hornet fighter jets from 3 Wing to welcome Santa as he enters Canadian airspace. As Santa flies into western Canada, two CF-18 Hornets from 4 Wing will greet the sleigh and eventually escort Santa out of Canadian airspace, where NORAD will turn over tracking duties to the Continental U.S. NORAD Region for the next leg of Santa's Yuletide trip.

Children can also receive updates on Santa's Christmas Eve journey by calling the traditional "NORAD Tracks Santa" telephone hotline at 1-877-HI NORAD, or by emailing NORAD at noradtrackssanta@gmail.com. Last year, the NORAD Tracks Santa website received millions of visitors from hundreds of countries and territories around the world. Volunteers answered more than 73,000 phone calls and over 6,000 e-mails from children around the globe.

NORAD is a bi-national United States and Canadian organization, charged with the missions of aerospace warning and aerospace control for North America. NORAD performs its mission 365 days-per-year, but on Christmas Eve, NORAD performs an additional mission – tracking Santa around the world.

To arrange an interview with an escort pilot, please contact:
- Captain Nicole Meszaros, 4 Wing Public Affairs, at (780) 840-8000 ext. 8121
- Captain Jean-Philippe Gaudreault, 3 Wing Public Affairs, at (418) 677-4000 ext. 7031

To arrange an interview with a radar operator, please contact:
- Lieutenant Leah Pierce, 22 Wing Public Affairs, at (705) 494-6011 ext. 2822

For more information on the NORAD Tracks Santa program, please contact:
- Lieutenant Jordan Woodman, Canadian NORAD Region Public Affairs, at (204) 833-2500 ext. 2028

E X H I B I T 3-3C   Post Event News Release

NORTH AMERICAN AEROSPACE DEFENSE COMMAND

Press Release
Directorate of Public Affairs, Headquarters, North American Aerospace Defense Command, 250 Vandenberg, Suite B016,
Peterson AFB, Colorado Springs, Colo. 80914-3808; Phone (719) 554-6889, DSN 692-6889; NORAD website: www.norad.mil

FOR IMMEDIATE RELEASE   December 29, 2008

NORAD TRACKS SANTA MISSION A SUCCESS

PETERSON AIR FORCE BASE, Colo. – North American Aerospace Defense Command announced today that Christmas Eve 2008 marked another successful year for NORAD Tracks Santa.

The NORAD Tracks Santa Operations Center kicked into high gear at 6 a.m. EST Dec. 24, 2008. More than 1,200 Santa tracking volunteers cycled through the center answering telephone calls and emails from children around the world wanting to get a fix on Santa Claus' whereabouts. 73,872 telephone calls and 6,086 emails from around the world were answered in the center by a NORAD Santa tracker.

The NORAD Tracks Santa website, www.noradsanta.org, garnered 8,785,186 unique visitors to the site since going live on Dec. 1, 2008, and received 15,828,663 visits. The website featured information about tracking Santa in seven different languages and was viewed by visitors from 225 countries and territories, which generated 63,056,261 pageviews of the site. The site featured an interactive Kid's Countdown Village which included games and activities for children of all ages as well as the interactive Santa tracking map, which began Dec. 24.

"365 days a year, NORAD provides aerospace security for North America, and we are proud of our mission and what we accomplish. But Christmas Eve is always a special day for the personnel at NORAD who are able to bring this program of good will to children around the world," said Air Force Maj. Stacia Reddish, NORAD Tracks Santa Project Officer. "We thank not only our many volunteers who answer phones and e-mails, but we wish to thank all our corporate partners as well for making this program possible. We are looking forward to tracking Santa again next year."

Contact Information:
NORAD and NORTHCOM Public Affairs: 719-554-6889.

Courtesy NORAD Public Affairs

EXHIBIT 3-3D   **Promotional Poster on NORAD Santa Tracker**

Courtesy NORAD Public Affairs

4

Social Media

For many communications campaigns, public relations professionals must use and adopt best practices in social media communication strategies. Social media involves three distinct components. First, there is a new level of two-way engagement with key target audiences. Today, people expect a voice and expect to be heard using social media venues as their speaker's dais. Second, the communication process is powered by ever changing and evolving digital technologies. Twitter, Facebook, and YouTube have a very short life compared to legacy communication systems like newspapers, but they will shortly be supplemented, or even supplanted, by a host of new capabilities. Smart phones will eventually give way to a new generation of mobile devices that enhance communication and connectivity. Third, the technologies offer an ease and simplicity of publishing and producing information that allows digital savvy citizens to easily contribute to the public discourse. For example, viral emails circulated among friends become published commentary and connect people and ideas. Satirical videos shot on a smart phone and posted on YouTube may be seen by millions within hours. Taken together, social media involves *communication, connections, conversations, collaboration,* and *multi-media.*

The communication technologies underpinning social media have changed both the speed of the exchange of information and also the very nature of the dialogue among people, and the public's interaction with organizations, with corporations and with governments. These changes are manifested in such terms as Web 1.0 for the posting of information online and audiences as content consumers; Web 2.0 describing the use of technology promoting participation, conversations, and the exchange of user-generated content; and Web 3.0 referring to the Semantic Web with technologies working to enhance meaning for publics. Therefore, social media isn't just focused on digital technologies that enhance connections and conversations, but also about a shift in thinking about communication and how publics make meaning from communication. It is also about a shift in our perspective. As attributed to communication theorist Marshall McLuhan, "the medium is the message." The new tools surrounding social media can be seen as changing our very perception of reality. The very process of using social media affects our view of political engagement, relationships with others, relationships with products/brands, and the spread of ideas.

Social media enhances *conversations* and *connections* every day. For example, an elusive terrorist nemesis of the United States is killed by a military commando team and even before the official announcement by the president, a flash mob gathers outside the gates of the White House to celebrate based upon a Twitter feed that quickly was passed from friend to friend on digital networks. While attending the Royal wedding, thousands of people sent messages and photographs to their friends to "share in the moment."

Even though exchanging information with others is as old as gatherings around the first campfires, digital technologies allow social dialogue across vast distances, among tribes and people of very different backgrounds. It both helps us maintain ties to our friends and also helps us establish new tribal connections with those who have common interests with us.

Affinity groups with common interests have been banding together to exchange ideas and information on the Internet since the earliest days of the World Wide Web. Discussion boards and chat rooms made popular in the 1990s have evolved into Facebook and similar sites as new technologies allowed more ease of interaction and information flow. These affinity groups range from model railroaders to Blue Grass music devotees. Just one regional chapter of DC Metro Moms on Yahoo Groups has 250 members and many sub-groups around interest areas such as scrapbooking and challenges facing professional moms. In one community, there is an online group for contracting attorneys and an advocacy group for those individuals living with HIV/AIDS. Breast cancer patients may use social media to connect with others to establish information exchanges and support networks. Public relations seeks to join these social media conversations to discuss client services, products, or initiatives.

The communication technology that generated the current form of social media isn't static. The next generation of digital technologies is using geographical tags based upon Global Positioning Satellite (GPS) data to further enhance connections and conversations. Those connected via new social media technology will not only see simplified communication with friends but also be updated on the location of friends. Instead of serendipitously running into a person at the grocery store, smart phones and mobile tablets will let you know when a friend is in the neighborhood. Marketers are quickly finding ways to use this information to promote goods and services near your location. Public relations practitioners are similarly aware of the benefits of using these same tools for a campaign.

Are social media *conversations* really different? Weber suggests social enterprises are radically transparent entities that engage honestly and openly with the stakeholder communities in a way that other organizations wouldn't dream of or have the capability of doing. They are building long-term relationships with customers and other key constituents, primarily through vibrant digital communities where they connect personally and regularly.[1] The social media world is based upon the capacity to engage with audiences in genuine two-way dialogues. The dialogue and conversations describe the world of Web 2.0 where it isn't just more information via evolving technologies, but technologies transforming the very nature of communications. Public relations strategists must operate in a new world where people expect transparent communication. The speed of communications means people expect quick and ready answers from PR professionals. The technology seems to also impact our "patience" quotients. We like answers quickly. There is one other important issue about the speed of digital communication. Surprisingly, many organizations still aren't geared for the rapid response for effective social media operations. They don't have in place monitoring services for listening to dialogues that may impact their organization. They also haven't established policies that expedite the approval process for responding quickly to online threats to organizational reputation.

Collaboration is the norm for social media operations. Technology established Wikis with their ability for audiences to contribute and contribute to online publications. Wikipedia and its two million subject entries established an expectation that the power of citizen contributions were as good as the experts. Online movie reviews have usurped the power of newspaper movie critics. When 500 movie goers post a review of a new film on rottentomatoes.com, those individuals planning on going to see the film pay attention and trust in the judgment of the crowd. We trust the experience of others and scan the reviews for plumbing services and restaurants. Newspaper readers scanning the online version respond to the implied recommendations in "most popular" or "most emailed" articles. This is the power of the social media to use a collaborative voice to inform and influence.

Technology also allows the production of new multi-media. In the *New York Times*, Thomas Friedman said: "When everyone has a blog, a MySpace page or Facebook entry, everyone is a publisher. When everyone has a cell phone with a camera in it, everyone is a paparazzo. When everyone can upload video on YouTube, everyone is a filmmaker…. The blogosphere has made the global discussion so much richer—and each of us so much more transparent."[2]

A key characteristic of Web 2.0 is this ease of self-publishing and expressing of ideas. Information and ideas about an organization, product, service, or campaign may come from any person and from any direction.

The challenge for social media campaigns involves trying to carry on a meaningful dialogue in this free-for-all exchange. This challenge involves getting your story heard and acted upon in an environment punctuated by noise, opinions posing as information and provocative style over substance. This chapter on social media is also based upon an assumption that excellent communication relies on a variety of technologies and ways to reach audiences simultaneously. It isn't a matter of either using social media or traditional communication methodologies like media relations. It isn't just using one or the other approaches. The strategic goals of a communication campaign will influence the appropriate communication strategies, and the thrust of the cases in this chapter reveal a concentration on social media but in reality most campaigns are a blend of approaches to achieve strategic communication objectives. The PR practitioner must analyze the situation to determine when and if social media and digital tools are appropriate for a campaign and a client.

RESEARCH

The research process for social media also begins with an analysis of the practitioner's client or organization, of the opportunity or problem that accounts for a communication program, and of the various audiences themselves to be targeted for the PR effort and the messages and narrative story that may be most effective with the audience.

Client Research

Besides thoroughly understanding the client's organization and overall mission, the analysis should begin with a measure of the client's current presence within the social media world. Determine whether prior social media campaigns have been conducted or if any effort has been made to engage in dialogue on social media platforms.

Assess the social media world's current discussions about the client. Is perception about the organization positive, negative, or neutral? What is the intensity of the feelings about the client? How large is the public engaged in the dialogue about the client? Are there identifiable opinion leaders orchestrating the discussion?

Also, understand the client's real interest and overall capabilities to engage in the social media process. Some organizations think they must jump into the social media pond because so many of their friends are happily splashing about. They want to jump in because everyone else is doing it. However, they may not even own a swim suit, social media skills, or even know if their prime audience likes to swim. Or they treat social media as if it is a checklist. Are we on Facebook? Check. Are we on Twitter? Check. This approach is incorrect because they aren't stopping to think what the best platforms are for their target audience or distinguishing whether they can be an effective creator. Often times, organizations should consider just listening if they can't create content on a consistent basis.

Organizations also may be interested in online engagement with audiences without much thought about the real investment in time and resources to maintain a long-term presence in appropriate social media settings. Other organizations don't really understand the underlying purposes for online engagement and conversations. Also, determine if the organization is really committed to the process. Finally, a capability to conduct quality social media campaigns takes digital expertise, social media audience expertise, multi-media expertise whether messaging or producing videos appropriate to a campaign and the audience. See what they know and who in the organization could be useful in a campaign. Finally, see if there are policies in place that establish some guidelines in terms of content, conduct, and engagement. If there are none, this may be a starting point for the campaign to ensure a unified and focused effort by the organization and its people.

Do not forget to examine the past social media campaigns conducted by the organization and whether analytics had been used to determine whether the campaign was a success. All of these elements will provide a useful foundation for advising a client and ensuring that the return on investment (ROI) of the campaign is successful.

Opportunity or Problem Research

First, is there a real strategic reason for a campaign? Look at the potential initiatives by the organization that could merit participation on social media. Opportunities may revolve around reaching a special audience, which has a high rate of participation on social media. It may also depend upon a product, service, or campaign initiative that lends itself to online dialogue and activities.

Look at similar campaigns by other organizations to see if they were successful and see which factors contributed to the success or failure of the campaign. Also, monitor current events that could have an impact on people's perceptions of your initiative. For example, a campaign for a new geospatial tracking service may encounter huge public policy debates about privacy concerns for teens. In essence, keep alert to special problems that may impede a campaign.

Audience Research

Understanding the target public for social media campaigns can be exceptionally challenging. Practitioners must clearly identify the appropriate audience, and many times it is a micro-audience. As appropriate, slice the audience in terms of technographics, geographics, and demographics.

First, be wary of oversimplifying the audience. Social media may not just be the terrain of a younger demographic. In my recent undergraduate classes, most, but not all, students were active to various degrees on Facebook, yet very few were engaged on Twitter. It has been a challenge for young people to let their grandparents join their friendship circle on a social media site.

Start by identifying the digital skills (technographics) of a potential audience. Forrester Research categorizes individuals by the degree of social technology participation and profiles groups that range from "inactives" to "creators." The PEW Internet and American Life Project research identified ten different technology user types. "The ten groups that emerge in the typology fit broadly into a 'high end,' 'medium users,' and 'low-level adopters' framework."[3] The research cautions practitioners against treating most audiences as social media engaged and savvy. In 2007, a PEW study found 49 percent of those surveyed having few tech assets or capabilities and 15 percent were not even "connected" to the Internet or digital world. Find data that identifies the range of social and technological skills for your prime audience.

Audience values also inform a social media campaign. Li and Bernoff suggest there are many reasons for participation on social media and these motivations may help target the right public[4]:

- Making new friends
- Succumbing to social pressure to join
- Sites are useful and person may wish to contribute
- Altruistic impulse (charitable)
- Prurient impulse (people watching)
- Creative impulse
- Validation impulse (be seen as knowledgeable)
- Affinity impulse (common base of experiences).

Each motivation may offer a tactical approach to reach a specific audience.

Finally, like other campaigns, there are some members of the online social world who are much more influential than others. The celebrity Ashton Kutcher has more than six million followers on Twitter. The volume of followers or friends may be one indication of influence. If many respected blogs and websites link to a blog, that would also be a measure of merit for engaging the blogger during your campaign. Those individuals who exhibit a creative ability or seem to express wisdom will be likely additions to a list of influentials. There are knowledge experts in given fields that should be cultivated. However, the volume of friends may be deceptive as there are joiners who are not real connectors or creators. Also, don't overlook the value of journalists during a social media campaign as many media outlets now encourage their reporters to be engaged online.

Finally, listen to the tone and tenor of existing conversations on social media, both concerning your client and similar organizations. Find out the type of discussions and the range of opinions that are being expressed. See what types of discussions are being emailed, 'liked' and recommended to friends. As in media relations, the list of audiences should be detailed and well understood before starting the social media engagement process.

OBJECTIVES

Social media campaigns use both impact and output objectives around a clear, overarching strategic focus. Changing awareness, attitude or behavior of an online public is involved with the objectives. Using technology is not the objective. Here are typical examples of both impact and output objectives in a social media campaign.

Impact Objectives

Impact objectives represent the desired outcomes of modifying the awareness, attitudes, and behaviors of target audiences. In social media campaigns, they may include such statements as:

1. To develop 50 percent more online reviews of your product.
2. To increase positive mentions by credible bloggers by 25 percent.
3. To have at least 100,000 views of a client video on YouTube.
4. To have 50,000 members participate in a video game featuring your product.
5. To increase support of tray-less meals by 25 percent in the student dining hall on campus.

For each objective, a specific audience could be identified.

Output Objectives

Output objectives in social media campaigns involve efforts made by the practitioner on behalf of the client. These statements suggest activities intended to support the client's desired influence on audiences. Output objectives may include:

1. To create an online presence that encourages participation in a discussion forum.
2. To produce a stream of ten daily Twitter posts per day about a new organizational initiative for 45 straight days.
3. To coordinate five blogger interviews with organizational officers.
4. To develop and publish a new CEO blog for the organization
5. To distribute three videos on YouTube.

PROGRAMMING

Programming for social media relations includes many of the same planning and execution elements used in other forms of public relations: (1) theme and messages, (2) actions or special events, (3) uncontrolled or controlled media, and (4) principles of effective communication. The primary strategy in social media programming is to engage in a dialogue with an online community appropriate to your campaign goals, or develop your own online community. An organization may create a presence on social media, and then maintain the presence and enable relationships. Li and Bernoff say the five basic strategies with social media include: *listening* to better understand, *talking* to spread messages, *energizing* through enthusiastic participants who use their word of mouth to tell your story, *supporting* customers, and *embracing* by integrating your customers into the way your business works.[4] Taken together, social media programming also involves communication, connections, conversations, collaboration, and multi-media.

Theme and Messages

The ability to develop a compelling story often differentiates the high impact social media campaigns from those that don't make a ripple on the social media pond. For example, the campaign around BMW's Mini Cooper talks about "driving down the highway in *big gulps* and helping out others along the way." There is even a "Motoring Hearts" site with a mini-storybook and a way to volunteer in your area. The messages and visuals convey values and passion. A promotion for the documentary "Powerful Noise" included an online petition and Tweet-a-thon to make powerful noise about the film and the issue of women helping their families out of poverty. The message connects with audience altruistic values and engages them in the campaign.

The messages for social media campaigns may rely on the same standards for newsworthiness as used in journalism. Do the messages weave an interesting and engaging story based upon drama, conflict, human interest, and notable personalities? Similarly, messaging strategies can use best persuasive practices in public speaking: think about reinforcing similarities with the audience, conveying respect for the audience, using vivid description and imagery, and using extended narratives as a powerful way to evoke emotional response.[5] Also, expect Web citizens to question authority and expect honest and transparent dialogue. Therefore the tone of messages needs to be conversational and personable. However don't take it personally when your organization faces a barrage of rather tart comments to your messages. It is usually best to keep your cool and to avoid provoking other social media communities to action.

Like other aspects of programming, theme and messages should be governed by the practitioner's understanding of what is newsworthy and engaging for a specific audience.

Action(s) or Special Event(s)

The use of special events and contests on social media can attract interest for a client's product or issue. A soft drink company had people vote online for their favorite causes and awarded grants to charities based upon the votes. The campaign was also promoted via traditional media relations and advertising. Another soft drink manufacturer constructed a social media campaign around fan-made flavors and let the fans engage in promotion of the new flavors via Twitter. Celebrities may attract additional awareness for a campaign. Brand Affinity Technology research suggests "celebrity-endorsed Facebook messages resulted in a 50 percent improvement in cost-per-action over non-endorsed Facebook advertising."[6]

Uncontrolled Media

For social media, much of the communication is controlled and the messaging is developed by the organization for posting online, yet the content quickly generates responses from the audience which are more typical of uncontrolled media. The lines between Controlled and Uncontrolled Media are quite blurred with social media.

Photograph and Video Opportunities

Visuals count on social media. The Red Cross posts images of disaster recovery operations on Flickr to promote an awareness of a natural disaster and encourage people to volunteer or donate to relief efforts. Videos structured for online sites such as YouTube are able to convey an organization's message through a story board or presentation by a corporate CEO. Dominos Pizza was able to counter a prank video by employees spoofing the sanitary practices of food preparation through a CEO "for the record" video presentation on YouTube. One company wished to promote the superior power of their blender so they made a single, low-budget video showing the blender blending an iPhone that significantly increased sales. Similarly, video opportunities must offer compelling visuals that tell a real story and accent key themes for a client. Think in terms of a story with drama, challenges, and resolution. Good narrative visual storytelling involves planning the messages and carefully outlining a script. For some videos, follow the style of the classic film narrative with its beginning, where a problem is introduced, middle, with repeated attempts to solve the problem, and an ending where just in the nick of time the hero or heroine solves the problem and all live happily ever after. Other videos use humor or parody to highlight issues. Why do talking babies attract attention for a stock broker? Figure it out and use your own video hook. Also, be prepared to respond on appropriate social media venues if warranted. How would you respond to a YouTube post called "People of Walmart" that portrays colorful and sometimes rather tacky attire by store patrons? One element of your social media policy is having systems in place to evaluate the appropriateness of a response to videos that seriously damage the organization's reputation.

Controlled Media

There are many elements of social media campaigns involving controlled media, however, given the Web citizens propensity to post comments and engage in the dialogue, a controlled post is only the first stage in the conversation. Expect to monitor and respond to comments and videos posted in respond to the organization's material. Don't expect to control the conversation.

Many social media campaigns start with blogs. The writing should be informational and useful to the audience. Like a news release, a blog should make "news." Let people know how the organization thinks about an issue. Get members of the online community to subscribe to RSS feeds (Really Simple Syndication) and widgets that tell them when you have added content to your website or blog. Writing a blog follows the rules of rhetoric. Establish your credibility, use emotion and stories to capture attention, and use logic to convince. Have a voice. Think about expanding the scope of blogs in the organization. Encourage experts in the organization to blog about their area of expertise. If your company specializes in technology, then train a tech expert on the principles of good blog writing.

A Facebook or MySpace page offers avenues to engage audiences. The goal is to gain "friends" or those who want to belong to your affinity group because of information or benefits associated with membership. Also explore the value of LinkedIn with professional audiences or MySpace, Piczo for graphics and images, Orkut (popular in India and Brazil), Bebo (blog early and blog often), or Hi5 (focused on social gaming).

Twitter offers a way to provide a stream of controlled messages. The messages or micro-blogs, are limited to 140 characters. The better Twitter feeds are informative and engaging. News organizations now post a short teaser announcing a story along with a few details about the story. Hash tags are similar to "keywords" in blogs and identify the subject matter in the Tweet. Use the service of a URL shortener to provide links to websites. Also, a single message doesn't establish a presence on Twitter. Think in terms of a string of messages over days or weeks so people will start to "follow" the organization's Twitter feeds. Again, the Twitter feeds provide information of value to others. Make sure that posts are not promotional in nature, and that they have a personal voice. Journalists may even follow the organization to develop stories for later publication.

Effective Communication

With social media, many of the nine principles of effective communication discussed in Chapter 2 apply.

Most important, the social media communication process can be aptly described as a two-way. Kent and Taylor outline elements of value to this two-way, dialogic, process and suggest it is a product of ongoing communication and relationships that involves trust, risk, and vulnerability[7]:

1. Mutuality—recognition the organization and publics are tied together and characterized by collaboration and inclusion.

2. Propinquity—spontaneity of interaction with publics involves engagement and consultation.

3. Empathy—supportive and confirmation of common goals and interests.

4. Risk—the willingness to interact with publics on their own terms.

5. Commitment—willing to keep engaged in the process.

Expect social media publics to respond to online engagement with your organization based upon their perceptions around these elements. If a client is listening and respectful of the public's opinions, the public will assume the dialogue is based upon mutuality, empathy, and commitment.

Source credibility clearly is applicable in the case of social media. Demonstrate that your client is trustworthy and reliable.

Opinion leaders are key elements for social media interactions. Such organizations as Klout, have devised measures around "social influence." The Klout Score integrates "reach" (number of people adding you to lists), "amplification" (diversity of those that

@ message you on Twitter, velocity of retweets, and activity such as tweets generating new followers), and "network influence" (the influence scores of those who follow you). Having opinion leaders to promote your product or ideas through social media venues can significantly expand the influence of your message and campaign.

Salient information is crucial for the online community. When the information provided by an organization is timely and relevant to an audience, the messages have greater impact. For example, a pregnant woman may start to pay closer attention to nutritional information or childcare issues. Make your messages and narratives compelling and interesting.

The selective exposure principle clearly applies on social media. Don't expect to be very successful influencing the flamers who clearly vent with venom in their "comments."

On the other hand, the group-influence principle is a dominant issue for social media. People follow the lead of their affinity groups. They want to know what others are thinking and doing about your issue. Notice how quickly you click on the "most popular" or "most emailed" story on a news organizations website. Group endorsements carry weight with social media audiences.

Finally, the audience participation principle is valid and useful in social media. When introducing new product lines, for example, many companies may invite individuals to join a Facebook community or even vote for a new theme song. People love to add comment to blogs and videos and post to the "wall" on your Facebook page.

Thus, most of the principles of effective communication apply to social media to some degree.

EVALUATION

With social media, monitoring the impact of a campaign is as relevant as any other campaign. In fact, there are many monitoring services offering customized research to review the social cloud's response to a campaign. A campaign needs to understand where conversations are occurring about the campaign issue, who is engaged in the conversation, and what people are saying. The following list offers an example of these services yet barely represents the approximate 200 offerings on the market with many likely to emerge as the list of social media analytics expands: Radian6, ListenLogic, SocialCast, Lithium Social Media Monitoring, Sysomos, Looxi, Jive, and Visible Technologies. In addition, specific platforms have their own measurements such as Facebook analytics, TweetReach, TwitterCounter, or We Follow.

Evaluating Impact Objectives

With the social media campaign working engagement and dialogue with key audiences, measurement is more complex than a traditional media relations campaign and print impressions to measure the reach for "awareness." Awareness objectives can be evaluated using views for a Facebook page or a video on YouTube. Attitude objectives may be seen through the number of new "friends," "followers," or "like" responses for your product or organization. The organization may also conduct a traditional survey of attitudes toward the product or client as a measure of success. Marklein suggests tracking engagement and impressions in parallel as data is readily available on the number of views for an online video or the number of people who "friend" your organization.[8] He also suggests contextualizing data as engagement with an influential blog with 10,000 daily readers is more valuable than many other sites.

Behavioral impact metrics still involve the traditional measures of increased sales, attendance at an event, or surveys of changed behavior, such as reduced accidents caused by texting while driving following a campaign targeted at young drivers.

During the 2011 Academy Awards show, two new hosts for the event were selected to attract more young viewers. It is easy to measure the success of the campaign (increase viewership among 18- to 26-year-olds) through the Nielsen ratings. Also as the social media was used to promote the new MC's with the target audience, social media discussions would provide additional measures of success. CNN did a story ("Oscars: The bomb heard round the Internet"— February 28, 2011) about the cloud of Twitter feeds around the social media response to the event's new MCs—it was not favorable. A content analysis of the Twitter feeds related to your campaign would provide a valuable source of feedback on the *tone, sentiment,* and *volume* of comments. These same measures are valuable in other social media campaigns.

Tap the many other analytic tools for online engagement campaigns. Google Alerts provides keyword searches for issues and products in your campaign. Icerocket helps you keep watch over Twitter, blogs, web, and news stories. Addict-o-matic allows searches across blogs, Twitter, Digg, and Flickr. Boardtracker finds "buzz" about your organization in message boards and online group forums. HootSuite and Seesmic manage conversations across Twitter, Facebook, MySpace, WordPress, Foursquare, and LinkedIn. TweetDeck and HootSuite monitor profiles across Twitter, Facebook, LinkedIn, Foursquare, and Google Buzz and allow for scheduled posts.

Expect the organization to expect a ROI for a social media campaign.

Valuating Output Objectives

Along with the measurement of impact objectives, practitioners want to determine the effectiveness of their social media output objectives. It is straightforward to measure the number and quality of blog posts, videos distributed, or Twitter feeds.

SUMMARY

Social media provide an important arena for public relations campaigns. The rules and style of communication may be a bit unruly for some organizations, yet the digital technology offers valuable tools to reach audiences. Also, the very nature of social media may have changed your audience's expectations for dialogue and engagement with your organization. Operating in social media takes special skills with not only the technology, but the forms of *communication, connections, conversations, collaboration,* and *multi-media.* Programming for social media involves engaging in a dialogue with online communities appropriate to your campaign goals, or developing your own online community. For effective communication, the principles of two-way communication and identifying key influential members of the online social media community are important to the success of a campaign. Finally, there are many tools or social media analytics, to help monitor online conversations about your organization and to measure the success of a campaign.

The four-stage process is as useful in social media campaigns relations as it is in other forms of public relations. Essentially, social media engagement involves establishing a favorable working relationship between an organization and it's online communities upon which success or failure is determined.

ENDNOTES

1. Weber, Larry. *Everywhere: Comprehensive Digital Business Strategy for the Social Media Era.* Hoboken, NJ: John Wiley & Sons, 2011, p. 31.

2. Friedman, Thomas (June 27, 2007). "The Whole World is Watching." *The New York Times,* A23.

3. Horrigan, John. "A Typology of Information and Communication Technology Users." Pew Internet and American Life Project (May 6, 2007). www.pewinternet. org/Reports/2007/A-Typology-of-Information-and-Communication-Technology-Users.aspx, accessed March 24, 2008.

4. Li, Charlene, and Josh Bernoff. Groundswell: Winning in a world transformed by social technologies. Boston: Harvard Business Press, 2008.

5. Benoit, William L., and Pamela J.Benoit. *Persuasive Messages*, Malden: MA: Blackwell, 2008, p. 151.

6. "Social Media Ad Performance Surges with Celebrity," News Release by Brand Affinity Technologies (March 9, 2011), www.brandaffinity.net/pressandnews_viewrelease?article=030911, accessed.

7. Kent, Michael L., and Maureen Taylor. "Toward a dialogic theory of public relations," *Public Relations Review*, 28.1 (February 2002): 21–37.

8. Marklein, Tim. "The big shift: Moving from impressions to engagement," *Public Relations Tactics* 18.5 (May 2011): 13.

READINGS ON SOCIAL MEDIA

"A World of Connections," The Economist (January 28, 2010). www.economist.com/node/15351002, accessed March 14, 2011.

Beaubien, Greg. "In social media era, companies can't hide truth" *Public Relations Strategist* 16.4 (Fall 2010): 4.

Bernoff, Josh and Ted Schadler. *Empowered: Unleash your employees, energize your customers, transform your business.* Boston: Harvard University Press, 2010.

Briones, Rowena L., Beth Kuch, Brooke Fisher Liu, and Yan Jin. "Keeping up with the digital age: How the American Red Cross uses social media to build relationships," *Public Relations Review* 37.1 (March 2011): 37–43.

Evans, Angelica, Jane Twomey, and Scott Talan. "Twitter as a public relations tool," *Journal of Public Relations* 5.1 (Winter 2011).

Kaplan, Andreas M. and Michael Haenlein. "Users of the World, Unite! The Challenges and Opportunities of Social Media," *Business Horizons* 53 (2010): 59–68.

Kent, Michael L., and Maureen Taylor. "Toward a dialogic theory of public relations," *Public Relations Review,* 28.1 (February 2002): 21–37.

Levinson, Paul. *New New Media,* Boston: Allyn & Bacon, 2009.

Li, Charlene, and Josh Bernoff. *Groundswell: Winning in a world transformed by social technologies.* Boston: Harvard Business Press, 2008.

Lichtenstein, Jesse. "Digital Diplomacy," *New York Times Magazine* (July 16, 2010).

Marken, G.A. "Social Media … The Hunted Can Become the Hunter," *Public Relations Quarterly* 52.4 (2009): 9–12.

Marklein, Tim. "The big shift: Moving from impressions to engagement," *Public Relations Tactics* 18.5 (May 2011): 13.

McCorkindale, Tina. "Can You See the Writing on My Wall? A Content Analysis of the Fortune 50's Facebook Social Networking Sites." *Public Relations Journal* 4.3 (Summer 2010). www.prsa.org/Intelligence/PRJournal/Documents/content_analysis_of_the_fortune_50s_facebook.pdf, accessed March 14, 2011.

Radick, Steve. "The power of social networks: Reviving the intranet," *Public Relations Tactics* 18.1 (Jan 2011): 18.

Rybalko, Svetlana and Trent Seltzer. "Dialogic communication in 140 characters or less: How Fortune 500 companies engage stakeholders using Twitter," *Public Relations Review* 36.4 (November 2010): 336–341.

Schultza, Friederike, Sonja Utz, and Anja Göritz. "Is the medium the message? Perceptions of and reactions to crisis communication via twitter, blogs and traditional media," *Public Relations Review* 37 (March 2011): 20–27.

Scott, David Meerman. *The New Rules of Marketing and PR: How to Use News Releases, Blogs, Podcasting, Viral Marketing and Online Media to Reach Buyers Directly.* Chichester, UK: John Wiley and Sons, 2010.

Smith, Brian G. "Socially distributing public relations: Twitter, Haiti, and interactivity in social media." *Public Relations Review,* 36.4 (November 2010) 329–335.

Solis, Brian and Deidre Breakenridge. *Putting the Public Back in Public Relations: How Social Media Is Reinventing the Aging Business of PR.* Boston: Pearson, 2009.

Weber, Larry. *Everywhere: Comprehensive Digital Business Strategy for the Social Media Era.* Hoboken, NJ: John Wiley and Sons, 2011.

Wright, D. K., and Hinson, M. D. "Examining how public relations practitioners actually are using social media," *Public Relations Journal 3.3* (2009): 1–33.

Zuk, Ryan. "Communication journeys: Where PR pros are heading with the social Web" *Public Relations Tactics* 17.12 (Dec 2010): 7.

Social Media Cases

Case 4-1

Super events command audiences that warrant superior communication efforts. Using social media to generate added audience participation and conversations just multiplied the publicity. Exhibit 4-1A is a news release announcing the winner of the contest.

Doritos Crashes the Super Bowl: How a Leading Snack Brand Put the Power to its People and Changed Madison Avenue Forever

FritoLay with Ketchum

SITUATION ANALYSIS

Imagine a brand taking a risk so daring that Las Vegas set odds on whether it would pay off. That brand is Doritos. With a motto "go big or go home," Doritos pioneered and proved the power of consumer-created content by boldly airing fan-made Super Bowl spots in 2007 and 2008. Both ads placed No. 4 in *USA Today's* prestigious ad meter, which ranks Super Bowl ads from most to least favorite. But, this year, Doritos elevated the stakes, taking a chance on its consumers that could lead to unprecedented success or a significant let down. Doritos put up $1 million for the fan whose home-made Doritos Super Bowl ad could trump Madison Avenue and become the first-ever user-generated commercial to take the top spot in *USA Today's* ad meter. No brand, even with the backing of top-notch ad agencies, had been able to beat Budweiser for the No. 1 ranking for the past decade. Could a Doritos fan actually dethrone the king? With millions in broadcast advertising dollars and the brand's reputation at stake, public relations served a lead role in driving high-quality submissions and strong ROI. The PR strategy turned what could have been only a one-week news cycle into six months of coverage that drove entries and overall awareness of the David vs. Goliath moments on Super Bowl Sunday and the next day, when *USA Today* revealed Doritos was No. 1, turning the unemployed winners into millionaires and media darlings over night.

106

RESEARCH
Primary

- Commissioned internal and external researchers to obtain insight into Doritos' core consumer group
- Evaluated consumer feedback shared via Doritos website/forum and the blogosphere

Secondary

- Analyzed recent media coverage and surveys on the evolving consumer-generated content trend and media consumption habits of Doritos' core and broader target audiences
- Identified top trends in current news cycle to determine best PR positioning of program

Key Research Insights

Research efforts confirmed that the most influential media to reach the core target were blogs, social networking, and viral video sites. But, it also revealed that traditional media and local print, radio, and TV news still needed to be a vital part of a communications campaign to this audience. Given the media's focus on the economic downturn and presidential election, a cash prize in the contest and themes of hope, optimism and the power of people to make change were deemed the most newsworthy angles.

Target Audience Analysis

The Doritos target consumer is between the ages of 16 and 24, and is a member of a technology-savvy group that has mastered multi-tasking with media. The Internet is the second most-consumed medium by this group and they spend approximately three hours online per day. Due in large part to the 24/7 availability of unfiltered feedback online, Doritos' target has developed a higher tolerance and respect for honest and authentic messaging. In the quest to control their stimulation, Doritos' consumers embrace media as a form of self-expression.

PLANNING
Objectives

- Drive consumer engagement in contest via submissions and video views on program website.
- Sustain six-month news cycle of Doritos contest coverage.

Media Goal:

Generate 600 million media impressions in mainstream and youth media.

Target Audiences:

Core: 16 to 24 year olds; Broader: 18 to 45 year olds

Strategies

The research led to a daring idea that put Doritos fans in complete creative control of the brand and dangled a reward so sweet it would motivate consumer and media engagement like never before:

- Invite America to develop Doritos' Super Bowl ads and award the winning creator with $1 million if he or she can beat the professionally produced spots and place No. 1 in *USA Today*'s ad meter.
- Implement a two-prong media outreach approach to simultaneously reach Doritos' core target audience and likely entrants while maintaining ongoing coverage in mainstream news outlets.
- Prepare messaging and media opportunities for all potential *USA Today* result scenarios.

EXECUTION
Strategy 1:

Invite America to develop Doritos' Super Bowl ads; and Award $1 million for top ad meter spot

- Challenged fans to create and submit a Doritos ad to www.crashthesuperbowl.com for a chance to have it air during Super Bowl XLIII, unedited by Doritos
- Invited consumers to vote online for their favorite ad among the five finalists selected by Doritos
- Aired two consumer-created and consumer-selected Doritos Super Bowl ads

Strategy 2:

Implement a two-prong media outreach approach

- Secured exclusive launch story in *Wall Street Journal* to spark David vs. Goliath news story early on
- Targeted college newspapers, top film schools, and largest universities; utilized viral video/photo sites (e.g., Flickr, You Tube, etc.); targeted blogs and podcasts for core consumers (16-24), film makers and ad industry, generated news around finalist grassroots, and social networking efforts
- Distributed national audio news release on 1,000+ favorite youth radio shows nationwide; targeted ad, sports and lifestyle reporters at broadcast, print, and online media; promoted finalists to hometown media outlets; created and distributed b-roll; positioned Doritos as user-generated content pioneer in Super Bowl ad co-op video news release and conducted satellite media tour (SMT) with finalists

Strategy 3:

Prepare messaging and media opportunities for all potential result scenarios

- Developed multiple messages to control internal and external communications around various outcomes (e.g., Doritos takes top spot, Doritos places in top five, Doritos places low, etc.).

- Conducted extensive outreach to national and local-market media to line-up post-game press; arranged SMT onsite in Tampa to handle potential influx of interview requests, pending outcome.

- Based on Doritos turning two unemployed brothers from "small town" America into millionaires overnight, extended typical 24-hour post-game news cycle into a two-week, multi-city media tour, culminating in a press conference, and party in their hometown of Batesville, Indiana on February 12, 2009.

EVALUATION

Just as a Doritos fan trumped Madison Avenue, PR also gave the ad world a run for its money. **Publicity efforts** marketed Doritos tortilla chips so extensively that the total earned media impressions were **valued at nearly 13 times the cost of an average Super Bowl ad.** Through the power of pitching, Doritos ads aired thousands of times as part of news coverage at no cost. From *Today* to *The Tonight Show* and everything in between, **PR made Doritos the No. 1 news story post-game.**

Best success indicator: significant year-over-year lift in Doritos sales the week post-game.

The consumer-created Doritos ad, "Free Doritos," placed first in *USA Today*'s ad meter, turning its talented but unemployed creators (Joe Herbert and Dave Herbert, brothers from Batesville, IN) into millionaires and media darlings over night. Just weeks post-Super Bowl, they are already evaluating countless job opportunities and remain in the news as a result of their widespread exposure.

Objective 1:

Drive consumer engagement in contest via submissions and video views

- Received 1,900 entries, twice the number of submissions from year one of the program.

- Doubled number of unique website visitors from year one of the program.

- Engaged thousands of Doritos enthusiasts on social networking sites (Facebook, You Tube, etc.).

- Doritos was the No. 2 brand capturing share of blog discussions about Super Bowl ads.

- Consumer engagement with Doritos was evident in these top consumer-controlled ad rankings:

  - No. 1 on YouTube Super Vote, No. 1 on MSNBC Ad Poll; most tweeted Super Bowl ad.

OBJECTIVE 2:

Generate 600 MM impressions in mainstream and youth media.

- Generated more than 2X our earned media impressions goal and beat media results from first year of the contest.
- 25 national print/wire features, including *USA Today* (five stories), *Wall Street Journal* (three stories), *New York Times* (three stories), Associated Press (two stories), and Reuters
- 108 national TV and radio segments, including winner interviews on *Today* show and *The Tonight Show* and coverage on *Good Morning America, CNN Headline News,* and NPR.
- More than 360 online news stories including the Yahoo.com home page, Time.com, MSNBC.com, CNBC.com, Forbes.com, CNNMoney.com, TheStreet.com, AdWeek.com, and Brandweek.com.
- More than 2,200 local TV/radio mentions, including multiple airings in the top 20 markets.

E X H I B I T 4-1A   News Release

For Immediate Release

Contact:
Chris Kuechenmeister
Frito-Lay
214-422-8901 cell
Chris.Kuechenmeister@fritolay.com

DORITOS FAN TRUMPS ADVERTISING PROFESSIONALS AND WINS $1 MILLION SUPER BOWL ADVERTISING CHALLENGE

*First-Ever Consumer-Created Ad Takes No. 1 Spot in
USA TODAY's Annual Super Bowl Ad Meter*

PLANO, Texas (Feb. 2, 2009) —The Doritos brand today announced that its consumer-created Doritos commercial "Free Doritos," which aired for the first time nationally during yesterday's Super Bowl XLIII broadcast, ranked No. 1 in *USA TODAY's* annual Super Bowl Ad Meter. The tortilla chip brand is now giving Joe Herbert, the ad's talented creator, a $1 million payout for claiming the coveted title many ad pros strive to attain each year.

Nationwide consumer votes put "Free Doritos" in the Super Bowl limelight from amongst nearly 2,000 entries and five finalist ads in the third annual Doritos "Crash the Super Bowl" program. Now, too, in the Super Bowl spotlight is finalist Eric Heimbold. Doritos surprised viewers by also airing his commercial "Power of Crunch," which placed No. 5 in the *USA TODAY* ad meter.

"We've said it before and we'll say it again, Doritos goes big or goes home," said Ann Mukherjee, group vice president, marketing, Doritos. "We knew Joe could take on the pros and now he has the financial resources to pursue his dreams. We are extremely proud of Joe's accomplishment and believe this is the best million dollars the Doritos brand has ever spent."

The brand also announced that it will continue to give control of its broadcast advertising air time to its fans. Doritos will also air all five finalist commercials as its national Doritos TV campaign to continue to shine the spotlight on their makers and their budding careers. In addition to "Free Doritos," the other finalists' ads that will be at the center of Doritos' TV advertising campaign are: "Power of the Crunch," "The Chase," "Too Delicious," and "New Flavor Pitch."

"We believe in our fans and will continue to provide them with opportunities to be discovered and live out their dreams," adds Mukherjee. "Doritos feels, as a brand, it should break the rules for it fans so they can make the impossible become possible."

Joe and his co-creator and brother Dave Herbert returned to meet the newly raised stakes of the third annual Doritos "Crash the Super Bowl." From shattering a vending machine full of Doritos with a snow globe to throwing the "crystal ball" at the Boss, the inspiration for their commercial is based on ideas the brothers felt would evoke laughter and emotion from the audience at different points of the commercial.

"To have 'Free Doritos' exposed on the Super Bowl stage was already amazing enough," exclaimed Herbert. "But, to now claim No. 1 on the *USA TODAY* Ad Meter and win $1 million is unbelievable and affirmation that we can and will fulfill our dreams. This means so much to my brother and I. We are very thankful to Doritos, our friends, our family, and everyone else who supported us and believed in us."

The *USA TODAY* Super Bowl Ad Meter tracks the second-by-second responses of a panel of viewers to ads during the national broadcast of the Super Bowl and ranks them favorite to least favorite. Created in 1989, *USA TODAY's* Ad Meter has been regarded as the most influential Super Bowl ad rating in the advertising industry.

Eric Heimbold, a graduate of the film department at Pasadena Art Center College of Design, was hoping to challenge himself as a film-maker when he rallied old friends from school to create a Doritos ad that told a sexy, Super Bowl-worthy story. "Power of the Crunch" is a comedic take on the idea that people are corrupted by ultimate power. In less than 30 seconds, his main character spirals through a series of extreme indulgences and ultimately self-destructs. For Eric, this was a great opportunity for him to do something that is of meaning to him personally and appreciated in a well-structured public forum.

The "Crash the Super Bowl" campaign is the evolution of the Doritos brand allowing consumers to be in control. In 2007, the Doritos brand aired its first consumer-created commercial during Super Bowl XLI, as part of the first Doritos "Crash the Super Bowl" challenge. That same day, the brand aired a second commercial to kick-off the first-ever consumer-created Doritos brand television ad campaign, in which all five of the Doritos "Crash the Super Bowl" finalists' ads aired on national television. Last year Doritos launched the music career of one of its talented fans by airing her original song in a music video during its Super Bowl XLII air time as part of its second annual "Crash the Super Bowl" program.

In addition to the Doritos "Crash the Super Bowl" challenge, in 2007 the brand put consumers in control with programs such as Doritos "Fight for the Flavor," which invited Doritos fans to determine which of two new flavors survived on store shelves and which one was pulled. Then, the brand launched the Doritos "X-13D Flavor Experiment," where consumers had a chance to name a new mysterious flavor of Doritos tortilla chips, followed by "Unlock Xbox," which empowered fans to design the first-ever consumer-created Xbox LIVE® Arcade game. In 2008, "THE QUEST" campaign gave Doritos lovers a unique opportunity to choose how and when to get engaged in a multi-faceted program that had online and real world challenges. Fans were in control of how they participated in "THE QUEST" in everything from guessing a mystery flavor to solving virtual puzzles and competing in real-life adventures. In addition, Doritos put control into the hands of its consumers through a programming partnership with MTV.

Frito-Lay North America is the $11 billion convenient foods business unit of PepsiCo, which is headquartered in Purchase, NY. In addition to Frito-Lay, PepsiCo business units include Pepsi-Cola, Quaker Foods, Gatorade, and Tropicana.

# # #

Courtesy FritoLay and Ketchum

Case 4-2

Harnessing the power of crowdsourcing with a desire to change the world, a company introduces an innovative new corporate social responsibility initiative. Exhibit 4-2A is a social media summary, Exhibit 4-2B is an overview of the allocation of funds for individual projects and Exhibit 4-2C features highlights from the program.

Refreshing Change: Pepsi Refresh Project Brings Good Ideas to Life

PepsiCo with Edelman and Weber Shandwick

SUMMARY

Positioning itself as the optimistic catalyst for idea creation, the Pepsi Refresh Project (PRP) invites the public to Do Good. An exercise in digital media democracy; using social and earned media to engage and empower consumers, Pepsi has made the process engaging and asked those with ideas to harness the power of their networks—over 10,000 projects to date having motivated and received more than 58 million votes from the American public. The Project drives conversation and builds credibility in the social enterprise and innovation arenas through a dynamic, real time "campaign" which democratizes the process of turning ideas into reality, earning more than 3 billion audience impressions to-date positively enhancing the Pepsi brand. Recent data from Marketing Evolutions reveals that knowledge of PRP (36 percent) remains high compared to comparable social innovation campaigns.

SITUATION ANALYSIS

"That's a good idea." All your life, you've heard this simple statement that celebrates a small moment of what might be sheer genius. A "good idea" can happen at any time, and given the right circumstances, change everything. Imagine if people across the United States had just one idea to make the world better. **Now imagine if they had the means to bring their ideas to life.**

Pepsi believes in optimism and the power of people to move communities forward. It comes down to a simple reality: **people plus ideas can bring about change; people plus ideas plus Pepsi can refresh the world.**

Though consumers love when their favorite brands support good causes, they want those causes to resonate personally. To empower people and their ideas the Pepsi Refresh Project (PRP) is awarding more than $20 million in grants in 2010 to support ideas that will make a difference. Pepsi is asking people to step up and share their ideas for improving communities, then letting them decide which of those ideas PRP should move forward. In the process, the public's longtime relationship with the brand will deepen and become refreshed itself.

RESEARCH/PLANNING

To have an impact, Pepsi needed to evolve the Refresh Everything campaign, launched in 2009, to turn good ideas into action. The following research and statistics were consulted in developing the Pepsi Refresh Project:

- Today's consumers scrutinize every dollar they spend—much less give (Iconoculture). 84 percent of consumers want to select their own causes; 83 percent say personal relevance is key (2008 Cone Cause Evolution Study).
- 95 percent of Millennials were still very optimistic about their lives—despite what was happening around them (2008 Pepsi Optimism Project). 94 percent percent of Americans agreed that optimism is important in creating ideas that can have a positive impact, and the best ideas come from "normal people" (66 percent) versus public figures (2009 Pepsi Optimism Project).
- Based on these findings, Pepsi needed to create a forum off and online where social innovation could become personal and help move ideation to implementation in a worthwhile, fun, and contagious context.

Objectives

The Pepsi Refresh Project was designed to give away more than $20 million in the U.S. to fund good ideas, big and small, that move communities forward. With roles clearly defined by the client, Edelman and Weber Shandwick collaborated closely and formed a nearly seamless team to support implementation and meet the communication objectives of the Pepsi program.

1. Raise awareness and interest in the Pepsi Refresh Project; Position Pepsi as the optimistic catalyst for idea creation with consistency and alignment of program messages across all media channels
2. Generate a steady stream of national, local, and online media buzz to support business and brand goals
3. Drive Americans to *RefreshEverything.com* to register and submit their ideas or vote and promote ideas that they care about.

Audience Analysis

PRP targeted U.S. Millennial, Gen Y, and Boomer men and women. For Boomers to Millennials, positive change is a priority. Nearly two-thirds (71 percent) of people globally believe brands spend too much on marketing and should invest more in good causes. Consumers will not only recommend brands that support good causes (64 percent), but more than half (59 percent) will then help that brand promote its products (2009 Good Purpose Study).

Strategy

Edelman and Weber Shandwick worked with Pepsi and agency partners to create a strong communications plan to drive media and voting around the launch of PRP:

- Create intellectual capital around "where ideas come from"; position Pepsi as a credible motivator to empower the everyday American to be the next social entrepreneur
- Cast a national spotlight on the implementation of ideas for refreshing change by announcing the diversion of funds to implement the Project
- Collaborate with employees, bottling and retail partners to generate local news angles, drive awareness
- Raise awareness and increase participation at grassroots level through Hispanic and English language press
- Promote **RefreshEverything.com** as the online destination; encourage individuals to submit ideas and vote
- Encourage online engagement with the Project on Facebook or on Twitter
- Develop national partnerships to raise broad awareness of the Project to tell stories of Project impact and reach.

EXECUTION

Edelman and Weber Shandwick oversaw the following program elements that led to a successful media rel ations campaign this year with the Pepsi Refresh Project:

- **Research**: Published op-ed from CMO Jill Beraud on HuffingtonPost
- **Media Blitzes:** Conducted media relations surrounding milestones: POP, Super Bowl, Ambassadors, Grant recipients
- **RefreshEverything.com:** Positioned as premiere resource for consumer-generated ideas.

Idea Kick-Off:

CEO and PRP team rang NYSE opening bell to signify opening of PRP. Leveraged celebrity spokespeople for brainstorm with in-house and online audiences to ignite idea conversation on national scale.

Refresh Challenges:

Worked with popular culture influencers to generate their own ideas for PRP Grants in collaboration with SxSW, NFL.com, MLB.com, U.S Men's National Team, Nascar.com.

Engagement Events:

Collaborated with celebrities, performing artists to inspire youth to develop ideas.

Do Good For the Gulf:

Doubled commitment of PRP in support of ideas to refresh Gulf communities

Thought Leadership:

Hosted Social Good Conversation with philanthropy influencers; speaking opportunities

Digital Engagement:

Monitored conversation provided real-time responses, fostered dialogue, engaged key voices.

EVALUATION/RESULTS/ROI

Objective 1: Raise awareness and interest in PRP

> Pepsi became one of the **most talked-about brands at Super Bowl** despite not advertising (Nielsen)
>
> **37 percent of Americans now aware** versus 12–21 percent for similar cause marketing programs (Marketing Evolutions)
>
> Correct PRP knowledge is **25 percent** (versus 5—12 percent)

Objective 2: Generate a steady stream of media buzz

> Surpassed media impressions goal by nearly 12-fold, **generating over 2.9 billion audience impressions** in eight months
>
> More than 140,000 tweets, while Facebook "likes" have increased by more than 600 percent (300,000 to over 2 million)
>
> Interaction with refresheverything.com **significantly increased brand attributes** including favorability, intent, and trust along with **intent to purchase among Millennials** (Dynamic Logic)

Objective 3: Drive Americans to RefreshEverything.com

> **Over 17 million unique visitors** to RefreshEverything.com, January–November
>
> Over 10,000 projects have received votes
>
> More than 4.5 million Americans have voted, on track for over 5 million in 2010
>
> **58 million votes cast**, on track for over 75 million in 2010
>
> **1.2 million** online comments to date.

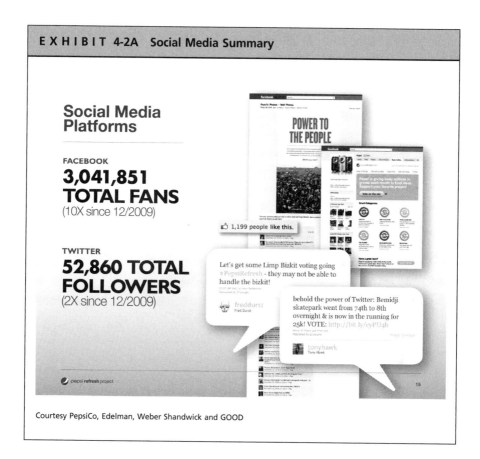

EXHIBIT 4-2A   Social Media Summary

Courtesy PepsiCo, Edelman, Weber Shandwick and GOOD

EXHIBIT 4-2B   Overview of Allocation of Funds

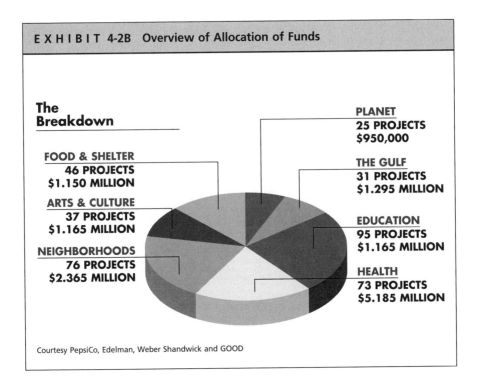

The Breakdown

FOOD & SHELTER
46 PROJECTS
$1.150 MILLION

ARTS & CULTURE
37 PROJECTS
$1.165 MILLION

NEIGHBORHOODS
76 PROJECTS
$2.365 MILLION

PLANET
25 PROJECTS
$950,000

THE GULF
31 PROJECTS
$1.295 MILLION

EDUCATION
95 PROJECTS
$1.165 MILLION

HEALTH
73 PROJECTS
$5.185 MILLION

Courtesy PepsiCo, Edelman, Weber Shandwick and GOOD

E X H I B I T 4-2C   Pepsi ReFresh Highlights

1000 Grantees and Counting

Rocking North Carolina

With Pepsi's help, 17-year-old Austin Halbert turned his Refresh idea—a community concert—into a kick-off celebration for an anti-violence student organization, backed by the mayor, with chapters throughout the county.

In 2010, the Pepsi Refresh Project awarded **$6,200,000** to **139 projects** supporting youth across the country.

Courtesy PepsiCo, Edelman, Weber Shandwick and GOOD

Case 4-3

Twitter may limit content to just 140 characters, but conveying a message, value and meaning in a "one-second ad" seems to be an X Prize contest for social media users. Again, a national super event with millions of viewers is an enticing platform for this innovative approach. Exhibit 4-3A is a news release on the campaign. Exhibit 4-3B is a screenshot of the winning ad.

The Miller High Life One-Second Ad
Miller High Life with Dig Communications

BACKGROUND

The Super Bowl is THE marketing event of the year. Companies spend millions in a competitive battle to be the most talked about brand. Not only is the Super Bowl an annual advertising showcase, it also is a major beer-drinking occasion. The Super Bowl is viewed by more than 100 million people, and 28 million of those viewers host Super Bowl parties, resulting in $11.7 billion spent.

However, since Anheuser-Busch (A–B) has secured category exclusivity on national advertising during the Super Bowl telecast, it is a big challenge for competing beer brands to break through during this period. Realizing its financial and competitive obstacles, the Miller High Life brand turned to its advertising agency (Saatchi & Saatchi) its internal PR team and Dig Communications to develop a multi-faceted, integrated campaign that made High Life the toast of the Super Bowl, reinforced its "**common sense in a bottle**" positioning and drove **unprecedented sales growth** during this key beer-selling occasion.

RESEARCH

As a high quality, low cost beer, Miller High Life has adopted a brand positioning focused on value and common sense. Due to a limited marketing budget, as well as the financial and competitive obstacles to Super Bowl advertising, High Life typically retreats and goes dark well into April. However, riding a wave of momentum from its popular beer deliveryman advertising, High Life decided it would not sit on the sidelines in 2009. Instead, the brand charged its agencies and PR team with developing a newsworthy, attention-getting, beer-selling campaign that would overcome the competitive challenges and help High Life break through the clutter before, during, and after the big game.

Courtesy of MillerCoors and Dig Communications

The team conducted extensive research to uncover the consumer insight that led to the unique campaign, as well as research to ensure its campaign would resonate with targeted consumers, while reinforcing the brand's common sense, value positioning.

- The High Life team conducted a **Segmentation research study** to find out more about the target audience (males 30-45) and their feelings about the economy, Super Bowl spending, media consumption habits, and interests/activities. A consistent theme arose among participants: Anxiety over the poor state of the economy, leeriness over corporate spending, and a backlash against pretentiousness and phoniness.

- The High Life PR team then coordinated informal **focus groups** with a variety of key audiences, including Miller Brewing local market managers, beer distributors, consumers, retailers, media, and bar owners, to find out more about opportunities and obstacles surrounding the Super Bowl in the retail world and beyond.

- The High Life **media team researched opportunities** or loopholes that would allow the brand to gain exposure despite A-B's exclusive sponsorship. After extensive digging, they found that despite category exclusivity, competing brands can purchase airtime on the Super Bowl directly through **local market NBC affiliates.**

- To gain additional understanding of the campaign's impact, the Miller High Life brand team conducted pre- and **post-campaign research** to track sales and brand equity impact.

PLANNING

Equipped with valuable research, an intriguing consumer insight, a **$110,000** budget and a greater understanding of the opportunities and obstacles surrounding the Super Bowl, the High Life team and Dig Communications began laying out plans for a PR-led campaign, aiming to accomplish the following objectives:

Objectives

- Generate extensive media coverage and **build consumer buzz** for Miller High Life before, during and after the Super Bowl

- Drive significant media coverage in the top 20 key High Life markets and create at least **three national placements**

- Help drive **2 percent sales growth** for Miller High Life during the key Super Bowl selling period—an extremely challenging goal, considering the recent struggles and declines of full-calorie, mainstream beers. In fact, sales of full-calorie, mainstream beers decreased an average of 3 percent in 2009

- Incorporate a viral, online component to expand the campaign's reach, attracting at least **500,000 visits**.

Strategy

Building off the team's research, obstacles, opportunities, and objectives, the team focused on developing a program that would drive sales and break through A-B's exclusivity. And once the team settled on an idea, everyone immediately understood its potential:

Miller High Life would create a **one-second television ad** that would air during the Super Bowl, purchasing airtime from individual NBC network affiliates in key markets. Beyond being unique and creative, the concept gave High Life a chance to highlight the brand's value and common sense positioning, while **juxtaposing** its approach to Anheuser-Busch, which planned to air 10 TV ads, valued at $3 million for every 30-second ad. The campaign's theme and main message focused on the fact that High Life has **too much common sense** to spend **$3 million for 30 seconds** of air time:

Miller High Life is a high quality beer and a great value. The brand stands for common sense. So it wouldn't make sense for High Life to pay $3 million for a 30-second ad. Just like our consumers, High Life strives to make smart choices. We'd rather invest that money in brewing a great beer. Plus, one second should be plenty of time to remind viewers that High Life is a good, honest beer at a tasty price.

The team realized that although a TV ad was at the heart of the concept, this was a PR play all the way. Knowing that media outlets focus just as much on Super Bowl advertising as they do the game, the PR team and Dig Communications developed a strategic, multi-faceted execution plan to maximize the impact of this unique marketing idea.

EXECUTION

In order to achieve each business objective, the High Life team's comprehensive communications plan focused both on internal audiences (employees, retailers, and beer distributors) and external audiences (consumers and media). Activities included:

- Launched the campaign with an exclusive *USA Today* story, including interviews with the MillerCoors CMO and the popular High Life deliveryman from the existing "Take Back the High Life" TV campaign.

- Distributed a national **social media news release**, featuring embedded video, images, and hyperlinks to a teaser site.

- Coordinated hundreds of radio, print, TV, and online **interviews** in key local markets for the High Life brand manager, the MillerCoors CMO, local market managers and the High Life deliveryman.

- Developed an **Online Media Kit** as a one-stop-spot where media could obtain high-res images, broadcast-quality video footage, news releases, and sound bytes.

- Vigorously promoted campaign details with corporate employees, field sales reps, beer distributors, and retailers, encouraging major High Life **Super Bowl retail displays.**

- Coordinated high-profile national interviews for the campaign's famous beer deliveryman, including on the **"Tonight Show with Jay Leno."**

Additional national media coverage included *ABC News Tonight, Good Morning, America, The Bonnie Hunt Show,* and *Fox & Friends.*

- Used social media tools to launch a **viral campaign**, including a teaser website featuring outtakes and "one-second ads that didn't make the cut," as well as a one-second-ad-themed YouTube channel.

- Utilized the **MillerCoors intranet** and system-wide emails to share High Life football-themed point-of-sale signage and ideas for leveraging the One-Second Ad campaign at retail.

- Aired an **attention-getting one-second** ad during the Super Bowl in key regions, covering 75 percent of the country. The ad, which was the talk of the Super Bowl before, during and after the game, simply featured the beer deliveryman enthusiastically shouting **"High Life!"** Although we did not downplay the ad's regional buy, media ignored that aspect, and focused on the unique idea, which resonated even further with national media and consumers due to the country's difficult economic environment.

EVALUATION

The team's research and strategic approach to planning, unveiling, communicating, and leveraging the *High Life One-Second Ad* paid off, allowing the brand to surpass each of its objectives:

Objectives	Results
Generate **extensive media coverage** and build consumer buzz for Miller High Life	More than **5,000** newspaper, television, radio, and online stories featured the Miller High Life One-Second Ad campaign!
Drive significant media coverage in the top 20 key High Life markets and create at least **three national placements**	The team secured placements in the top **250 High Life** markets, and generated national coverage on *The Tonight Show with Jay Leno, ABC World News Tonight, The Bonnie Hunt Show,* and *GMA.*
Help drive **2 percent sales growth** for Miller High Life during the key Super Bowl selling period	Miller High Life sales during the Super Bowl selling period increased an **unprecedented 9 percent**. Furthermore, sales maintained the dramatic increase during each of the three months following the campaign!
Incorporate a viral component to expand reach, attracting at least **500,000 visits**	The teaser website and YouTube videos combined to attract more than **3 million visits!**

EXHIBIT 4-3A   News Release

For more information, contact:

Tom Ryan
MillerCoors
414.931.3377
Ryan2.Thomas@MillerCoors.com

Jody Breier
Dig Communications
312.577.1757
jbreier@digcommunications.com

Common Sense Says Length Doesn't Matter

*One Second was all Miller High Life Needed to Make its
Point During the Big Game*

MILWAUKEE (Feb. 1, 2009) – While it took four quarters of gridiron action to learn who the best football team in the nation is, it only took Miller High Life one second to remind viewers around the country that High Life is common sense in a bottle.

In contrast with other companies that spent an estimated $3 million for 30 seconds of airtime, Miller High Life broke from conventional commercial formatting and aired a 1-second spot during the Big Game, which can now be viewed online at www.1SecondAd.com.

"The overwhelmingly positive response we've received leading up to tonight's commercial debut shows that consumers are embracing our message of a quality beer at a tasty price," said High Life Senior Brand Manager Kevin Oglesby. "We didn't need to spend millions of dollars for half-a-minute when our common sense philosophy can be conveyed in just one second."

To build anticipation for the debut of the one-second ad, Miller High Life began airing a 30-second teaser ad on Jan. 20 and launched www.1SecondAd.com. The website features the Big Game ad, several of the 1-second ads that didn't make the final cut, as well as the 30-second teaser spot. The Big Game ad, featuring the popular High Life deliveryman, aired throughout the majority of the country on local NBC network affiliates.

Miller High Life Big Game Ad
February 1, 2008
Add One

Editor Note: Broadcast-quality videos of the ad and hi-res images are available for media to download by visiting www.epkzone.com/millerhighlife.

About MillerCoors

Built on a foundation of great beer brands and more than 288 years of brewing heritage, MillerCoors continues the commitment of its founders to brew the highest quality beers. MillerCoors is the second largest beer company in America, capturing nearly 30 percent of U.S. beer sales. Led by two of the best-selling beers in the industry, MillerCoors has a broad portfolio of highly complementary brands across every major industry segment. Miller Lite is the great tasting beer that established the American light beer category in 1975, and Coors Light is the brand that introduced consumers to refreshment as cold as the Rockies. MillerCoors brews full-calorie beers Coors Banquet and Miller Genuine Draft; and economy brands Miller High Life and Keystone Light. The company also imports Peroni, Grolsch, Pilsner Urquell and Molson Canadian and offers innovative products such as Miller Chill and Sparks. MillerCoors features craft brews from the Jacob Leinenkugel Company, Blue Moon Brewing Company and the Blitz-Weinhard Brewing Company. MillerCoors operates eight major breweries in the U.S., as well as the Leinenkugel's craft brewery in Chippewa Falls, Wis., and two microbreweries, the Leinenkugel's 10th Street Brewery in Milwaukee and the Blue Moon Brewing Company at Coors Field in Denver. MillerCoors vision is to become the best beer company in America by driving profitable industry growth. MillerCoors insists on building its brands the right way through brewing quality, responsible marketing and environmental and community involvement. MillerCoors is a joint venture of SABMiller plc and Molson Coors Brewing Company.

###

Courtesy of MillerCoors and Dig Communications

E X H I B I T 4-3B   Screenshot of One-Second Ad

Courtesy of MillerCoors and Dig Communications

Case 4-4

Digital communication using social media opens doors to new audiences and establishes new conversations with those audiences. Exhibit 4-4A is a news release. Exhibit 4-4B is a screenshot of the app.

Volkswagen GTI Becomes The World's First Car Launched Exclusively on a Mobile Device

Volkswagen of America, Inc. and MWW Group

SUMMARY

Volkswagen of America, Inc., an operating unit of Volkswagen Group of America, Inc., ("VWoA") challenged its partners develop a national strategy for the 2010 GTI® launch that was as powerful, stylish, and innovative as the car itself and do it all without paid media support of any kind. The solution: become the first car in the world to be launched on an iPhone® and use a mobile gaming strategy to reach its 25-40 year old technophile male target. The results include 800 percent ROI, $2M in media value, a #1 app in 36 countries, and more than 80 percent increase in leads, quotes, and test drives. Through the effort, 85 cars were sold.

RESEARCH

Evaluating VWoA's primary industry research and purchasing data painted a clear picture of the GTI buyer as predominantly male, between the ages of 21-35. They are gamers and own an iPhone. They play games on their iPhone. They get their news through the Web and base purchasing decisions on third-party endorsement and through peer recommendation. A unique overlap was recognized between the GTI and iPhone audience.

Apple research showed there were 4.5M men aged 25-44 who owned an iPhone. On average, they downloaded more than 20 applications and 45 percent play downloaded games or browser games. In fact, this group factored heavily in making 12 of the top 25 apps games. Comparing to automotive industry research, 6 percent of males, aged 25-44, who were "in the market" for a new car, and also owned an iPhone. This overlap established the business case for how a VWoA iPhone app would help sell cars.

VWoA's research and audience insights, led to the creation of an iPhone and iPod Touch app by mobile agency AKQA, that would exclusively launch the 2010 GTI models via a mobile platform, making VW the first auto manufacturer to do so.

PLANNING

The core objectives of the program were to support the Volkswagen brand pillar of innovation, to engage VWoA's core enthusiast audience in a new way, to generate buzz and consideration in the GTI audience of technophile men (age 25-40), and to use media attention to drive retail sales by gathering hand-raisers and qualified leads.

The strategy to meet these objectives was to leverage a unique launch platform (mobile only) and event to generate media attention for the game (and subsequently, the GTI), while driving game participation to funnel consumers to the Volkswagen brand.

The project's public relations budget was $250,000, which would need to cover the cost of a media immersion event, social media integration, press materials, and agency fees for planning, execution, and tracking.

EXECUTION

VWoA launched the GTI via a customized racing app for the Apple iPhone and iPod Touch platform called Real Racing GTI. The game would be made available globally at no cost. The racing game borrowed many attributes of the GTI to provide the feeling of a high-speed test drive. Users could post videos on YouTube and an online leaderboard tracked rankings. In the showroom, customers learned about the new GTI. Using the iPhone's GPS function, fans could easily locate the nearest VWoA dealer and schedule a test drive.

The launch was driven solely by publicity - no paid media, not a single online banner, print ad, or broadcast spot. MWW Group launched the campaign with a press, blogger and influencer event in New York at the Classic Car Club of Manhattan, which married a beautiful raw space SoHo with the smell of gasoline. VWoA's mobile only strategy and Real Racing® GTI game was announced. No advanced access or pre-interviews were granted. Instead, the event took place on the eve of the availability of the game and car, making the entire event a sneak peek.

The team worked closely with Apple PR to leverage their audience of iPhone supporters and app development media.

Guests could play the game on iPhone devices tethered to HDTVs throughout the event space and even try their skills on the main stage on a theater-sized screen. Custom cocktails named for key attributes of the car and game helped liven the spirits of guests while culinary expressions of classic "guy food" fed the energy.

Since VWoA is not in the gaming business, they wanted a host whose involvement would legitimize Real Racing GTI for the gaming elite and lend credibility to attract new players. MWW selected Olivia Munn, host of "Attack of the Show" on G4 TV. Olivia was the hottest name in gaming and her following was predominantly within VWoA's target demographic. In addition, Olivia's Twitter following of more than 175k gaming fanatics was a valuable property when considering the host. Olivia introduced the game to guests, played head-to-head on the theater screen with VWoA's then vice president of marketing, Tim Ellis, and then stayed to challenge guests throughout the evening. Her tweets from the event helped engage her followers and kicked off a spike in conversation. Gobos showing the event hashtag (#gti2010) and screens throughout the space showed tweets from around the world (and in the room) appearing live on Twitter. Grammy Award-winning DJ Questlove of The Roots, set the mood as DJ and helped make the VWoA GTI launch the event of the evening.

More than 125 journalists, bloggers and influencers joined VWoA to celebrate the launch of the GTI and to experience the Real Racing GTI game. Following the event, Tim Ellis went on the media circuit speaking to business, marketing, and automotive press, while Charlie Taylor, director of digital marketing at VWoA, spoke to all technology, mobile, gaming, and social media outlets as well as bloggers covering the launch. At the conclusion of week one, MWW shifted gears from communicating Real Racing GTI to promoting the car as the hero. Utilizing six prize cars, media relations to drive visibility surrounding the winners and their customized GTI models became top priority resulting in automotive and enthusiast press focusing on the styling and performance of the 2010 GTI.

EVALUATION

VWoA's primary goals for the program were to create national buzz around the launch to increase consideration of the GTI amongst consumers, and to use the unique launch platform to drive retail sales interest. The program exceeded expectations in both categories. The program ran for six weeks and during that time, generated more than 255 million media impressions. Over 125 press, bloggers and influencers joined VWoA at the launch event in New York City to take Real Racing GTI—and VW's alternative marketing strategy—for a spin. Coverage highlights included *The New York Times* App of the Week column, *The New York Times* Wheels Blog, *BusinessWeek*, *USA Today*, ABC News, *Wired*, TIME.com and AdAge, and endorsements from top tech and gaming sites including Engadget, Joystiq, Kotaku, and CNET.

Total media relations efforts returned $2M in equivalent ad value to VWoA (an 800 percent return on its public relations investment). To make the car successful, VWoA first had to make the app a phenomenon. With the bar set at 1.5 million downloads, the numbers far exceeded expectations. Real Racing GTI saw more than 3.7 million downloads (nearly 800,000 in the 4 days following the launch event). Real Racing GTI became the #1 free app on Apple iTunes App Store within 5 days, the #1 free global app on Apple iTunes for 36 of 59 countries and a Top 5 free app in all countries where the iTunes Store is available.

In addition to media impressions, the VWoA program hashtag (#gti2010) reached #6 on the global trending topics on Twitter during launch week (ahead of Balloon Boy). More importantly, the business results proved even more effective. Over the course of the campaign, VWoA saw an 81 percent increase in weekly leads for the GTI from vw.com, an 86 percent increase in "Get a Quote" submissions for the GTI and an 80 percent jump in test drives at dealers. Most rewarding, a total of 85 cars were sold via leads generated exclusively by Real Racing GTI, as tracked through VW direct sales match backs.

E X H I B I T 4-4A News Release

Volkswagen Becomes First Auto Manufacturer To Launch a Car Exclusively on a Mobile Device

Free Real Racing GTI Game Brings Volkswagen All-New 2010 GTI to iPhone® and iPod touch®

Six U.S. Players Will Each Win One of Six Customized Limited-Edition GTI MkVI Vehicles Through December 2

HERNDON, Va., October 22, 2010 /PRNewswire/ – Volkswagen of America, Inc. today announced the launch of the all-new 2010 GTI via the App Store by making available a free version of the popular Firemint Real Racing game that exclusively features the all-new 2010 GTI. This is the first time an automotive manufacturer has used the App Store to launch a new vehicle. Additionally, users of the Real Racing GTI App in the United States can compete for the chance to win one of six, limited-edition 2010 GTIs that are fully-customized inside and out.

(Photo: http://www.newscom.com/cgi-bin/prnh/20091022/DE96311-a)

(Photo: http://www.newscom.com/cgi-bin/prnh/20091022/DE96311-b)

The free Real Racing GTI App is available worldwide and spares no detail, allowing players to experience every thrilling aspect of the all-new 2010 GTI right in the palms of their hands on iPhone and iPod touch. From the redesigned exterior with more aggressive headlights and the famous red-striped grille, to the sporty interior with a race-inspired steering wheel, the all-new 2010 GTI races its way to life on the screen for a thrilling gaming experience.

"With the personalization of media and the challenges inherent with reaching constantly connected consumers, we tasked ourselves to rethink the way we launch vehicles in order to engage our consumers in a meaningful way," said Tim Ellis, Vice President of Marketing, Volkswagen of America, Inc. "The GTI customer is a tech-savvy consumer who enjoys social networking, playing games and spending time on mobile devices—most often an iPhone. Launching the all-new 2010 GTI via the Real Racing GTI App allows us to connect with this savvy GTI consumer within his or her everyday life in a way that no 30-second spot ever could."

U.S.-registered players enjoying the action of the Real Racing GTI App will be challenged to put their skills to the test for a chance to win one of six limited-edition 2010 GTI models. The more they play, the more chances they have to win. Each week for six consecutive weeks beginning today, one player will be chosen to win the ultimate racing prize: the exclusive GTI MkVI, an individually-numbered, specially-tuned version of the legendary hatchback. Each model includes the GTI's 2.0T 200hp four-cylinder engine, a performance tuned suspension finished with black, Volkswagen motorsport 18-inch all-new wheels, and special interior touches, including carbon fiber-look trim, a numbered dash plaque, and unique stitching in the front headrests. For more information on the competition please visit: www.vw.com/RealRacingGTI.

Given the ever-increasing prominence of social networking in the lives of the games' target consumers, Real Racing GTI includes several features designed to foster social connectivity. These include the ability of players to send messages to their competitors via Twitter and to capture and upload videos of their best laps to the game's YouTube channel for international bragging rights. Additionally, GTI MkVI buyers will also be able to configure their vehicles, modeled after the six prize cars, at participating Volkswagen dealerships throughout the United States.

The Real Racing GTI App is available for free from the App Store on the iPhone and iPod touch or at www.itunes.com/appstore/. No purchase is necessary to enter the contest, which officially ends on December 2 at 11:59PM.

For more about the 2010 Volkswagen GTI, the *Real Racing GTI* game, and an in-depth look at the six GTI prize editions that are waiting to hit the streets, please visit www.media.vw.com.

About Volkswagen Group of America, Inc.

Founded in 1955, Volkswagen Group of America, Inc. is headquartered in Herndon, Virginia. It is a subsidiary of Volkswagen AG, headquartered in Wolfsburg, Germany. Volkswagen is one of the world's largest producers of passenger cars and Europe's largest automaker. Through its Volkswagen division, VWGoA sells the Golf, GTI, New Beetle, New Beetle convertible, Jetta, Jetta SportWagen, Eos, Passat, Passat Wagon, CC, Tiguan, Touareg, and Routan through approximately 600 independent U.S. dealers. All 2010 Volkswagen models come standard-equipped with Electronic Stabilization Program. This is important because the National Highway and Traffic Safety Administration (NHTSA) has called ESC the most effective new vehicle safety technology since the safety belt. Visit Volkswagen of America online at www.vw.com or www.media.vw.com to learn more.

About Firemint

Firemint creates fun, addictive games. The studio has worked with the industry's leading publishers developing over 30 titles from notable franchises as well as originals. Firemint's first self-published iPhone game Flight Control has been a world-wide #1 App Store hit. Firemint's second self-published iPhone game, the high-end 3D pro racing title Real Racing, has been critically acclaimed as a triumph for the platform. Founded in 1999 by CEO Robert Murray, Firemint is located in Melbourne, Australia's games development hub, and employs 35 people. For more information about Firemint, please visit www.firemint.com.

SOURCE: Volkswagen of America, Inc.

Photo: http://www.newscom.com/cgi-bin/prnh/20091022/DE96311-a
http://www.newscom.com/cgi-bin/prnh/20091022/DE96311-b
http://photoarchive.ap.org
AP PhotoExpress Network: PRN2 3
PRN Photo Desk, photodesk@prnewswire.com

SOURCE: Volkswagen of America, Inc.

Courtesy Volkswagen of America and MWW Group

E X H I B I T 4-4B Screenshot of Mobile App

Courtesy Volkswagen of America and MWW Group

5

Internal Communications

Public relations conducted inside organizations falls into two general categories: employee relations and member relations. Employee relations includes all communications between the management of an organization and its personnel. Member relations refers to communications inside a membership organization between the officers, staff, and members.

EMPLOYEE RELATIONS

Research, objectives, programming, and evaluation are useful problem-solving tools in employee relations. Good management of an organization is often measured by the quality of communication within the organization. Senior leaders also understand that well-informed employees form the basis for many strategic communication initiatives with external publics.

RESEARCH

Research for employee relations concentrates on client research, studying the reason for communication, and identifying the employee audiences to be targeted for communication.

Client Research

Client research for employee relations focuses on *information* about the organization's personnel. What is the size and nature of the workforce? What reputation does the organization and its senior leadership have with its workforce? How satisfied are the employees? What employee communications does the organization regularly use? Are any special forms of communication used? How credible and effective are the organization's internal communications? Has the organization conducted special employee relations programs in the past? If so, what were the results of such programs? What are the organization's strengths, weaknesses, and opportunities regarding its workforce? These questions might guide the initial research in preparation for an employee relations program.

Opportunity or Problem Research

A second focal point for research is the *reason* for conducting an employee relations program. Is a new program really necessary? Most organizations have regular and ongoing channels of internal communications that are used to convey management information, so this question should be answered with care because it justifies the necessary expenditure for a program. Would the program be reactive—in response to a problem that has arisen in employee relations, or would it be proactive—taking advantage of an opportunity to improve existing employee relations?

A survey of employee attitudes may reveal a variety of issues, including low levels of satisfaction and morale, dislike of the physical surroundings, and/or frustration with internal policies. The survey results may thus demonstrate a strong need for a reactive employee relations program.

Audience Research

The final area of research involves precisely defining the *employee audiences* to be targeted for communication. These audiences can be identified using the following terms:

Management

    Upper-level administrators

    Mid-level administrators

    Lower-level administrators

Nonmanagement (staff)

    Specialists

    Clerical personnel

    Executive assistants

Operational personnel

    Equipment operators

    Transportation providers

    Security personnel

    Customer service representatives

    Other support personnel

Union representatives

Other nonmanagement personnel

Effective research on employee relations is built on an understanding of the client's personnel, the opportunity or problem that serves as a reason for communication with the workforce, and the specific identification of the employee audiences to be targeted for communication.

OBJECTIVES

Objectives for employee relations include the two major categories of impact and output. Employee relations objectives may be specific and quantitative to facilitate accurate measurement. Optional percentages and time frames are included here in parentheses.

Impact Objectives

Impact objectives for employee relations include informing employees or modifying their attitudes or behaviors. Some typical impact objectives are:

1. To increase employee knowledge of significant organizational policies, activities, and developments (by 60 percent during March and April)
2. To enhance favorable employee attitudes toward a new organization program (by 40 percent during the current fiscal year)
3. To accomplish (50 percent) greater employee adoption of ride sharing (in a three-month period)
4. To make (20 percent of) the employee force organizational spokespersons in the community (during the next two years)
5. To receive (50 percent) more employee feedback from organizational communications (during the coming year).

Behavioral, informational, and attitudinal impact objectives may be used in any combination in a public relations plan. The chosen objectives should be carefully determined so they demonstrate the program's goals.

Output Objectives

Output objectives in employee relations constitute the efforts made by the practitioner to accomplish such desired outcomes as employee recognition and regular employee communication. Some examples include:

1. To recognize employee accomplishments and contributions in (80 percent of) employee communications (during the current year)
2. To prepare and distribute employee communications on a weekly basis
3. To schedule interpersonal communication between management and a specific employee group each month (specify groups and months).

PROGRAMMING

Programming for employee relations should include the careful planning of theme and messages, action(s) or special event(s), uncontrolled and controlled media, and execution, using the principles of effective communication.

Theme and Messages

The theme and messages for employee relations depend on the reason for conducting the campaign or program. Both of these elements should grow out of the opportunity or problem that accounts for the particular program. That is, themes and messages usually grow out of the problems faced by companies and the methods chosen to solve them. For example, a practitioner working for a company that is moving its facilities and offices to a new building could produce a brochure entitled "A Company on the Move," and a series of emails and blog posts by senior leaders explaining the change.

Action(s) or Special Event(s)

Action and special events used in employee relations programs include:

1. Training seminars
2. Special programs on safety or new technology
3. An open house for employees and their families
4. Parties, receptions, and other social affairs
5. Other employee special events related to organizational developments.

A bank, for example, could sponsor a surprise Dividend Day for participants in the employee stock program, and a company moving into a new facility could arrange an employee open house and party. The chief executive officer (CEO) can host a company-wide town meeting to signal an important announcement.

Uncontrolled and Controlled Media

The use of uncontrolled media in employee relations is usually limited to sending news releases or announcements about employees' accomplishments to outside mass and specialized media as warranted. Actually, this is media relations, not employee relations, but it is often considered part of the employee relations program, as a news report is often perceived by employees as a credible source of information about the organization.

Controlled media, on the other hand, are used extensively in employee relations programs. The most frequently used controlled media are email, voice mail, websites, and memoranda. Also often used are employee publications such as magazines, newspapers, and newsletters addressed to particular groups or levels of employees in larger organizations. These publications are often highly professional and creative, both in writing and in design.

In addition to email, voice mail, websites, and house publications, employee relations programs use a variety of other forms of controlled media, such as:

1. Bulletin boards
2. Displays and exhibits
3. Telephone hot lines or news lines

4. Inserts accompanying paychecks
5. Internal television/video
6. Executive blogs
7. Meetings
8. Teleconferences
9. Audiovisual presentations and videos
10. Booklets, pamphlets, and brochures
11. Speakers' bureaus (employees address community groups)
12. Talking points distributed to managers.

The use of media in employee relations differs from that in other forms of public relations because of the heavy emphasis on controlled media.

Effective Communication

Principles of effective communication are virtually the same for employee relations as for most other forms of public relations, although two-way communication and audience participation should be stressed. Special events are an excellent way to use these elements in employee relations.

EVALUATION

Impact and output objectives in employee relations can be evaluated using the same tools of measurement as in other forms of public relations (see Chapter 2). In addition, a variety of research techniques have been developed to deal exclusively with internal organizational communication.

Follow-up surveys were used in most of the case studies in this chapter. These yield quantitative measures of the stated objectives. Objectives were also assessed through publicity placement and employee participation in the programs.

Again, remember that to be effective and useful to the organization, research—both initial and evaluative—should be conducted by trained, experienced professionals who work for reputable research firms.

SUMMARY

The ROPE process provides a useful approach to the planning and execution of employee relations programs.

Research for employee relations concentrates on demographic data about the organization's workforce, existing levels of employee satisfaction, the state of relations between management and employees, and the effectiveness of employee communication. The uniqueness of research in this form of PR is, of course, the focus on information gathering about the workforce itself.

Both impact and output objectives are generally used in employee relations programs. Impact objectives include such desired outcomes as increasing employee knowledge of organizational matters and eliciting favorable employee attitudes and behaviors toward the organization. Output objectives are the efforts of practitioners to recognize employee contributions, distribute employee communications effectively, and otherwise enhance the impact objectives.

Programming for employee relations may include catchy, inspirational themes, special events such as training seminars, special employee campaigns or programs, or social events for employees, and controlled media such as email, voice mail, websites, memoranda, house publications, bulletin boards, displays, meetings, and a variety of electronic means of communication to include use of social media.

Evaluation of employee communication should refer back to each stated objective. Follow-up surveys are a popular means of evaluating attitudinal and behavioral objectives.

Each element of the ROPE process should be tailored for the particular situation, as we will see in this chapter's cases.

READINGS ON EMPLOYEE RELATIONS

Barkow, Tim. "Blogging for Business," *Public Relations Strategist* 10 (fall 2004): 40-43.

Buffington, Jody. "Can Human Resources and Internal Communications Peacefully Coexist?" *Public Relations Strategist* 10 (fall 2004): 33-36.

Charland, Bernie. "The Mantra of Metrics: A Realistic and Relevant Approach to Measuring the Impact of Employee Communications," *Public Relations Strategist* 10 (fall 2004): 30-33.

Charles, Melissa. "Lessons from the Best in Fortune: Changing the Way You Look at Employee Publications," *Public Relations Tactics* 12 (January 2005): 21.

Corman, Steven R., and Marshall Scott Poole, eds. *Perspectives on Organizational Communication.* New York: Guilford Publications, 2001.

Crescenzo, Steve. "What Is the Role of the Corporate Editor?" *Communication World* 22 (September–October 2005): 12-142.

———. "Employees: PR Ambassadors, or Your Worst Nightmare?" *Communication World* 22 (May–June 2005): 10-11.

Dowling, Michael J. "Adapting to Change: Creating a Learning Organization," *Public Relations Strategist* 10 (spring 2004): 10-14.

Downs, Cal W., and Allyson D. Adrian. *Assessing Organizational Communication: Strategic Communication Audits.* New York: Guilford Publications, 2004.

Eisenberg, Eric M., H. L. Goodall, and Angela Trethewey. *Organizational Communication: Balancing Creativity and Constraint,* 6th ed. New York: Bedford/St. Martin's, 2009.

Ewing, Michelle E. "An Engaged Work Force—Selling the Value and Incorporating Best Practices of Employee Communications," *Public Relations Tactics* 12 (March 2005): 10-12.

Frey, Thomas. "Employee Relations: The Facade of Communication," *Public Relations Strategist* 10 (fall 2004): 22-24.

Friedla, Julia and Ana Tkalac Verčič. "Media preferences of digital natives' internal communication: A pilot study," *Public Relations Review* 37.1 (March 2011): 84-86.

Gargiulo, Terrence L. *The Strategic Use of Stories in Organizational Communication and Learning.* Armonk, NY: M. E. Sharpe, 2005.

Grates, Gary F. " 'Why Don't I Know?' The Strategic Role of Today's Internal Communications," *Public Relations Strategist* 10 (fall 2004): 14-18.

Greene, Barbara and Susan Balcom Walton. "Showing the White Sail: Making Employee Communication a Priority in Times of Crisis," *Public Relations Strategist* 14 (Summer 2008).

Guiniven, John. "Inside Job: Internal communications in tough times," *Public Relations Tactics* 16 (November 2009): 6.

Harris, John. "Employee Engagement: An Easy Investment with Large Returns," *Public Relations Tactics* 11 (January 2004): 13.

Harris, Thomas E. *Applied Organizational Communication: Principles and Pragmatics for Future Practice*, 2d ed. Mahwah, NJ: Erlbaum, 2002.

Keyton, Joann. *Communication and Organizational Culture.* Thousand Oaks, CA: Sage Publications, 2004.

Klein, Karen E. "A Company Blog Keeps People Connected," *Business Week Online* (August 21, 2006): 5.

Madlock, Paul E. "The Link Between Leadership Style, Communicator Competence, and Employee Satisfaction," *Journal of Business Communication* 45 (January 2008): 61-78.

Manchester, Alex. *How to Use Social Media to Engage Employees.* London: Melcrum Publishing, Ltd., 2006.

Miller, Katherine. *Organizational Communication: Approaches and Processes.* Belmont, CA: Wadsworth, 2008.

Papa, Michael J., Tom D. Daniels, and Barry K. Spiker. *Organizational Communication: Perspectives and Trends.* Thousand Oaks, CA: Sage Publications, 2007.

Parker, Glenn. *Team Players and Teamwork*, 2d ed. San Francisco: Jossey-Bass, 2008.

Perkins, Lisa. "Inspiring Change and Driving Results: What Can your Employee Publication Do for You?" *Public Relations Tactics* 12 (May 2005): 10.

Rayburn, Jay. "A Matter of Trust (And More)," *Public Relations Tactics* 14 (March 2007): 21.

Sanchez, Paul. "Defining Corporate Culture," *Communication World* 21 (November–December 2004): 18-21.

Schell, Robin; Smith, Stacey. "Communicating to Employees During Difficult Economic Times," *Public Relations Strategist* 16. 1 (winter 2010): 12.

Thilmany, Jean. "Showing Up Happy," *Mechanical Engineering* 126 (November 2004): 3-5.

"Using social media for internal innovation networks," *Knowledge Management Review* 9 (January/February 2007): 7.

Voeller, Greg, and Kelly Groehler. "Employees—Always the Primary Audience," *Public Relations Strategist* 10 (fall 2004): 27-30.

Wright, Marc. "Moving into the Mainstream," *Communication World* (January/February 2008): 22-25.

Employee Relations Cases

Case 5-1

Setting a vision and obtaining employee support for that vision involves a challenge for organizational leaders. Customizing the communication process by region is novel and revolves around an understanding of the special issues surrounding differentiated audiences.

Allstate Insurance Company Southeast Region Employee Engagement Strategy
Allstate Insurance Company

SUMMARY

Allstate's Southeast Region created an Employee Engagement Committee (EEC) to improve employee engagement, to focus on driving a cultural shift through grassroots communication, and to increase positive responses on an employee engagement survey. As tactics, this committee introduced employee events including: community workdays, a regional library, Bring Your Child to Work Day, and Lunch and Learn sessions. The team was successful in leading an overall positive engagement shift and contributed to moving Southeast regional employees from second tier agreement levels ("agree") to top line agreement ("strongly agree") on engagement index questions.

BACKGROUND

Allstate introduced a new initiative to align its employees around its vision for the future. Since this rollout would require a culture change throughout the company, Allstate's leadership asked Allstate regional leaders to implement engagement plans in all 14 of Allstate's operating regions. Allstate's Southeast region is headquartered in Atlanta, and the Southeast assistant field vice president contacted

Allstate's Corporate Relations (CR) internal communications consultant for assistance. Since highly engaged team members are usually informal opinion leaders within an organization, the Southeast leadership team saw the need to engage employees to drive this cultural shift from a grassroots level to augment this culture change initiative. Although this employee engagement project initially began to assist with the initiative implementation, it expanded to become a vehicle to drive overall employee engagement. The primary goal was to increase employee engagement as measured by EEC surveys and annual Quality Leadership Measurement Survey (QLMS) results.

RESEARCH

Primary Research

The employee focus group, which later evolved into the EEC, was the primary research vehicle to help the region determine how best to align the region with Allstate's updated vision and to increase employee engagement. This group was made up of 12 non-managerial employees, and care was taken to ensure diverse representation. A pre-focus group meeting survey was conducted with all committee members. The EEC examined a variety of topics:

a. what engagement means to employees,

b. what is the current perception of employee engagement within the region, and

c. how do regional employees feel that they could improve engagement.

Specific questions were geared toward what is defined as an "Engagement Index" to measure an employee's connectedness to the company, willingness to exert extra effort, and desire to remain with the organization.

Highlights of the survey—confirmed by discussion—included opportunities within the areas of:

- Career development: Less than 70 percent of the group felt that the company and region were interested in advancing their career development. Further group discussion in this area revealed interesting point—not all development has to lead to advancement. A number of members, while most comfortable in their current position, considered the opportunity to branch out, learn and grow as development. This point also led to the idea that there is business value (via engagement) in assisting with emotional/life development of employees as well.

- Work/life balance: General discussions with the group revealed a desire to incorporate family into work life during occasional events. The statement was shared that people naturally become more connected to one another when they can get to know the person outside work. The region did not have integrated activities where employees could interact outside the work environment (such as intramural sports or community projects).

- Communication regarding company programs/services: Many employees were not aware of existing programs and offerings the company already has in place to support employees.

Secondary Research

Allstate surveys its employees yearly via a QLMS to gauge overall employee satisfaction with the company work environment, and this data was used to serve as a baseline for measurement of regional efforts to improve engagement and identify potential opportunity areas.

Outside Research

A number of Web/periodical articles were researched before beginning focus groups. The best conversation starter article was a *Wall Street Journal* article that outlined activities of highly engaged companies. Web research was used in order to prepare CR representative for task ahead and to use as a pre-read for focus groups to spark conversations, thoughts, and ideas.

Planning

The creation of the EEC was an idea that resulted from the extensive research phase. For example, one of the companies mentioned in the *Wall Street Journal* article employed a similar entity. Focus group findings, reinforced by QLMS data, pointed to certain opportunity areas which would be the main focus of the EEC with a target audience of regional employees and regional leadership:

- Employee development (including career, emotional, and life development).

- Communication regarding existing programs and offerings the company already has in place to support employees, as well as enhanced two-way communication to allow EEC members to advocate for company initiatives while also providing anonymous, real-time feedback to regional leadership without formal surveys.

- *Esprit de Corps*: Promote, encourage, create, and execute activities that promote connectedness and interconnectedness among Southeast regional employees. The general plan was that a CR consultant, armed with findings from the QLMS and focus group, would present the proposal to Southeast region leadership to allow for formal creation of the EEC. The CR consultant would serve as committee chair and liaison between leadership and EEC with an approved budget of $14,000. This EEC offered a unique measurement challenge because Allstate's Southeast regional employees already had strong numbers on engagement index questions. For example, the region scored in the low 90th or high 80th percentile on majority of questions such as 93 percent favorable response to question Q.29: "Considering everything, how would you rate your overall satisfaction with Allstate?" The EEC goal was to make employee engagement even stronger—as measured by QLMS and compared with 2007 level used as baseline.

The opportunity areas (lower scores from 2007) included:

- Q.38 *How would you rate Allstate as a company to work for compared to other companies?* (83 percent said either "above average" or "one of the best"—this represented a 9 percent drop from 2006)
- Q.28 *If the choice is mine I will be working for Allstate in 3 years.* (82 percent favorable)
- Q.21 *How do you rate your overall benefits program?* (84 percent favorable)
- Q.16 *I feel I am paid competitively for the work I do.* (61 percent favorable).

Goals: Five percent top line movement across all engagement index questions and to improve all questions identified as EEC opportunity areas.

EXECUTION

With the permission of regional leadership, the EEC was formed. The committee:

- Developed a set of bylaws to govern operation.
- Formed sub-committees with chairs acted as team leads for committee initiatives.
- Promoted committee with theme "Everyone Counts" and logo.
- Secured time in each quarterly regional meeting to discuss committee activities/projects.
- Collaborated with other regional committees such as Well & Fit Fitness and Helping Hands volunteerism committees.
- Rolled out committee initiatives such as book clubs, regional blog, regional library, lunch and Learns, Quarterly Community Work Days, and Bring Your Child to Work Day.

EVALUATION

The EEC contributed to positive 2008 Southeast regional employee engagement results. There were no 2008 decreases from 2007 survey levels with any of the employee engagement index questions; instead, the team led an overall positive engagement shift and contributed to moving Southeast regional employees from 2nd tier agreement levels ("agree") to top line agreement ("strongly agree") on engagement index questions.

Case 5-2

The passion of the founder of a national chain inspires the creation of a major Foundation but each year becomes a new challenge to engage employees in the cause. The communication goal is to inspire the same level of passion and caring among employees even in its 15th year. Exhibit 5-2A is the Foundation website promoting the Adoption Friendly Workplace and Exhibit 5-2B are images from a public service announcement.

Best Adoption-Friendly Workplace and Foster Care Adoption Outreach

Dave Thomas Foundation for Adoption with Paul Werth Associates

OVERVIEW

The Dave Thomas Foundation for Adoption strives to dramatically increase adoption of children in foster care. Every year about 129,000 children in the U.S. foster care system are eligible for adoption because parental rights have been terminated. Yet, nearly 25,000 reach the age of 18 without finding a permanent family. Created by Wendy's founder and adoptee Dave Thomas, the Foundation reaches out to potential adoptive parents, adoption advocates, and officials involved in the foster care system to help these children obtain permanent, loving homes. The Foundation has teamed with Paul Werth Associates to support these goals since 2007.

RESEARCH

To gain a better knowledge of Americans' opinions on foster care adoption, the Foundation commissioned Harris Interactive to survey 1,600 Americans. The results showed two-thirds of those considering foster care adoption were unnecessarily concerned that biological parents could return to claim their children. In addition, nearly half of Americans mistakenly believed foster care adoption was expensive, when in reality the adoptive parents incur few costs. Many also thought children available for adoption were juvenile delinquents. This research was used to develop message points on the realities of foster care adoption.

Noticing that no organization provided surveys of the quality of adoption benefit packages in American businesses, the Foundation researched existing workplace-related surveys to develop best practices for the development of America's Best Adoption-Friendly Workplace list, beginning in 2007. *Fortune Magazine's* "100 Best Companies to Work For" and *Working Mother Magazine's* "100 Best Companies" were identified as the main models. The Foundation reviewed all aspects, including data collection, methodology, and publicity. The Foundation also interviewed a focus group of HR professionals to learn what was important to them, their companies, and their employees regarding adoption benefits. This secondary research resulted in a success metric for the survey: an increase in benefits year-over-year as an indicator that more organizations were offering more adoption benefits.

PLANNING

Working with Werth, the Foundation focused on three objectives:

- Make adoption more affordable for families as measured by an increase in the employee benefits provided to adoptive families.

- Educate potential adoptive parents to overcome misconceptions and present the facts about foster care adoption as measured by the inclusion of message points in media coverage, on the website and in outreach opportunities, such as speeches.

- Raise awareness of the 129,000 children available for adoption in foster care to the general public and policymakers as measured by an increased number of adoptions on National Adoption Day, the number and scope of events celebrating foster care adoption, the quantity of media coverage for these events and the number of online hits for the website.

Two major strategies supported these objectives:

- The creation and promotion of America's Best Adoption-Friendly Workplace (ABAFW) survey.

- A year-round public relations campaign, involving adoption advocates, culminating in National Adoption Day (NAD) to celebrate foster care adoption.

EXECUTION

To develop its Best Adoption-Friendly Workplace list, the Foundation mailed survey invitations to 40,000 business leaders, surveyed HR professionals at conferences and inputted data from an online survey on the Foundation's website. Using data collected from 919 U.S. employers, rankings were based first on the maximum amount of financial reimbursement per adoption, and second, on the maximum number of weeks of paid leave per adoption. Employers who offered both were ranked higher than those providing only monetary support.

Rankings were created by business size, industry and state location, as well as an overall Top 100 list, generating substantial interest upon release in April 2007. The Foundation began to receive inquiries from companies asking how they could improve benefits to rise up the 2008 list.

For the second annual survey, released in April 2008, the team again focused on celebrating top-ranked companies by promoting them to specific trade media for their industries, such as hospitality, legal, retail, and construction, and their own communities. Werth also enlisted several survey partners and media outlets to extend the survey's reach. These included *Employee Benefit News*, the leading trade for benefits decision makers, the National Restaurant Association, and the Ohio Chamber of Commerce. The team distributed targeted media pitches as well as national, regional and industry-focused press releases, generating more than 20 million impressions through coverage in outlets such as *TIME* and CNBC.

As work on the survey concluded, Werth began in May to build national enthusiasm among adoption advocates and families for National Adoption Day on November 15. Werth revamped the Foundation website, launching a social networking program to encourage adoptive parents and advocates to share their stories and interact at adoptionday.ning.com. The site encouraged advocates to register local NAD events and provided event toolkits. The campaign also featured a 30-second PSA, print PSA placements and traditional media outreach. A Twitter page was created to keep adoption advocates and national media abreast of event happenings and NAD news. The national event, held at Queens Family Court in New York, featured the Foundation's executive director and local judges speaking on the realities of foster care adoptions and the positive impact of the ABAFW. A former foster child, actress Victoria Rowell, spoke to the New York media, including *The Today Show*, on these message points as well.

A five-member Werth team and the Foundation's marketing director made the most of public relations budgets of $40,000 for the ABAFW survey and $157,500 for NAD in 2008.

EVALUATION

Employers who made the Top 100 ABAFW list in 2008 offered more robust adoption benefit packages than in 2007, with more than 50 organizations establishing or enhancing benefits for 580,470 employees. Thirty-three of the survey participants established new adoption benefit policies in 2008, and 26 used the Foundation's free adoption resources. The 2008 list influenced 92 organizations to improve adoption benefits for 2009, and 33 used the Foundation's free adoption resources. Media coverage of the 2008 list included more than 200 stories delivering over 20 million impressions.

The NAD campaign exposed more than 120 million Americans to the Foundation's positive messages about foster care adoption through editorial placements in prominent consumer and trade media. The campaign culminated in the adoption of 4,600 foster care children during 325 NAD events held in all 50 states, Puerto Rico and the District of Columbia, an increase of 65 events and 250 adoptions from 2007. The campaign also delivered more than 400 earned media placements throughout the United States, including *Women's Day*, *The New York Times*, and The Today Show, generating 100 million impressions.

Of the 423 earned media placements, 342 (80 percent) featured the targeted message points the Werth team and the Foundation set as top priority. As a result of the Werth team's efforts in preparing concise, accurate, and thorough talking points for spokespeople, the media reported on adoption's affordability, shattered stereotypes, and raised awareness for the 129,000 children in foster care. The NAD website received a record number of visits as a result of garnered media placements and Werth's supporting social media efforts. As a result of coverage from The Today Show on November 14 and the Werth team "tweeting" live from the NYC event on November 15, the site had almost 4,000 visitors during the two-day period.

Overall, site visits remained high for the rest of November—adoption month.

The 2009 ABAFW survey and NAD planning are now in progress. The success has sparked even more enthusiasm in the team for helping foster children find permanent homes.

EXHIBIT 5-2A Foundation Website

Adoption-Friendly Workplace

A Signature Program of the Dave Thomas Foundation for Adoption

Adoption-Friendly Workplace works to make adoption an affordable option for every working parent. Our goal is to provide companies with the support needed to provide adoption benefits to employees and recognize the forward-thinking employers that already have adoption benefits in place.

Adoption-Friendly Workplace Toolkit

Make your office an Adoption-Friendly Workplace with our toolkit that helps you propose an adoption benefits policy to your employer.

Learn more about free Adoption-Friendly Workplace toolkits.

Best Adoption-Friendly Workplaces List

We celebrate companies with the best adoption benefits for their employees. Every year, we compile a list of the top 100 adoption-friendly workplaces—the best small, medium, and large employers.

Stay tuned for our announcement of the 2011 Best Adoption-Friendly Workplaces list later this year. See last year's winners. Learn more about the Best Adoption-Friendly Workplaces list.

Adoption Benefits Survey

Does your company offer adoption benefits? Let us know and we can tell the world. We celebrate all employers with adoption benefits on our website, and we honor the nation's best with our annual Best Adoption-Friendly Workplaces list. It's easy to participate. Simply complete our two-minute survey online, by phone, by mail or email. Although this year's survey is closed, keep watching this page for information on the 2011 list announcement and for the 2012 survey dates.

Learn more about the adoption benefits survey.

Employers and Benchmarks

We recognize all adoption-friendly employers by posting a complete list of every employer who has completed our adoption benefits survey. We also provide benchmarks, with the company's permission, about specific adoption benefits offered by employers of a specified size, state, or industry.

Learn more about employers and benchmarks.

Courtesy Dave Thomas Foundation for Adoption and Paul Werth Associates

EXHIBIT 5-2B   Public Service Announcement

Courtesy Dave Thomas Foundation for Adoption and Paul Werth Associates

Case 5-3

The value of a firm for investors is largely based upon the quality of senior leaders and employees. Given the potential for pessimism surrounding the economy, a company kept employees focused on key long-term goals for the economic health of the organization. Exhibit 5-3A is the intranet microsite for the program, Exhibit 5-3B is a collection of banners and posters and Exhibit 5-3C are the communication tools that were used to implement the campaign.

Rise to the Challenge: Overcoming the Great Recession of 2009

Newell Rubbermaid

SUMMARY

The Great Recession of 2009 was a make-or-break year for Newell Rubbermaid (maker of brands such as Sharpie pens, Rubbermaid food containers, Calphalon cookware, and Graco strollers). Investors had lost confidence due to plunging sales and a bloated cost structure. Communications, partnering with Senior Management, motivated employees to "Rise to the Challenge" and focus on five key behaviors necessary to achieve the company's financial commitments. Newell Rubbermaid CEO Mark Ketchum credits the campaign with lifting employee morale and helping the company exceed its 2009 financial commitments, which fueled a tripling of the company's stock price.

SITUATION ANALYSIS

As the economic downturn worsened in late 2008, consumer spending evaporated and Newell Rubbermaid sales plunged by double digits. To make matters worse, a bloated cost structure, excess inventories, and a looming $700 million debt refinancing put the company's very survival in doubt. After two dividend cuts in two months and with the company's stock price plunging from a high of $32 to an eventual low of $4.54, investors had clearly lost confidence and analyst reports were openly questioning management. Meanwhile, employee morale plummeted after layoffs of 10 percent of the company's workforce were announced two weeks before Christmas 2008.

RESEARCH

Primary Research

- Financial analyst reports indicated doubt the company would meet its financial goals.
- A February 2009 employee survey bolstered what Human Resources was hearing from the field:
  - Employees who strongly agreed/agreed with the statement that teamwork is recognized and rewarded dropped nearly 20 percent since January 2008. A team decreased by almost ten percent since January 2008.

Secondary Research

- Investor calls and meetings indicated a high level of concern about deteriorating fundamentals.
- Human Resources reported employees were near the breaking point: fearful about their own futures, burdened with extra work as colleagues were laid off, and forced to tighten their belts at home as prices rose and spouses' jobs were in jeopardy.
- Discussions with senior management validated a need for increased communications and management visibility to support the organization in a challenging environment.
- Informal benchmarking indicated a number of Fortune 500 peers used an annual theme to motivate employees and set the tone for the year.

PLANNING

Objective: Rally a disheartened organization to deliver the following 2009 financial goals, thus restoring investor confidence and lifting employee morale:

- Salvage flat earnings growth—despite falling sales—by gaining market share from competitors
- Reduce overhead expenses by $100 million
- Generate operating cash flow of $400 million

Strategy: Use a clear and actionable theme and behaviors to mobilize and inspire employees and show them exactly what was needed to achieve the company's financial commitments.

Primary Audience: Global professional employees who could help the company meet or exceed its financial commitments and who had asked for reward and recognition for their successes.

Secondary Audience: Analysts/shareholders who believed the company may not meet its commitments.

As the team began brainstorming a solution, the analogy of climbing Mount Everest fit perfectly with the situation. Mountain climbing takes teamwork, preparation, and willpower. Moreover, it is a global sport. With that in mind, we decided on the theme, "Rise to the Challenge." To brand it, we created a logo that showed climbers striving for the peak of a large mountain. Bold colors added impact. HR leaders in every global region reviewed translations to ensure the theme's intended meaning was preserved.

Next, working with the CEO and other senior management, we developed five clear and actionable behaviors that were essential to delivering the company's financial commitments:

1. Simplify work

2. Reduce cost

3. Conserve cash

4. Gain market share

5. Develop yourself and others

Budget: $50,000 for video development, translations, and sign printing—not including salaries for the seven-member communications team. Program-to-date spend is $18,500, reflecting a focus on developing a large volume of stories and tools that could be output locally on ordinary printers at low cost.

EXECUTION

To maximize employee awareness and understanding, and ensure the Rise to the Challenge campaign would be sustainable throughout 2009, Communications strategically launched the theme and behaviors by cascading them through the company's global locations as follows:

Phase 1: Introduce to Top Leadership At Executive Retreat (goal: educate VPs and above)

- CEO launched theme via dramatic video, walked onstage in climbing gear, gave inspiring speech.

- Project teams presented example case studies to educate the organization on the five behaviors.

- Attendees were asked to cascade Rise to the Challenge content to their employee teams.

Phase 2: Launch Global Education Campaign (goal: cascade program to global organization).

- CEO email and call to action urged employees to Rise to the Challenge.

- Intranet microsite educated employees on the behaviors, with case studies and videos.

- Manager toolkit assisted managers in hosting local staff meetings to develop action plans.

- HR community helped cascade by putting up posters translated into languages for all locations.

Phase 3: Drive Employee Adoption (goal: use reminder messages to convert awareness to action)

- Steady drumbeat of intranet stories maintained awareness of theme and message.

- Rise to the Challenge messaging included in all other employee-facing communications.

- CEO touted campaign on quarterly earnings calls to investors, which employees listened to.

Phase 4: Celebrate Success (goal: show the campaign is working and publicize achievements)

- Publicized 23 most-impactful case studies spanning all business units and global regions via the company intranet and monthly posters in all global locations.

- Challenges: given the economic situation, it was critical that the campaign have a balance between looking professional and not appearing expensive or frivolous. Many teams were working with reduced staffs, so putting up posters or being interviewed for a case study was not always a priority. Frequent communication and easy-to-access materials alleviated the pressure of an increased workload.

EVALUATION

We exceeded our objective and had measurable success in all five campaign behaviors outlined in our strategy. Newell Rubbermaid CEO Mark Ketchum credits the campaign with lifting employee morale and helping the company exceed its financial commitments in 2009:

- Earnings grew by 8 percent vs. a goal of flat, with market share gains in 60 percent of categories

- Overhead expenses were slashed by $128 million vs. a goal of $100 million

- Cash flow soared to $603 million vs. a goal of $400 million.

On an absolute basis, the best measure of investor confidence is the company's stock price.

Newell Rubbermaid shares tripled from a March low of $4.54. Three financial analysts have upgraded their rating on the company, citing metrics related to the Rise to the Challenge campaign. While we will not administer another employee survey until 2011, we have measured a positive impact on morale via direct employee feed-back to Senior Management, Human Resources, and Communications.

Here are the results in terms of the five campaign behaviors, for which we gath-ered and internally publicized 23 case studies from employee teams around the world:

1. Simplify work: contributed to reducing overhead expenses and anecdotally was cited by employees when eliminating unnecessary activities.

2. Reduce cost: overhead expenses were cut by $128 million.

3. Conserve cash: cash flow rose 32 percent to $603 million.

4. Gain market share: 60 percent of the company's businesses grew market share during the year.

5. Develop yourself and others: unlike at many companies, training programs were not cut; usage grew 3 percent on a constant-employee basis despite the increased workload after layoffs.

E X H I B I T 5-3A **Microsite Home Page**

Courtesy Newell Rubbermaid

EXHIBIT 5-3B Banners and Posters

Courtesy Newell Rubbermaid

EXHIBIT 5-3C   Campaign Tools

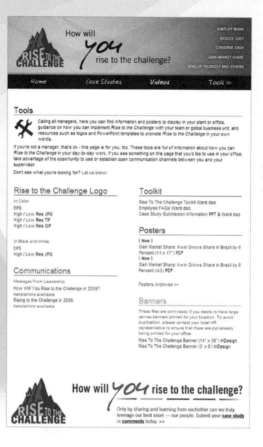

Courtesy Newell Rubbermaid

MEMBER RELATIONS

Membership organizations include trade associations, professional associations, labor unions, interest groups, social and religious organizations, and thousands of other groups, large and small, which dot the landscape. Each has a need for communication between its leaders and members. This process is called member relations.

RESEARCH

Research in member relations includes the client, the opportunity or problem, and the member audiences to be targeted for communication.

Client Research

As a prerequisite for the member relations program, the practitioner needs a thorough understanding of the membership organization conducting the program. The precise nature of the organization, its purpose, its headquarters organization and personnel, its financial status, its reputation with the general public and especially with its own members, its present and past public relations practices, and its public relations or image strengths and vulnerabilities will be part of the organizational profile the practitioner must construct.

Opportunity or Problem Research.   As in all other forms of public relations, the second research objective of member relations is a determination of the reason for conducting the program. Will it be a long-range, proactive program, or will it address a particular problem? As membership is voluntary, major changes in programs or restructuring initiatives require the support and buy-in from the members or their elected representatives. It is crucial to gauge the level of commitment and support for new ideas. The expenditure necessary for the program should be thoroughly justified at this point.

Audience Research.   Identification of audiences to be targeted for communication is the last of the three aspects of research in member relations. Member publics can be categorized into six groups:

> Organization employees
>> Headquarters management
>> Headquarters nonmanagement (staff)
>> Other headquarters personnel
> Organization officers
>> Elected officers
>> Appointed officers
>> Legislative groups
>> Boards, committees

Organization members

    Regular members

    Members in special categories, such as sustaining, emeritus, students

    Honorary members or groups

    Prospective organization members

State or local chapters

    Organization employees

    Organization officers

    Organization members

Prospective organization members

Related or other allied organizations

Member relations research, then, consists of an examination of the client or organization conducting the program, the opportunity or problem that necessitates the program, and the member audiences targeted for communication.

OBJECTIVES

Impact and output objectives are used in member relations and, as in other forms of public relations, objectives should be specific and quantitative as far as possible.

Impact Objectives

For member relations, impact objectives consist of the desired outcomes of informing or modifying the attitudes and behaviors of the members of an organization. Some examples are:

1. To increase members' knowledge of organizational developments, policies, or activities (by 50 percent during the current year)
2. To engender (30 percent) more favorable member attitudes toward the organization (during the months of October and November)
3. To gain support (favorable vote) for a new programmatic initiative.

Impact objectives, in member relations, as in all types of communication, should be developed carefully for they are the standard against which the success of a program will be evaluated.

Output Objectives

Output objectives in member relations refer to the distribution or execution of essentially controlled forms of communication. Some examples are:

1. To prepare and distribute three membership communications concerning the current initiative
2. To prepare and execute membership conventions, seminars, and other meetings on a timely basis.

PROGRAMMING

Programming for member relations includes theme and messages, action(s) or special event(s), controlled media, and the use of effective communication principles. These factors are the same for member relations as for employee relations except for the types of action(s) or special event(s) and the types of communication used.

Actions or special events for member relations concentrate on conventions, seminars, conferences, and similar meetings. The headquarters management of an organization has an obligation to schedule and execute such gatherings for the membership.

Other actions on the part of the headquarters officials of an organization usually include the promotion of industry research, preparation of industry statistics and data, development of professional standards and ethical codes, development of in-service education and training for members, and promotion of standards of safety and efficiency among the members or in the industry.

Member communications are usually limited to controlled media. These usually consist of phone calls, email, websites, Twitter feeds, newsletters and other member publications, reports, industry brochures, pamphlets, and other printed materials, some of which can be distributed to the members' clients. For example, the American Dental Association publishes dental care brochures for patients, and the American Heart Association prints materials for individuals who want to lower their levels of cholesterol. Other associations may establish an online professional forum for members to share information and initiatives.

Uncontrolled media in the form of news releases about employees or members are often considered part of the internal communication program. Strictly speaking, however, such communication falls into the category of external media relations.

Principles of effective communication are the same in member relations programs as in other forms of public relations. Association will use trusted, influential members for "source credibility" and two-way communication is usually effective with members.

Thus, programming for member relations shares many similarities with that for employee relations.

EVALUATION

Evaluation of member relations directs attention back to the objectives established for such programs.

Success for programs may be directly linked to the objectives—informational, behavioral, and/or attitudinal—stated at the outset of a program. Was there favorable reaction from the membership? Did the number of members increase or decrease? Have members actively supported a new initiative with their time and money? Have requests for membership information increased?

SUMMARY

Member relations is communication between the officers (management) of a membership organization and its members.

Research in member relations focuses on the demographics, information levels, attitudes, and behaviors of the organization's membership.

A complete member profile should be constructed through such research, with special attention to the typical member's attitudes and behaviors toward the organization itself.

Both impact and output objectives are used in member relations.

Impact objectives include the desired programmatic outcomes of favorable member attitudes and behaviors toward the organization.

Output objectives catalog desired PR practices, such as effective planning, preparation, and distribution of member communications.

Programming for member relations usually includes such events as conventions, conferences, seminars, and such actions as promotion of industry research, preparation of industry statistics and data, and general promotion and development of the industry or profession represented by the membership.

Common forms of communication are email, websites, member publications, reports, printed materials, audiovisual materials, and meetings.

As in other forms of public relations, evaluation consists of measuring stated objectives through surveys, observation, or other appropriate means suggested by the objectives themselves.

READINGS ON MEMBER RELATIONS

"Association Public Relations" (special issue), *Public Relations Quarterly* 37 (spring 1992).

Encyclopedia of Associations. Detroit, MI: Gale Research, published annually.

Cutlip, Scott M., Allen H. Center, and Glen M. Broom. "Nonprofits, Trade Associations, and Nongovernmental Organizations." In *Effective Public Relations*, 10th ed. Englewood Cliffs, NJ: Prentice-Hall, 2009.

Dixon, Tom. *Communication, Organization and Performance*. Norwood, NJ: Ablex Publishing, 1996.

Levy, Ronald N. "Association PR: Techniques of Great PR Teams." *Public Relations Quarterly* 44 (winter 1999): 19–21.

Miller, Katherine *Organizational Communication Approaches and Processes*, 5th ed. Belmont, CA: Wadsworth, 2008.

Tucker, Mary L., G. Dale Meyer, and James W. Westerman. "Organizational Communication: Development of Internal Strategic Competitive Advantage," *Journal of Business Communication* 33 (April 1996): 51ff.

6

Community Relations

O ne of the most important audiences an organization has is its community, the home of its operations. Traditionally, maintaining good relations with the community entails management and employees becoming involved in and contributing to local organizations and activities. However, community relations may involve broader engagement with a community through support for community activities and organizations or even donations to charitable causes. In addition, the organization may communicate with the community by distributing house publications or meeting with community leaders. Often community relations activities involve face-to-face interaction between an organization and a public, one of the most powerful forms of influencing attitudes.

Solving community relations problems may follow the usual sequence of research, objectives, programming, and evaluation.

RESEARCH

Research for community relations includes investigation to understand the client, the reason for the program, and the community audiences to be targeted or engaged through communication.

Client Research

Client research for community relations concentrates on the organization's role and reputation in the community. It often involves finding answers to basic questions. What is the organization's level of credibility? Have there been significant community complaints in the past? What are the organization's present and past community relations practices? What changes in the community and political landscape are affecting relations with the organization? What are its major strengths and weaknesses in the community? What opportunities exist to enhance community relations? These questions provide a helpful framework for a community relations program.

Opportunity or Problem Research

Why have a community relations program in the first place? Considering the cost and benefits involved, this is a question worthy of detailed justification. The public relations practitioner should assess problems the organization may have had with community groups and make a searching analysis of community relations opportunities. Many organizations conduct ongoing proactive community relations as a form of insurance against any sudden problem requiring a reactive public relations solution. It is often easier to communicate with an organization's current community network than to build a new communication program from scratch.

Audience Research

The final aspect of community relations research consists of carefully identifying audiences to be targeted for communication and learning as much about each audience as possible. Community publics can be subdivided into three major groups: community media, community leaders, and community organizations. These categories can then be further subdivided as shown in Exhibit 6-a.

E X H I B I T 6-a   Community Publics

Community media
    Mass
    Specialized
Community leaders
    Public officials
    Educators
    Religious leaders
    Professionals
    Executives
    Bankers
    Union leaders
    Ethnic and racial group leaders
    Neighborhood leaders
Community organizations
    Civic —7 exist for community well being
    Business
    Service
    Social
    Cultural
    Religious
    Youth
    Political
    Special interest groups
    Other

In conducting community relations programs, it is important for the practitioner to develop contact lists of journalists, community leaders, and organizations. The lists are then rank ordered by importance and influence within the community. For example, two organizations or civic leaders may be far more influential than 40 other groups.

The media contact lists will be similar to those discussed in Chapter 3, on media relations. These lists should include the type and size of audience reached by each media outlet in the community, the type of material used by each outlet, the name and title of appropriate editors who handle organizational news, and deadlines. Don't neglect the publisher or owner of the media outlet as they could also be key players in community politics.

The list of community and organization leaders should be equally thorough. It should include the name, title, affiliation, address, and telephone number of all important community leaders. These data should be categorized according to occupational fields, such as public officials, educators, or religious leaders. In addition to a listing of leaders alone, there should be a list of organizations that includes frequently updated names of officers, their addresses, and telephone numbers. It is often a real challenge to identify the influentials or opinion leaders who have exceptional credibility with others in the community through reputation, expertise, economic clout, or political power. Because of their voice in community affairs, some activist groups would be considered influential members of the community. It is not always those individuals in "official positions of leadership." For example, the president of the local Parent Teacher Association (PTA) may be important, but the real power behind decisions about education may be a former school board member or a highly respected principal. When these people talk, others are careful to listen.

Research for community relations, then, consists of investigation of the client, the reason for the program, and the target audiences in the community.

OBJECTIVES

Impact and output objectives for community relations, like those for other forms of public relations, should be specific and quantitative.

Impact Objectives

Impact objectives for community relations involve informing the community audiences or modifying their attitudes or behaviors. Some examples are:

1. To increase (by 30 percent this year) community knowledge of the operations of the organization, including its products, services, employees, and support of community projects

2. To promote (20 percent) more favorable community opinion toward the organization (during a specified time period)

3. To gain (15 percent) greater organizational support from community leaders (during a particular campaign)

4.   To encourage (20 percent) more applications for philanthropic grants (during the current year)

5.   To increase the number of employees participating as leaders in local youth sport programs by 20 percent.

Output Objectives

Output objectives consist of the efforts made by the practitioner to enhance the organization's community relations. Some illustrations are:

1.   To prepare and distribute (15 percent) more community publications (than last year)

2.   To create (five) new community projects involving organizational personnel and resources (during this calendar year)

3.   To schedule (five) meetings with community leaders (this year).

Thus, both impact and output objectives are helpful in preparing community relations programs. They serve as useful and necessary precursors to programming.

PROGRAMMING

Programming for community relations includes planning the theme and messages, action or special event(s), and using effective communication principles.

Theme and Messages

The theme and messages for community relations are situational and grow out of research findings related to the organization, the reason for conducting the program, and the existing and past relationships with the targeted community audiences.

Action(s) or Special Event(s)

Actions and special events most often associated with community relations are:

1.   An organizational open house and tour of facilities

2.   Sponsorship of special community events or projects

3.   Participation of management and other personnel in volunteer community activities

4.   Purchase of advertising in local media

5.   Financial support for community organizations or causes

6.   Meetings with community leaders

7.   Membership of management and personnel in a variety of community organizations—civic, professional, and/or religious

8.   Cause related support tied to the organization's mission.

Involvement of the organization, its management, and its other personnel in the affairs of the community is the most significant aspect of a community relations program.

Uncontrolled and Controlled Media

In the communications part of a community relations program, the practitioner should think first of servicing community media outlets with appropriate uncontrolled media, such as placing news stories, photographs or photo opportunities, and interviews of organizational officers with local reporters.

The use of controlled media, on the other hand, should include sending copies of house publications to a select list of community leaders or sending email links to digital media developed by the organization. The practitioner should also help the organization develop a speakers bureau, and publicize the availability of organizational management and expert personnel to address meetings of local clubs and organizations. It is also appropriate to target community leaders on a timely basis for selected direct mailings, such as important announcements or notices of organizational involvement in community affairs.

Above all, the organization must develop an informative and appropriate Internet presence. This can be used for both uncontrolled and controlled communication. Journalists should be able to obtain background information and up-to-date news about the organization on the website. This should include background on organizational leaders and facilities as well as other important and relevant data.

Both uncontrolled and controlled media in the community relations program should be tied to specific campaigns of community involvement.

Effective Communication

Three principles of effective communication deserve special attention in community relations programs.

First, the targeting of opinion leaders or community leaders for communication is crucial to the success of such a program. The leadership provides the structure and substance of the community itself.

Second, group influence plays a substantial role in effective community relations. Organizations exercise varying degrees of cohesiveness and member conformity. The community relations program must cultivate community groups, their leaders, and their memberships. The effective speakers bureau is a primary means for accomplishing this.

Finally, audience participation is highly significant. Targeted community media, leaders, and groups can be encouraged to participate in the client's organizational events. Most important, the client should reach out to the community by sponsoring attractive activities.

EVALUATION

If the objectives of the community relations program have been phrased specifically and quantitatively, their evaluation should be relatively easy. For example, it is simple to measure the number of presentations by the organization's speakers bureau or to measure the number of people attending special events sponsored by the organization. The success of a program should be directly linked to its attainment of the objectives stated at the program's outset.

SUMMARY

Research for community relations assesses the organization's reputation and its existing and potential problems with the community. Targeting audiences usually includes a detailed analysis of community media, leaders, and organizations.

Impact objectives for community relations are such desired outcomes as informing or influencing the attitudes and behaviors of the community. Output objectives consist of a listing of public relations efforts to enhance the organization's relations with the community.

Programming concentrates on organizational involvement with the community through sponsorship of events, employee participation in community activities, contributions to community causes, meetings, and the like. The uncontrolled media used in community relations are aimed at engaging local journalists with appropriate news releases, photographs, and interviews with organizational officers. Controlled media usually include house publications, online video postings, speaker's bureaus, and appropriate direct mailings to community leaders.

It is also important for the organization to develop an attractive and informative community-oriented online presence and even social media tools for community engagement.

Evaluation of stated objectives uses methods appropriate to the type of objective. Impact objectives are usually measured by a survey or other appropriate quantitative methods, while output objectives may call for simple observation of whether the desired output was achieved.

READINGS ON COMMUNITY RELATIONS

Bete, Tim. "Eight Great Community Relations Ideas," *School Planning and Management* 37 (May 1998): 49ff.

Bruning, Stephen D. "Examining the Role That Personal, Professional, and Community Relationship Play in Respondent Relationship Recognition and Intended Behavior," *Communication Quarterly* 48 (fall 2000): 437–448.

Bruning, Stephen D., and Meghan Ralston. "Using a Relational Approach to Retaining Students and Building Mutually Beneficial Student-University Relationships," *The Southern Communication Journal* 66 (summer 2001): 337ff.

Burke, Edmund M. *Corporate Community Relations: The Principle of the Neighbor of Choice.* Westport, CT: Quorum Books, 1999.

Few, Roger. "Containment and Counter-Containment: Planner/Community Relations in Conservation Planning," *The Geographical Journal* 167(2) (June 2001): 111–124.

Flocks, Joan, Leslie Clarke, Stan Albrecht, Carol Bryant, Paul Monaghan, and Holly Baker. "Implementing a Community-Based Social Marketing Project to Improve Agricultural Worker Health," *Environmental Health Perspectives* 109 (June 2001): 461–468.

Forrest, Carol J., and Renee H. Mays. "The Practical Guide to Environmental Community Relations," *Journal of Environmental Health* 67 (January–February 2005): 30ff.

Gaschen, Dennis J. "Play Ball: Community Relations and Professional Sports," *Public Relations Tactics* 7 (August 2000): 10.

Hall, Margarete R. "Corporate Philanthropy and Corporate Community Relations: Measuring Relationship Building Results," *Journal of Public Relations Research* 18 (2006): 1–21.

Holtzhausen, Derina R. "Public Relations Practice and Political Change in South Africa," *Public Relations Review* 31 (September 2005): 407–416.

Keswick, Renée, and LaDon McNeil. "Reaching out to the Arabic Community," *Behavioral Healthcare* 26(11) (November 2006): 32.

Lattimore, Dan, Otis Basking, Suzette T. Heiman, and Elizabeth L. Toth. "Community Relations," Public Relations: The Profession and the Practice. New York: McGraw-Hill 2011.

Ledingham, John A., and Stephen D. Bruning. "Building Loyalty Through Community Relations," *Public Relations Strategist* 3 (Summer 1997): 27–29.

Lukaszewski, James E. "Getting to 51 Percent: Building Community Relationships That Gain and Maintain Public Consent," *Public Relations Tactics* 12 (May 2005): 11.

Matson, Judy. "Creating the Intersection Between Corporate Values and Community Service," *Public Relations Strategist* 10 (Summer 2004): 30–31.

McDermott, David. "The 10 Commandments of Community Relations," *World Wastes* 36 (September 1993): 48ff.

Milstein, Eric, and David S. Coles. "Don't Hate San Francisco! Engage, Don't Estrange," *U.S. Naval Institute Proceedings* 134(1) (January 2008): 88.

Parker, Rani. "Community Impacts of Corporate Social Responsibility in the Mining Sector: Examples from Peru, Canada and Mali," Conference Papers—International Studies Association (2007): 1.

Poston, Patty. "Grassroots Communications Reconsidered," *Public Relations Tactics* 9 (September 2002): 12–13.

Schultz, David L. "Strategic Survival in the Face of Community Activism," *Public Relations Strategist* 7 (Spring 2001): 36–38.

Wiser, Nancy. "After the storm: PR efforts help quell public frustration in Kentucky," *Public Relations Tactics* 11 (January 2004): 11–12.

Community Relations Cases

Case 6-1

This communication campaign engaged the community in an energy conservation effort using a variety of special events, media relations and social media to develop a synergy of effort. Exhibit 6-1A is a news release launching the campaign and Exhibit 6-1B is a flyer with the contest details and tour dates.

Puget Sound Energy's Rock The Bulb Tour

Puget Sound Energy and Colehour+Cohen

SUMMARY

Washington State's oldest local energy utility, Puget Sound Energy, aimed to create a deeper relationship with its customers and become their most trusted energy efficiency resource. As a result, PSE and Colehour+Cohen developed PSE's "Rock the Bulb" campaign, which included weekend bulb exchange events, a vast door-to-door CFL bulb distribution effort and an energy-efficiency contest. PSE exceeded its bulb distribution goal by 28 percent—topping 511,500 CFL bulbs. Installed, these bulbs saved more than 118.3 million kWh of electricity and 130 million lbs of greenhouse gas emissions, equal to taking more than 10,800 cars off the road. Washington State's oldest local energy utility, Puget Sound Energy, aimed to create a deeper relationship with its customers and become their most trusted energy efficiency resource. As a result, PSE and Colehour+Cohen developed PSE's "Rock the Bulb" campaign, which included weekend bulb exchange events, a vast door-to-door CFL bulb distribution effort and an energy-efficiency contest. PSE exceeded its bulb distribution goal by 28 percent—topping 511,500 CFL bulbs. Installed, these bulbs saved more than 118.3 million kWh of electricity and 130 million lbs of greenhouse gas emissions, equal to taking more than 10,800 cars off the road.

Courtesy Puget Sound Energy and Colehour+Cohen

RESEARCH

Puget Sound Energy is Washington State's oldest local energy utility, serving more than 1 million electric customers and nearly 750,000 natural gas customers. In 2009, PSE engaged Colehour+Cohen to help develop and execute an innovative customer engagement and education campaign focusing on motivating customers to be more energy-efficient at home, starting with energy-efficient lighting in the form of compact fluorescent bulbs (CFL bulbs).

The team pulled from three research sources to help plan the campaign:

- An evaluation report of a 2008 PSE CFL give-away pilot program that identified the pros and cons of distributing free CFLs to customers through events.

- A detailed customer segmentation study that identified attitudes, beliefs and current energy efficiency behaviors.

- Market intelligence surveys that analyzed customer segments in terms of type of media used and geography.

The research identified two primary audience segments that would be most receptive to changing their energy use behaviors: Green Idealists (~14 percent of PSE customers) who believe that it is socially responsible to limit energy use and are very educated about environmental issues; and Practical Idealists (~ 23 percent of PSE customers) who think it's important to limit energy use but are more motivated by practical reasons to do so (i.e. saving money).

Both audience segments may have made some changes to reduce energy use, but are busy and may not have had time to fully learn about what they can do. They trust PSE and welcome help in becoming more energy-efficient but are not broadly aware of the wide range of programs and services offered by the utility. They use online search engines, the PSE website and bill inserts, and newspaper, TV and radio to get energy efficiency information.

PLANNING

The research showed an opportunity for PSE to create a deeper relationship with the target customers and become their "trusted resource" for energy efficiency information. To do this, PSE and C+C developed one of the most comprehensive CFL bulb giveaway programs in the country: PSE's "Rock the Bulb"—an effort that included weekend bulb exchange events, a vast door-to-door CFL bulb distribution effort and an energy-efficiency contest and promotions. PSE's Rock the Bulb concept used the promise of free CFL bulbs to engage customers in energy efficiency practices, required an incandescent bulb in exchange for a free CFL, used a four-month-long contest to continue customer engagement, and used festival-like events and door-to-door outreach to engage customers directly with PSE's efficiency experts.

Through Rock the Bulb, PSE aimed to help its customers think about cutting emissions and preserving resources—all while saving on electricity bills and having fun! The team established the following program objectives:

Objective #1: Distribute 400,000 CFL bulbs through exchange events and door-to-door efforts

Objective #2: Engage 12,500 customers through attendance at Rock the Bulb exchange events

Objective #3: Recruit 5,000 customers to show energy-efficiency commitment by participating in a contest

Objective #4: Inspire 1,000 volunteers to engage with PSE to deliver bulbs door-to-door in their communities.

Budget: $2.6 million, including: door-to-door and community event distribution of 275,000 bulbs; creation and production of all campaign materials; media relations/events; social media; planning, staffing, materials and rentals for 32 retail events; and a website with at-event login and customer ability to track energy usage online.

EXECUTION

Four central tactics drove participation and engaged customers:

- PSE's Rock the Bulb Tour included 32 weekend bulb exchange events for PSE electric customers at select Lowe's and Ace Hardware stores. Customers exchanged up to 10 incandescent bulbs for free CFL bulbs in various styles and sizes. The events had a family-friendly, music festival-like atmosphere with music, snacks, energy-efficiency games and activities, and PSE's Energy Advisors on hand. To stretch the campaign budget, events were staffed by 12 paid staff and 12 volunteers.

- Project Porchlight PSE and non-profit Project Porchlight delivered 275,000 CFL bulbs door-to-door and at community events 1-3 weeks ahead of each Rock the Bulb Tour event, and worked with community officials and local organizations to build grassroots support of the campaign.

- The Be an Energy Rock Star Contest PSE secured $45,000 in prizes from their bulb vendor to award to customers who earned the most points by exchanging bulbs, participating at a Rock the Bulb Tour event; volunteering with Project Porchlight; reducing their home energy use; and recruiting up to 20 friends to participate.

- Website A campaign Website (www.rockthebulb.pse.com) was created to publicize the events, allow contest participants to track their points and provide customers with links to PSE's energy efficiency tips and information.

A Social Media PSE created a Golden Bulb promotion that utilized Twitter, Facebook and the campaign blog. To drive participation in the campaign, PSE and the C+C team employed a variety of traditional and grassroots tactics. Advertising

- Web. The team placed banner ads promoting the contest and events, customized for each week's upcoming event.

- Radio. The team partnered with three radio stations to drive participation, with radio spots promoting the events, contest, social media promotion, and volunteering elements; live remotes at select PSE Rock the Bulb events; and other efforts such as blog postings, listener emails and in-studio interviews.

- TV. The team partnered with Comcast to run a 'zoned' :60 spot, customized for each region to run before each event. PSE also partnered with the local Univision affiliate to reach Spanish-speaking populations.

- Print. Print ads were placed in major regional publications, as well as smaller community papers in each community hosting an event—including Spanish language paper *La Raza del Noroeste*.

Internal PSE Media

The team held a kick-off event for PSE employees and ran several articles for PSE's media vehicles including: Customer communications: bill inserts, Energy at Home email newsletter, EnergyWise customer newsletter. Employee communications: Friday Focus employee newsletter, and weekly campaign updates on the company's Intranet, PSEWeb.

Media Relations

- Launch Media Event. Media were invited to the opening event in Bellevue with the city's mayor and PSE officials in order to see kids from the local YMCA participating in event activities. All four local TV affiliates covered.

- News Advisories and Releases. Issued at launch, before every weekend event and at key milestones. These were followed up with outreach to local reporters, and follow ups about each weekend's events, with photos of notable volunteers (mayors, sports stars, etc.) distributing CFL bulbs door-to-door.

- Magicians (Mid-Campaign Event). To further mid-campaign buzz, PSE hired a magician to perform campaign-themed magic tricks at local transit stations and on buses, and handed out free CFLs and campaign information.

- ENERGY STAR Media Event. EPA's ENERGY STAR program selected PSE's Rock the Bulb tour as one of four locations in the country for the ENERGY STAR Exhibit House in 2009. Prior to this event, the team held a media event at a local home that included kids from the local Boys and Girls Club.

- Culmination Media Event. PSE announced the winner of the Be an Energy Rock Star Contest at a media event at the winners' home in Bellevue,

Wash. The event showed how the winning family reduced their energy use by 94 percent during the contest!

- Web/Social Media. Social media was used to help keep the campaign fresh and engaging. Tactics included a blog, Facebook page and Twitter account. The blog and Facebook page were updated several times a week. PSE created a Golden Bulb promotion where 20 yellow CFL bulbs were hidden throughout PSE's service area. Clues were sent several times a day via Twitter, Facebook and on the blog—winners received a $250 gift card to a partner retailer.

Challenge

The team found out at 2 p.m. the day before the first event that the CFL bulbs were stuck in California and would not make it to the event until late Saturday. To ensure we had enough stock for our first event, the team went to eight Lowe's stores and purchased CFL bulbs, which were later reimbursed by the bulb vendor.

EVALUATION

Objective #1: Distribute 400,000 CFL bulbs through events and door-to-door efforts. Result: PSE exceeded its bulb distribution goal by 28 percent—more than 511,500 CFL bulbs were distributed. Installed, these bulbs equal more than 118.3 million kWh of electricity saved; over $22 million saved on energy bills; and more than 130 million lbs of greenhouse gas emissions avoided, equal to taking more than 10,800 cars off the road.

Objective #2: Engage 12,500 customers through attendance at Rock the Bulb exchange events. Result: Objective exceeded. Almost 25,000 PSE customers had exchanged bulbs at a PSE Rock the Bulb event.

Objective #3: Recruit 5,000 customers to expand their energy-efficiency commitment by participating in a contest. Result: Objective exceeded. More than 7,600 customers had signed up for the contest.

Objective #4: Inspire 1,000 volunteers to engage with PSE to deliver CFL bulbs door-to-door in their communities. Result: Objective exceeded. Over 1,100 volunteers handed out bulbs to their friends and neighbors.

Other measures of success included earned media impressions of 4.8 million with a media value of $213,700. In addition, the post-campaign survey showed that 83 percent of participants were more interested in PSE's energy efficiency services and programs after Rock the Bulb, and 91 percent found that information disseminated about the campaign was useful or helpful.

EXHIBIT 6-1A   News Release

PUGET SOUND ENERGY
The Energy To Do Great Things

NEWS RELEASE

For Immediate Release:

July 17, 2009

Media Contact:

Rebekah Anderson
1-888-831-7250

PSE's Rock the Bulb campaign to give away 400,000 free CFL bulbs to residential electric customers from July through October

First of its kind utility campaign will feature 16 local weekend events, neighborhood outreach and prizes to help consumers save energy, money and the environment

BELLEVUE, Wash. – Puget Sound Energy today is kicking off a four-month-long campaign called PSE's Rock the Bulb Tour to promote home energy efficiency by encouraging PSE residential electric customers to switch from incandescent lighting to ENERGY STAR® qualified, energy-efficient compact fluorescent light (CFL) bulbs. PSE's Rock the Bulb Tour will demonstrate easy ways for residents to lower their home energy use as a first step to saving money, energy and the environment.

PSE's Rock the Bulb Tour will distribute 400,000 energy-saving CFL bulbs to PSE customers through 16 weekend bulb exchange events at local hardware stores, door-to-door outreach with nonprofit partner Project Porchlight and at community events in neighborhoods in the utility's electric service area.

"We want our customers to get excited about saving energy," said Cal Shirley, vice president of Energy Efficiency Services for PSE. "PSE's Rock the Bulb Tour is a family fun way to help our customers switch out incandescent bulbs for CFL bulbs to experience first hand what a difference energy efficiency can make to saving energy, money and the environment.

"CFL bulbs use 75 percent less electricity than old-fashioned incandescent light bulbs and last up to 10 times longer," explained Shirley. "Every light bulb changed will save $40 or more in electricity costs over its lifetime."

Putting the 400,000 CFLs distributed through PSE's Rock the Bulb Tour into service in customer homes will result in overall savings of more than $17 million in energy costs and a reduction of more than 101 million pounds of greenhouse gas emissions—the equivalent of taking more than 8,000 cars off the road each year.

"Lighting makes up 20 percent of the average home's energy bill, and by replacing the 10 most frequently used lights in the home with CFL bulbs, residents can save $400 or more in energy costs over the life of the bulbs," explained Shirley. "That's big savings per home and for the region."

There are four ways PSE customers can participate in PSE's Rock the Bulb Tour campaign:

- PSE's Rock the Bulb Tour—Unplugged Events—16 weekend energy efficiency fairs and light bulb exchange events at local hardware stores where PSE residential electric customers can exchange up to 10 incandescent bulbs for the same number CFL bulbs, choosing from among six different styles, and participate in fun and educational activities that show how to lower home energy use.
- PSE's Be an Energy Rock Star Contest - offers PSE customers the chance to win prizes for reducing home energy use and participating in energy efficiency activities.

- Project Porchlight Puget Sound—PSE customers can volunteer to help distribute 275,000 ENERGY STAR CFLs door-to-door and at community outreach events.
- The Golden Bulb Promotion—PSE has placed yellow bulbs—Golden Bulbs—throughout the PSE service area. Starting July 17, PSE will send out clues on Twitter, Facebook and the campaign blog to lead participants to bulb locations. Bulb finders will receive a $250 gift certificate to either Lowe's or Ace Hardware.

PSE's Rock the Bulb Tour—Unplugged Events

The 16 weekend events at local retailers offer PSE residential electric customers an opportunity to learn about and embrace energy efficiency in a family-friendly, festival-like atmosphere. The events feature games and activities, displays about choosing the proper CFL, energy-efficiency advice from PSE's Energy Advisors, and up to 10 free CFL bulbs in exchange for the same number of incandescent bulbs.

PSE's weekend Rock the Bulb Tour—Unplugged events will be held at the following locations, Saturday and Sunday from 10 a.m.–4 p.m.:

- July 11–12   Renton Lowe's Store
- July 18–19   Bellevue Lowe's Store
- July 25–26   Issaquah Lowe's Store
- Aug. 1–2   Silverdale Lowe's Store
- Aug. 8–9   Bremerton Lowe's Store
- Aug. 15–16   Port Orchard Lowe's Store
- Aug. 22–23   Anacortes Ace Hardware Store
- Aug. 29–30   Oak Harbor Ace Hardware Store
- Sept. 12–13   Mt Vernon Lowe's Store
- Sept. 19–20   Bellingham Lowe's Store
- Sept. 26–27   Federal Way Lowe's Store
- Oct. 3–4   Kent Lowe's Store
- Oct. 10–11   Auburn Lowe's Store
- Oct. 17–18   Puyallup Lowe's Store
- Oct. 24–25   Lacey Lowe's Store
- Oct. 31–11/1   Olympia Lowe's Store

PSE's Be an Energy Rock Star Contest

PSE's Rock the Bulb Tour also offers its customers The Be an Energy Rock Star Contest where customers can earn points for a chance to win part of $45,000 in prizes, awarded as Lowe's and Ace Hardware gift cards for more energy efficiency home upgrades, provided by our energy efficiency bulb partner Feit Electric. PSE residential electric customers can enter the contest at one of the 16 weekend events or online at rockthebulb.pse.com.

Participants earn points for activities such as participating in a PSE Rock the Bulb Tour—Unplugged event, exchanging incandescents for CFL bulbs, taking the ENERGY STAR pledge to save energy at home, recruiting others to participate, and by reducing their electric bill during the month of October 2009.

Winners will receive gift cards to Lowe's or Ace Hardware, and Grand and Second prize winners also receive a free PSE HomePrint energy audit.

Project Porchlight Puget Sound

PSE is working in partnership with Project Porchlight to distribute 275,000 free CFL bulbs from July through October to PSE's residential electric customers door-to-door and at community events. PSE volunteers will distribute free CFLs in the communities of Port Townsend, Redmond, Bothell, Ferndale, Kirkland, Bainbridge Island, Poulsbo, Burlington, Renton, Bellevue, Issaquah, Silverdale, Bremerton, Port Orchard, Anacortes, Oak Harbor, Mt. Vernon, Bellingham, Federal Way, Kent, Auburn, Puyallup, Lacey and Olympia. PSE customers can register to volunteer online at projectporchlight.org.

The Golden Bulb Promotion

Throughout the PSE service area, PSE has given several regional VIP's yellow CFL bulbs known as Golden Bulbs. Starting July 17, Golden Bulb Promotion participants can receive clues at twitter.com/PSERockthebulb that will lead them to the Golden Bulbs. Each day of the promotion, PSE will tweet two or three clues about the whereabouts of the Golden Bulbs. Participants who follow the clues and find a Golden Bulb will receive a $250 gift certificate to either Lowe's or Ace Hardware.

Since PSE began its energy-efficient lighting program in 2002, the utility has distributed more than 10 million CFL bulbs within its electric service area, an average of 10 CFL bulbs per household. The PSE Rock the Bulb Tour should push that number past 11 million.

For more information about PSE's Rock the Bulb Tour, go to rockthebulb.pse.com or follow the campaign on Twitter at twitter.com/PSERockthebulb.

To learn more about how homeowners can save energy and take advantage of PSE rebates for energy efficiency home improvements, visit PSE.com or call a PSE Energy Advisor at 1-800-562-1482.

About Puget Sound Energy

Washington state's oldest local energy utility, Puget Sound Energy serves more than 1 million electric customers and nearly 750,000 natural gas customers in 11 counties. A subsidiary of Puget Energy, PSE meets the energy needs of its growing customer base through incremental, cost-effective energy conservation, procurement of sustainable energy resources, and far-sighted investment in the energy-delivery infrastructure. PSE employees are dedicated to providing great customer service and delivering energy that is safe, reliable, reasonably priced, and environmentally responsible. For more information, visit www.PSE.com.

###

Courtesy Puget Sound Energy and Colehour+Cohen

EXHIBIT 6-1B Contest Flyer

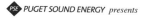 PUGET SOUND ENERGY *presents*

ROCK THE BULB

PSE'S BE AN ENERGY ROCK STAR CONTEST
$45,000 IN PRIZES!

Want to be an energy rock star? Enter PSE's Be an Energy Rock Star contest and rise to energy-saving stardom!

Earn points by taking energy-saving actions at home and in your community. Those with the most points have the opportunity to win some great prizes!

PRIZES
- 1 Grand Prize: $7,500 gift card to Lowe's or Ace Hardware and a free PSE HomePrint home energy audit
- 2 Second Prizes: $2,500 gift card to Lowe's or Ace Hardware and a free PSE HomePrint home energy audit
- 65 Third Prizes: $500 gift card to Lowe's or Ace Hardware

WAYS TO ENTER:
- Online at rockthebulb.com
- Come to one of PSE's 16 Rock the Bulb Tour—Unplugged events to get registered and start earning points towards the contest. Don't forget your old incandescent bulbs—you'll be able to exchange up to ten of them for free energy-saving CFLs!
- Sign up for the contest with a Project Porchlight volunteer if they come to your door with a free CFL!

Track your points at ROCKTHEBULB.PSE.COM!

PSE.com

PSE PUGET SOUND ENERGY
The Energy To Do Great Things

EARNING POINTS:

PARTICIPATE IN A ROCK THE BULB TOUR—UNPLUGGED EVENT!

At these 16 weekend events, you can:

- Exchange up to 10 incandescent bulbs for free CFL bulbs (50 points)
- Visit three lighting activity stations (25 points)
- Stop by the PSE HomePrint booth and talk with a PSE Energy Advisor and/or attend a 15 minute on-site class about energy conservation (25 points)

TAKE THE ENERGY STAR PLEDGE!

Pledge to save energy at home at energystar.gov/changetheworld or at a Rock the Bulb Tour—Unplugged event (5 points)

VOLUNTEER WITH PROJECT PORCHLIGHT

Join PSE partner Project Porchlight to hand out free energy-saving bulbs in your community, either door-to-door or at a community event. Sign up at porchlight.org (30 points).

RECRUIT FRIENDS AND FAMILY

Recruit others to sign up for the contest at rockthebulb.com (5 points per recruit up to a maximum of 100 points).

SAVE ENERGY

Reduce your home's electricity use during month of October 2009, as compared to October 2008 (20-100 points):

- Top 10% of Savers (100 points)
- Second 10% of Savers (80 points)
- Third 10% of Savers (60 points)
- Fourth 10% of Savers (40 points)
- Final 60% of Savers (20 points)

Visit **ROCKTHEBULB.PSE.COM** or call 1-888-362-0363 for more information

PSE.com

PSE *PUGET SOUND ENERGY*
The Energy To Do Great Things

Courtesy Puget Sound Energy and Colehour+Cohen

Case 6-2

Development projects require multiple tiered approaches with many publics to achieve success. Here is a campaign involving working with civic leaders and neighborhood communities for the expansion and renovation of a shopping center in San Diego. Exhibit 6-2A is the project fact sheet, Exhibit 6-2B is a fact sheet enumerating "green issues," and Exhibit 6-2C is an e-blast announcement.

The New UTC: Building Community Support for a $1 Billion Shopping Expansion and Revitalization

Westfield with Southwest Strategies

OVERVIEW

Southwest Strategies (SWS) was hired by Westfield Corporation in 2003 to develop a community relations program to advocate the public and develop build support for the company's proposed $1 billion expansion and renovation of its UTC shopping center in San Diego. To proceed, Westfield needed to secure a vote of approval from the San Diego City Council. The project, dubbed The New UTC, would add three new department stores, 150 specialty shops, up to eight new restaurants, two food courts, a new 14 screen movie theater, a $22 million transit center, 10 acres of solar power on parking garages, and 250 housing units to the existing site. The New UTC would be one of the largest privately financed development projects in the history of San Diego.

RESEARCH

SWS initially recommended a comprehensive research program to better understand the community's perception of the existing shopping center, as well as to help identify potential messages that would resonate with the public. Previous efforts to develop a message platform were unsuccessful because the company's message was fragmented. As a result, a more focused effort was developed, which was comprised of four parts. Ultimately, this resulted in more than 1,000 personal

Courtesy Westfield and Southwest Strategies

contacts with shoppers, local residents, business owners, elected officials, and key opinion leaders. Each is described below:

- Key opinion leader audit: SWS interviewed 20 elected officials and key opinion leaders to get a perspective from those who shape policies and make decisions in San Diego. The results were crucial in developing the right kind of information for opinion leaders. Smart growth, infrastructure and traffic were top issues of concern for this group.

- Public opinion survey: Various concerns emerged from telephone interviews with more than 400 San Diegans throughout the city. This target audience was far more concerned with entertainment options and specific stores that might be offered at the new shopping center. Participants also expressed concerns about increased traffic and how the development would impact the quality of life in surrounding neighborhoods.

- Dial session/focus group: SWS also worked with Westfield to coordinate an enhanced focus group with a handheld dial that allowed participants to measure their support or opposition to specific issues in real-time by turning the device in different directions. Through this session, Westfield learned that shoppers and other important audiences wanted a "green" shopping center that used sustainable materials and designs.

- Parent survey: Nearly 300 parents at the UTC playground were also interviewed. The purpose was to determine how Westfield could improve amenities for local families. The most common response was more shaded areas for parents.

To address the results of the research, four distinct messages were developed. They were....

The New UTC:

1. represents the evolution of a place that is casual, yet sophisticated;
2. integrates environmentally friendly practices and sustainable designs;
3. boosts the regional economy by creating jobs and generating tax revenues; and
4. preserves the convenient, hassle-free nature of the shopping center.

Using this information, SWS developed a targeted community relations program.

PLANNING

Due to the sheer size of the project, SWS recommended that Westfield secure third-party support both locally and regionally. Local support would be particularly important given that many of Westfield's neighbors had previously expressed concerns about the projected increase in traffic and degradation of their quality of life resulting from the project. In addition, opponents would quickly seize on the idea that approving this project would set a bad precedent for the community, allowing other developers in the surrounding areas to seek major expansions of their properties. As a result, Westfield and SWS agreed on a plan to identify, educate, and mobilize credible third parties that would be able to reinforce the project messages (or strengths). It was also decided that project support would be measured by collecting signed support cards and letters of support in favor of the project. Plan details are discussed in the following section.

Objective

SWS initially established a goal of identifying 2,000 support cards (500 neighbors) from San Diegans and securing endorsements from influential regional organizations.

Strategy

Recognizing the project would face stiff local opposition, SWS set out to "break even" with local neighbors, while winning the support of regional leaders.

Target audiences

UTC shoppers, neighbors, key opinion leaders, regional organizations, San Diego City staff, the San Diego City Planning Commission, and the San Diego City Council were all audiences.

Materials

In conjunction with Westfield, SWS developed a number of materials. These included a project website, presentation boards, a PowerPoint presentation, fact sheets, direct mail pieces, brochures, and regular e-Blasts.

EXECUTION

SWS started by creating a comprehensive database that allowed the team to segment project supporters by City Council districts. The database was also designed to track those supporters willing to write letters to key decision-makers and those willing to testify at critical public hearings. Community relations tactics used include:

- Community presentations: SWS conducted more than 50 presentations with homeowners groups, trade associations, civic organizations, labor unions, and neighborhood groups.
- Direct mail: Westfield and SWS developed and distributed three separate direct mail pieces with tear off response cards aimed at local residents.
- The UTC Experience: Westfield opened the UTC Experience, an interactive design studio and lounge with project renderings and a project model, which was open seven days a week at the shopping center.
- Strategic partnerships: As noted, the Westfield/SWS team also determined early on that forming strategic partnerships with key regional organizations could also play a role in demonstrating widespread support for the project. Realizing that projected traffic from the expansion was a potential area of vulnerability for Westfield, SWS encouraged the company to seek the support

of the Metropolitan Transportation System (MTS) and the San Diego Association of Governments (SANDAG), the two regional government agencies responsible for transportation planning in San Diego. Forging a unique partnership with MTS and SANDAG, Westfield agreed to provide nearly two acres of the shopping center to accommodate a state-of-the-art $22 million transit center. This deal resulted in support from both MTS and SANDAG and helped neutralize criticism from opponents about increased traffic.

- Key groups that could reinforce the project messages: In terms of generating support from key groups that could reinforce the project messages, SWS took the unusual step of approaching organizations that typically steer clear from development proposals. For example, the American Lung Association wrote a letter of support because of the project's focus on transit, sustainability and solar power. The United States Green Building Council also supported The New UTC in part because of water conservation and on site affordable housing.

- Media relations campaign: Westfield and SWS also engaged in a media relations campaign that started with the launch of the final project design in August 2007. The launch, intended to focus on the "green" elements of the project, was covered by every major television station in the region, and the headline in the largest print publication read, "UTC to go Green." The successful launch served as a media catalyst that resulted in numerous positive stories leading up to public hearings, editorial board support from the largest newspaper in the region and several favorable opinion editorials from local residents.

- e-Blast and letter writing campaign: Finally, an aggressive e-Blast and letter writing campaign in support of the project was launched in the weeks leading up to the final City Council vote. The Westfield/SWS team also met personally with each of the eight City Council members, delivering copies of signed support cards (tracked in our master database) from constituents in each of their districts.

EVALUATION

On July 29, 2008, after nearly five years of hard work, the San Diego City Council voted 7-1 to approve The New UTC. The approval represents one of the largest land development projects ever supported in San Diego's history.

SWS easily exceeded its objective in terms of support, identifying more than 3,000 from San Diegans (and more than 800 from neighbors within one mile of the shopping center). In addition, more than 500 letters and e-mails were sent to each City Council member, and more than 200 people attended the public hearing and wore green t-shirts in favor of The New UTC. SWS also secured the support of virtually every influential regional group in the County, including the Asian Business Association, the San Diego Housing Commission, the San Diego County Taxpayers Association, the San Diego County Parent Connection, the San Diego Cinema Society, the San Diego Regional Chamber of Commerce, the San Diego Regional Economic Development Corporation, and the San Diego Chapter of the California Restaurant Association.

The wide-ranging support sparked one City Councilmember during the final hearing to say, "The UTC project is not only a model for how to build a project in San Diego, it is a prototypical example about how to run a community relations campaign in favor of a development project."

EXHIBIT 6-2A "Imagine a New UTC" Fact Sheet

Westfield Imagine the New UTC

Fact Sheet

Project Background

Westfield is excited to revitalize the UTC shopping center, the first enhancement since 1984. The project will include an exciting range of shops and restaurants, and a family environment reflecting the unique San Diego lifestyle.

- Three new anchor stores
- 150 new stylish shops and specialty boutiques
- Five new restaurants plus a wine bar and bistros
- A new state-of-the-art movie theater
- Revitalization of existing center
- More parking and a new transit center
- 250 new housing units with a variety of choices
- New enhanced public ice skating rink
- Recreational spaces such as trails and picnic areas

Environmentally Friendly

By using environmentally friendly designs and green building principles, UTC will be a smart growth project and a model of sustainability. Westfield is proud to announce that the New UTC will be the first shopping center project in the United States to be approved by the U.S. Green Building Council at the Gold level under the new LEED-ND (Neighborhood Development) pilot program. Other specific green features include:

- Not using a single drop of additional potable water by using recycled water for landscape irrigation
- Use of "cool roof" technology to reduce the need for air conditioning
- Recycling of construction and everyday waste generated by the shopping center
- Exploring a large scale solar rooftop project on parking garages and retailers

Economic Benefits

Millions of dollars in revenue will be created by the New UTC each year for the City of San Diego, along with thousands of new jobs for residents, all at no expense to taxpayers. After completion, a revitalized UTC will generate:

- More than $10 million a year for vital City services such as police, firefighters, parks and libraries
- More than 2,500 new full- and part-time jobs
- $40 million for transportation and other public works projects

Learn More

Visit www.thenewutc.com to learn more, or stop by the UTC Experience, a design studio and gallery at UTC (adjacent to the food court) featuring project renderings and videos.

Westfield UTC • 4545 La Jolla Village Drive, Suite E25 • San Diego, California 92122 • (858) 453-2930

Courtesy Westfield and Southwest Strategies

EXHIBIT 6-2B "Green Vision for the New UTC" Fact Sheet

 Westfield   # A Green Vision for the New UTC

thenewutc   ## Fact Sheet
A Revitalization of Westfield UTC

Westfield's goal for the New UTC is simple: Build the greenest shopping center possible. Westfield's plans incorporate energy efficiency, water conservation and sustainable materials in multiple ways in the project's design. We are proud to announce that the New UTC is the first shopping center project in the United States to be approved by the U.S. Green Building Council at the Gold level under the new LEED-ND (Neighborhood Development) pilot program.

Water Conservation

By not using a single drop of additional potable water, Westfield will make better use of one of Southern California's most precious resources. Water-smart features include:

- Use of recycled water for all irrigation on the site, instead of drinking water.
- Use of water-conserving plumbing fixtures throughout the project.
- Use of indigenous, drought-resistant landscaping to minimize irrigation needs

Energy Efficiencies

The New UTC will reflect Westfield's global values that have made us a leader in energy conservation. Energy-saving plans include:

- Building solar panels on parking structures and retail rooftops, potentially generating up to two megawatts of clean, renewable power.
- Constructing all new buildings to be a minimum of 10 percent more energy efficient than California standards.
- Using 'cool roof' technology to reduce heat absorption, minimizing the need for air conditioning.

Sustainable Materials and Practices

Widespread use of environmentally friendly materials and construction practices will lay a sustainable foundation for the New UTC. Examples of this thinking include:

- Use of accredited timber products and locally sourced, low-impact materials.
- A minimum of 50 percent of all construction and demolition waste recycled (target 75 percent).
- Recycling station on-site for operational waste.

For more information on Westfield UTC's green vision, call 858.453.2930, or visit thenewutc.com.

Courtesy Westfield and Southwest Strategies

EXHIBIT 6-2C   E-blast Announcement

Courtesy Westfield and Southwest Strategies

Case 6-3

Connecting a faux political campaign with the local animal society may sound like a stretch, yet demonstrates the way unusual pairings can generate much needed publicity and local community involvement for an organization. Exhibit 6-3A is a news release announcing the contest, Exhibit 6-3B is a promotional poster, and Exhibit 6-3C is the Facebook site for the campaign.

Spike & Biscuit Rebrand for the Charleston Animal Society

Charleston Animal Society with Rawle Murdy

SUMMARY

The non-profit John Ancrum Society for the Prevention of Cruelty to Animals (JASPCA) struggled with an overcrowded facility, virtually no name recognition, and a poor community profile. Rawle Murdy helped the JASPCA redefine its image and raise community awareness of its mission and new location. The campaign rebranded the organization, increased visitation, boosted adoptions, and educated area residents on issues like spaying/neutering by building buzz through a fun, interactive presidential election between a dog and cat. The campaign successfully repositioned the Charleston Animal Society as a positive force in the community culminating in a record number of adoptions in 2008.

SITUATION ANALYSIS

When the John Ancrum Society for the Prevention of Cruelty to Animals (JASPCA) prepared to open a new $11 million center, it faced a tough reality. Although the non-profit group had found good homes for great animals for more than a century, it was virtually unknown in the greater Charleston, S.C. community. Recognizing the new center as a landmark opportunity, Rawle Murdy volunteered to help JASPCA leadership redefine its image and raise community awareness of its mission. The ensuing pro bono campaign set out to increase visitation, boost adoptions, and educate area residents on messages like the importance of spaying/neutering.

RESEARCH

Rawle Murdy set out to uncover why pet owners historically have not turned to JASPCA. We conducted our own primary research by surveying 100 locals, conducting on-the-street interviews, and speaking with vets and pet store owners. Secondary research involved mining the Internet for historical information and local message boards for opinions, as well as reviewing JASPCA's historical data and comment cards.

This research indicated Charleston County residents barely knew the JASPCA existed. An estimated one in three locals owned a pet, but most either adopted them through rescue centers and newspaper ads or purchased them at pet stores and breeders. The few familiar with the JASPCA believed it was an old, run down, dirty "kill" shelter for diseased and unwanted animals. In fact, this non-profit has been the place for Charleston animals in need of care since 1880. No animals are turned away ... ever,—a strong point of differentiation from other local shelters. Moreover, many mistook the center as a government-funded facility when it actually depended on private donations.

PLANNING

Rawle Murdy's challenge was to create a campaign that didn't use the guilt strategies commonly employed by animal shelters nationwide to drive adoptions and donations. We worked closely with JASPCA staff to identify business goals and communication objectives that would drive the strategic campaign and effect meaningful change.

Business goals:

1. Build positive credibility
2. Boost the number of animal adoptions.
3. Educate the public on the importance of spay/neuter and other JASPCA messages.

Rawle Murdy recommended changing JASPCA's name to the much more identifiable Charleston Animal Society (CAS).

We then shook up its approach to public outreach, using humor and irreverence in messaging and collateral.

Through research we knew the target audiences were:

1. Local animal lovers who have adopted or purchased pets elsewhere, supported other organizations, were unfamiliar with JASPCA or have supported JASPCA in the past and needed to know about the upcoming name change.
2. Pet-related businesses.
3. Veterinarians.
4. Media.

The public relations objectives were to:

1. Establish consistent messaging to tell the positive story and build excitement.
2. Identify 1-2 speaking opportunities or public engagements each month where CAS could demonstrate community leadership.
3. Secure 5-7 local placements prior to and 5-7 post the new center opening.
4. Plan and execute a grand opening event.
5. Identify 5 key pet-related businesses for potential partnerships.

Rawle Murdy's awareness strategy contained four essential elements:

- Build buzz and entertain locals through a fun, interactive political campaign tapping into the current climate (S.C. was an early presidential primary state).
- Intrigue people to seek more details online.
- Stage a mock presidential election between a dog and a cat.
- Spread CAS key messages via candidates' platforms on a continuous basis instead of a one-time re-naming and center opening announcement.

Paid media and production vendors doubled our limited budget by matching the spend 2:1 across the board.

EXECUTION

In late 2007 and early 2008, the U.S. presidential candidates and primaries trans-fixed Charleston. In the midst of this chatter, we unleashed the CAS's rebranding campaign. With our tongues firmly planted in cheek (and a nod to Stephen Colbert), we offered up two additional candidates for president, Spike the dog and Biscuit the cat. These two CAS alumni—both successfully adopted into loving homes—on November 27, 2007 announced their respective candidacies for president of the newly-renamed Charleston Animal Society and its new center for animals. The intensive, four-month public relations campaign served up a political race, mimicking and spoofing storylines playing out in national headlines. Through the combination of public relations, community relations, social media, paid media, and grassroots strategies, word spread quickly.

Each candidate developed platforms (Spike: Adoption and Animal Rights. Biscuit: Healthcare and Owner Education). Weekly updates from each campaign announced key endorsements, introduced new campaign commercials and sometimes even alleged dirty tactics. They candidates made public appearances and mobilized the College of Charleston vote with a campus information booth. Political posters were displayed in more than 100 stores and restaurants, and campaign collateral hit 75 local veterinarians, kennels, groomers, and pet stores—both at the start of the campaign and again before Election Day/Grand Opening. Biscuit's spokes-human the CAS Director of Outreach garnered exposure for Biscuit's campaign on her weekly radio and TV appearances, while

Spike's spokes-human CAS Board of Directors Chairman used his influence to gain local mayoral endorsements.

Rawle Murdy supported both efforts by "scratching up" Biscuit and Spike endorsements from numerous key community leaders. The spikeVSbiscuit.org website was the hub for campaign details and information, linking to the candidates' diaries on Facebook, campaign commercials on YouTube, and to charlestonanimalsociety.org for building construction updates and campaign contributions. As word continued to build, profiles on Catster and Dogster emerged, and the weekly YouTube videos were distributed via eNewsletter, news releases, and virally. Billboards, print ads, interactive media, and radio traffic sponsorships also helped leverage the public relations effort.

The ensuing buzz was unlike any the area—and the country, it soon became clear—had seen from a non-profit marketing campaign before. Media covered the hype, community leaders took sides and citizens began donning campaign buttons. A reporter from *The New York Times*—among many outlets that covered the race was among the first to call the morning after the final poll, eager to find out who won. Rawle Murdy planned to have a third party candidate enter the race as a "dark horse" candidate, but that happened naturally when Hissy the Snake jumped in and called a local radio station. Several bunnies were write-in candidates on Election Day.

The new center for animals opened on March 8, 2008, with local leaders, elected officials, and the Charleston community pouring in to show their support and adopt pets in record numbers. A small army of Rawle Murdy and CAS volunteers hosted center tours, games, and pet fashion shows while supporters donated free refreshments.

During the grand opening ceremony, which Rawle Murdy wrote and produced, Spike was declared the winner and first ever president of the Charleston Animal Society by 86 votes, out of a total 3,780 votes. The crowed cheered when he graciously invited Biscuit to serve as vice president, and again when staff, community leaders, animals, and their guardians together pulled a giant dog toy (instead of cutting a ribbon) to officially open the new center.

EVALUATION

We measured the success of the campaign by:

1. Adoptions compared to 2007.
2. Media hits and key and the presence of key messages.
3. Social media penetration: Daily voting on website; website click throughs and page views; Facebook, Catster, and Dogster friends; YouTube viewing of candidate videos; opens on eNewsletters.
4. Fulfilling PR objectives. The entire campaign revitalized the center with an ongoing brand, successfully positioning the Charleston Animal Society as a positive force in the community.

Adoptions: CAS had record-breaking adoption numbers for the opening weekend—29 adoptions on Saturday and 13 on Sunday. CAS had 82 more adoptions in March 2008 than from the March prior. In April, that number increased to 114 more than the year before. In 2008, 4,407 animals were saved compared to 3,944 in 2007—a 12 percent increase and a 22 percent increase from 2006.

Media Hits: 38 print, radio, TV, and online media hits were secured almost three times the goal with an estimated ad equivalency value of $297,486. And more importantly, all stories included messages related to the name change, the organization's mission, the services available to the community, and the need for support.

Social Media Penetration: The spikeVSbiscuit.org pages were viewed more than 10,000 times, and traffic to the Charleston Animal Society website increased a sustained 100,000+ monthly visitors year over year, surging to more than 680,000 hits in March 2008. More than 268 people signed on as "friends" of Spike or Biscuit on their respective Facebook pages, and a "Vote for Spike!" fan group even formed. Campaign commercials posted to YouTube racked up more than 4,300 views. Over the course of the campaign, a total of 3,780 online votes were cast.

The campaign surpassed all five objectives

1. messaging/build excitement;
2. public engagements;
3. media placements;
4. grand opening event; and
5. relationships with key pet businesses.

In the ultimate compliment, the New York ASPCA, which announced Charleston as the only city in the nation to be awarded a special grant in 2008, "borrowed" the pet presidential race concept and is currently staging its own version.

EXHIBIT 6-3A   Spike versus Biscuit News Release

For Immediate Release
November 27, 2007

TWO CHARLESTON HOPEFULS ANNOUNCE CANDIDACY FOR PRESIDENT

Election '08 is predicted to be a close race

CHARLESTON, S.C. – Forget Stephen Colbert, Charlestonians now have two new candidates vying for the Presidency. In an unprecedented joint announcement today, the political opponents appeared side by side to launch their respective campaigns.

Spike the Dog, channeling the podium-pounding energy of Howard Dean, announced his desire to represent Lowcountry animals as the next president of the revitalized Charleston Animal Society (formerly known as the John Ancrum SPCA). Not to be outdone, Biscuit the Cat declared the time is right for the leadership of a strong woman president, and she will mold her presidency after her role models, Margaret Thatcher and Golda Meir.

Both candidates believe it is time for a change and feel they are the right animal for the job. Votes should be cast before March 1 online at www.spikevsbiscuit.org and the public can pick up campaign information at locations across Charleston County.

About the Candidates:

Spike the Dog, a Charleston Animal Society success story, has defined his platform by claiming to be the "dog's dog." **The cornerstones of his campaign are adoption and equal animal rights.** "Since his adoption by a West Ashley family, Spike truly understands the power of adoption," said his spokesperson Charlie Karesh. "And, he really believes in the importance of welcoming *all* animals—dog, cat, horse, bunny, bird or lizard—at the Charleston Animal Society."

Spike's campaign stances are tied closely together, as he strongly feels that every great animal, regardless of type, deserves proper care and the opportunity to find a great home.

Presidential Hopefuls
1st Add

Spike, a Boxer mix, was rescued from a back alley off Savannah Highway and taken to the Charleston Animal Society. Soon afterwards, he was adopted by a loving family in West Ashley, who whole-heartedly supports his candidacy. When he isn't on the campaign trail he's living a happy, healthy life as their family pet.

Biscuit the Cat brings feline sensibility and strong leadership to the Charleston Animal Society (CAS). **Biscuit has shaped her campaign around two key issues: education and health care.** "Biscuit knows the future of animals in the Lowcountry begins with the education of our children. When children know more about animals and how to care for them, it builds a strong foundation for a lifetime," said campaign spokesperson, Kay Hyman. "Biscuit's been a big proponent for the multi-purpose space for public education at the Charleston Animal Society's new center for animals."

From first-hand experience, Biscuit understands the need for quality health care for the Lowcountry's animals and is an advocate for the new facility's advanced surgical suites and spay/neuter clinic. Biscuit was discovered by a delivery man behind a grocery store and he brought her to the Charleston Animal Society. Her outgoing personality has made her a favorite at the Charleston Animal Society and although she will be missed, Biscuit is available for permanent adoption.

There are rumors circulating about a third hopeful for president—a dark horse candidate—but a representative could not be reached for comment.

Presidential Hopefuls
2nd Add

About Election 2008

The 2008 Election opens with the announcement of the organization's new name: **The Charleston Animal Society.** Formerly known as the JASPCA (John Ancrum Society for the Prevention of Cruelty to Animals), the Charleston Animal Society now has a name that more accurately reflects the organization's mission to protect, save and find good homes for great animals in the Lowcountry every day.

The Charleston community can vote for president of the Charleston Animal Society online at www.spikevsbiscuit.org. "Polling" locations will include campaign information at local pet stores, businesses and veterinary offices across the Lowcountry. Voting officially opens on December 1 and the campaigns will kick-off at the Charleston Animal Society's Annual Celebrity Chili Cook-Off and will close on March 1, the day the new center opens. There is no age requirement to vote and voters do not have to currently own a pet.

About the New Center

In addition to the new name, Charleston's leading animal organization will also have a new space opening March 2008. The new center for animals is more than double the size of the previous main facility on Leeds Avenue. The new space, conveniently located in North Charleston on Remount Road near the airport and I-26, will have climate-controlled rooms, natural light, 140 cat kennels, 162 dog kennels, a small animal room, large outdoor play and exercise areas, surgical suites, a spay/neuter clinic, getacquainted rooms, and multi-purpose meeting and education spaces.

About the Charleston Animal Society

The Charleston Animal Society was founded in 1880 and is the Lowcountry's leading not-for-profit animal protection and welfare organization. Soon to be located in a new, 33,000-square-foot, state-of-the-art center near the intersection of Highways I-26 and 526, the Charleston Animal Society is dedicated to protecting, saving and finding good homes for all animals in the Lowcountry. For more information or to make a donation, visit www.charlestonanimalsociety.org.

###

Media Contacts:
Ashley Bedford Weckback
Rawle Murdy—452.6925; abedford@rawlemurdy.com

Claire Gibbons
Rawle Murdy—577.7327; cgibbons@rawlemurdy.com

Courtesy Charleston Animal Society and Rawle Murdy

EXHIBIT 6-3B   **Promotional Poster**

Courtesy Charleston Animal Society and Rawle Murdy

E X H I B I T 6-3C **Facebook Page**

Courtesy Charleston Animal Society and Rawle Murdy

7

Public Affairs and
Government Relations

M any U.S. corporations have subsumed what was formerly known as government relations within the broader enterprise now called public affairs. To add
further semantic confusion, the U.S. government in the early 1980s decreed that the
term public affairs would replace public information in all its departments and
agencies.

Our principal concern here will be with how the enactment of legislation is
influenced and the influence of the public policy process. This process includes the
creation of political coalitions, direct and indirect lobbying, political action and
political education activities, communication on political issues, and political support activities.

RESEARCH

The research process of public affairs includes investigation of the practitioner's
client or organization, the opportunity or problem that accounts for the need for
communication—including the important area of issues management—and the
audiences to be targeted for public affairs programs.

Client Research

Client research for public affairs starts with background information about the client or
organization, including its personnel, financial status, and reputation, especially with
government and community audiences. The practitioner should pay particular
attention to past and present relations with the government and the community, along
with any particular client strengths or weaknesses in these areas, such as identifying

extremely credible and trusted voices within the organization or its friends. Finally, the practitioner should catalog all opportunities for profitable communication with government or community audiences.

Opportunity or Problem Research

In public affairs programs, the process of issues management can help with identification of opportunities or challenges. *Issues management* consists of listing and giving priority to all issues of interest to the client and then determining options and strategies for dealing with them. This process includes assessing political risks and monitoring social and political developments of concern to the client at the local, state, national, and international levels. An examination of each of these areas on a priority basis is a useful means of targeting the client's public affairs program.

Audience Research

The final aspect of research for public affairs consists of identifying target audiences, the necessary data regarding each one, and the methods of research necessary to obtain this information.

Public affairs programs target three audiences: community publics, government, and ancillary publics—this last group consisting of client allies, constituents of legislators, and media that reach both of them. Community publics were examined in the preceding chapter (see Exhibit 6-a). Government publics can be considered at the federal, state, county, or city level; they and the ancillary publics are listed in Exhibit 7-a.

Data necessary for understanding members of the legislative branches of government include officials' voting records on issues of concern to the client; their general attitudes or past and present reactions to the client; the size, location, and general demographics of their voting constituencies; their committee assignments; and their general interests and areas of expertise. Government officials in the executive branch may or may not hold elective office; this is their single most important characteristic. Beyond that, the nature and authority of the offices they hold, along with as much background about them as possible, should prove helpful. For example, a senior official in a state department of environmental protection may be a key player in the legislative process for environmental policy. For officials in both legislative and executive positions, of course, the highest priority information about them is their degree of involvement with each issue or piece of legislation affecting the client, along with their stand, and how they are expected to vote. Officials often rely on key staff and advice from leaders in organizations specializing in public policy issues, to include coalitions of activist groups. It is valuable to determine who has the ear of a representative or government official, and to analyze what values underlie their advice.

Methods of gathering information about government officials are usually nonquantitative. Voting records or accomplishments are public knowledge and easily accessible. Beyond that, conducting surveys among officials is usually not feasible. Thus, the practitioner must rely on other sources of information, such as conversations with staff people, the officials' past behavior, and their public statements regarding issues of concern to the client.

E X H I B I T 7-a   Government and Ancillary Publics

Government Publics

   Federal

      Legislative branch

         Representatives, staff, and committee personnel

         Senators, staff, and committee personnel

         Executive branch

         President

         White House staff, advisers, and committees

         Cabinet officers, departments, agencies, and commissions

   State

      Legislative branch

         Representatives, delegates, staff, and committee personnel

         Senators, staff, and committee personnel

         Executive branch

         Governor

         Governor's staff, advisers, and committees

         Cabinet officers, departments, agencies, and commissions

   County

      County executive

      Other county officials, commissioners, and departments

   City

      Mayor or city manager

      City council

      Other city officials, commissions, and departments

   Ancillary Publics

   Allies

   Think tanks

   National/local public policy activist groups

   Constituents of legislators

   Media

      Mass media

      Specialized media

      Trade publications

   Allied organizations' publications

   Constituent media

Research on the ancillary publics listed in Exhibit 7-a is also of considerable value. Allies of the client must be identified and cultivated with the goal of building a coalition. Coalitions frequently bring both real and perceived strength to issue advocacy. The home districts, communities, and constituents of legislators must also be identified and studied. Old friends, business or professional partners, and local civic leaders are trusted sources of grassroots information for a legislator. Government leaders maintain close connections with their constituents to capture a sense of local concerns. They monitor local media in their district to gain a pulse on the body politic. Try to monitor these same sources. Finally, mass and specialized media for reaching constituents and client allies should be identified, and media contacts lists should be prepared, as discussed in Chapter 3.

OBJECTIVES

As in other forms of public relations, objectives for public affairs programs should be specific and quantitative.

Impact Objectives

A sampling of impact objectives for public affairs includes such statements as:

1. To increase knowledge of the client's current activities and field of operations among legislators (by 50 percent during the current year)
2. To create or enhance favorable attitudes toward the client's new initiative among officials (by 30 percent before the February vote)
3. To influence a favorable vote on a bill (by 30 members of the House of Representatives during the current session).

Output Objectives

Output objectives represent the effort of the practitioner without reference to potential audience impact. Such objectives might use such statements as:

1. To make oral presentations to 30 lawmakers
2. To distribute issue papers to 45 lawmakers.

PROGRAMMING

Public affairs programming includes the same four planning and execution elements used in other forms of public relations: (1) theme and messages, (2) action(s) or special event(s), (3) uncontrolled and controlled media, and (4) principles of effective communication.

Theme and Messages

Always be aware that government audiences may be the most knowledgeable and sophisticated of all audiences for public relations communication. For this reason, the use of catchy themes or slogans may not be helpful; at times, they can even be counterproductive, yet the framing of issues with precise language and values will be appreciated. When addressing public affairs programming to ancillary audiences, however, more traditional use of themes or slogans may be appropriate. Messages, of course, should be carefully coordinated with the program objectives and actions or special events. To be most effective, conduct appropriate research on the working of your themes and messages.

Action(s) or Special Event(s)

Public affairs programming, like other forms of public relations, is structured around actions and special events. The practitioner should review the types found in Exhibit 2-c. The actions unique to public affairs programming are:

1. Fact-finding
2. Coalition building
3. Direct lobbying
4. Grassroots activities (indirect lobbying)
5. Political action committees
6. Political education activities
7. Communications on political issues
8. Political support activities.

Fact-finding.   Information gathering is an important aspect of public affairs. It includes attendance at openly conducted hearings, generally scheduled by both the legislative and the executive branches of government when considering legislation or regulations. This monitoring function is indispensable for all public affairs programs.

In addition to monitoring hearings, fact-finding often includes exchanging information with government officials, representatives of trade associations or interest groups, and other sources of reliable data. Fact-finding may also include participation in social events attended by legislators where the atmosphere may be conducive to an informal exchanging of information.

A final aspect of fact-finding is the reporting of data and findings to the client, along with recommendations for appropriate communication actions.

Coalition Building.   It is useful to organize groups or individuals with a common interest in the passage or defeat of legislation or regulations. Such coalitions can be much more effective in attaining goals than groups or individuals working alone. The power of a coalition is often based on the "perceived" cohesiveness and political clout of the group. Some coalitions will claim a large number of members to enhance the credibility of the organization, even though many members may actually be relatively small local activist organizations. Coalitions can pool such resources as staff time, legal help, and printing and mailing costs. Working together, they can set priorities and devise operational strategies more effectively. The use of social media offers additional venues for building coalitions. In brief, the building of coalitions is one of the most important and effective tactics in public affairs.

Direct Lobbying.   The two "core" activities of public affairs are direct and indirect lobbying. In direct lobbying, the practitioner contacts legislators or officials who can influence the passage or defeat of a bill or proposed regulation. It is an overt advocacy process, although it takes the sometimes subtle forms of information exchange and hospitality.

Information exchange includes providing the lawmaker or official with data about the client's field of interest and the effect the proposed legislation or regulation would have on this field. The practitioner, or lobbyist, usually makes an authoritative oral presentation, including the publicity potential for the legislator or official and the potential interest or impact of the proposals on constituents. These two aspects—*publicity value* and *constituent interest*—strike the most responsive chords in the ears of legislators or officials. They should always be central to a public affairs presentation. In addition to presentations, the practitioner usually offers the official a sample draft of the proposed legislation or regulation that incorporates the views of the client. Position and background papers are a staple of information exchange. Some organizations also host informational sessions for legislators and staff members to meet with subject area experts on an issue.

Finally, information exchange may include providing authoritative testimony or offering witnesses for the hearings that are usually held in conjunction with proposed legislation or regulations. The practitioner often writes the testimony that is usually given by the client or the chief executive officer of the client's organization.

The second form of direct lobbying is still more subtle than information exchange. It involves offering *hospitality* to the legislator or the agency official. However, in an era of increased transparency and "sunshine laws," legislators and agency officials are sensitive to the potential for media news stories about untoward political influence by moneyed interests or wrongdoing in high places. Nonetheless, hospitality still plays an important role in public affairs or, more particularly, in lobbying. Lawmakers and agency officials often accept invitations to social functions sponsored by influential associations or corporations. Personal relationships are still the realm of many political decisions and face-to-face exchanges work well in convincing an official of the merits of your initiative.

These social gatherings provide a relaxed and conducive atmosphere for the subtle conduct of the business of public affairs.

Now, more often than not, the legislator provides the hospitality in the form of thousand-dollar-a-plate breakfasts, lunches, dinners, or other special events at which the corporation, association, or union representatives pay or make large contributions to attend, and thus gain access to the lawmaker.

Access is a major goal of all lobbying, and to an increasing degree, hospitality events—usually linked to fund-raising for the legislator—have become the most used avenue for reaching this goal.

Grassroots Activities (Indirect Lobbying).   Indirect lobbying, or grassroots activities, is the second of the two core aspects of public affairs. This form of indirect lobbying involves mobilizing support for or opposition to proposed legislation or regulations at the state or local level, especially in the home districts of elected legislators. In the case of government departments or agencies, this grassroots level may be the location where a large agency is considering constructing or closing an installation that will profoundly affect the local economy.

Grassroots activities include working with national, state, or local media; the use of interpersonal communication; and the orchestration of campaigns to bring constituent pressure on legislators or officials.

The grassroots use of the mass media includes publicizing the client's position in national, state, or local media, demonstrating that this position will be beneficial to the media audience. This action is usually performed in cases where an elected official is in opposition to the client's position or is uncommitted. The practitioner, on behalf of the client, will use all feasible forms of media, including paid advertising, to generate news coverage about the situation. If the legislator has taken a stand contrary to that of the client's, the media messages will call attention to that, to voting records, and to the harm such a position will bring to the constituency. A second effective type of grassroots activity is the use of various forms of interpersonal communication at the national, state, or local level. This includes targeting key groups of opinion leaders in the home districts of legislators and getting expert and highly credible representatives of the client's viewpoint invited to their meetings, conferences, or conventions as guest speakers.

In addition to addressing important grassroots audiences, the client can meet with key executives at breakfast, with editorial staffs of newspapers, or with small groups of community leaders. Dyadic interactions may include interviews and meetings with key public officials, executives, and/or union leaders.

Interpersonal communication, then, in the form of speeches, small group meetings, or dyadic interactions can be a highly useful form of grassroots activity. When organizations host annual conventions in Washington, they arrange short meetings between legislators and association members who are constituents. The constituents arrive with specific talking points related to the organization's public policy agenda.

Finally, grassroots activities culminate in the orchestration of campaigns at the national, state, or local level designed to bring pressure from constituents directly on legislators or officials. These campaigns can be orchestrated by small or large membership groups, associations, or other affected groups. They may take the traditional form of organized letter writing to a legislator from home district constituents; or they may use more contemporary forms, such as email, faxing, social media posts or telephone calls to activate public response. The "telephone tree" consists of groups of constituents who each may call 5 to 10 friends, who in turn each call 5 to 10 more friends, and so on, all of whom then call or otherwise communicate with the office of the lawmaker with a common request or purpose. Viral emails have the same intent.

The National Rifle Association (NRA) is a membership group that uses all of these forms of constituent communication effectively to influence the course of national legislation. The NRA boasts the ability to mobilize its membership within 24 hours to flood Congress with enough constituent communication to shape the course of gun legislation.

Of the two public affairs core methods, grassroots activities usually prove more effective. These actions—working with mass media, interpersonal communication, and constituent communication campaigns—can provide legislators and other officials with unmistakable evidence regarding the will of the electorate.

Political Action Committees.   Political action committees (PACs) are groups established for the purpose of contributing an organization's money toward the election of political candidates. The Federal Election Commission (FEC) permits PACs to contribute a maximum amount per candidate per election. FEC limits are indexed for inflation and adjusted for every election cycle.

Since their inception in the mid-1970s, PACs have enjoyed phenomenal growth. Each year PACs provide funds to several thousand candidates for federal office. Such money may be solicited (but not coerced) from an organization's employees. Large groups, such as the banking and finance industry, labor unions, and the insurance industry, have the resources of hundreds of PACs at their disposal. Of course, PAC money can be used collectively for candidates who support legislation favorable to an entire industry.

The use of such funds to support the campaigns of elected officials guarantees access to those officials. Thus, PACs have become a significant force in public affairs.

Political Education Activities.   Organizations may also attempt to politicize their employees. They issue newsletters on the major political issues confronting given industries along with the company's positions on these issues. Employees and members may be instructed in the methods of grassroots lobbying: emailing or writing letters to legislators, taking action through membership groups, or visiting legislators in their home district offices. Moreover, some large organizations provide their employees with political education seminars. Elected officials and candidates are invited to corporate facilities, where they make presentations and meet groups of employees. In return, the officials are often given honoraria, usually in accordance with legally allowable limitations. Political education activities, then, play an increasingly important role in the conduct of public affairs programs.

Communications on Political Issues.   Organizations communicate on political issues chiefly through advocacy advertising and targeted communications, such as direct mail to community leaders or special audiences or promoting issues on social media pages.

Advocacy advertising has become increasingly popular since the early 1970s, when Herbert Schmertz, vice president for public affairs of Exxon Mobil, decided that major media outlets seemed interested only in condemning large oil companies for their alleged role in the creation of the gasoline shortages of the day. Schmertz abandoned the use of news releases and other uncontrolled media to give the oil companies' side of the controversy. Instead, he began to buy advocacy advertising space in the nation's most prestigious newspapers and later bought time on cooperative broadcast networks. Schmertz's success in calling attention to his corporation's political views gave rise to a boom in the corporate use of advocacy advertising. Expect to see advocacy ads not only in national newspapers such as the *Washington Post* with its political emphasis in the Capital, but in the local newspaper of a legislator who is the target of a campaign.

Their proliferation has probably diminished their effectiveness, but they remain a major vehicle for corporate communication on political issues.

Political communications can also be aimed at community leaders or occupational groups. Professors of communication, for example, are frequently the recipients of reprints of speeches by the chief executive officers of television networks and other corporations. A Twitter feed may promote a link to a recent news story that slants an issue in favor of an issue advocacy group. These reprints and online connections are but a few ways to engage with community leaders and members of various professions.

Political Support Activities. A final public affairs action is the support a corporation, association, or other organization offers an incumbent legislator or a candidate. Some organizations offer free media training. Another association provides technical expertise on an issue. Some organizations provide volunteers to work on political campaigns. Additionally, political support can be offered in the form of expertise and other services needed for orchestrating election campaign events such as fund-raisers and testimonial dinners. Donations of facilities, recruiting celebrities to appear at the events, and any number of other services can be offered.

Like other forms of public affairs activities, political support can ensure access to the officeholder at a later time.

Another form of political support called "soft money" became the hottest—and most controversial—form of lobbying in the 1990s. Corporations and individuals were allowed to give unlimited amounts of money to national political parties for voter registration, television advertising, get-out-the-vote campaigns, and other party activities. This unlimited "soft money" could be contributed to support the party, but not specific candidates. Federal legislation passed in 2002, however, now prohibits corporations, unions, and individuals from giving unlimited contributions to national political parties. But this ban on "soft money" does not apply to independent groups or PACs. They are free to raise as much money as corporations, unions, or individuals will give them. They can spend unlimited sums of money to influence federal elections as long as they operate independently of election campaigns, stop short of calling for a specific candidate's election or defeat, and stop airing advertising within 30 days of a primary election and 60 days of a general election.

To counter the flow of this "soft money," the 2002 Bipartisan Campaign Reform Act limited the flow of large contributions to the political parties, but groups soon exploited Section 527 of the Internal Revenue Code, which had been added in 1974 to allow tax-exempt contributions for political activities, including voter mobilization efforts and issue advocacy. The 527 groups claimed to rely on grassroots efforts by small donors to encourage civic engagement, yet one study found the biggest 527s got 44 percent of their contributions from just 25 deep-pocket donors. During the 2004 political campaigns, MoveOn.org and the Swift

Boat Veterans for Truth were some of the most visible and passionate in activating political engagement; however, neither was in the top 5 among all 527 groups that raised an estimated $550 million to influence the political process. Each election cycle reveals major donations by other groups. During the 2008 campaign, U.S. Senators Barack Obama and John McCain expressed concern about the role of these independent groups in presidential campaigns and urged their donors to not support these groups. "Hard money" contributions to candidates for federal office continue to be strictly limited by the Federal Election Committee. However, with increasingly close relationships between candidates, especially incumbents, and PACs, it is likely that multimillion-dollar contributions of "soft money" to PACs will become the most certain of all paths to officeholder access.

Uncontrolled and Controlled Media

The practitioner's communication with public officials must largely be direct and interpersonal. The lobbyist or practitioner of public affairs uses uncontrolled media at the grassroots level by working with the media to place news stories favorable to their approach to an issue. However, all forms of controlled media can be used both in direct contact with lawmakers and in grassroots communication with constituents. In general, then, the uniqueness of public affairs communication lies in the interaction that occurs directly with lawmakers and officials. To be effective, it should emphasize interpersonal, preferably one-on-one, communication.

Effective Communication

The communication flow in public affairs is best described as triangular (see Exhibit 6-b). The flow is targeted ultimately at lawmakers, in the legislative branch, or at regulation-makers, in the executive branch. Thus, communication is generally initiated from the private sector and flows appropriately toward those two targets. In many cases, however, communication is initiated in the executive branch. Presidents, governors, and mayors may lobby their respective legislative branches for the passage or defeat of a law. Sometimes officials in the executive branch lobby a particular audience in the private sector to bring pressure on the legislative branch. Legislators often refer to this as "going over their heads to the people." Some U.S. presidents have been particularly fond of this form of lobbying.

The nine principles of effective communication discussed in Chapter 2 all apply in public affairs. Of special concern, however, is *selective exposure*. Public affairs, more than other forms of public relations, deals with legislation and regulations that are controversial. Therefore, it is important that the practitioner categorize the targeted receivers based on their agreement or disagreement with the public affairs messages. As suggested in Chapter 2, the terms that coincide with the Likert scale can be useful in this process. Thus, targeted legislators or other officials should be rated as "positives," "somewhat positives," "undecideds," "somewhat negatives," or "negatives." The selective exposure principle is applicable in this situation. The practitioner should thus begin persuasive efforts with the positives. Next to be targeted are the somewhat positives, then the undecideds, and last, if at all, the somewhat negatives. The pure negatives

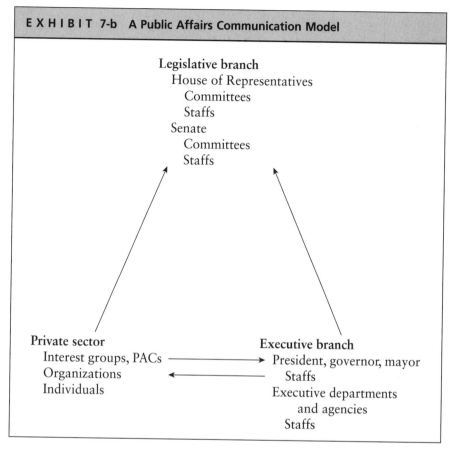

EXHIBIT 7-b   A Public Affairs Communication Model

Legislative branch
House of Representatives
Committees
Staffs
Senate
Committees
Staffs

Private sector
Interest groups, PACs
Organizations
Individuals

Executive branch
President, governor, mayor
Staffs
Executive departments
and agencies
Staffs

have hardened attitudes against the practitioner's cause and should not be targeted for communication. To communicate with those strongly opposed to the message is usually counterproductive; it simply makes them more determined and sometimes more active in their opposition.

Thus, the selective exposure principle of effective communication bears reiteration because of its special significance in public affairs. It is not necessary to convince everyone, just a few key votes that will swing the outcome. During presidential elections, selective exposure largely explains how some areas of the country seldom saw a political advertisement while other "swing states" were bombarded with thousands of ads and a flood of direct mail appeals. The campaigns know that trying to influence some electorates isn't worth the effort.

All other principles of effective communication should also be observed. Each one can contribute to the success of public affairs programs.

EVALUATION

In public affairs, the measurement of impact and output objectives is somewhat different from the general methods of assessment presented in Chapter 2.

Evaluating Impact Objectives

There are two differences in the measurement of impact objectives for public affairs. First, message exposure, message comprehension, and message retention are not measured in the same way. The primary target audiences for public affairs are legislators and officials. The media, however, are used essentially to reach the *constituents* of these public officials. And though the officials themselves are usually media sensitive, message exposure in public affairs usually refers to *constituent* exposure.

The second difference in the measurement of impact objectives is that surveys or other quantitative methods of research cannot be used with the primary target audiences because legislators and officials will not usually take the time to respond to such PR surveys. Thus, nonquantitative measurements of message exposure and message retention are used in assessing the results of informational objectives.

Message comprehension, of course, can be measured, as usual, by the application of readability formulas. This will give the practitioner an indication of the *potential* for comprehension, not actual audience comprehension, which can be measured using nonquantitative research methods.

These same generalizations are applicable to attitude and behavioral objectives. Surveys among the primary audience are generally impossible, so the practitioner must rely on the nonquantitative research methods discussed earlier in this chapter— voting records or accomplishments, conversations, use of the practitioner's materials, and public statements by the targeted legislators or officials. At the grassroots level, of course, surveys are useful and should be employed to evaluate the impact objectives.

Evaluating Output Objectives

The practitioner needs to evaluate both forms of public affairs objectives. Output objectives can be measured through counting presentations and materials and through making qualitative value judgments. Having three personal meetings with a legislator and the member's key staff would be such a measure.

Evaluation of public affairs, then, ultimately focuses on observing the voting behavior or actions of legislators and other public officials. The practitioners in this chapter's cases accomplished all of their stated objectives remarkably well. In addition to informing their various targeted audiences, they also met their legislative or regulatory goals.

SUMMARY

Research for public affairs concentrates on problem assessment through issues management and on identifying and understanding target audiences. Audiences are usually in the legislative or executive branch of government, at various levels. Information about these officials consists of voting records, accomplishments, and public stands on issues.

Impact and output objectives are both useful in public affairs. Impact objectives consist of providing the target audience with information or influencing its attitudes or behavior, in this case, voting behavior. Output objectives catalog the practitioner's communication efforts without reference to the desired impact.

The most essential activities in public affairs programming are fact-finding, coalition building, direct lobbying, grassroots (indirect) lobbying, the use of PACs, political education, communications on political issues, and political support activities. Of special significance in lobbying is the principle of selective exposure. Lawmakers to be lobbied should be categorized as "positives," "somewhat positives," "undecideds," "somewhat negatives," or "negatives." The positives through the undecideds should be targeted for lobbying; the somewhat negatives should be targeted with caution, and the negatives, not at all.

Evaluation is not the same for public affairs as for other forms of public relations. Media exposure or placement does not ensure contact with legislators, and legislators and officials are often unresponsive to PR surveys. Nonquantitative measurements of impact objectives are thus more useful. Output objectives, of course, are measured by the same means as usual—observation and quantification. The ultimate means of evaluation in public affairs, however, is the voting behavior of the target audience.

READINGS ON PUBLIC AFFAIRS

"The Advocacy Book: Directory of Public Affairs & Grassroots Lobbying Firms," *Campaigns & Elections* 26 (2005): 84–95.

Alexander, Robert M. *Rolling the Dice with State Initiatives: Interest Group Involvement in Ballot Campaigns.* Westport, CT: Praeger, 2002.

Amidei, Nancy. *So You Want To Make a Difference?* Seattle, WA: CreateSpace, 2010.

Beaubien, Greg. "Grassroots Campaigns Need Social Media to Succeed," *Public Relations Strategist* 16.3 (Summer 2010): 4.

Brown, Clyde, and Herbert Waltzer. "Organized Interest Advertorials," *Harvard International Journal of Press/Politics* 9 (Fall 2004): 25–48.

Cigler, Allan J., and Burdett A. Loomis. *Interest Group Politics,* 7th ed. Washington, DC: Congressional Quarterly, 2007.

Cook-Anderson, Gretchen. "Effectively Winning over Young Voters," *Public Relations Tactics* 11 (July 2004): 12.

Goldstein, Kenneth M. *Interest Groups, Lobbying and Participation in America.* Port Chester, NY: Cambridge University Press, 1999.

Graziano, Luigi. *Lobbying, Pluralism, and Democracy.* New York: Palgrave, 2001.

Grefe, Edward A., and Martin Linsky. *The New Corporate Activism: Harnessing the Power of Grassroots Tactics for Your Organization.* New York: McGraw-Hill, 1996.

Grossman, Gene M., and Elhanan Helpman. *Special Interest Politics.* Cambridge, MA: MIT, 2001.

Guyer, Robert L. *Guide to State Legislative Lobbying.* Gainesville, FL: Engineering THE LAW, 2003.

Hallahn, Kirk. "Inactive Publics: The Forgotten Publics in Public Relations," *Public Relations Review* 26 (Winter 2000): 499.

Harris, Phil, and Craig S Fleisher, eds. *Handbook of Public Affairs.* London: Sage Publications, 2005.

Heath, Robert L. (ed), and Michael James Palenchar (ed). *Strategic Issue Management: Organizations and Public Policy Challenges,* 2d. Thousand Oaks, CA: Sage Publications, 2009.

Kaid, Lynda Lee, ed. *Handbook of Political Communication Research.* Mahwah, NJ: Erlbaum, 2004.

Kramer, Tony, and Wes Pedersen, eds. *Winning at the Grassroots: A Comprehensive Manual for Corporations and Associations*. Washington, DC: Public Affairs Council, 2000.

Ledingham, John A. "Government-Community Relationships: Extending the Relational Theory of Public Relations," *Public Relations Review* 27 (Fall 2001): 285.

Lerbinger, Otto. *Corporate Public Affairs: Interacting With Interest Groups, Media, and Government*. Mahwah, NJ: Erlbaum, 2005.

Levin, David. "Framing Peace Policies: The Competition for Resonant Themes," *Political Communication* 22 (January–March 2005): 83–108.

Murray, Bobbi. "Money for Nothing," *The Nation* 277 (September 8, 2003): 25.

Ortega, Felix. "Politics in the New Public Space," *International Review of Sociology* 14 (July 2004): 205–207.

Pinkham, Doug. "What it Takes to Work in Public Affairs and Public Relations," *Public Relations Quarterly* 49 (Spring 2004): 15ff.

Richards, Barry. "The Emotional Deficit in Political Communication," *Political Communication* 21 (July–September 2004): 339–352.

Seltzer, Trent and Weiwu Zhang. "Toward a Model of Political Organization–Public Relationships: Antecedent and Cultivation Strategy Influence on Citizens' Relationships with Political Parties" *Journal of Public Relations Research* 23 (2011): 24–45.

Solomon, Dan. "Getting Involved: Health Care Reform in a Web 2.0 World," *Public Relations Tactics* 15 (March 2008): 14.

Smith, Catherine F. *Writing Public Policy*. New York: Oxford. 2010.

Taibbi, Matt, "Four Amendments and a Funeral." *Rolling Stone Magazine*. August 25, 2005.

Thomson, Stuart, Steve John, and George J. Mitchell. *Public Affairs in Practice: A Practical Guide to Lobbying*. London: Kogan Page. 2007.

Traub, James. "The Statesman, Why and How, Bono Matters," *New York Times Magazine* (September 18, 2005).

Trento, Susan. *Power House: Robert Keith Gray and the Selling of Access and Influence in Washington*. New York: St. Martins Press, 1992.

Ward, Hugh. "Pressure Politics: A Game-Theoretical Investigation of Lobbying and the Measurement of Power," *Journal of Theoretical Politics* 16 (January 2004): 31–52.

Public Affairs and Government Relations Cases

Case 7-1

Public policy agendas are often shaped by distant forces, especially when an event quickly starts to affect people's pocket books as well the overall welfare of the economy. Managing a campaign may require raising awareness about an issue and then mobilizing political action to correct a problem. Exhibit 7-1A is campaign news release calling for "action", Exhibit 7-1B is a print advertisement for the campaign, and Exhibit 7-1C is an open letter to airline customers.

Stop Oil Speculation Now
Air Transport Association with Xenophon Strategies

BACKGROUND

In June 2008, the U.S. airline industry was in crisis. Record-high fuel prices endangered the industry's future. Economic analysis indicated that unregulated speculation added as much as $30 to $60 to a barrel of oil. Airlines were desperate to reduce these costs. Unfortunately, neither Congress nor the American public was knowledgeable about speculation or the lack of transparency in the complex commodities futures markets. The Air Transport Association (ATA), the premier trade group of the principal U.S. airlines, enlisted Xenophon Strategies and 720 Strategies to develop a public affairs campaign to help lower fuel prices. ATA hoped to accomplish this by exposing unregulated oil speculation and influencing the Congressional energy debate. Two weeks of intense strategic planning resulted in the creation of a multi-industry campaign called Stop Oil Speculation Now (SOS Now), which consisted of 85 businesses, associations, and labor groups united in support of lower energy prices. The coalition included representatives from agriculture, aviation, trucking, mass transit, travel, and energy industries. The coalition used multiple communications components including earned media, coalition building, Web outreach, and grassroots advocacy to reach its target audiences. By August, more than 50 percent of Americans blamed speculators for the energy crisis, up from only six percent in May, according to a Gallup poll.

Courtesy Air Transportation Association and Xenophon Strategies

This public outrage helped pop the oil price bubble, saving coalition members billions of dollars in fuel, and reducing pump prices nationwide.

RESEARCH

The price of oil nearly tripled between January 2007 and June 2008. Never before had oil prices increased so quickly. Economists testified that speculative investors poured billions into the commodities markets in 2008, wildly inflating the cost of oil. Many financial experts predicted oil prices would reach $200 a barrel before the year ended. The airline industry expected to lose as much as $15 billion in 2008 as a result. By June, the crisis had forced nine airlines into bankruptcy, caused 14,000 layoffs, and eliminated air service to nearly 90 communities. According to an independent Gallup poll conducted in May, only six percent of Americans blamed speculators for high oil prices. ATA believed Congress would not focus on this issue without increased constituent awareness.

PLANNING

In June, ATA worked with Xenophon Strategies and 720 Strategies to design an intense, short-term campaign with a limited budget to influence public policy on oil market speculation as quickly as possible. To multiply the campaign's impact, ATA united with other organizations to build a multi-industry coalition. The coalition developed an aggressive outreach program to capture the public's attention through media and grassroots advocacy. The goal of the campaign was to help reduce oil prices by influencing the Congressional energy debate and shining sunlight on the issue of unregulated oil speculation.

EXECUTION

The SOS Now coalition used public affairs tactics to influence public policy. This included media relations, grassroots engagement, digital outreach, opinion polling, and coalition building. These tactics resulted in constant media attention, public outcry, and Congressional action. Concerned citizens sent 1.64 million advocacy emails to members of Congress through the SOS Now website. Every national news network reported on the campaign, while coalition-influenced articles and editorials prominently ran in targeted outlets including the Associated Press, *Wall Street Journal*, *New York Times*, *Washington Post*, *USA Today*, *Politico*, Reuters, and Bloomberg. Wire articles mentioning the coalition ran in at least 650 media outlets nationwide.

Highlights of the Campaign Included:

- Coalition Building: ATA recruited 85 organizations to the SOS Now coalition from a wide variety of industries including agriculture, aviation, trucking, mass transit, travel, and energy.

- OS Now website: The coalition designed a website with easy-to-understand information on speculation. The website included an electronic newsletter sign-up, a function for emailing Congressional representatives, Spanish-language accessibility, a link to the SOS Now Facebook group, links to relevant news stories, a compilation of third-party quotes, and a posting function allowing people to "share their story" on high energy prices.

- Airline Frequent Flyer Call to Action: The SOS Now campaign launched with an open letter to airline customers signed by 12 CEOs, an unprecedented feat. Airlines used the letter to deliver unified messages on speculation to millions of frequent flyers by email.

This was the first and only time that airlines jointly emailed an industry-wide message to frequent flyers. The email generated widespread news media response and grassroots communications to Congress. The airlines continued advocating to frequent-flyers by including oil-speculation columns in their in-flight magazines and by linking to www.StopOilSpeculationNow.com from their websites.

- Grassroots Advocacy: The coalition delivered informational and advocacy emails to concerned citizens, which resulted in grassroots supporters sending 1.64 million emails to Congressional representatives through the SOS Now website, and turning out hundreds of supporters to attend local congressional town hall meetings during the August recess. These communications resulted in blog postings as well as social media groups on sites such as Facebook, Twitter, and LinkedIn. The coalition provided "Web stickers" for activists and coalition members to post on their websites, which increased links and traffic to the SOS Now site. This grassroots advocacy helped pressure Congressional representatives to take action against speculation.

- Coalition Media Toolkit: The coalition designed a media/grassroots toolkit to help coalition members understand the complex issues surrounding commodities trading. Coalition members used the toolkit for media relations and employee advocacy. The toolkit helped multiple, diverse industries deliver consistent messaging to target audiences.

- Coalition Press Conference: The coalition held a press conference announcing solutions for reducing oil prices. Four spokespersons discussed how energy prices affected their industries, while renowned commodities analyst Michael Masters announced proposals for stopping speculation. Broadcast and print media widely covered the press conference, resulting in an influential *Wall Street Journal* article that defined the issue in future media coverage.

- Public Opinion Poll: The coalition conducted a national opinion poll on oil speculation that showed Americans were supportive of the campaign. The coalition used the results for earned media and Congressional outreach.

- Congressional Information Packets: The coalition provided informational packets to members of Congress including district-specific news articles and testimonials from constituents protesting high energy costs.

EVALUATION

The public exposure of unregulated oil market speculation helped energy costs quickly return to normal levels—even before the financial crisis began. The threat of regulatory action resulted in investors pulling $39 billion out of the commodities markets during the first seven weeks of the campaign, which reduced oil prices by 35 percent.

Financial experts predict U.S. airlines might return to profitability in 2009 as a result of lower fuel costs. The SOS Now campaign gained considerable media, grassroots, and political traction. An independent Gallup poll conducted five weeks into the campaign showed more than 50 percent of Americans believed speculation contributed to high oil prices. This was a significant jump from before the campaign when only six percent of Americans blamed speculators for high fuel prices, according to a Gallup poll. Members of Congress repeated SOS Now messages during floor debate and the U.S. House passed anti-speculation legislation with 283 votes. A similar Senate bill introduced by the Majority Leader received 50 votes, but could not overcome election-year political hurdles. Congress reintroduced speculation legislation in 2009.

EXHIBIT 7-1A   News Release

www.StopOilSpeculationNow.com

For Immediate Release
Contact: XXXXXXXXX
202–626–4205
XXXXXXXXX
202–626–4141

'STOP OIL SPECULATION NOW' COALITION CALLS FOR ACTION

WASHINGTON, July 11, 2008 – Record-high oil prices are hurting American families and damaging our nation's economy. In response to this growing crisis, 38 organizations have joined together to push for effective short-, mid- and long-term solutions to help materially reduce unnecessarily high energy prices.

"This country is experiencing its worst energy crisis ever, driven by a confluence of factors, including a weak U.S. dollar, geopolitical tensions, limited supplies, strong global demand and the lack of a cohesive and comprehensive national energy policy," ATA President and CEO James C. May said, speaking on behalf of all of the coalition members. "This crisis deserves the full attention of Congress—now—not next week, next month or next year. It is too important to wait. We believe that the fastest way to get oil prices under control in the short term is by reducing reckless and unfair speculation in the futures markets while, at the same time, enacting measures for the mid and long term to expand oil supplies, enhance efforts to advance alternative and renewable energy sources and improve energy conservation across the board."

"Without question, energy futures markets, when functioning with proper oversight, serve a useful purpose, especially to bona fide hedgers. But in today's distorted market, rampant oil speculation is devastating both businesses and consumers," the coalition asserts. "Reasonable financial controls and transparency, which have been eliminated at the urging of the big speculation market players, need to be reestablished," said May.

"Numerous experts from around the world peg the impact of oil speculation at $20 to $60 per barrel. That translates into between $0.48 and $1.43 at the gas pump. In recent months, the number of "paper barrels" traded by speculators has risen dramatically, peaking at 22 times the physical market on June 6, when crude oil shot up $11 in one session. Interestingly too, that spike came immediately on the heels of a prediction of $150 per barrel oil by one of the speculators with the most to gain by the increase."

"Oil speculation has upset the traditional balance between supply and demand," said Michael W. Masters, short equity hedge fund portfolio manager and founder of Masters Capital Management, LLC. "If Congress would pass meaningful speculation reform, oil prices would drop significantly within a matter of days or weeks."

The Stop Oil Speculation Now coalition, in addition to its mid- and long-term supply and conservation elements, is calling for Congress to push for lower prices immediately by:

- Strengthening regulations weakened by the Enron Loophole and other loopholes
- Limiting the amount of oil that individuals or groups can trade speculatively in the energy futures markets while unfairly driving up prices
- Requiring reporting by unregulated, secret markets like the swaps market: All markets should have basic regulations that report the amount of oil people are buying, no smatter who they are or where they reside
- Make foreign traders follow U.S. rules and laws, just like everyone else who does business in the United States

"This campaign will result in one million messages being sent to Congress in just the last three days by concerned citizens mobilized by the SOS Coalition," said May. "This movement is just beginning to grow and we predict it will not stop until Congress acts."

The Stop Oil Speculation Now coalition is a diverse and growing organization of industries, businesses, labor groups and ultimately concerned citizens united in support of responsible energy policies and prices. The coalition includes:

Members of the Stop Oil Speculation Now Coalition: ABX Air, Inc.; Agricultural Retailers Association; Air Carrier Association of America; Aircraft Owners and Pilots Association; Air Line Pilots Association, International; AirTran Airways; Air Transport Association; Alaska Airlines, Inc.; American Airlines, Inc.; American Association of Airport Executives; American Bus Association; American Trucking Associations; Association of Corporate Travel Executives; ASTAR Air Cargo, Inc.; Atlas Air, Inc.; Cargo Airline Association; Continental Airlines, Inc.; Delta Air Lines, Inc.; Evergreen International Airlines, Inc.; Federal Express Corporation; Frontier Airlines, Inc.; Gasoline & Automotive Service Dealers of America; Hawaiian Airlines; JetBlue Airways Corp.; Midwest Airlines; National Business Travel Association; National School Transportation Association; Northwest Airlines, Inc.; Petroleum Marketers Association of America; Regional Airline Association; Southwest Airlines Co.; Spirit Airlines, Inc.; TripplerTravel.com; International Brotherhood of Teamsters; United Airlines, Inc.; United Motorcoach Association; UPS Airlines; and US Airways, Inc.

To learn more about oil speculation and its effects on America's economy, or to tell your member of Congress now that you demand action, now, please visit www. StopoilSpeculaionNow.com

EXHIBIT 7-1B   Print Advertisement

DO YOU:

Drive to work?

Buy food?

Take the kids to see grandma each summer?

Plan on heating your home this winter?

If you do any of these things, gas and oil speculation hurts you and your family.

Today speculation in oil markets hurts most Americans. Speculation is driving up the price of oil to historic levels. And it hurts all of us—from what you pay at the pump to how much it costs to heat your home to the price of putting food on your table.

It just isn't fair.

We need to increase domestic supply, exploration, alternative energy sources and conservation. But we also need fair markets, curbing excessive speculation with tough, fair rules that protect consumers and lower prices.

Log on to StopOilSpeculationNow.com and ask Congress to act now! In the next 30 days, Congress can make a real difference in lowering costs for all Americans.

www.StopOilSpeculationNow.com

PAID FOR BY THE COALITION TO STOP OIL SPECULATION NOW

Courtesy Air Transportation Association and Xenophon Strategies

EXHIBIT 7-1C   Action Letter

An Open letter to <u>All</u> Airline Customers:

Our country is facing a possible sharp economic downturn because of skyrocketing oil and fuel prices, but by pulling together, we can all do something to help now.

For airlines, ultra-expensive fuel means thousands of lost jobs and severe reductions in air service to both large and small communities. To the broader economy, oil prices mean slower activity and widespread economic pain. This pain can be alleviated, and that is why we are taking the extraordinary step of writing this joint letter to our customers.

Since high oil prices are partly a response to normal market forces, the nation needs to focus on increased energy supplies and conservation. However, there is another side to this story because normal market forces are being dangerously amplified by poorly regulated market speculation.

Twenty years ago, 21 percent of oil contracts were purchased by speculators who trade oil on paper with no intention of ever taking delivery. Today, oil speculators purchase 66 percent of all oil futures contracts, and that reflects just the transactions that are known. Speculators buy up large amounts of oil and then sell it to each other again and again. A barrel of oil may trade 20-plus times before it is delivered and used; the price goes up with each trade and consumers pick up the final tab. Some market experts estimate that current prices reflect as much as $30 to $60 per barrel in unnecessary speculative costs.

Over seventy years ago, Congress established regulations to control excessive, largely unchecked market speculation and manipulation. However, over the past two decades, these regulatory limits have been weakened or removed. We believe that restoring and enforcing these limits, along with several other modest measures, will provide more disclosure, transparency and sound market oversight. Together, these reforms will help cool the over-heated oil market and permit the economy to prosper.

The nation needs to pull together to reform the oil markets and solve this growing problem.

We need your help. Get more information and contact Congress by visiting www.StopOilSpeculationNow.com.

Robert Fornaro
Chairman, President and CEO
AirTran Airways

Bill Ayer
Chairman, President and CEO
Alaska Airlines, Inc.

Gerard J. Arpey
Chairman, President and CEO
American Airlines, Inc.

Lawrence W. Kellner
Chairman and CEO
Continental Airlines, Inc.

Richard Anderson
CEO
Delta Air Lines, Inc.

Mark B. Dunkerley
President and CEO
Hawaiian Airlines, Inc.

Dave Barger
CEO
JetBlue Airways Corporation

Timothy E. Hoeksema
Chairman, President and CEO
Midwest Airlines

Douglas M. Steenland
President and CEO
Northwest Airlines, Inc.

Gary Kelly
Chairman and CEO
Southwest Airlines Co.

Glenn F. Tilton
Chairman, President and CEO
United Airlines, Inc.

Douglas Parker
Chairman and CEO
US Airways Group, Inc.

S.O.S. NOW
www.StopOilSpeculationNow.com

Courtesy Air Transportation Association

Case 7-2

Public health is a major policy issue and changing state and local regulations for a new medical facility involves a major communication effort. Exhibit 7-2A is a promotional ad, Exhibit 7-2B is an announcement for a "letter writing rally," Exhibit 7-2C is a print ad about choice, Exhibit 7-2D is a letter asking for support at a hearing and Exhibit 7-2E shows a few presentation slides used at the hearing.

Two Hospitals for Williamsburg: Building Support for State Approval of a New Hospital

Riverside Health System with Ron Reid
Public Relations

SUMMARY

In what one local newspaper editor called a "stunning" event and a turn-around of considerable proportions, Riverside Health System won state approval (after two previous attempts) to build a new hospital in Williamsburg, VA, largely because of a thoroughly researched, strategically sound, and professionally executed PR-based communications campaign that generated more than 2,200 letters of support sent to the state health commissioner, endorsements by all local governments, and a record crowd of supporters at a decisive public hearing. This campaign shows once again the power of PR and communications to move people to action and make things happen.

BACKGROUND

Riverside Health System wanted to build a 40-bed hospital to serve the residents of the Williamsburg, VA, area. Any new hospital construction in Virginia must receive state approval in the form of a Certificate of Public Need (COPN) from the State Health Commissioner. The approval process demands that the applicant satisfy 21 criteria, covering a range of requirements from financial and service plans

Courtesy Air Transportation Association and Xenophon Strategies

Courtesy Riverside Health System and Ron Reid PR

to those of Criterion 21, which says the application must "In the case of proposed health services or facilities, (show) the extent to which a proposed service or facility will increase citizen accessibility, demonstrate documented community support and introduce institutional competition into a health planning region." Riverside attempted to gain COPN approval in 2005 and 2006. Both efforts failed. In 2008, it launched a third campaign to gain approval, spurred by the new importance given to demonstrated public support by the "21st Criterion," as the regulation came to be known. The company filed its application for COPN approval in June of 2008. In July, it launched a public relations campaign to build public support for DOCTORS HOSPITAL OF WILLIAMSUBUG. In October, the state's COPN Division staff recommended approval. In February of 2009, the state health commissioner gave the green light to Riverside's application, citing the outpouring of community support as a major reason for her approval.

RESEARCH

Research conducted by Riverside from 2005 through 2007 drove every aspect of the campaign. In fact, the name Doctors Hospital of Williamsburg was selected based on research showing residents strongly favored physician involvement in healthcare management. Demographic research (secondary) guided the attitudinal research. (Data showed, for example, that adults above age 55 have a much stronger interest in health care issues.) Primary research not only measured public opinion and levels of support, the findings also translated directly into key messages of the campaign.

Riverside conducted the following primary research:

- In-depth personal interviews with more than 50 community leaders in 2005.
- A mailed survey of 250 physicians in 2005.
- Telephone surveys of residents (age 50+) in 2005 and 2006.
- Telephone surveys of residents (age 50+) in 2005 and 2006.
- Telephone survey of residents (age 50+ in selected areas) in late 2007 for the 2008 public campaign.

The findings of the resident surveys remained remarkably consistent from 2005 through the 2007 research. About 75 percent of those surveyed believed a second hospital would benefit the community. However, a majority were satisfied with the community's health services. Support was broad, but neither deep nor intense, for a second hospital.

Research provided the foundation for message development. Those surveyed were most concerned or felt most intense about the following issues:

- Choice of healthcare facilities and services.
- Convenient access to services, especially emergency room services.
- Competition in healthcare.

- Local control and physician involvement in healthcare decisions for the community.

Finally, secondary research of the market and healthcare trends indicated that a tightly targeted campaign would be most efficient and effective, a campaign directed to:

- Residents age 50+ because they are most in need and most concerned about health issues.
- Older residents because they are more likely to vote, to take part in community issues and actions.
- Residents closest to the Doctors Hospital site, especially those in low-income, medically underserved areas.

PLANNING

Research guided every aspect of strategic planning from the development of theme and key messages to target audiences and media/methods used to reach them. The requirements of the state COPN criteria predicated in large measure the campaign's goals and specific objectives.

Goals

- Win state approval of Riverside Health System's application for a Certificate of Public Need (COPN) to construct a new hospital (DOCTORS HOSPITAL OF WILLIAMSBURG).
- Generate and document a level of public support sufficient to meet the public support requirement of Criterion 21 for granting COPN approval.

indirect

indirect

Specific Objectives

- Generate 2,000 individual letters of support mailed to the Virginia Health Commissioner by October.
- Fill the Public Hearing room with Doctors Hospital supporters.
- Secure the active support of Williamsburg physicians.
- Secure endorsements of Williamsburg City Council, JCC Supervisors, Fire and Police, etc.

Target Audiences

The focus was primarily on those audiences most likely to actively support Doctors Hospital; in other words, those who will see direct benefit to them if the hospital is built. Specifically, those audiences include:

- Past supporters of Doctors Hospital (existing mailing list).
- Residents of Doctors Hospital's service area age 50+ or who live in designated underserved districts.

- Physicians, especially those affiliated with Riverside Medical Group.
- Community leaders, elected officials, fire, and safety officers.

Overall Strategy

The overall strategic approach focused on creating an energizing theme and set of messages to ignite passion for a second hospital. The campaign emphasized the need for two hospitals rather than positioning the issue as a battle between two health systems.

From that premise came the campaign's theme: TWO HOSPITALS FOR WILLIAMSBURG—The Care You Need. The Choice You Deserve.

All communications focused on three key messages that supported and reinforced the theme:

- A second hospital will improve ACCESS to vital services older residents and underserved areas.
- A second hospital will bring the benefits of COMPETITION to the market: lower cost, better quality.
- A second hospital will give residents a CHOICE of services best suited to their needs and location.

Message delivery strategies centered around three key points:

- Use media appropriate for the primary target audience (older residents of Williamsburg).
- Keep messages simple, direct, and very focused around the central theme.
- Make it as easy as possible for people to take action.

EXECUTION

Because of the thorough research and planning, execution was simple, smooth, and without major complications. Although a range of traditional tactical methods were employed to carry out the program—personal contact with key reporters and editors (news releases were little used in the small market), individual meetings with city council members, supervisors and other key leaders, appearances before civic and business clubs, etc.—three things were paramount in achieving the campaign's goals and objectives:

- A substantial communications program using a combination of media coverage, advertising, and mail correspondence to energize supporters and move them to take action (write a letter).
- More than 20 "Write a Letter Rally" events that brought in more than 2,200 individual letters.

- A mail campaign to get supporters to the public hearing and a superb case presentation at the hearing. The Doctors Hospital "team" included Riverside communications executives and staff, PR agency staff, plus many community volunteers who went literally door-to-door urging their neighbors to write letters.

EVALUATION

This was a campaign with a clear beginning and end, and the only evaluation measurements that ultimately mattered were the achievement of goals and objectives. Were they achieved? Yes!

- Riverside received a Certificate of Public Need and planning is now underway on the construction of Doctors Hospital of Williamsburg.
- The campaign generated public support sufficient to meet the requirements of the 21st Criterion. Quoting the COPN staff report, "With minimal documentation of opposition, there has been significant if not an overwhelming outpouring of support for the Doctors' Hospital project." DCOPN has received more than 2,000 letters of support ... from the residents of the Williamsburg service area, local business leaders, physicians, state and local elected officials, and major healthcare insurance companies.
- The objective of 2,000 letters was exceeded by more than 200; there were only 29 letters opposed.
- Endorsements were gained from Williamsburg City Council, the county supervisors, police and fire chiefs in the city and county, many area pastors and municipal leaders, and 14 past chiefs of the medical staff at the former community hospital.
- The Public Hearing literally overflowed with Doctors Hospital supporters. Of the nearly 350 people in attendance, more than 320 signed in as "in favor" of Riverside's application. The title slide of Riverside's formal presentation generated a standing ovation from the assembled crowd—most likely a first ever for a Public Hearing.

By more qualitative measurements, the campaign set a tone, a theme, and a strategic approach from the earliest stages of planning that carried through to the successful completion of the task. It is an excellent demonstration of the basic premise that if research is good and thorough, if goals and objectives are clear and measurable, if strategies are sound, and if execution is professional, YOU WILL SUCCEED.

EXHIBIT 7-2A   Advertisement

TWO HOSPITALS
FOR WILLIAMSBURG

IT'S ABOUT TIME!

Look at the map. Think about where you live.
Which hospital will give you faster access to
medical and emergency services?

If your answer is DOCTORS HOSPITAL OF
WILLIAMSBURG, please write a letter of support.
For your convenience, our WRITE-A-LETTER
DESK at Riverside Healthcare Center will be
open through **October** 3.

DOCTORS HOSPITAL
of WILLIAMSBURG
Affiliated with RIVERSIDE
The Leader in Lifelong Health

Visit our WRITE-A-LETTER DESK
Riverside Healthcare Center ■ **120 Kings Way** ■ **Main Lobby**
Monday through Friday ■ **9**AM **to 5**PM

Courtesy Riverside Health System and Ron Reid PR

EXHIBIT 7-2B Flyer for Rally

TWO HOSPITALS
FOR WILLIAMSBURG

Make Your Voice Heard!

Riverside Health System seeks approval from the
State Health Commissioner to build DOCTORS
HOSPITAL OF WILLIAMSBURG.

Community support for this new hospital will make a
big difference in whether or not Riverside's application
is approved.

SO WHAT CAN YOU DO?
You can write a letter to the State Health
Commissioner! Join us in The Cove this Friday
for a special **LETTER WRITING RALLY**.

The Riverside folks will help you write, print and mail
your personal letter to the Commissioner supporting
Doctors Hospital. **And it takes less than 10 minutes.**

HOSTED BY:
Linda and Joe Gyorog, Shirley and Bob Rumer.

DOCTORS HOSPITAL
of WILLIAMSBURG

Affiliated with RIVERSIDE
The Leader in Lifelong Health

Where: The Cove
When: This Friday, Sept. 12,
anytime between 11:30AM and 2:30PM

LETTER WRITING RALLY

Courtesy Riverside Health System and Ron Reid PR

E X H I B I T 7-2C **Advertisement Promoting Choice**

TWO HOSPITALS
FOR WILLIAMSBURG

THE CARE YOU NEED. THE CHOICE YOU DESERVE.

Clyde Haulman
Professor of Economics, College of William & Mary
Vice Mayor of Williamsburg

CLYDE HAULMAN BELIEVES WE NEED
DOCTORS HOSPITAL OF WILLIAMSBURG

Numerous studies of hospital markets show that competition leads to "substantially lower cost and to significantly lower rates of adverse outcomes." They also find that the entry of new providers "leads to markets quickly becoming competitive" and "increases quality." Importantly for Williamsburg, "the most striking effects of entry come from having a second and possibly a third firm [hospital] enter the market."

That's why I believe strongly that a second hospital ensuring the benefits of free-market competition would be good for the health of our community.

PLEASE WRITE A LETTER OF SUPPORT
If you agree that two hospitals will bring the benefits of competition to our community, please write a letter supporting approval of Doctors Hospital of Williamsburg and mail it to:

Karen Remley, M.D., M.B.A.
State Health Commissioner
P.O. Box 2448
Richmond, Virginia 23218-2448

DOCTORS HOSPITAL
of WILLIAMSBURG

Affiliated with RIVERSIDE
The Leader in Lifelong Health

To find out more about how you can help ensure healthy competition in medical services for Williamsburg, call Dave Tate at 345-3081 or email him at David.Tate@rivhs.com.

COMPETITION

Courtesy Riverside Health System and Ron Reid PR

E X H I B I T 7-2D   Letter

Doctors Hospital Needs your Support at a Public Hearing on October 16.

Thank you for writing a letter supporting approval of our application to build Doctors Hospital of Williamsburg. The outpouring of community support for the proposed hospital is truly remarkable. So far, more than 2,100 people like you have written letters to the State Health Commissioner. This effort will have a significant impact on the final decision.

   The next step in the approval process is a Public Hearing on Thursday, October 16. **WE NEED TO FILL THE ROOM WITH CITIZENS LIKE YOU WHO SUPPORT DOCTORS HOSPITAL.** We must make it absolutely clear to the Health Commissioner that the community wants and needs this hospital.

   The hearing begins at **11:00 a.m. in the Tidewater Room of the Williamsburg Lodge.** Before it starts, you may sign up to speak in favor of approval, or you can simply record your support for Doctors Hospital and listen to the proceedings. We welcome your participation.

   Once again, thank you for your support.

   Sincerely,

David Tate
Senior Vice President, Development
Riverside Health System

Directions: The Williamsburg Lodge is located at 310 South
                     England St. in the historic area. From downtown, take
                     Francis St. heading east. Turn right onto South
                     England St. The Lodge will be on your right directly
                     across from the Williamsburg Inn.

Parking: You may park in the Williamsburg Inn parking lot
                     across South England St., or in the Williamsburg
                     Lodge parking garage. To enter the garage, turn right
                     on Newport Ave. (the first street past the Lodge).
                     Take another immediate right to enter the garage.

Courtesy Riverside Health System and Ron Reid PR

EXHIBIT 7-2E Hearing Presentation Slides

COMMUNITY SUPPORT

75% Public Support (3 Surveys)

Williamsburg City Council

James City County Board of Supervisors

14 Former Chiefs of Medical Staff

Fire, EMS & Safety Officials

TWO HOSPITALS FOR WILLIAMSBURG

- Independent phone surveys conducted in 2005, 2006, and late 2007 showed consistently that roughly 75 percent of area residents supported the need for two hospitals in the community.
- Every year, the Williamsburg City Council and the James City County Board of Supervisors passed unanimous resolutions of support.
- Former Chiefs of the Medical Staff at Community Hospital have consistently supported approval of DOCTORS HOSPITAL.
- Fire, Emergency Medical Service teams, and other safety officials in the area support our application.
- Many other business, civic and community leaders have come forward in strong support of DOCTORS HOSPITAL.

Courtesy Riverside Health System and Ron Reid PR

Pastor William Dawson

*"There are many in Williamsburg and southeastern James City County who don't have emergency care and hospital services they can access readily, particularly the **elderly and the economically disadvantaged**. We must provide quality, accessible medical and emergency services for these members of our community."*

TWO HOSPITALS FOR WILLIAMSBURG

8

Investor and Financial Relations

Corporations that sell shares to the public must conduct a specialized form of public relations with the investment, or financial community. Investor and other financial relations cannot be managed in the same aggressive manner that characterizes other forms of public relations. The U.S. Securities and Exchange Commission (SEC) prohibits the promotion of corporate stock under certain circumstances, and it has detailed regulations regarding the issuance of annual and quarterly reports and the timely disclosure of all information that will affect the value of publicly traded corporate shares. After scandals involving accounting irregularities by large corporations such as ENRON, Congress passed the Sarbanes-Oxley Act in 2002 to set standards for corporate responsibility and internal audit practices. It included measures requiring chief executive officers (CEOs) and chief financial officers (CFOs) to certify financial and other information in their companies' quarterly and annual reports and to force disclosure of non-GAAP (Generally Accepted Accounting Principles) financial measures. Coupled with SEC policy changes making company information more transparent for the general investor, investor relations is a challenging communications field.

How, then, does our four-stage process apply to this highly specialized form of public relations?

RESEARCH

Investor relations research includes investigation of the client, the reason for the program, and the audiences to be targeted for communication.

Client Research

The public relations practitioner needs to focus first on the company's past and present financial status, its past and present investor relations practices, and its strengths, weaknesses, and opportunities specifically related to the financial community. Both internal management initiatives and external factors such as new pressures from competitors, changes in the cost of goods, and unfounded rumors may all affect decisions by the investment community and will need to be explored.

Opportunity or Problem Research

The second area of research involves assessing the need for a program of financial public relations. Most corporations engage in ongoing investor relations programs that may involve routine communication with the financial media, the annual report to shareowners, the annual meeting, as well as regular conference calls with analysts and shareholders. When problems develop with particular publics, special programs may be devised reactively. Thus, the need for the program should be clearly justified and explained in this phase of research.

Audience Research

Finally, research for investor relations involves identification of key audiences or groups that make up the financial community:

Shareowners and potential shareowners

Security analysts and investment counselors

The financial media

> Major wire services: Dow Jones, Thomson Reuters Economic Service, AP, UPI, Bloomberg
>
> Major business magazines: *BusinessWeek, Forbes, Fortune*—mass circulation and specialized
>
> Major national and international newspapers: *The New York Times, The Wall Street Journal, Financial Times*
>
> Statistical services: Standard & Poor's, Moody's Investor Service
>
> Private wire services: PR Newswire, Business Wire, and PRIMEZONE
>
> Major broadcast networks: CNNfn, CNBC, Fox Business, Bloomberg TV
>
> Regional, and local business publications

Securities and Exchange Commission

OBJECTIVES

Investor relations objectives, both impact and output, should be as specific and as quantifiable as possible.

Impact Objectives

Impact objectives for investor relations include informing investor publics and affecting their attitudes and behaviors. Some examples are:

1. To increase the investor public's knowledge of significant corporate developments (by 40 percent during the current year)

2. To enhance standing in a national reputation index (by 30 percent this year)

3. To create (40 percent) more interest in the corporation among potential investors (during this year)

4. To raise (20 percent) more capital through the investor relations program (by our deadline of December 1)

Output Objectives

In investor relations, output objectives constitute the distribution and execution of program materials and forms of communication. Examples are:

1. To distribute corporate news releases to 12 major outlets among the financial media

2. To make 18 presentations to security analysts during the months of March and April

Output objectives for investor relations are much simpler to evaluate than impact objectives.

PROGRAMMING

As in other forms of public relations, the element of programming for investor relations includes planning the theme and messages, the action(s) or special event(s), the uncontrolled and controlled media, and the use of effective principles of communication in program execution.

Theme and Messages

The theme and messages for an investor relations program will be entirely situational. Such programs usually provide assurances of credibility and attempt to enhance relations between the company and the financial community.

Action(s) or Special Event(s)

Actions and special events unique to investor relations include:

1. An annual shareowners' meeting

2. An open house for shareowners or analysts

3. Meetings with members of the financial community

4. Teleconference or webcast with investors and analysts

5. Special seminars or other group meetings with analysts

6. Special visits to corporate headquarters or plant tours for analysts and shareowners

7. Presentations at meetings or conventions of analysts, in and outside of New York City

8. Promotional events designed to enhance the company's image in the financial community

Uncontrolled and Controlled Media

Uncontrolled media most frequently used in investor relations include:

1. News releases or feature stories targeted to the financial and mass media
2. CEO interviews with the financial and mass media
3. Media relations with key members of the financial press to stimulate positive news coverage of the company and its activities

Controlled media most often found in investor relations programs are:

1. Printed materials for shareowners, including the annual report, quarterly and other financial reports, newsletters, magazines, special letters, dividend stuffers, and announcements; much of this sent by email and placed on the Web site
2. Company promotional videos
3. CEO and other corporate officers' speeches to key audiences in the financial community and professional blogs
4. Company financial fact books, biographies and photographs of corporate officers, special fact sheets, and news releases
5. Shareowner opinion surveys
6. Financial advertising
7. The company website, a repository for all of the above

Several examples of uncontrolled and controlled forms of communication are included with the cases in this chapter. Each element of a campaign should contribute to corporate reputation and brand management.

Effective Communication

The most relevant communication principles for investor and financial relations are source credibility and audience participation.

Much of the effort of the investor relations program is directed toward enhancing the credibility of the corporation inside the financial community. The financial media, security analysts, shareowners, and potential shareowners must have a favorable image of the corporation. To accomplish this, organizations have changed their stock offerings from regional exchanges to the NASDAQ, the American, or the New York Stock Exchange; have upgraded their promotional materials, incorporating designs to convey a more "blue-chip" image; and have stepped up presentations to security analysts. Much of the value associated with a stock is often attributed to the quality of senior leadership in the corporation. Thus, corporate credibility must always be a paramount concern.

Audience participation is also a vital aspect of such programs. Prospective shareowners, financial media people, security analysts, and others targeted for communication are invited to as many corporate functions as possible. The ultimate form of "audience participation," of course, is the actual purchase of shares in the company.

EVALUATION

Evaluation of investor relations programs should be goal oriented, with each objective reexamined and measured in turn. Although there is a great temptation to cite analyst reports about the company and the company's performance, especially its stock price/earnings (P/E) ratio, these measures may not be related to investor relations programming, or there may be other intervening variables that overshadow the influence of such programming. Some firms use external measures of reputation to gauge success. These include such lists as the *Financial Times'* "World's Most Respected Companies," *Fortune's* "100 Best Places to Work," and *Washington Technology's*, "Fast 50" list of fastest growing technology firms.

SUMMARY

Research for investor relations aims at understanding the publicly owned company's status in the financial and investment community, the need for communicating with that community, and the makeup of that community as a target audience. The audience components are shareowners and potential shareowners, security analysts and investment counselors, the financial press, and the SEC.

Both impact and output objectives are used in investor relations. Impact objectives are oriented toward informing or influencing the attitudes and behaviors of the financial community, while output objectives cite distribution of materials and other forms of programming as desired outcomes.

Programming for investor relations usually consists of such actions and events as annual shareowners' meetings, an open house for shareowners, special meetings with analysts or other members of the financial community, and promotional events designed to enhance the company's image in the financial community. Uncontrolled and controlled media used in investor relations include news releases, interviews, printed literature, Internet posting to include social media sites, audiovisual materials, and/or speeches directed to targeted segments of the financial community.

Evaluation of investor relations should return to the program's specific, stated objectives and measure each one appropriately. Some practitioners attribute enhancement of the corporation's P/E ratio to the efforts of the investor relations program. However, the presence of intervening variables should always be suspected in such cases.

READINGS ON INVESTOR AND
FINANCIAL RELATIONS

Bragg, Steven. *Investor Relations: The Comprehensive Guide.* Centennial, CO: Accounting Tools, 2008.

Casteel, Lynn. "Investing in an Effective Annual Report," *Public Relations Tactics* 9 (November 2002): 10.

Cole, Benjamin Mark. *The New Investor Relations—Expert Perspectives on the State of the Art*. Princeton, NJ: Bloomberg Press, 2003.

Fernando, Angelo. "When Rumor Has It (or Not)," *Communication World* 22 (July–August 2005): 10-11.

Gaschen, Dennis John. "Restoring Public Confidence—The Challenges of Conducting Investor Relations in Today's Volatile Market," *Public Relations Tactics* 9 (November 2002): 8.

Guiniven, John. "About loyalty, trust and the bottom line," *Public Relations Tactics* 16.4 (Apr 2009): 6.

Hassink, Harold, Laury Bollen, and Michiel Steggink. "Symmetrical Versus Asymmetrical Company-Investor Communications Via the Internet," *Corporate Communications* 12 (Spring 2007): 145-160.

Heiby, Tom. "Litigation and Your Board: Assigning Order to Chaos," *Public Relations Strategist* 13.3 (Summer 2007): 42-43.

Higgins, Richard B. *Best Practices in Global Investor Relations*. Westport, CT: Greenwood Publishing Group, 2000.

Hong, Youngshin, and Eyun-Jung Ki. "How Do Public Relations Practitioners Perceive Investor Relations? An Exploratory Study," *Corporate Communications* 12 (Spring 2007): 199-213.

Jordan, Allan E. "Strategic Communication Plan Reassures Jittery Gold Investors," *Communication World* 20 (August/September 2003): 42ff.

Jones, Charles P. *Investments: Analysis and Management*, 10th ed. Somerset, NJ: Wiley, 2007.

Kanzler, Ford. "Poised for Public Offerings? Start Your Public Relations Efforts Now," *Public Relations Quarterly* 41 (Summer 1996): 23ff.

Kim, Sora, Jae-Hee Park, and Emma K. Wertz. "Expectation gaps between stakeholders and web-based corporate public relations efforts: Focusing on Fortune 500 corporate web sites," *Public Relations Review*, 36.3 (September 2010): 215-221.

Marconi, Joe. "Taking Stock Understanding Investor Relations," in *Public Relations: The Complete Guide*. Mason, OH: South-Western, 2004.

Marston, Claire. "Investor Relations Meetings Evidence from the Top 500 UK Companies," *Accounting and Business Research* 38 (2008): 21-48

McDonald, Lynette M., Beverley Sparks, and A. Ian Glendon. "Stakeholder reactions to company crisis communication and causes," *Public Relations Review* 36.3 (September 2010): 263-271.

Nekvsil, Charles. "Getting the Most Out of Your Investor Relations Conference Calls," *Public Relations Tactics* 6 (August 1999) 10ff.

Parnell, Larry. "Making the Business Case for Corporate Social Responsibility: Why It Should Be Part of a Comprehensive Communications Strategy," *Public Relations Strategist* 11 (Spring 2005): 49-51.

Savage, Michelle. "New Standards in Communicating to Financial Audiences—Why You Need to Understand XBRL," *Public Relations Strategist* 11 (Winter 2005): 10-12.

Schneider, Carl W., Joseph M. Manko, and Robert S. Kant. *Going Public Practice, Procedure and Consequences*. New York: Browne Publishing, 2002.

Silver, David. "PR Professionals as Assets: Communication Is Key During Distressed Mergers and Acquisitions," *Public Relations Strategist* 15.1 (Winter 2009): 6.

_____ "Creating Transparency for Public Companies: The Convergence of PR and IR in the Post-Sarbanes-Oxley Marketplace," *Public Relations Strategist* 11 (Winter 2005): 14–17.

Turnock, Madeline. "IR and PR Come Together," *Public Relations Strategist* 8 (Spring 2002): 13–15.

Walton, Susan Balcom. "The art of anticipation: Developing effective Q-and-As," *Public Relations Tactics* 13.12 (Dec 2006): 14.

Waters, Richard D. "Redefining stewardship: Examining how Fortune 100 organizations use stewardship with virtual stakeholders," *Public Relations Review* 37.2 (June 2011): 129–136.

Investor Relations Cases

Case 8-1

Corporate reputation is often tied to the perceived leadership expertise and style of the CEO. Pay for performance and compensation packages are frequent points of contention in a corporation and among shareholders. Exhibit 8–1A is a news release on the program and Exhibit 8–1B is the compensation recommendation for the shareholder meeting.

Aflac Gives Shareholders
A "Say on Pay"
Aflac with Fleishman-Hillard Inc.

SUMMARY

Inspired by a desire to illustrate Aflac's commitment to transparency, CEO Dan Amos made a strong push for a shareholder vote on executive pay. Prior to the vote, Aflac's communications team was charged with reinforcing (via business media coverage) the company's rationale for setting compensation for the CEO and other senior executives, the commitment by Aflac to pay-for-performance as well as its loyalty to shareholders. As a result, Aflac became the first major U.S. public company to conduct a shareholder vote on executive compensation.

SITUATION ANALYSIS

In August 1990, Daniel Amos became the chief executive officer of Aflac. Since then, the company has increased its profits and become a household name. In 2006, inspired by a desire to illustrate the company's commitment to transparency, Amos made a strong push for a shareholder vote on executive pay, commonly known as "Say on Pay." Amos also was responding to inquiries from a shareholder rights advocacy group. Aflac is the first major U.S. public company to permit a shareholder vote on executive compensation. Prior to the vote, Aflac's communications team was charged with reinforcing (via business media coverage) the company's rationale for setting compensation for the CEO and other senior executives, the commitment by Aflac to pay-for-performance as well as its loyalty to shareholders. As a result, Aflac became the first major U.S. public company to conduct a shareholder vote on executive compensation. A whopping 93 percent of shareholders voted to affirm executive pay in 2008. Even more remarkable: 97 percent of shareholders voted to affirm executive pay in 2009.

RESEARCH

2007 Corporate Board Effectiveness Survey reported that about one in three directors of U.S. based public companies said CEO pay is "too high in most cases." Most directors (about 90 percent) said they doubt the rules—designed to give investors and corporate watchdogs better, timelier information about pay and other compensation for top executives—are meeting investors' needs. The 2008 Report on Directors' and Investors' Views on Executive Pay and Corporate Governance, which surveyed 163 directors and 72 investment and pension-fund managers, found 63 percent of directors think the pay system is improving, compared to just 36 percent of investors. The Compensation of Senior Executives as Listed Companies: A Manual for Investors, a 2006 study done by CFA Institute, provided information to frustrated shareholders on analyzing the fairness, transparency, and long-term effectiveness of executive compensation agreements.

PLANNING

- Negotiate exclusive national release of news of the history-making announcement of "Say on Pay" in February 2007 to help improve placement and prominence (*USA Today,* Feb. 14, 2007).

- Refer reporters to pertinent shareholder activists (typically critics of corporate governance) to provide a counterintuitive aspect to the story (*Newsweek,* June 4, 2007).

- Reiterate the "Say on Pay" story throughout the year leading up to the shareholder vote in quarterly earnings (*The Wall Street Journal,* Feb. 18, 2007).

- Negotiate unprecedented access to the chief executive officer for select national media ("CBS Evening News," April 29, 2007).

- Make CEO Amos available for in-person interviews (Fox News "Huckabee," Jan. 4, 2009).

- Leverage adjacent news trends/events to tell Aflac's "Say on Pay" story (*The Boston Globe,* June 24, 2009).

EXECUTION

Target national and regional business media, print, and broadcast, regarding the "Say on Pay" vote with various story angles throughout the year:

- "Aflac Adopts Non-Binding 'Say On Pay' Shareholder Vote," announced plan for vote, originally scheduled for 2009 (Feb. 14, 2007).

- "Aflac Moves Up 'Say on Pay' Shareholder Vote to 2008," changed vote date from 2009 to 2008 (Nov. 14, 2007).
- "First 'Say on Pay' Vote Goes to Aflac Shareholders," announced date of vote and mentioned proxy statement (March 25, 2008).
- "Aflac Shareholders Have Their 'Say on Pay'," announced results of vote (May 6, 2008).
- "Aflac CEO Amos given up golden parachute," announced Dan Amos' decision to decline $13 million bonus and severance package (Nov. 14, 2008).
- "Pay debate, part II," positions Aflac as thought leader on executive compensation (June 24, 2009).
- Schedule a CEO media tour to national business media.
- Proactively pitch the story and offer CEO interview to any reporter who had written/aired items on corporate governance during the previous five years.
- Target regional media initially to test effectiveness of messages before approaching national business media.
- Heavily research issue to arm CEO with talking points that effectively justified fairness of compensation
- For example: missing text or needs rewording from the time Amos became CEO in August 1990, Aflac's total return to shareholders, market value, and total revenues increased substantially.

Media highlights include:

- Appearance on Fox News program "Huckabee" on January 4, 2009.
- Feature in *The Washington Post* on December 23, 2008.
- Feature in *The Boston Globe* on June 24, 2009.
- Nearly 10 minutes on ABC News' "Nightline" on June 11, 2007.
- More than 4 minutes on "CBS Evening News" on April 29, 2007.
- More than 4 minutes on the "Today Show" with Matt Lauer on March 28, 2008.
- Appearances on CNN shows "Issue #1" and "Your $$$$$."
- Eight appearances on various CNBC shows including "Closing Bell," "Kudlow & Company," "Squawk Box," and "The Call."
- Two appearances on "Fox Business News" with Neil Cavuto.
- An appearance on PBS "Nightly Business Report."
- Feature announcing "Say on Pay" program in *USA Today* on Feb. 14, 2007.
- Features in *The Wall Street Journal, The New York Times, Newsweek,* and *Time.*

EVALUATION

From February 2007 through February 2010, the Aflac "Say on Pay" story was well covered:

- Placements: 236 media items including print, television, radio, and online coverage.
- Circulation/audience/viewers: 413,371,900.
- Advertising value: $4,465,620.10.
- Media value (ad value X credibility multiple 2.5): $11,164,050.29
- And, most importantly, 97 percent of shareholders voted to affirm executive compensation in 2009, up six percentage points from the 2008 vote.
- Aflac leapt from number seven in 2008 to number one on Fortune's 2009 list of the World's Most Admired Companies in the Health and Life Insurance category.
- Aflac has twice been named as one of the World's Most Ethical Companies by *Ethisphere* magazine, and was named by Reputation Institute in 2008 as the Most Respected Company in the Global Insurance Industry.
- In 2009, *CRO* magazine named Aflac to its list of 100 Best Corporate Citizens, based on the company's high level of public disclosure and transparency.

E X H I B I T 8-1A   News Release

News Release

Aflac Moves Up 'Say-on-Pay' Shareholder Vote to 2008

Columbus, Ga., Nov. 14/PRNewswire/– Aflac Incorporated today announced that its board of directors has approved a resolution that accelerates the adoption of what is commonly referred to as "say on pay" to 2008. The say-on-pay resolution will give Aflac shareholders an opportunity to cast a non-binding advisory vote on the company's pay-for-performance compensation of the top-five named executive officers.

In February 2007, Aflac became the first company in the United States to adopt a resolution giving shareholders this type of advisory vote on compensation. At that time, the company had indicated the first advisory vote would occur in 2009 because it is the first year that executive compensation tables in the proxy statement will contain three years of data that reflect the Securities and Exchange Commission's new compensation disclosure requirements implemented during the most recent proxy season. However, after evaluating Aflac's compensation disclosures in the 2007 proxy statement, the board of directors concluded two years of comparable compensation data would be adequate for our shareholders to make an informed vote. As a result, the board changed the timing of the first say-on-pay vote from 2009 to 2008.

"We believe that our shareholders have embraced the expanded disclosure on executive compensation and it gives them the information they need to make an informed decision as they weigh pay versus performance," said Dan Amos, Aflac Chairman and CEO. "Aflac has a long history of generating strong returns for its shareholders and we remain committed to being transparent and responsive to our owners."

From the time Mr. Amos became chief executive officer in August 1990 through October 2007, Aflac's total return to shareholders, including reinvested cash dividends, has exceeded 3,863%, compared with 694% for the Dow Jones Industrial Average and 582% for the S&P 500. During the same period, the company's market value has grown from $1.2 billions to more than $30 billion. Total revenues have grown from $2.7 billion in 1990 to $14.6 billion in 2006.

For more than 50 years, Aflac products have given policyholders the opportunity to direct cash where it is needed most when a life-interrupting medical event causes financial challenges. Aflac is the number one provider of guaranteed-renewable insurance in the United States and the number one insurance company in terms of individual insurance policies in force in Japan. Our insurance products provide protection to more than 40 million people worldwide. Aflac has been included in *Fortune* magazine's listing of America's Most Admired Companies for seven consecutive years and in *Fortune* magazine's list of the 100 Best Companies to Work For in America for nine consecutive years. Aflac has also been recognized three times by both *Fortune* magazine's listing of the Top 50 Employers for Minorities and *Working Mother* magazine's listing of the 100 Best Companies for Working Mothers. Aflac Incorporated is a Fortune 500 company listed on the New York Stock Exchange under the symbol AFL. To find out more about Aflac, visit aflac.com.

(Logo: http://www.newscom.com/cgi-bin/prnh/20041202/CL TH019LOGO)

Analyst and investor contact—Kenneth S. Janke Jr., 800.235.2667—option 3, FAX: 706.324.6330, or kjanke@aflac.com

Media contact - Laura Kane, 706.596.3493, FAX: 706.320.2288, or lkane@aflac.com
SOURCE Aflac Incorporated

CONTACT: Investors, Kenneth S. Janke Jr., +1-800-235-2667 option 3, +1-706-324-6330 (fax), kjane@aflac.com, Media, Laura Kane, +1-706-596-3493, +1-706-320-2288 (fax), lkane@aflac.com, both of Aflac Incorporated

Courtesy Alfac and Fleishman-Hillard, Inc.

E X H I B I T 8-1B   Annual Meeting Material

COMPENSATION DISCUSSION AND ANALYSIS

I. Introduction

The Company's compensation philosophy is to provide pay for performance that is directly linked to the Company's results. We believe this is the most effective method for creating shareholder value, and that it has played a significant role in making the Company an industry leader. The performance-based elements of our compensation programs apply to all levels of Company management, including our executive officers. In fact, pay for performance components permeate every employee level at the Company. The result is that we are able to attract, retain, motivate, and reward talented individuals who have the necessary skills to manage our growing global business on a day-to-day basis, as well as for the future.

The Company has a history and a well-earned reputation with its shareholders as a very transparent organization. That commitment to transparency on all levels was certainly a driving force in our decision last year to allow shareholders a "say-on-pay" advisory vote. As a Company, we pride ourselves on incorporating ethics and transparency into everything we do, including compensation disclosure. With the in mind, we are pleased to provide the following CD&A.

IV. Executive Compensation Philosophy and Core Principles

The following table highlights the primary components and rationale of our compensation philosophy and the pay elements that support such philosophy

Philosophy Component	Rationale/Commentary	Pay Elements
Compensations should reinforce business objectives and values	One of the Company's guiding principles is to provide an enriching and rewarding workplace for our employees. Key goals are to retain, motivate and reward executives while closely aligning their interests with those of the Company and its shareholders. Our compensation practices help us achieve these goals.	All elements (salary, non-equity incentive awards, equity linked compensation, retirement, and health and welfare benefits)
A majority of compensation for top executives should be based on performance	Performance-based pay aligns the interest of management with the Company's shareholders. Pay for top executives is highly dependent on performance success. Performance-based compensation motivates and rewards individual efforts, unit performance, and Company success. Potential earnings under performance-based plans are structured such that greater compensation can be realized in years of excellent performance. Similarly, missing goals will result in lower, or no, compensation from the performance-based plans.	Merit salary increases, annual non-equity incentive awards, and equity-linked incentive compensation (stock options, time-based restricted stock, and performance-based restricted stock)

Compensation should be competitive	The Compensation Committee has retained Mercer Human Resource Consulting as an adviser to assist the Committee with assessing pay practices and peer group performance, at least annually, in order to maintain competitive compensation relative to the Company's industry. The Consultant uses a combination of proxy data and market surveys to assess the competitiveness of the Company's executive pay within the industry. Company philosophies and cultural practices also affect the overall compensation policies for the executive officers.	All elements
Key talent should be retained	In order to attract and retain the highest caliber of management, the Company seeks to provide financial security for its executives over the long term and to offer intangible non-cash benefits in addition to other compensation that is comparable with that offered by the Company's competitors.	Equity-linked incentive compensation, retirement benefits, employment agreements, and change-in-control provisions
Compensation should align interests of executives with shareholders	Equity ownership helps ensure that the efforts of executive are consistent with the objectives of shareholders.	Equity-linked incentive compensation and stock ownership guidelines

Courtesy Aflac and Fleishman-Hillard, Inc.

Case 8-2

Even with a stable investor base, there may be a need for constant updates to communication plans. Exhibit 8-2A is a news release on the quarterly financial results, Exhibit 8-2B is a news release on a business acquisition and Exhibit 8-2C is a stock chart.

No Brakes for Monro Muffler!
Monro Muffler Brake, Inc. with FD

SITUATION ANALYSIS

Over the past two years, the automotive industry has been hit particularly hard by the economic downturn, with dealers closing in record numbers, small aftermarket retail shops being put under pressure, and consumers struggling to keep older cars on the road while rapidly losing trust in the industry as a whole. As a result, many consumers were left to find trustworthy, yet affordable, providers to maintain their automobiles, and Monro Muffler Brake (NASDAQ: MNRO) saw this as an opportunity to differentiate itself through its proven business model and marketing tactics.

Leading up to and during the height of the economic downturn, and despite the multitude of problems plaguing consumers, the automotive aftermarket industry, and the auto industry in general, FD helped Monro position the equity as a quality as a quality investment for Wall Street. While Monro already had a stable investor base and strong relationships with many of its existing investors, FD worked with the company to further capitalize on this success by executing a strategic financial media and investor relations campaign to raise awareness of Monro. Consequently, the company experienced a boom in business and was positioned to emerge as a strong regional winner in a tough market.

RESEARCH

Based on interactive dialogue with senior management, as well as active monitoring of peer messages and communications tactics, FD aligned the company's internal strategy with external perceptions and concerns. In addition, FD completed a thorough company and peer analysis to monitor changes in investor base, as well as sell-side analyst coverage and media analysis. This analysis was

Courtesy Monro Muffler Brake, Inc. and FD

used to help develop potential sell-side analyst, investor, and media target lists as well as to inform key message creation and communications vehicles that were used as part of the program. Given that this was a very fluid process, FD regularly reviewed the shareholder bases of the company and peers, and re-evaluated Monro's communications tactics in order to ensure that the company was utilizing the most appropriate tools available to them.

Planning/Objectives

The primary objectives of FD's integrated communications program were to:

- Protect and enhance Monro's corporate valuation during a period of very volatile market conditions.
- Develop a targeted financial media program to reinforce the Monro story, clearly differentiating its business model and growth strategy from its peers and the struggling automotive industry.
- Leverage new and existing media relationships to convey key points about Monro's unique business model, advertising strategy, and strong growth in order to boost the company's visibility in the marketplace.
- Uncover economic, automotive, and auto repair industry trends that benefit Monro and reveal these trends to selected reporters, resulting in key coverage in top tier media that would normally not cover a company of Monro's limited size.
- Define and communicate clear messages and articulate a compelling investment proposition that highlighted Monro's insulation from the struggling automotive industry.
- Continue to establish visibility for Monro in the investment community and form strong relationships with existing and new sell-side analysts as well as current and prospective shareholders to continue to build interest in the stock.

To successfully accomplish the intended goals, it was important that the program developed by FD address the different audience groups within the investment community and business media through the appropriate communications vehicles. While the audiences could be reached through some of the same methods of communication, FD also employed more individualized and direct outreach. Business, financial and select industry trade reporters were key targets as FD looked to use media coverage as a vehicle to reinforce Moro's messaging with the investment community and attract new investors. For instance, FD targeted business media such as Dow Jones, *The Wall Street Journal*, Bloomberg, The Street.com, Jim Cramer's Mad Money, and the Associated Press, and successfully established relationships for Monro that continue to be ongoing and valuable today. In addition, to improve the investment community's perception and understanding of Monro, FD targeted existing sell-side analysts and shareholders as well as potential new sell-side analysts and investors and identified specific speaking venues, meetings, and direct company communications that could be used with each of these audience groups.

EXECUTION

FD and Monro successfully used the financial media to raise awareness of Monro, in addition to increasing the Company's prescience among new and existing investors. Tactics included:

- **Facilitate introductions and/or secure interviews to top tier business reporters:** FD worked with reporters to educate them about Monro's unique position given the economy and facilitated interviews with the CEO. Monro received interest from six prospective, quality investors in the week following the *The Wall Street Journal* article and the stock rose six percent while the Dow dropped two percent.

- **Provide ample visibility into business:** In addition to earnings releases, FD worked with Monro to issue business updates to provide mid-quarter insight into the business.

- **Increase visibility within the investment community:** FD secured Monro invitations to the following investment community conferences and helped to arrange one-on-one investor meetings at each conference.

  - Wachovia First Union Consumer Growth Conference
  - Gabelli & Company, Inc. Automotive Aftermarket Symposium
  - Sidoti & Co. Emerging Growth Institutional Investor Forum
  - Susquehanna Financial Group Consumer Focus Forum
  - Piper Jaffray Consumer Conference
  - Oppenheimer & Co. 9th Annual Consumer, Gaming, Lodging & Leisure Conference
  - BB&T Capital Markets 1-on-1 Conference
  - Sidoti & Company West Coast Institutional Investor Forum
  - C.L. King and Associates Best Ideas Conference
  - Thomas Weisel Consumer Conference

- **Garner sell-side interest:** FD scheduled meetings between Monro and prospective analysts.

EVALUATION

- **Drove industry trend story:** FD helped the media to uncover a trend in which Americans were opting to fix their old cars rather than buy new ones.

- **Achieved strategic media coverage:** Through FD's outreach to targeted reporters, the company was appropriately positioned in industry coverage, key messages were strategically used, and the company's earnings were positively highlighted.

- **Successfully positioned numerous strategic acquisitions:** As a result of the relationships that FD had fostered and nurtured with key reporters, the company's acquisitions were covered extensively in the media.

- **Broadened equity sponsorship:** FD aided Monro in attracting new sell-side attention, which resulted in coverage initiations by Gilford Securities and Avondale Partners, as well as invitations to present at investment conferences hosted by non-covering sell-side firms.

- **Increased institutional ownership:** FD assisted Monro in arranging investor meetings and conferences, and as a result institutional interest increased with existing holders significantly expanding their positions over time and new holders entering the stock.

- **Successfully positioned Monor and drove exceptional stock performance:** FD helped to refine messages and educate key constituencies about strength within the category, growth opportunities, and long-time viability. This led Monro's stock to appreciate over 30 percent and reach numerous all-time trading highs, including on 12/17/08; 12/30/08; 3/26/09, 4/2/09; 9/16/09; 9/21/09; 10/7/09; 10/12/09; and 10/20/09.

EXHIBIT 8-2A   News Release on First Quarter Financial Results

CONTACT:
Robert Gross
Chairman and Chief Executive Officer
(585) 647-6400

Catherine D'Amico
Executive Vice President—Finance
Chief Financial Officer
(585) 647-6400

Investors: Caren Villarreal
Media: Diane Zappas
FD
(212) 850-5600

For Immediate Release

**MONRO MUFFLER BRAKE, INC. ANNOUNCES RECORD FIRST QUARTER
FINANCIAL RESULTS**

~ Comparable Store Sales Increase 6.2% ~
~ Operating Income Increases 21.7% to a Record $17 Million ~
~ Second Quarter 2010 Estimated EPS Range of $.43 to $.48 vs. $.38 Prior Year ~

ROCHESTER, N.Y. – July 23, 2009 – Monro Muffler Brake, Inc. (Nasdaq: MNRO), a leading provider of automotive undercar repair and tire services, today announced financial results for its first quarter ended June 27, 2009.

First Quarter Results

Sales for the first quarter of fiscal 2010 increased 6.4% to a record $128.0 million compared to $120.4 million for the first quarter of fiscal 2009. Sales growth was driven by strong in-store sales execution as well as continued highly effective advertising campaigns. Comparable store sales increased 6.2%, on top of 5.6% growth for the first quarter of the prior year, and were at the high end of the Company's previously estimated range of 4% to 7%. Comparable store sales increased approximately 6% for brakes, 6% for maintenance services and 7% for tires.

Gross margin increased to 44.1% in the first quarter from 42.3% in the prior year quarter due to price increases that were implemented in response to increased material costs. Other contributing factors were increased vendor rebates, reduced labor costs, and leveraging of fixed occupancy costs. The expansion in gross margin was partially offset by the shift in sales mix towards the lower-margin tire and maintenance services categories. Total operating expenses were $39.4 million, or 30.8% of sales, compared with $36.9 million, or 30.7% of sales, for the same period of the prior year.

Operating income for the quarter increased 21.7% to a record $17.0 million from $14.0 million in the first quarter of fiscal 2009. Interest expense was $1.9 million compared with $1.5 million in the first quarter of fiscal 2009.

Net income for the first quarter increased 20.7% to a record $9.4 million compared to $7.8 million for the prior year period. Diluted earnings per share for the quarter increased 17.9% to a record $.46, compared to diluted earnings. Per share of $39 in the first quarter of fiscal 2009, and came in at the high end of the company's estimated range of $.42 to $.47. Net income for the first quarter reflects an effective tax rate of 37.8% compared with 37.6% for the prior year period.

The Company opened 30 locations during the quarter, ending the first quarter with 740 stores, which includes the 26 Autotire Car Care Center ("Autotire") locations acquired in June 2009.

Robert G. Gross, chairman and chief executive officer stated, "We are pleased with our results for the quarter and our ability to extend our strong performance of last year into the new fiscal year, especially given ongoing challenges in the economic environment. Our team's exceptional execution led to comparable store sales growth of 6.2% as well as continued expansion in gross margin and substantial growth in operating income. Our advertising strategy continued to effectively complement our low-cost and efficient business model and helped to drive an approximate 2% increase in store traffic. Additionally, we further expanded our market share as we integrated the recently-acquired Autotire business and continued to benefit from reduced competition and dealership closures. As a result, we broadened our customer base to include new groups of customers with whom we have begun to build long-term, trust relationships."

Company Outlook

Based on current visibility and business and economic trends, the Company anticipates comparable store sales growth in the range of 5% to 7% for the second quarter of fiscal 2010. The Company also expects diluted earnings per share for the second quarter to be in the range of $.43 to $48, compared with $.38 for the second quarter of fiscal 2009.

For fiscal 2010, the Company continues to anticipate comparable store growth in the range of 4% to 7%. The Company continues to expect total fiscal 2010 sales in the range of $515 million to $530 million. The Company positively adjusted its estimated range for fiscal 2010 diluted earnings per share to $1.35 to $1.45 from its previously estimated range of $1.30 to $1.45. The estimate is based on 20.4 million weighted average shares outstanding.

Mr. Gross concluded, "We are pleased to have delivered another strong quarterly performance and delighted that the solid traction that our business has gained in fiscal year 2009 is continuing into the new fiscal year. Currently, our July comparable store sales are up approximately 7%, on top of 7.7% growth for last July. Further, we are pleased with the progress that we have made in integrating Autotire into the Monro family and believe we are positioned to take advantage of additional value-added acquisition opportunities as they arise. We remain optimistic about our prospects for continued growth and market share expansion, and expect that our company-operated stores and low cost business model will allow us to continue to produce solid results. That said, we recognize that the economic environment remains uncertain, which may further impact consumer confidence and spending as we head into the Fall."

Earnings Conference Call and Webcast

The Company will host a conference call and audio webcast today, July 23, 2009 at 11:00 a.m. Eastern Time. The conference call may be accessed by dialing 888-797-2996 and using the required pass code 9131407. A replay will be available approximately one hour after the recording through Thursday, July 30, 2009 and can be accessed by dialing 888-203-1112. The live conference call and replay can also be accessed via audio webcast at the Investor Info section of the Company's Website, located at www.monro.com. An archive will be available at this website through July 30, 2009.

About Monro Muffler Brake

Monro Muffler Brake operates chain of stores providing automotive undercar repair and tire services in the United States, operating under the brand names of Monro Muffler Brake and Service, Mr. Tire, Tread Quarters Discount Tires, and Autotire. The Company currently operates 739 stores in New York, Pennsylvania, Ohio, Connecticut, Massachusetts, West Virginia, Virginia, Maryland, Vermont, New Hampshire, New Jersey, North Carolina, South Carolina, Indiana, Rhode Island, Delaware, Maine, Missouri, and Illinois. Monro's stores provide a full range of services for brake systems, steering and suspension systems, tires, exhaust systems and many vehicle maintenance services.

The statements contained in this press release that are not historical facts may contain statements of future expectations and other forward-looking statements made pursuant to the Safe Harbor provisions of the Private Securities Litigation Reform Act of 1995. Forward-looking statements are subject to risks, uncertainties, and other important factors that could cause actual results to differ materially from those expressed. These factors include, but are not necessarily limited to, product demand, dependence on and competition within the primary markets in which the Company's stores are located, the need for and costs associated with store renovations and other capital expenditures, the effect of economic conditions, the impact of competitive services and pricing, product development, parts supply restraints or difficulties, industry regulation, risks relating to leverage and debt service (including sensitivity to fluctuations in interest rates), continued availability of capital resources and financing, risks relating to integration of acquired businesses and other factors set forth elsewhere herein and in the Company's Securities and Exchange Commission filings, including the report on Form 10-K for the fiscal year ended March 28, 2009.

###

E X H I B I T 8-2B New Release on Acquisition

CONTACT:
Robert Gross
Chairman and Chief Executive Officer
(585) 647-6400

Catherine D' Amico
Executive Vice President—Finance
Chief Financial Officer
(585) 647-6400

Investors: Caren Villarreal
Media: Diane Zappas
FD
(212) 850-5600

For Immediate Release

MONRO MUFFLER BRAKE, INC. ANNOUNCES TWO ACQUISITIONS AND PROVIDES BUSINESS UPDATE

~ Acquisitions Expected to Add Approximately $60 Million in Annual Sales ~
~ Company Narrows Second Quarter EPS Guidance to High-End of Previously Expected Range ~
~ Expected Second Quarter Comparable Store Sales Increase of Approximately 7.0! ~

ROCHESTER, N.Y.—September 24, 2009—Monro Muffler Brake, Inc. (Nasdaq: MNRO), a leading provider of automotive undercar repair and tire services, today announced two tire store acquisitions. The Company has signed a definitive agreement to acquire the assets of Tire Warehouse Central, a privately-owned tire store chain serving five New England states ("Tire Warehouse"). Monro has also completed the acquisition of the assets of Midwest Tire & Auto Repair, a small independent tire chain in northwest Indiana ("Midwest Tire"). Separately, the Company provided a business update for the second quarter of fiscal 2010.

John Van Heel, president, commented, "We believe that the acquisitions of both of these businesses fit well into our stated strategy of seeking value-priced transactions that expand our market share. We are delighted to add Midwest Tire and Tire Warehouse to the Monro family and look forward to capitalizing on the significant opportunities presented by the addition of 50 stores, nearly $60 million in sales, and an additional 500,000 tire units. Coupled with our acquisition of Autotire earlier this year, we have added 76 stores and $90 million of annual sales or approximately 18% top line growth through acquisitions so far this year."

TIRE STORE ACQUISITIONS

The total purchase price for Tire Warehouse, which consists of 40 tire stores and six tire franchise locations, is $34 million. The purchase price includes real estate assets for 12 store locations and a distribution center located in Swanzy, New Hampshire. Tire Warehouse, which focuses solely on tires and related services, generated annual net sales of approximately $53 million in 2008. Management expects the Tire Warehouse business to be slightly accretive in the first 12 months following the acquisition and $0.06 to $0.08 accretive in the second 12 months of Monro ownership. The transaction is expected to close in early October. Following the acquisition and initial integration of the business, the Company intends to further leverage the Tire Warehouse store presence and distribution facilities by converting 50 of its existing Monro service stores in these markets to its Black Gold format. Black Gold is a program designed to increase sales in Monro's service stores, particularly of tires, and related services.

The total purchase price of the Midwest Tire business was $2 million. Midwest Tire consists of four tire locations in northwest Indiana that generated annual net sales of approximately $6 million in 2008. Management expects that Midwest Tire, which will be converted to the Mr. Tire brand name, will operate at a breakeven level in the first 12 months following the acquisition.

Taken together, the acquisitions will bolster the Company's tire store footprint in New Hampshire, Massachusetts, Rhode Island, Vermont, Maine and Indiana. Both acquisitions will be funded through the Company's existing line of credit. It is management's intention to retain the store employees of the acquired businesses. The impact of the acquisitions is not included in the Company's previously provided guidance for fiscal 2010.

BUSINESS UPDATE

For the second quarter of fiscal 2010, the Company expects a comparable store sales increase of approximately 7.0%, which is at the high-end of the Company's previously anticipated range. The Company now expects diluted earnings per share for the second quarter of 2010 to be in the range of $0.47 to $0.48, narrowed to the high-end of its previously expected range of $0.43 to $0.48. This estimate compares to $0.38 in the prior year quarter and is based on 20.4 million weighted average shares outstanding.

Robert G. Gross, chairman and chief executive officer, commented, "We are pleased with our continuing momentum and performance in the second quarter of fiscal 2010 with an expected quarterly comparable store sales increase of 7.0%. We are encouraged by these strong sales trends which indicate that consumers continue to return to Monro, their trusted service provider, for their car repairs. In addition, we look forward to integrating our two acquisitions into our low-cost business model and are eager to capitalize on the economies of scale that we expect to gain from the higher volume of tire unit sales, which we expect will positively impact our gross margin going forward."

The data provided for the second quarter is based on preliminary unaudited internal results and is subject to change as the Company completes the preparation of full consolidated financial statements for the period. The Company plans to release its second quarter fiscal 2010 results on October 26, 2009.

INVESTOR CONFERENCE

Monro announced that Mr. Gross will participate in the Thomas Weisel Consumer Conference on Thursday, October 1, 2009 at 9:10 a.m. at the New York Palace Hotel in New York City. The presentation will be webcast live during the conference and available for 30 days after the conference ends via the Investor Information section of the Company's Website at www.monro.com.

About Monro Muffler Brake

Monro Muffler Brake operates a chain of stores providing automotive undercar repair and tire services in the United States, operating under the brand names of Monro Muffler Brake and Service, Mr. Tire, Tread Quarters Discount Tires and Autotire. The Company currently operates 740 stores in new York, Pennsylvania, Ohio, Connecticut, Massachusetts, West Virginia, Virginia, Maryland, Vermont, New Hampshire, New Jersey, North Carolina, South Carolina, Indiana, Rhode Island, Delaware, Maine, Illinois, and Missouri. Monro's stores provide a full range of services for brake systems, steering and suspension systems, tires, exhaust systems and many vehicle maintenance services.

###

EXHIBIT 8-2C   Stock Chart

Monro Muffler Brake Stock Chart
January 1, 2009 through February 24, 2010

⬤ 52-week high

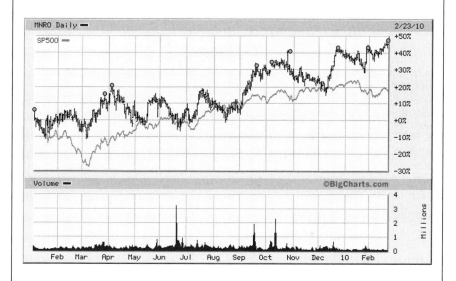

Courtesy monro muffler Brake, inc. and FD

Case 8-3

Corporate reputation can be enhanced by "thought leadership," whether for new products or research and development. And credibility can be established by using the tools that the target audience trusts. Exhibit 8-3A is a customized blog for the new program, Exhibit 8-3B is the Facebook page, and Exhibit 8-3C is a news release announcing a new feature of the program.

The Debt Diva Campaign
CareOne Services with RLF Communications

SUMMARY

CareOne Services, the nation's largest credit counseling and debt management company, needed to accomplish two objectives in 2008—establish third-party credibility and more effectively reach young female consumers. Clarky Davis, a certified credit counselor and spokesperson for CareOne, was transformed into the Debt Diva. The Debt Diva rose to prominence through national TV coverage and explosive growth on social media sites. Nearly 9,000 consumers, most of them young women, used the Debt Diva platform as the basis for starting work with CareOne, and the company was well on its way to establishing its thought leadership position in the industry.

RESEARCH

After CareOne laid out its key objectives for 2008, RLF conducted both primary and secondary research to prepare a communications strategy. They examined CareOne's proprietary database with information from more than a quarter-million customers, interviewed customer service specialists, they benchmarked all competitors and evaluated social media presence.

Based on our research, they created the Debt Diva. Aimed primarily at reaching women ages 18 to 40, they targeted media outlets and social media sites with unique messages distinct from other personal finance experts. They found many prominent experts offer advice that is beyond the reach of our target audience. How many younger women can realistically amass a savings cushion of six months worth of their living expenses during good times, much less in this economy? Our goal was to offer personal finance tips on saving, budgeting, and paying down debt that were actionable and inspiring to our target audience. The Debt Diva's advice: live frugally and fabulously.

Courtesy CareOne Services and RLF Communications.

PLANNING AND EXECUTION

Based on our research they created a media relations campaign aimed at consumer and lifestyle outlets, offering useful personal finance tips geared to specific topics, holidays, and current events. They created online content (ww.thedebtdiva.com) and developed a strategy for search engine optimization.

Objectives

We established four key objectives for measuring our campaign:

- Book two interviews with national media outlets to establish credibility for the Debt Diva in the first year.
- Increase traffic to CareOne's Website by 50 percent through increased search engine optimization in the first year.
- Create an online presence for the Debt Diva though the use of social media tools, measuring friend activity in numbers for the first six months, and then switching to drive engagement comments during the second half of 2008.
- Increase CareOne's customer base by 3,000 new consumers though unique visits to the Debt Diva website in the first year.

Tactics and Collateral

- RLF created a caricature of the Debt Diva to serve as the logo and style icon for our campaign.
- They created a printed and downloadable Debt Diva Financial Guide with goals, planning exercises, household budget worksheets, a spending and savings plan and a monthly calendar.

Media Relations

- RLF created a media kit with a launch release, the Debt Diva Financial Guide, as well as a business card to introduce the Debt Diva to targeted contacts.
- We wrote topical news releases related to budget planning and trend news coverage. RLF distributed these releases via Business Wire to increase search engine optimization, posted them on the Debt Diva Website, and sent them directly to target media.
- RLF proactively responded to articles about related consumer debt themes and developed relationships with these reporters who needed to be aware of the Debt Diva as a source. Debt Diva minisite new and expanded content. (www.thedebtdiva.com).
- RLF developed and maintained a blog on the site for the Debt Diva to share her thoughts, tips and advice with consumers.
- We posted Debt Diva print and broadcast media coverage to the website.

- RLF created a Debt Diva download section with PDF available of the financial guide, holiday guide and holiday planning pages. Social media/online presence.

- We created accounts for the Debt Diva on Facebook, Twitter, Squidoo, and MySpace.

- RLF created a Debt Diva YouTube video channel.

- RLF produced short videos featuring Debt Diva lifestyle advice, posted them on YouTube and promoted them via her blog, Facebook, Twitter, and MySpace.

RESULTS

Within two weeks of launching the Debt Diva, Clarky Davis made her first media appearance—on national TV—visiting "Fox & Friends Weekend." The campaign only picked up from there.

- RLF's "Frugal Is the New Black" news release messaging resulted in a second "Fox & Friends Weekend" appearance.

- That "Frugal Is the New Black" media appearance, the news release and supporting content on the Debt Diva Website brought Clarky Davis to the attention of T.J. Maxx, an off-price retailer. T.J. Maxx was searching for a spokesperson for a fall "Smart Shopping" campaign and media tour. RLF Communications brokered a contract for Davis, which resulted in $76,000 in revenue for CareOne Services, for T.J. Maxx's use of the Debt Diva as a spokesperson.

- ABC "Nightline" segment: the Debt Diva's money-saving secrets won a holiday shopping competition, beating Consumer Reports' Tightwad Tod in December 2008. (3 million media impressions/$885,263 calculated ad value).

- Featured in an *Essence* magazine cover story, December 2008.

- The Debt Diva has been featured in news segments on ABC, NBC, CBS, FOX, and CW affiliates in top 25 markets.

- The Debt Diva's personal finance advice has been quoted in consumer stories in many daily newspapers, including *The Dallas Morning News, St. Paul Pioneer Press, St. Petersburg Times, Kentucky Herald-Leader,* and *The Daily Record* (Md.).

- The Debt Diva has also been featured numerous times in blogs, mostly dealing with living a frugal lifestyle, such as A Woman$ Worth, Finally Frugal, and The Lean Green Family. In total, the Debt Diva media relations portion of the campaign resulted in 13.3 million media impressions and a total one-to-one media value of more than $3.5 million.

Social Media

- Facebook profile grew to 2,000 friends in two months.
- Twitter profile jumped from 28 to 1,500 in one moth.
- RLF used social networking conversations to drive traffic from these outposts to the Debt Diva blog and back again.
- Our holiday gift card giveaway increased followers and conversation on social networks.
- Short videos offered advice on smart shopping and affordable holiday gift baskets.

Twitter and Facebook cross-promotion also increased views on the Debt Diva's YouTube channel. The Debt Diva minisite and social networking pages continue to drive traffic to the CareOne Website. From June to December 2008, the Debt Diva minisite had 54,232 unique visitors, a 264 percent increase in traffic to the CareOne Website, which hosts the minisite. As a result, 8,711 consumers who visited the Debt Diva minisite clicked on a CareOne link and started an application for financial services with CareOne, a value of approximately $300,000 to CareOne Services. More than two thirds of them were young women, our target audience.

The Rewards

- $300,000 in sales, $76,000 in other revenue and $3.5 million in one-to-one media value.

EXHIBIT 8-3A Blog

My CareOne | My Messages | My Program | My Profile   Community: Forums | Blogs | Groups

mycareOne
1-888-888-CARE   **Manage your debt. Change your life. Sign in now!**
▶ Member Log-In ▸ New User?

CareOne Home ▸ My CareOne ▸ Blogs ▸ Debt Diva Blog ▸ Keeping Clean on a Budget   ❓ Help

Blog Post   ⬚RSS ⬚Share

Keeping Clean on a Budget

Now that summer is here, many of my family members are taking advantage of their vacation days and planning trips to Raleigh, NC for a visit. This has forced me to stop procrastinating and start sprucing up my home. My first priority has been to clear out the cobwebs and start cleaning! I would never describe myself as an organized neatnick; however, I have been hard at work trying to get my home nice and tidy for my future guests.

Cleaning supplies are very pricey, and I've got some great tips for you how you can save money and still make your home sparkly! Best of all, they are environmentally friendly.

1. Make your own home cleaner: Cleaning supplies can break your budget. Did you know you could make your own cleaning solution at home? With a little baking soda, white vinegar and water you have a powerful all-purpose cleaner for less than store bought products. Vinegar is known to kill germs and bacteria. It's also a proven stain fighter. Just be sure to test any homemade solutions on a small area. Check out Frugal Living for other household cleaning recipes.

2. Rent instead of buying: Your home's exterior and lawn may need sprucing up for summer. Pressure washing your home's exterior and reseeding the lawn require machines with muscle and some hefty dollars to boot. Consider renting a pressure washer, tiller or spreader as an alternative to making a long-term, monetary investment. You can also find carpet cleaning and floor polishing equipment to help spruce up your home's interior. Your local grocers or home improvement stores rent these machines for a relatively low price. Consider renting other machinery such as lawn mowers and garden tillers for heavy duty jobs.

3. Find low cost alternatives for everyday cleaning: Instead of using paper towels, reach for old wash cloths or retired bath towels instead of paper towels. You're not only saving money on paper products, but this is also a great way to reduce household waste. If you need to make a purchase, look at local dollar stores or big box retailers for deals on cleaning supplies.

I'd love to hear your frugal cleaning tips! Please leave them for me in the Comments!

Posted 07-01-2009 6:51 PM by DebtDiva

Comments

ELLESERENE wrote **re: Keeping Clean on a Budget**
on 07-03-2009 12:41 PM

If you do rent a piece of equipment to clean the carpet, yard, exterior, etc., find a friend who wants to use it the same day. You can split the cost of the rental in half, and both have a helper for the heavy work (such as moving furniture or ladders).

jenmcveigh wrote **re: Keeping Clean on a Budget**

Search

Enter Search Term
Search ▸

Debt Diva Blog
▸ Home
▸ About

Syndication
▸ RSS for Posts
▸ Atom
▸ RSS for Comments
▸ Email Notifications
Your Email Address Go

Recent Posts
▸ Spooktacular Halloween Costume Savings!
▸ How You Can Stay Frugally Healthy!
▸ Cool Savings on Power Bills: Join Me for #FrugalChat Sept. 15
▸ More Savings Tips for the Back to School Smart Shopper
▸ Taking Control of Back to School Expenses

Tags
back to school bargains
budget
contest control
debt diva

Courtesy CareOne Services and RLF Communications

E X H I B I T 8-3B   Facebook Wall

Courtesy CareOne Services and RLF Communications

EXHIBIT 8-3C   News Release

For immediate release

Contact:
Stephanie Skordas
Phone: (336) 553-1803
E-mail: sskordas@rlfcommunications.com

The Debt Diva's Frugal Fitness Guide

Break a sweat without breaking the bank to stay frugal and fit in 2009

Columbia, MD (February 18, 2009) – More than 80 million Americans go on diets each year, taking a pledge to lose weight, but getting in gear and joining a gym can add up during these tough economic times. But you don't have to break your healthy resolution because it's breaking your bank. The Debt Diva, offers some great ways to stay in shape on budget in the new Debt Diva Frugal Fitness Guide.

The Frugal Fitness Guide outlines ways consumers can save money in all areas of their routine. Ordinary items in the home can become workout tools, turning a living room into a gym.

"You'd be surprised at how differently you can look at your couch, a dinner table and even a wall," says Davis on turning your home to your very own gym. "Everyday items around the home can be used as props to hold your feet, keep you balanced and most importantly, help you get in shape you fulfill your resolution to get fit and fabulous, frugally."

Consumers can also learn smart ways to buy the right foods to stay healthy without spending a fortune. The Debt Diva's Guide points consumers to community resources they can use on a regular basis to help them save money and stay on track. Davis also suggests ways to lock in a routine alone or with a workout buddy.

Davis offers some great alternative ways to get fit. Stay on top of your fitness goal in 2009 with these tips from The Debt Diva:

1. The best thing you can do for yourself is just to get up and start moving! Taking a few minutes each day to stretch out before you start any exercise is a great way to start any workout whether it's cardio or strength training.
2. The American Heart Association says that a simple 20 to 30 minute walk three times a week will make you feel more energetic, happier, and calmer. You mostly want to increase your heart rate when you're working out, because the more it increases, the more calories your burn. And the more you burn, the more fat you'll lose.
3. If you have a limited amount of time and are jumping into a workout routine for the first time, start with squats, lunges, pushups, and crunches. And best of all, these are all things you can do in your home using ordinary items in your home for support – like the floor, a wall, your couch, or even a dining room chair.
4. A set of weights Is as close as your pantry. A regular can of soup weighs just about 2 pounds, which is fine to start with if you haven't done much exercise. If you've tried a can of soup, use water bottles for more mass, which can weigh about 3 to 4 pounds.
5. After you drink the water, dry out the bottle and fill it with rice to increase the weight.

6. When you've started to build your routine, try using plastic milk jugs filled with water (or just halfway) to increase the weights you are lifting. Just remember to tape the lids on securely or do these exercises on a linoleum or tile floor in case you have a spill.
7. Walking and jogging are great cardio exercises you can do around the house.
8. Cleaning your house also burns the calories just like walking and jogging. An hour of cleaning will burn about 200 calories!*Check out this nifty calculator* to see how many calories you're burning by doing chores!
9. Work out with a friend. You'll help each other stay motivated and you'll most likely stick to a routine because you know someone else is counting on you.
10. Turn your workout into time for the family by incorporating activities for everyone. It can be as simple as a game of tennis or a visit to the playground.

"Getting fit on a budget can be fun and rewarding for your wallet and your health," says Davis. "Don't forget to set short term and long term goals for your workout. Your short term goal should be achievable within a month, while your long term goals can be achieved over an extended period of time. Reward your short term goals with a new work out challenge so you're not spending what you've saved. Then take the money you save and reward yourself in a big way, with a new outfit for example, when you achieve your long term goal."

To find more unique ways to turn ordinary items at home into your personal gym, download the entire Frugal Fitness Guide at www.thedebtdiva.com.

About The Debt Diva

Clarky Davis has more than five years of experience in the debt management industry and more than 10 years of hard-won personal experience with credit cards and debit cards. The money saving tips the Debt Diva offers have all been tested and proven by the glamorous girl herself. Davis now offers these hard-won insights to others seeking to maximize their tight budgets and deal with debt.

About CareOne Services

CareOne Services was formed in 2002 to provide consumers with multiple solutions to complex money problems. CareOne Services Inc. boasts a unique Financial Fitness Center that examines each consumer's individual financial situation and develops a personalized solution to help the consumer get out of debt and strengthen his or her financial footing.

Courtesy CareOne Services and RLF Communications

9

Consumer Relations

Consumer relations involves much more than just public relations campaigns during the launch of a new product. At each stage during the lifecycle of a product, there may be the need for new publicity to raise consumer awareness of changes to the product or to improve declining market share. A trend in consumer awareness may provide new opportunities to establish relationships with a wider spectrum of publics. For example, greater environmental concerns may open the door for a service to promote its "green" benefits to senior adults.

The promotion of goods and services usually falls under the terrain of sales and marketing. However, consumer relations can enhance brand loyalty and even a corporation's overall reputation. Therefore, consumer relations can even have a significant impact on market share.

Most organizations providing products and services must also work the ever changing relationships with consumer product protection groups, activist groups, and government regulatory agencies. The tension between producers and publics can be seen in the establishment of organizations such as the National Consumers League in 1899 followed by the creation of government regulatory agencies such as the Food and Drug Administration (FDA) and the Federal Trade Commission (FTC). By 1936, the Consumers Union and *Consumer Reports* were established.

Today, no corporation can ignore the need for a fully functioning program in consumer relations or, as it is often known, consumer affairs. The ROPE process model is a useful means of preparing and executing a consumer relations program.

RESEARCH

Research for consumer relations includes investigation of the client, the reason for the program, and the consumer audiences to be targeted for communication.

Client Research

In the case of consumer relations, client research will be centered on the organization's reputation in its dealings with consumers. How credible is the organization with activist consumer groups? Has it been a frequent target of their advocacy attacks? What are its past and present consumer relations practices? Does it have a viable program in place? What are its major strengths and weaknesses in this area? What opportunities exist to enhance the organization's reputation and credibility in consumer affairs? The practitioner should also understand the reputation of the organization's goods and services. The answers to these questions will provide a reasonably complete background for further development of a consumer relations program.

Opportunity or Problem Research

Explanation and justification of the need for a consumer relations program is part of the research process. The need grows out of the client research phase in determining past and present dealings with consumers. If problems already exist, a reactive program will be necessary. Based upon new products or potential issues affecting the organization's goods and services, the practitioner should consider preparing a proactive or strategic long-term program. The organization's "wellness" in its relations with consumers and stakeholder publics should be made a matter of priority concern to management. Also, opportunities and challenges are often connected to the competition faced by the organization. For example, other companies are vying for the same audience by capturing market share or consumer loyalty. Problems with a competitor's product lines could cause problems for your client's products.

Audience Research

The final aspect of research consists of identifying and examining audiences to be targeted in a consumer relations program. These audiences usually include:

Company employees

Customers

> Professionals
> Socio-economic segments
> Values and lifestyle segments
> Demographic segments
> Gender and minority specific segments

Other

> Activist consumer groups
> Consumer publications
> Community media—mass and specialized
> Community leaders and organizations

Information about the customer groups and activist consumer groups should be of particular interest. Their attitudes and behaviors toward the company and their media habits are especially important.

OBJECTIVES

Consumer relations programs may use both impact and output objectives.

Impact Objectives

Some likely examples of impact objectives are:

1. To increase consumers' knowledge about the company's products, services, and policies (by 30 percent during the current year)
2. To promote (30 percent) more favorable consumer opinion toward the company (before December 1)
3. To increase sales (15 percent) for a company's specific product or service (this year)
4. To introduce a new product and capture five percent of the market within three months.

Output Objectives

Output objectives for consumer relations involve the practitioner's measurable communication efforts with targeted audiences:

1. To distribute (10 percent) more consumer publications during the period June 1 to August 31
2. To develop three employee consumer seminars for this fiscal year
3. To establish three new online consumer engagement centers during the next six months
4. To prepare and distribute recipes for using the product to 12 major food editors in the state during the campaign.

PROGRAMMING

Programming for consumer relations includes planning the theme and messages, action(s) or special event(s), uncontrolled and controlled media, and effective communication principles to execute the program.

Theme and Messages

The theme and messages will grow out of the consumer relations situation and will reflect research findings and objectives for the program. For example, a new product should have a message accenting its distinctive elements to differentiate it from the competition.

Action(s) or Special Event(s)

Organizational actions and special events in a consumer relations program generally include:

1. Advising management and all employees about consumer issues
2. Developing an efficient consumer response system
3. Handling specific consumer complaints through a customer relations office
4. Maintaining liaison with external activist consumer groups
5. Monitoring federal and state regulatory agencies and consumer legislation that might affect the company
6. Developing emergency plans for a product recall
7. Establishing a consumer education program, including meetings, information racks with printed materials on product uses, training video on product uses, celebrity endorsements and tours, online interactive quiz, and paid advertising on consumer topics
8. Holding employee consumerism conferences, seminars, and/or field training
9. Establishing a presence on a social media or virtual world Internet platform.

Similarly, developing an "app" or application that provides regular updates to consumers on their portable tablets or smart phones.

These actions and events form the basis of a thorough consumer relations program.

Uncontrolled and Controlled Media

Community, and sometimes state or national, media should be targeted for appropriate news releases, photo opportunities or photographs, interviews, and other forms of uncontrolled materials reporting the company's actions or events in consumer affairs.

Controlled media for a consumer relations program usually include printed materials on the effective use of the company's products or on health, safety, or other consumer-oriented topics. In addition, specific printed materials are developed for meetings, conferences, and other special events. Audiovisual materials such as videos and DVDs are often used as vehicles for consumer education. One of the most important mechanisms for effective consumer communication is the company website and Internet presence. A Facebook site and the website can contain virtually unlimited amounts of information useful to consumers. The cases included in this chapter illustrate a variety of forms of both uncontrolled and controlled media.

Finally, interpersonal communication should play a significant role in any consumer relations program. Ideally, the company can employ a consumer affairs spokesperson whose tasks may include conferring with consumer groups, addressing community organizations, or even representing the company in mass media appearances, including paid consumer advertising. Interpersonal communications should also be used generously in the company's consumer response system, its customer relations office, and other meetings and conferences in the consumer relations program.

Effective Communication

The principles of special interest for effective communication in consumer relations are source credibility, two-way communication, and audience participation.

★ A major purpose of consumer relations programs is credibility enhancement. For example, a grocery chain employs a consumer adviser who listens to customers and produces a "weekly column" for radio stations. One woman held the position for more than 25 years and captured considerable name recognition and credibility for her nutritional and shopping information.

Consumers are increasingly quality conscious in their purchases of goods and services. For decades, U.S. automobile manufacturers suffered a loss of public confidence and credibility in comparison with the high-quality standards of their Japanese competitors. Because of this stiff competition, the U.S. companies have been forced to improve their quality controls, their warranties, and their treatment of consumers in general. Once lost, corporate credibility is difficult to rebuild, but effective programs in consumer relations can be a decisive factor in that rebuilding process. For example, automobile manufacturers conducted driving events where consumers could test drive the company's products and also their competitors as a way to prove the value of their reengineered product lines. The event was part of their consumer communication campaign.

★ Two-way communication and audience participation go hand in hand in consumer relations. There can be no substitute for direct, interpersonal communication in some situations. The proper treatment of consumers demands that their grievances be heard and, in most cases, personally resolved. The most effective consumer education programs are those that go beyond mere distribution of information on a website but engage in meaningful dialogue with consumers. The best programs involve the consumer personally in meetings, interviews, conferences, or on social media platforms that allow audience feedback and participation.

EVALUATION

There are no surprises and nothing out of the ordinary in the evaluation of consumer relations programs. The practitioner uses the previously discussed methods to evaluate the program's stated objectives. Measures of reputation and sales are frequent mainstays of evaluating successful programs.

SUMMARY

Research for consumer relations concentrates on an organization's reputation with its consumers and on the reason for conducting a program of this kind. In some instances, the consumer publics are segmented, with different messages and media designed for communication with each group.

Consumer relations uses both impact and output objectives. Impact objectives propose outcomes that increase consumers' knowledge or influence their attitudes and behaviors. Output objectives propose outcomes in terms of measurable practitioner efforts without regard to impact.

Programming involves organizational actions such as advising management about consumer affairs, developing consumer-oriented programs, and/or holding meetings or conferences about consumerism. Communication for consumer relations includes uncontrolled, controlled, and interpersonal formats. Although the use of controlled printed materials is often emphasized, interpersonal communication and social media engagement are increasingly being used.

Evaluation, as in other forms of public relations, consists of discovering appropriate measurements for the program's stated objectives.

READINGS ON CONSUMER RELATIONS

Abboud, Leila. "Stung by Public Distrust, Drug Makers Seek to Heal Image," *Wall Street Journal* 40 (August 26, 2005): sec. B.

Beaubien, Greg. "Marketers Hope 'New Retro' Branding Will Charm Consumers," *Public Relations Strategist* 16.4 (Fall 2010): 44.

Beaupre, Andre. "Getting Your Customers to Help with Public Relations," *Public Relations Tactics* 10 (October 2003): 9.

Benett, Andrew. "Consumers Are Watching You," *Advertising Age* 79 (April 7, 2008): 19.

Burke, Claire. "Inconspicuous consumption: 5 things you need to know about reaching consumers," *Public Relations Tactics* 17.11 (November 2010): 14.

Bush, Lee. "Focusing on Strategy: Moving Beyond Media Relations and Getting to the New Brand Marketing Table," *Public Relations Strategist* 13 (Spring 2007): 30–32.

Choi, Chong Ju, Tarek Ibrahim Eldomiaty, and Sae Won Kim. "Consumer Trust, Social Marketing and Ethics of Welfare Exchange," *Journal of Business Ethics* 74 (August 2007): 17–23.

Colgate, Mark R., and Peter J. Danaher. "Implementing a Customer Relationship Strategy: The Asymmetric Impact of Poor Versus Excellent Execution," *Journal of the Academy of Marketing Science* 28 (Summer 2000): 375ff.

Crawford, Alan Pell. "Why We Need to Begin Our Work With a Customer-First Approach," *Public Relations Tactics* 7 (April 2000): 12.

Ford, Rochelle L. "Marketing to dads," *Public Relations Tactics* 17.6 (Jun 2010): 6.

Greene, Richard. "Two Steps to New Product Success," *Public Relations Tactics* 11 (December 2004): 17.

Guiniven, John. "The Less-is-More Approach: Extending Campaigns' Lives," *Public Relations Tactics* 14 (April 2007): 6.

Hynes, Aedhmar. "Bridging the Trust Gap: How Public Relations Elevates Brand Value," *Public Relations Strategist* 15.4 (Fall 2009): 22.

Holtz, Shel. "Establishing Connections," *Communication World* 22 (May–June 2005): 9ff.

Hong, Soo Yeon, and Sung-Un Yang. "Effects of Reputation, Relational Satisfaction, and Customer-Company Identification on Positive Word-of-Mouth Intentions," *Journal of Public Relations Research* 21.4 (2009): 381–403.

Jacques, Amy. "The hills are alive with the sound of music: PR's role in building Bonnaroo," *Public Relations Tactics* 17.6 (June 2010): 8.

Krauss, Michael. "Create Customer Promoters, Avoid Detractors," *Marketing News* 40 (April 1, 2006): 8–9.

Laufer, Daniel and Jae Min Jung. "Incorporating regulatory focus theory in product recall communications to increase compliance with a product recall," *Public Relations Review* 36.2 (June 2010): 147–151.

Lee, Ki-Hoon and Dongyoung Shin. "Consumers' responses to CSR activities: The linkage between increased awareness and purchase intention," *Public Relations Review* 36.2 (June 2010): 193–195.

McNaughton, Melanie Joy. "Guerrilla communication, visual consumption, and consumer public relations," *Public Relations Review* 34.3 (September 2008): 303–305.

Miller, Steve. "Toyota CGM Exec Monitors the Good, the Blog, the Ugly," *Brandweek* 48 (September 3, 2007): 8.

Rappleye, Willard C., Jr. "Customer Relationship Management," *Across the Board* 37 (July 2000): 47ff.

Rhea, Darrel. "Understanding Why People Buy," *Business Week Online* (Accessed August 15, 2005), www.businessweek.com/innovate/content/aug2005/id20050809_077337.htm.

Schneider, Joan. "Countdown To Launch: 10 Lessons Learned About Publicizing New Products," *Public Relations Tactics* 8 (May 2001): 24.

Scott, David Meerman. *The New Rules of Marketing and PR: How to Use News Releases, Blogs, Podcasting, Viral Marketing and Online Media to Reach Buyers Directly.* Hoboken, NJ: Wiley, 2007.

Sernovitz, Andy. *Word of Mouth Marketing: How Smart Companies Get People Talking.* Chicago: Kaplan, 2006.

Stern, Barbara B. "Advertising Intimacy: Relationship Marketing and the Services Consumer," *Journal of Advertising* 26 (Winter 1997): 7–19.

"Target Practice," *Economist* (April 2, 2005): 13ff.

Thompson, Gary W. "Consumer PR Techniques in the High Tech Arena," *Public Relations Quarterly* 37 (Winter 1992): 21–22.

Trudel, Mary R. "Consumer Marketing Synergy: PR Comes of Age," *Public Relations Quarterly* 36 (Spring 1991): 26ff.

Ventura, Michael. "No Such Thing as a Free Lunch," *Advertising Week* 49 (May 12, 2008): 18.

Volmar, Philip. "New Consumers Say 'Less Is More'," *Public Relations Strategist* 16.3 (Summer 2010): 5.

Weber, Larry. *Marketing to the Social Web: How Digital Customer Communities Build Your Business.* Hoboken, NJ: Wiley, 2007.

Willing, Paul. "Be a Partner with Your Community" *Nursing Homes* 54 (August 2005): 14–16.

Consumer Relations Cases

Case 9-1

Here is a case connecting social responsibility to a consumer product. Exhibit 9-1A is a news release on the Honey Bee campaign and Exhibit 9-1B is a program summary of key campaign elements and future plans for a continued communication campaign.

Häagen-Dazs Loves Honey Bees: Let's Lick This Problem

Ketchum and Häagen-Dazs

OVERVIEW

The Häagen-Dazs® (HD) brand recognized that it was an iconic, strong brand that had lost relevance with its consumers, and was looking for a way to highlight its all-natural positioning that would resonate. They were looking for a different way to crack the nut!

The goal: to re-ignite consumer passion and boost annual sales growth by at least one percent and media impressions by 25 percent in 2008. At the essence of the brand is its commitment to all-natural ingredients. They uncovered an obscure problem, "disappearing honey bees" (referred to as Colony Collapse Disorder (CCDE)) threatening the existence of 40 percent of HD's natural ingredients. HD saw a unique opportunity to be the champion of an under-reported but critical cause. HD Loves HB was born to connect with consumers in an authentic way, be first to put the cause on consumers' radar in a major way, and underscore HD's "all natural" brand value proposition by inextricably linking the important relationship between honey bees and its ice cream.

HD created a new flavor in honor of the honey bees, placed a captivating bee logo on all products threatened by these pollinators, launched a new consumer education website, and produced print and TV advertising. But the biggest marketing lever of all for the campaign was public relations. The brand and Ketchum set the tone for the entire campaign, formed an expert advisory board, directed significant donation funds towards meaningful research, and created an avenue for consumers in mass numbers to plant bee-friendly habitats to help save the bees. The campaign exceeded all management expectations in getting consumers, retail sales, and media buzzing. HD experienced the highest sales increase in 12 months, garnered 277+ million impressions with $1.5 million in advertising equivalencies and increased consumer brand advocacy to 69 percent, the highest level among 19 different ice cream brands measured.

Objectives

The brand identified actionable business, awareness, comprehension, and behavior goals for year one of the HD Loves HB campaign. PR needed to bring instant awareness/clarity to the complex plight of the disappearing honey bees, and make a strong, direct connection in media coverage between the issue and the future of HD. HD hoped the campaign would become the long-term business solution to turning around stagnating sales and restoring the brand to its historically high rate of 7–10 percent annual sales growth by 2010.

Business Goals:

1. Drive sales of HD's new Vanilla Honey Bee and products carrying the honey bee "cause" symbol.
2. Increase 2008 revenue growth by 1 percent over 2007.

Awareness/Comprehension Goals:

1. Increase awareness of the honey bee issue and the HD loves HB campaign.
2. Increase consumer media impressions on the HD brand by 25 percent over 2007 levels (total media goal: 125 million impressions in year one).

Behavior Goals:

1. Convince consumers to plant bee-friendly habitats. Achieve HD's first-year goal of planting one million bee-friendly flowers.
2. Drive unique visitors to helpthehoneybees.com. (Achieve industry average of five page views per visit.)
3. Increase consumer recommendations of HD over Q1 levels.

RESEARCH

Primary: Focus groups were conducted to determine consumer awareness, engagement, and attitude toward the honey bee issue, and the brand's possible role in the cause. Focus group findings:

1. When consumers see HD supporting the cause and educating people about the issue, they feel positive about the brand and its involvement;
2. Creating awareness about the issue makes consumers feel that the brand truly cares and is not just interested in sales; and

3. The cause helps consumers feel more connected to the brand; there is a sense of "we're in it together."

Secondary research showed that while honey bees are essential to the U.S. food supply, no major food brands had adopted the issue. The research findings guided the communication strategy. To be authentic and create a reason for consumers to connect to the brand and advocate for it, the campaign needed to help raise awareness, educate consumers about the issue, and engage consumer and community groups. To be successful, HD needed to take advantage of its first-mover status and be the first national consumer brand to "own" the bee cause.

Target audience: age 35–54, most have children; male/female balanced; highly educated; affluent urban and suburban living; active.

Audience analysis: HD consumers care about what they eat, and where their food comes from. They pay attention to what they put in their mouths and the quality of food their families eat. They are happy and eager to do their part to contribute to a sustainable society—particularly if they can make an impact through small, enjoyable, hassle-free actions. They're also willing to support causes that are genuine and relevant, and are eager to find ways to teach their children about responsible sustainable living.

PLANNING

The team knew a cause-marketing campaign could help create an emotional connection between consumers and the brand and help make the brand more approachable, but the program needed to be more than just another ribbon on a carton. The cause had to be engaging while still directly relating back to HD's brand essence. The plight of the honey bees seemed obscure at first but after learning that bees play a pivotal role in pollinating ingredients in more than 40 percent of HD's flavors and moreover, that 1/3 of all foods are pollinated by honey bees, the team knew the cause was right.

Using the insights from research as a guide, the team set forth the following strategies: 1. Give consumers a compelling way to engage more genuinely and frequently with the brand by educating them about the honey bee plight, HD's concern and the brand's authentic reliance on honey bees. 2. Leverage first-mover advantage and become the first national consumer brand to support the issue and put the cause on consumers' radar in a major way; strategically use the brand name to raise awareness and underscore the brand's "all natural" brand essence by inextricably linking honey bees with HD.

EXECUTION

Donation:

After a deep-dive assessment of leading universities and organizations working to raise awareness and solve CCD, The brand decided to donate $250,000 to Pennsylvania State University (PSU) and the University of California, Davis (UCD) for sustainable pollination and CCD research, and an additional $10,000 donation to The Pollinator Partnership, an organization dedicated to preserving honey bee health.

Bee Board:

The brand created an advisory board comprised of PSU and UCD scientists to guide the brand and ensure communication was authentic and factual, and two beekeepers—one East Coast-based and one West Coast-based—to provide insight into the struggles beekeepers face. All Bee Board members served as media spokes-people to deliver campaign messages related to their specific area of expertise.

Flavor Launch:

HD launched a new bee-dependent flavor, Vanilla Honey Bee, and pledged a percentage of overall sales of this flavor and all other bee-dependent flavors to go towards CCD research. The brand also created a special logo that was featured on all bee-dependent products and printed CCD information under the lid of every bee-dependent pint.

Industry Outreach:

Prior to the official launch in early February, the brand announced the campaign to the beekeeping and scientific community at a key industry conference. As a result, experts were ecstatic about HD's involvement, and served as credible brand ambassadors who later spread the word about the program within the industry and to other influencers.

Media Outreach:

A comprehensive media strategy was created to ensure no media stone was left unturned. To expedite mass awareness, the team's strategy hinged on launching the story with a "media multiplier." The team allowed CNNMoney.com to break the launch date embargo, because the outlet directly feeds hundreds of others on the Web and drives broadcast and print coverage in local markets throughout the United States.

HD also understood the importance of education and expanded its media targets beyond the usual food and lifestyle outlets to include scientific, agricul-tural, environmental, gardening, and beekeeping trade outlets. The team: con-ducted national and regional print, broadcast, radio, and online outreach; developed B-roll featuring HD plant footage, comments from Bee Board mem-bers and bees pollinating crops and flowers, which was distributed to regional and national broadcast networks; and engaged Bee Board members as spokespeo-ple for magazine, television, and radio media tours.

Million Seeds Challenge:

The team outreached to bee supporters online using Craigslist and MeetUp.com and challenged them to help HD plant one million seeds to create bee-friendly habitats. Enthusiasts received "HD loves HB" seed packets for planting in back-yards and gardens.

Ice Cream Social on Capitol Hill:

During national Pollinator Week, the brand and The Pollinator Partnership hosted a briefing on Capitol Hill about the status of the plight of honey bees, and an HD-hosted ice cream social. Katty Pien, HD Brand Director, testified before the Subcommittee on Horticulture and Organic Agriculture on behalf of CCD to keep honey bees and beekeepers top-of-mind for legislators and decision makers. Additional media coverage ensued, resulting in two more nationally-syndicated wire stories and a front page *San Francisco Chronicle* feature in HD's own Bay Area backyard.

EVALUATION OF SUCCESS

Response to the campaign exceeded all expectations for a first-year cause marketing initiative and goal to change brand perception; HD Loves HB revived consumer interest in Häagen-Dazs and spiked retail sales. Results included:

Business Goals:

Drive sales of HD's new Vanilla Honey Bee/bee-dependent flavors; increase 2008 revenue growth by 1 percent over 2007:

- A 5.2 percent April sales increase—the largest single sales spike in a year and 4 percent growth sustained from April-July 2008.

Awareness/Comprehension Goals:

Increase consumer media impressions on the Häagen-Dazs brand by 25 percent over 2007 levels (total media goal: 125 million impressions in year one); increase awareness of the honey bee issue and the HB loves HB campaign:

- More than 277 million media impressions, worth nearly $1.5 million in advertising equivalencies. The HD loves HB story was featured or included in more than 1,097 unique news placements, including CNN, AP, NPR, *The Wall Street Journal*, Today, *The New York Times*, Everyday with Rachael Ray (HD was mentioned in the headline or the lead).

- In a media audit and ROI analysis, 93 percent of all media coverage was overwhelmingly positive toward the brand; virtually 100 percent carried brand name/product mentions and key PR messages proving HD dominated the cause.

- A strong 12-point increase in the level of PR and "buzz" was achieved over previous quarters.

- An Omnibus survey conducted at the end of year one for the campaign showed a large increase in honey bee awareness, knowledge and brand recall; an 8-point increase in awareness of the honey bee issue; a 6-point increase in accurate identification of the issue; HD had the highest unaided brand recall among consumers identifying companies/organizations working to help the honey bees.

Behavior Goals:

Convince consumers to plant bee-friendly habitats; drive unique visitors to the Website; increase consumer recommendations of HD over Q1 levels:

- The team surpassed their goal for one million seeds distribution with more than 1,200,000 bee-friendly flower seeds to community groups and individuals, including local businesses, garden clubs, and teachers.
- 469,798 unique visitors swarmed helpthehoneybees.com and engagement was high—visitors viewed 8 pages per visit (82 percent above industry average) and the number of new visits averaged 76 percent above industry standards.
- More than 950 consumers and organizations contacted HD with suggestions, offers to collaborate, requests for more information, and compliments on the program.
- HD experienced a 13 percent increase in its brand advocacy rating (between Q1 & Q2) to 69 percent, the highest in the category (exceeding Ben and Jerry's).

E X H I B I T 9-1A   News Release

hd ❤ hb

Häagen-Dazs loves Honey Bees

CONTACT:

Diane McIntyre, Häagen-Dazs
510.601.4338, dmmcinty@dreyers.com

Allyson Savage, Ketchum
415.984.2243, allyson.savage@ketchum.com

HÄAGEN-DAZS® ICE CREAM PLEDGES TO HELP SAVE NATURE'S UNSUNG HEROES

More than fifty percent of Americans are unaware of the honey bee crisis and the role honey bees play in the food supply

Oakland, Calif.—The food producer responsible for one of every three bites the average American eats is in crisis. And more than half of Americans are not even aware there is a problem.* Who is this mega food producer? Meet the humble honey bee.

Honey bees are responsible for pollinating more than 100 different crops, $15 billion worth annually in the U.S., and are a key factor in the agricultural industry's ability to provide food products to the rest of the world. But honey bees are dying at an alarming rate. Over the last several winters, more than 25 percent of the honey

*According to a recent survey conducted by Opinion Research Corporation on behalf of Häagen-Dazs

bee population in the United States has vanished, many under mysterious circumstances. Early reports from beekeepers show this phenomenon is continuing in 2008.

For Häagen-Dazs ice cream, the reality of this threat has spurred the superpremium ice cream maker to launch a national campaign to protect these tiny unsung heroes. Everything from poor nutrition to invasive mites to Colony Collapse Disorder (CCD)—a phenomenon where bees from a colony abruptly desert the hive and die—is affecting the bees. This disappearance has scientists stumped and has the potential to affect many of our favorite nuts, fruits and berries—key ingredients in some of the most popular Häagen-Dazs flavors. In fact, more than 40 percent of Häagen-Dazs all-natural ice cream flavors include ingredients dependent on honey bees for pollination.

To discover and prevent what's killing our honey bees, the Häagen-Dazs brand is launching the *Häagen-Dazs loves Honey Bees*™ campaign to fund sustainable pollination and CCD research at Pennsylvania State University and the University of California, Davis.

"Häagen-Dazs ice cream is made from the finest all-natural ingredients, and the plight of the honey bee could mean many of the ingredients used in our top flavors, like Vanilla Swiss Almond and Strawberry, would be difficult to source," said Häagen-Dazs brand manager Josh Gellert.

Putting all its marketing might behind the issue, the Häagen-Dazs brand will launch a website, print, television and online advertising dedicated to educating Americans about the problem and seeking their help to spread the word and join the campaign. The effort will also include information in retail stores and Häagen-Dazs® Shops and a full public relations campaign.

To further spotlight the issue, the Häagen-Dazs brand is launching a new honey bee-dedicated flavor in February 2008—Vanilla Honey Bee. The brand is also tagging all of its honey beedependent flavors—from Häagen-Dazs Wild Berry frozen yogurt to Caramelized Pear and Toasted Pecan ice cream—with a *HD loves HB*™ icon. A portion of the proceeds from the sale of the new flavor and all *HD loves HB* tagged flavors will be used to fund the $250,000 donation to UC Davis and Penn State.

Häagen-Dazs has recruited prominent university researchers and beekeepers to serve on a Häagen-Dazs Ice Cream Bee Board to provide insight and consultation on the complex honey bee situation. Häagen-Dazs Ice Cream Bee Board members include:

- Diana Cox-Foster, Ph.D., professor of entomology and CCD researcher at Penn State
- Dennis vanEngelsdorp, acting state apiarist with the Pennsylvania Department of Agriculture and bee specialist at Penn State
- Robert Berghage, Ph.D., associate professor of horticulture, bee garden expert, Penn State University
- Sue Cobey, bee breeder, geneticist and leader of the bee breeding program at the UC Davis Harry H. Laidlaw Jr. Honey Bee Research Facility
- Eric Mussen, Ph.D., extension apiculturist at the UC Davis Harry H. Laidlaw Jr. Honey Bee Research Facility
- Michael Parrella, Ph.D., professor of entomology and associate dean, College of Agricultural and Environmental Sciences, Division of Agricultural Sciences, UC Davis
- Randy Oliver, beekeeping expert and teacher
- David Hackenberg, beekeeping expert and owner of Hackenberg Apiaries

"Honey bee health and sustainable pollination is a major issue facing American agriculture that is threatening our food supply and endangering our natural environment," said Diana Cox-Foster, Ph.D., leading CCD researcher at Penn State and Häagen-Dazs Bee Board member. "Häagen-Dazs Ice Cream's generous donation to Penn State's research program will provide immediate funds for research, outreach and student training to help find a CCD solution and preserve our natural food supply."

"The Häagen-Dazs brand and UC Davis have a shared goal of preserving our local natural ingredients in a sustainable future and their donation to the UC Davis Laid-law facility will help us reach our goals through advances in research and community awareness programs," said Michael Parrella, Häagen-Dazs Ice Cream Bee Board member and associate dean, Division of Agricultural Sciences, College of Agricultural and Environmental Sciences, UC Davis.

There are several ways consumers can help save our favorite pollinators:

- Create a bee-friendly garden with plants that attract honey bees.
- Support the *Häagen-Dazs loves Honey Bees* program—a portion of the proceeds of the sale of all bee-dependent flavors will go toward helping the honey bees.
- Educate neighbors, schools and community groups about the severe situation the honey bees and our food supply are facing.

For full details on how the Häagen-Dazs brand is helping honey bees and how you can take part, please visit **www.helpthehoneybees.com.**

About Häagen-Dazs

Crafted in 1961 by Reuben Mattus in his family's dairy, Häagen-Dazs is the original superpremium ice cream. True to tradition, we are committed to using only the purest ingredients in crafting the world's finest ice cream. Truly made like no other, today Häagen-Dazs ice cream offers a full range of products from ice cream to sorbet, frozen yogurt and frozen snacks in more than 65 flavors. Häagen-Dazs products are available around the globe for ice cream lovers to enjoy. For more information, please visit www.Häagen-Dazs.com.

© HDIP, Inc.

Courtesy Häagen-Dazs and Ketchum

EXHIBIT 9-1B Program Elements and Future Plans

Program Elements

Many brands jump on the cause marketing bandwagon without a story to tell. For Häagen-Dazs, taking action to protect the bee population could not be a more authentic narrative. And so, an innovative marketing campaign – dubbed *HD loves HB*—wasborn. The highlights:

- **Vanilla Honey Bee Ice Cream** – A delicious, limited edition flavor was developed to help raise awareness and funding for the cause.

- **Packaging** – An *HD loves HB* symbol was created and placed on all products with ingredients that depend on honey bee pollination. Each bee-dependent flavor also had a special lid ring and underlid story.

- **Sustainable Pollination Research** – Walking the walk, Häagen-Dazs donated a total of $250,000 to Penn State and UC Davis to continue Colony Collapse Disorder research, the inexplicable threat to the bee population.

- **Getting buzz with opera singers and an original score** –Set to the rousing original score from Q Department, and the operatic voices of Kip Wilborn and Julianna Di Giacomo, Häagen-Dazs released a somber and dramatic live action and animated commercial tale of unrequited love between a flower and a honey bee. The commercial's intentionally edgy tone serves to remind viewers of the severity of this issue. The commercial debuted during the April 20, 2008 episode of *60 Minutes*.

- **Plant This Page Ad** – The brand also gave back to the honey bees with the first-of-its-kind "Plant This Page" sustainable interactive print advertisement. Printed on seed paper -- a 100 percent recycled linen paper embedded with flower seeds—the page can be torn right out of the June 9 "green" edition of select regional *Newsweek* issues and planted directly in the ground to sprout bee-friendly flowers.

- **Additional Print Advertising** –To further spread awareness and educate consumers, the Häagen-Dazs brand ran an additional print ad with the message "Honey, please don't go."

- **Bee Advertorials** – To break through clutter, the brand also developed two advertorials which ran in *Martha Stewart Living* and *National Geographic*, which highlighted specific bee-dependent ingredients. To further highlight the effect bees have on the food supply, the Häagen-Dazs brand also created a special one-third side-bar for *Gourmet* Magazine.

- **Interactive Website** – At www.helpthehoneybees.com, consumers are asked to imagine a world without honey bees and encouraged to pass along a "Bee-Mail" message to friends with a customizable bee avatar.

- **Million Seeds Program** – Häagen-Dazs is distributing packets of *HD loves HB* branded bee-friendly seeds to enthusiast groups to provide nutrition for honey bees in backyards and community gardens, with the goal of planting one million seeds around the U.S.

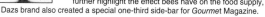

- **Häagen-Dazs Shops** – To further excite consumers and create a total brand experience around the program, Häagen-Dazs shops focused this year's New Flavor Day around Vanilla Honey Bee, including the creation of a new Honey Bee Sundae. The shops also marked all bee-dependent flavor tags with the *HD loves HB* burst and created special *HD loves HB* shirts for employees.

- **Employee Education** – The brand also educated employees with information packets and DVDs to highlight the importance of honey bees and the campaign. In turn, employees have become so excited and proud of the campaign that they have become active program representatives spreading honey bee information at local community groups and schools throughout the U.S.

- **Häagen-Dazs Bee Board** – To establish credibility, researchers and beekeepers who understand the issue were assembled to help direct Häagen-Dazs' messaging and explain the honey bee situation to media.

Partners

Contacted by hundreds of groups, the *HD loves HB* mission to help save the honey bees has resonated with a number of organizations ranging from national retail chains to local community members who have each reached out directly to Häagen-Dazs to offer support or suggest future partnership opportunities. The list includes:

- Pollinator.org
- Vanishing of the Bees Documentary
- Pittsburgh Garden Association
- *A NEW HIVE* Event at Earnest Sewn
- Beelogics

- Addison Elementary School (Palo Alto, CA)
- Entomological Society of America
- Brooklyn Beekeepers Group

- New York Taekwondo Clubs
- Association of Zoos & Aquariums
- Texas Botanical Gardens
- Hard Rock Café

What to look for the next 120 & beyond...

Häagen-Dazs will continue to be a leader in educating and raising awareness about the plight of the honey bee and ways consumers can make a difference to save these important pollinators and our food supply.

The Häagen-Dazs brand has partnered with Pollinator.org, an organization dedicated to preserving the health of honey bees and native pollinators in the U.S. The two organizations will host an "Ice Cream Social on the Hill" in Washington, D.C. during National Pollinator Week, June 22–28. To ensure honey bees and America's hardworking and struggling beekeepers stay top-of-mind for legislators and decision makers, Katty Pien will be giving testimony before the House of Representatives Committee on Agriculture.

Also during Pollinator Week, the brand is partnering with the Association of Zoos and Aquariums and local libraries to provide educational materials. The brand will also host a sampling event featuring Häagen-Dazs Vanilla Honey Bee ice cream at the Smithsonian (Washington D.C) and Dallas (Texas) zoos.

Häagen-Dazs is working with Whole Foods Markets to further spread awareness about the importance of honey bees. To show support Whole Foods will be handing out Bee-Friendly flower seeds, *HD loves HB* stickers and pins for employees. In addition, Vanilla Honey Bee ice cream with be placed in wrapped freezers on front end.

Häagen-Dazs has also partnered with Hyatt Hotels & Resorts to create A La Mode, a new decadent and stylish ice cream dessert menu, featuring Vanilla Honey Bee and other bee-dependent flavors.

Häagen-Dazs ice cream is also a sponsor of "The Vanishing of the Bees," a work-in-progress documentary that takes an investigative look at the bee crisis.

Looks Who's Buzzing about *HD loves HB*

Bee & Honey Industry

"The Häagen-Dazs gift is just awesome. **Last month at our national beekeeping conference, we gave a standing ovation to Häagen-Dazs for stepping forward to help us.**" – Jackie Park-Burris, California State Beekeepers' Association president, Palo Cedro, Shasta County, Calif.

"The National Honey Board fully supports the efforts of Häagen-Dazs to fund CCD research. We are excited to see this level of concern for the bees and recognition of their importance to our food supply. **This is an outstanding effort to deal with a critical and complex issue.**" – Bruce Boynton, CEO, National Honey Board

Courtesy Häagen-Dazs and Ketchum

Case 9-2

Companies often find new ways to engage customers and to customize their products, but seldom do they find one that resonates with personalized music. Exhibit 9-2A is a news release announcing the new "sound cards," and Exhibit 9-2B is a news release about the signing of a new recording artist.

Hallmark Sound Card Product Launch: Sweet Music!

Hallmark Cards with Fleishman-Hillard Inc.

SITUATION ANALYSIS

With the overwhelming growth of cell phones, Blackberries, and IMs, it has never been easier to communicate, And with more options than ever to say "Happy Birthday" or "Congrats" rather than using a traditional greeting card, many card companies realized they needed to work to remain relevant. Industry-wide, card sales have been flat for years. So how does a company whose brand is built on greeting cards grow sales?

In 2005, Hallmark Cards created the answer. The company set out to invent a new type of card—something that tapped into deep human emotion—and more specifically tied into our culture's music obsession. From iPods to ring tones, Hallmark knew personalized music was hot and there had to be a way to merge it with the emotion of greeting cards. The "sound card" was born.

Although a card that plays music was not new, Hallmark's approach with original songs by original artists—partnered with relevant editorial—was like nothing the industry had ever seen.

After an initial "test run" during Valentine's Day 2006, the 24 new sound cards were a hit ... leading Hallmark to embark on a mission to create 200 new cards in five months. With the ink still wet on the music licensing agreements, the expanded card line launched in summer 2006. Featuring recognizable songs selected for multi-generational appeal, it was the only sound card line to use original recordings by the original artists. And because of that, a key to success would be alerting music fans—potential new consumers—to the product.

One key strategy implemented by the Hallmark Cards and Fleishman-Hillard teams was to leverage extensive research about the consumer need/desire for the cards to raise awareness. The team showcased the cards via media sampling and unique direct-to-consumer tactics, In the end, the Hallmark Gold Crown-exclusive sound cards created *buzz,* drove traffic, and generated purchases from both Hall-mark Gold Crown Card (HGCC) members and non-members.

Specifically, the sound cards:

- helped card sales jump 9 percent over previous year's sales;
- formed the foundation of Hallmark's new "innovations" platform, demon-strating Hallmark cards' relevancy; and
- reminded consumers of the power of a card.

RESEARCH

Four research studies led to the expanded sound card line launch and were key to the communications strategies.

Product Research (2005)

Prior to the card line development, Hallmark researched the use of music as a marketing vehicle, finding trends in two areas:

- "Social expression" (personal playlists, favorite songs as gifts)
- "Brand relevance" (using music for branding).

Research showed we identify ourselves by our favorite music, which crosses gen-erations. Song cards are a way for adults to show kids they're hip. For kids, there's play value in the card.

Consumer Focus Groups (December 2005)

This research showed consumers believe the "wow" impact of a sound card is a motivator to purchase.

Sales Data Research (Valentine's Day 2006)

Preliminary results show broad appeal from both current HGCC consumers and new consumers.

- Equivalent appeal between HGCC consumers (49 percent) and non-HGCC (51 percent) consumers o Attracted "new" consumers, as HGCC members who bought song cards during Valentines 2006 but did not shop at HGC in Valen-tines 2005 were more likely to be newer to the HGCC program and younger.

Consumer Online Idea Exchange Research (April 2006)

Through an online study, Hallmark polled 1,000 consumers on what they liked/didn't like about the cards, showing:

- Song cards rated highest with 91 percent finding them appealing.
- 82 percent indicated they were likely to purchase song cards.
- The appeal is in the surprise or "wow" factor for many.

Research Findings

Through this research, Hallmark found consumers want to use music to communicate a unique message. The element of sound adds a whole new contemporary way of connecting—and it will surprise and delight both the giver and the receiver. With this finding, the team knew they had to showcase that "surprise and delight" element in the publicity tactics. In addition, the research showed these cards were a hit with a new, non-HGCC consumer, giving the team the ability to reach out to new consumers in new ways.

PLANNING

Objectives

- Raise consumer awareness of the new sound cards.
- Increase sales by driving traffic to Hallmark Gold Crown stores to try the new "shopping experience."

Strategies

- Create a sense of surprise and excitement to generate media attention, drive traffic, and attract consumers.
- Leverage product's ability to reach beyond the core target and speak to a "nontraditional" secondary audience.
- Use Hallmark's inherent creative experts to tell the story.
- Leverage cards themselves (demonstrate key attributes of product and sound technology) to garner media attention.

The target audience for the campaign was consumers who wanted a fun and unique way to enhance the experience of giving a greeting card. It included both current Hallmark consumers and new ones (music and pop culture fans).

The campaign was conducted over a 5-month timetable. Planning sessions took place in April/May 2006, and rollout occurred in July/August 2006.

EXECUTION

The team wanted to build excitement and awareness of the "wow" factor, and the cards were our best ambassadors. You didn't "get it" until you were able to experience it for yourself. Therefore, card samples were included with media materials and opened up to demonstrate during interviews. By providing samples and venues where key opinion leaders could "experience" the product, the team was able to combat the "song card" stereotype. (Prior to Hallmark's song card launch, most other products were poor sound quality and featured studio bands doing covers of songs.)

The team employed several non-traditional tactics to showcase the cards throughout the campaign. The key was to demonstrate the card—which worked best either direct-to-key-influencer or in a broadcast outlet—as the star.

These buzz-gen crating tactics reached new audiences for Hallmark:

- MTV Video Music Awards—To start building buzz among the music industry—and to attract new music artists to the concept—Hallmark provided sample products at the "AOL Style Suite" at the MTV VMAs. The sound cards were an unequivocal hit drawing comments such as "I have to have one of these," and "How can we get our band in a card?" More than 200 celebrities came through including Snoop Dogg, Fall Out Boy, The All American Rejects, and Panic! At the Disco. In addition, several music executives expressed interest in having their label's artists included in future song cards. To expand the buzz, celebrities ordered 100 holiday sound cards custom printed with a personal message to send to their friends and families.

- Fan club sites—The team targeted new consumers by reaching out to the fan sites of artists featured on the cards, leading to buzz-generating copy on sites for artists including Louis Armstrong, Blondie, Earth Wind & Fire, KISS, and The Village People.

- Radio trade-for-mentions—To generate more buzz among music fans, the team reached out to radio stations to offer "trade-for-mention" giveaways. The top 5 callers were given a "box set" of cards that matched the genre of that station. For example, R&B station listeners won "box sets" of cards featuring Earth Wind & Fire. The team also provided trivia questions that the DJ could use on air.

- Radio media tour—Key messages were delivered by Hallmark creative spokespersons. DJs received the cards prior to the interviews so they could play them on the air.

- Customized pitching—The team targeted media outlets with card samples and story ideas to fit their niche. As the campaign progressed, the team also pitched the top selling cards, posting them similar to Billboard's weekly music list.

- Satellite media tour—The success of the product line led to being featured in a "Best Products of 2006" SMT.

EVALUATION

Sales Results:

Ultimately, the success of the product launch was proven by sales results. In Hallmark Gold Crown stores, song cards fueled a 9 percent increase in sales of everyday cards compared with 2005.

The growth continued past the launch in July 2006 and into the holidays, the busiest season for Hallmark; o Total season greeting cards were up 9 percent

- Christmas counter card sales increased 10 percent; sound cards contributed 6 percent of counter sales.

- Sound cards contributed more than half of the counter card dollar increase.

More importantly, the success of song card sales helped overall sales for Hallmark Gold Crown stores. In 2006, total-store sales were up 3.1 percent.

Media Results:

The campaign successfully raised consumer awareness via national and local television, radio, newspapers, magazines, and Internet. As demonstrated by the enclosed clips, the media clearly communicated the message that Hallmark sound cards were a new way for consumers to communicate. PR strategies and tactics generated nearly 122 million trackable impressions.

- Radio/TV outreach resulted in more than 59 million impressions, including national hits on "The View," "The CBS Early Show," ABC News "Nightline," "CNN Headline News," Sirius Satellite Radio, and XM Satellite Radio, Local interviews were secured in cities ranging from New York to Seattle. As part of the radio trade-for-mention program, the team secured more than 50 giveaways of 270 "box sets" including WLTW, the No. 1 station in NYC, resulting in 45 million impressions.

- The print media outreach resulted in nearly 50 million impressions, including articles in key music industry publications such as *Billboard*, *Country Weekly*, and *Rolling Stone* (online). And, in addition to homerun hits in *The Wall Street Journal* and a positive *Associated Press* article, news about sound cards appeared in hundreds of newspapers across the country.

E X H I B I T 9-2A News Release on the Launch

FOR IMMEDIATE RELEASE
Contact: Deidre Parkes
(816) 274-5768 or dparke1@hallmark.com

Hallmark Has a Hit with Sound Card Collection
Expanded offering, includes new musical gift bags and gift-card boxes

(Kansas City, Mo., July 7, 2006) – Saying 'I love you' the first time can be nerve-wracking—but what if you had Willie Nelson or the Rolling Stones helping you out? Or what if you could cheer someone up by sending them the sounds of James Brown inside a card? Now, with a little help from Hallmark, you can.

This month, Hallmark Gold Crown® stores will offer an expanded collection of 223 sound cards featuring more than 100 original music artists as well as dialogue and theme songs from popular movies and TV shows. The collection also includes musical gift bags and gift-card boxes, as well as gift bags designed with pockets to hold a sound card.

Unlike any other cards in the market today, Hallmark sound cards feature CD-quality recordings of original music and sound clips. Each clip plays up to 30 seconds when the card is opened, and stops when the card is closed.

Tap into the Emotional Power of Sound

The addition of sound evokes more passion than a traditional card, according to Tim Bodendistel, art director for the line. "Music and favorite movie and TV shows evoke incredibly strong emotions," Tim says. "They recall memories, moments, times and feelings—so many tangible connections that the sender and recipient share. They allow you to share secret jokes from movies, relate to someone over an old TV show or evoke an emotion with a song.

Adding sound to a greeting card is a perfect way to help the card's sender express more meaning and to prompt that extra 'wow' from the recipient."

Hallmark sound cards are printed on high-quality card stock and feature a mix of special processes to make them sparkle, shimmer or stand out. The extraordinary sound quality from the cards' internal speaker is designed to be played again and again. The cards, priced at $4.99 each, are available exclusively in about 4,000 Hallmark Gold Crown® stores nationwide.

Appeal Across the Generations

The cards cover a range of sending situations including birthday, thinking of you, friendship, love, anniversary, encouragement, support, new baby, congratulations and cope. Clips featured in the cards have multigenerational appeal. The cards include classics songs such as "Unchained Melody" by The Righteous Brothers and "What a Wonderful World" by Louis Armstrong, as well as trendy tunes such as "All Star" by Smash Mouth, and "Wild Thing" by The Troggs.

Hollywood-themed cards feature sound clips and photos from popular movies, such as "Star Wars" and "Napoleon Dynamite." TV greetings showcase clips from shows such as "I Love Lucy" and "Law & Order." The clips include theme songs and well-known quotes from the TV show or movie.

The Hits Keep Coming

"When we introduced our original 24 sound cards last October, we approached two record labels and received licensing agreements for stock songs," says Tom Esselman, Hallmark greetings innovation director. "As word got out about the quality of our cards and their popularity with consumers, more record labels became interested in working with us. Today, we have much greater collaboration with everyone from major record labels to small publishing houses, and we're thrilled to introduce more than 180 new cards."

With this next generation of sound cards, "Hallmark has just taken the time and cared enough to make them meaningful—to get licensing rights to the original songs from the original artists and to put it together into a quality card that consumers love," Esselman says.

About Hallmark Cards, Inc

Kansas City-based Hallmark is known throughout the world for its greeting cards, related personal expression products, and television's most honored and enduring dramatic series, the Hallmark Hall of Fame. The company's Binney & Smith subsidiary, maker of Crayola® crayons and markers, is the leading producer of art materials for children and students. Through licensing leadership and joint ventures, Hallmark continues to expand its product formats and distribution avenues. The company publishes products in more than 30 languages and distributes them in more than 100 countries through a multi-national strategy. In 2005, Hallmark reported consolidated net revenues of $4.2 billion.

EXHIBIT 9-2B   News Release on New Recording Artist

New Faith Hill Hallmark Cards with Sound to Exclusively Benefit (RED)™
Share Faith Hill's music with a loved one and do some global good

KANSAS CITY, Mo. (June 16, 2008)—Hallmark Cards, Inc. today announced one of country music's top recording artists, Faith Hill, as the latest performer to be exclusively featured in Hallmark's (PRODUCT) RED™ Cards With Sound. The cards will feature five of Hill's originally recorded songs, and like other items in Hallmark's (PRODUCT) RED collection, the cards will raise money for the Global Fund to help eliminate AIDS in Africa.

"It's always great to find new ways for people to share music in a positive way," said Jill Rosen, Hallmark director of licensing. "To know that fans of Ms. Hill will save lives in Africa simply by purchasing a Hallmark card with one of her songs inside, that's a powerful thing."

Cards With Sound featuring Faith Hill's popular songs including "This Kiss," "If My Heart Had Wings," and "Breathe," are now available for $4.99 at Hallmark Gold Crown® stores nationwide.

With eight percent of net wholesale sales from all Hallmark (PRODUCT) RED products going to the Global Fund, the purchase of one Faith Hill Card With Sound results in a contribution equivalent to a single-dose treatment used to reduce the risk of transmission of HIV from mother to child during childbirth. Find out more about Hallmark's partnership with (RED) at Hallmark.com/RED and JOINRED.COM.

About Hallmark Cards, Inc.

Kansas City-based Hallmark has been helping people communicate, celebrate, and connect for nearly 100 years. Hallmark greeting cards and other products can be found in more than 43,000 places in the U.S. alone, with the network of Hallmark Gold Crown stores providing the very best selection. The Hallmark brand also reaches consumers online at Hallmark.com, on newsstands through *Hallmark Magazine,* and on television through Hallmark Hall of Fame original movies and the top-rated Hallmark Channel. In addition, Hallmark publishes products in more than 30 languages and distributes them in 100 countries across the globe. The company's Crayola subsidiary provides fun and imaginative ways for children to colorfully express themselves. In 2007, privately held Hallmark reported consolidated net revenues of $4.4 billion. Charitable giving of $16 million a year focuses on the well-being of children and families, vibrant arts and cultural experiences, and basic services for people in need in the communities where Hallmark operates. For more information about the company, visit http://corporate.hallmark.com.

###

Courtesy Hallmark Cards, Inc.

10

International Public Relations

During the past several decades, international public relations has become a major area of growth for practitioners. The two principal aspects of this field are counseling domestic clients in their programs to reach markets or audiences in other countries and counseling foreign clients, both corporate and governmental, in their efforts to communicate with American audiences. The process of international public relations is not just about translation, but also about deep cultural values and layered meanings in messages and connections with specific publics.

International public relations problems should be approached using the ROPE process.

RESEARCH

The research process for international public relations includes understanding the client, the opportunity or problem involved, and the audiences to be reached.

Client Research

A thorough investigation of the client will begin with background information on their nationality or home country. The next need will be for knowledge of the client's reputation and status in the country of its target audiences, along with past and present public relations practices in that country. Finally, the client's public relations strengths and weaknesses in the host country should be assessed.

Opportunity or Problem Research

In this phase of research, the practitioner should determine why and to what extent the client needs an international public relations program. The program may be either reactive in response to a problem experienced in the host country, or proactive in the interest of establishing a presence and creating goodwill in the host country.

Audience Research

Whether domestic or foreign, the client—and, more important, the practitioner representing the client—must understand various aspects of the target audience, including the language and its centrality to the culture of the host country, its cultural values, patterns of thought, customs, communication styles—both verbal and nonverbal—and the target audience's cultural norms. In addition, the public relations practitioner must become acquainted with the host country's various systems: legal, educational, political, and economic. Moreover, knowledge of the host country's social structure, heritage, and, particularly, its business practices will greatly benefit communicating with target audiences. Finally, audience information levels regarding the client and its products or services, audience attitudes and behaviors relevant to the client, and specific audience demographics and media-use levels should be gathered as part of the research for an international public relations program.

As in audience research for community relations, international practitioners will need to investigate and understand the media, opinion leaders, and major organizations of the host country. Collectively or singularly, they will often provide the key to success in communicating with a target international audience. Thus, audiences for international public relations can include those listed in Exhibit 10-a.

E X H I B I T 10-a   International Publics

Host Country Media

Mass

Specialized (print/broadcast/online)

Host Country Leaders

Public officials

Educators

Social leaders

Cultural leaders

Religious leaders

Political leaders

Professionals

Executives

Host Country Organizations

Business

Service

Social

Cultural

Religious

Political

Special interests

OBJECTIVES

International public relations programs may employ both impact and output objectives. They should be both specific and quantitative.

Impact Objectives

Impact objectives for international public relations involve informing target audiences or modifying their attitudes or behaviors. Some possible examples are:

1. To increase (by 20 percent) the international audience's knowledge of the client, its operations, products, or services (during a specific time period)
2. To enhance the client's image (by 15 percent during the current year) with the target international audience
3. To encourage (20 percent) more audience participation in the client's international events (during a particular program).

Output Objectives

Output objectives for international public relations consist of the practitioner's measurable efforts on behalf of the client. They may include such operations as:

1. Preparing and distributing (20 percent) more international publications (than last season)
2. Creating (five) new international projects (during the current calendar year)
3. Scheduling (eight) meetings with international leaders (during a specified time period)
4. Developing (three) special events for the public
5. Creating a digital presence on two social media platforms.

PROGRAMMING

Programming for international public relations includes planning theme and messages, action(s) or special event(s), uncontrolled and controlled media, and effective use of communication principles.

Theme and Messages

The nature of the opportunity or problem and the research findings in the situation will govern the messages and theme, if any, to be communicated in the international public relations program. Subtle differences in themes in countries may be required due to translation and cultural factors.

Action(s) or Special Event(s)

Client actions and special events for international programs often include:

1. Sponsorship of cultural exchange programs between the host and the client's countries

2. Establishment of institutes in the host country to teach the language and culture of the client's country

3. Meetings with leaders of the host country

4. Seminars or training programs held in schools, businesses, or institutions in the host country

5. Awards programs honoring leaders and other celebrities of the host country

6. Festivals in the host country celebrating the foods, dress, dance, art, or other aspects of the culture of the client's country. These may coincide with such holidays as creation of the client's country, its independence, victory in key battles or wars, birthdays of its founding fathers or heroes, and so on

7. Participation of the client organization, its management, and its personnel in the special holidays and events of the host country.

A major key to successful international public relations is the client involvement and interaction that actions and special events in the host country can provide.

Uncontrolled and Controlled Media

In international public relations, the practitioner should service the media of the host country with appropriate uncontrolled media such as news releases, interviews with officers of the client organization, and photo and video opportunities, all centered around the actions or special events composing the program itself.

Controlled media may also use the client's actions and special events as a major focus, with related print materials mailed or sent via email to a select list of leaders, posting video on a social media platform, and a speakers bureau created to provide important organizations in the host country with oral presentations from officers of the client organization. Both uncontrolled and controlled media should be centered on the client's involvement with, participation in, and contributions to the interests of the host country.

The client's website and online activities may play a significant role in the program. It may provide a wealth of information available in the language of the host country and reflect the client's interest in the host country. The website may also establish a channel for interactive dialogue and exchange of information. Social media interactions can open up avenues to new audiences.

Effective Communication

The most important communication principles involved in the programming of international public relations are source credibility, nonverbal and verbal cues, two-way communication, the use of opinion leaders, group influence, and audience participation.

Nothing is of greater importance in international public relations than the perceived credibility of the client organization in the host country. Target audiences must believe that the practitioner's client has their best interests at heart and is not simply exploiting local groups for personal gain. In such situations, credibility enhancement requires tangible and visible contributions to the host country on the part of the client organization, its management, and its personnel. These organizational representatives simply cannot set themselves apart as an elitist enclave or separate community in the host country and expect to maintain their credibility. They must become active and constructive participants in the life and culture of the host country. This will be best reflected in constructive actions and special events as part of the organization's public relations programming.

Effective use of verbal and nonverbal cues in the programming will include an understanding not only of the official language of the host country, but of that country's special applications or dialectical usage of the language. Although French is the official language of France, Canada's province of Quebec, and Haiti, its usage varies as widely among these countries as does Spanish usage from Madrid to Santo Domingo. The astute practitioner will understand such verbal nuances, as well as the many nonverbal cultural differences in the uses of time, spatial relationships, and visual and vocal cues. Failure to take these verbal and nonverbal distinctions into account can spell doom for international public relations programming.

Two-way, or interpersonal, communication is especially important in an international context. This presupposes the use of native speakers and writers in the public relations programming. The deadly public relations sin of overreliance on the mass media or other forms of one-way communication can take a serious toll on the effectiveness of international public relations efforts.

The inclusion of opinion leaders and groups is another indispensable element in international public relations programming. While important in most American contexts, attention to and communication with important leaders and groups can become magnified in the international context. This requires a thorough understanding of the complexities of the social and political context in the host country. It may require the employment of authoritative consultants in the host country. Though the cost of getting this right may be high, the cost of getting it wrong will, in the long term, be unbearable if not disastrous.

Finally, there can be no substitute in any public relations program for audience participation. If interactive programming is the norm for American public relations, it should be an absolute requisite of international public relations. This principle again underlines the significance of participative actions and special events as the core of effective programs.

Effective use of these communication principles cannot be overemphasized. They serve to heighten the practitioner's sensitivity to and awareness of the interactive and participative nature of public relations, especially in the international context.

EVALUATION

The evaluation of an international public relations program should be driven by the monitoring and final assessment of its stated objectives. Both impact and output objectives can be evaluated using the same measurement tools as in other forms of public relations (see Chapter 2). A significant difference may lie in the necessity to use research firms with credible reputations in the host country. It could be a serious mistake to bring in firms and employees from the client's country to conduct surveys, focus groups, and the like in the host country.

SUMMARY

The ROPE process is a useful format for the conduct of international public relations. In all aspects of the process, unusual precautions must be taken to observe the social, political, and cultural norms of the host country of the program's target audience. Not only must successful practitioners understand effective public relations principles, they must also become working cultural anthropologists and sociologists versed in the host country's history and politics.

READINGS ON INTERNATIONAL
PUBLIC RELATIONS

"An International Sensibility," *Public Relations Tactics* 6 (February 1999): 31.

Arfield, George. "As the World Changes, So Must Communicators," *Communication World* 10 June-July 1993): 33–34.

Bates, Don. "Update on Japan: Tips on Dealing with the Press," *Public Relations Journal* 50 (October-November 1994): 14.

Braun, Sandra L. "The Effects of the Political Environment on Public Relations in Bulgaria," *Journal of Public Relations Research* 19 (May 2007): 199–228.

Busch, Per-Olof, and Jörgens Helge. "The International Sources of Policy Convergence: Explaining the Spread of Environmental Policy Innovations," *Journal of European Public Policy* 12 (October 2005): 860–884.

Clarke, Terence M. "An Inside Look at Russian Public Relations," *Public Relations Quarterly* 45 (Spring 2000): 18ff.

Creedon, Pam, and Mai Al-Khaja. "Public Relations and Globalization Building a Case for Cultural Competency in Public Relations Education," *Public Relations Review* 31 (September 2005): 344–354.

Culbertson, Hugh M., and Ni Chen, eds. *International Public Relations A Comparative Analysis*. Mahwah, NJ: Erlbaum, 1996.

Curtin, Patricia A., and T Kenn Gaither. "Contested Notions of Issue Identity in International Public Relations: A Case Study," *Journal of Public Relations Research* 18 (January 2006): 67–89.

———. *International Public Relations: Negotiating Culture, Identity, and Power*. Thousand Oaks, CA: Sage, 2007.

———. "Privileging Identity, Difference, and Power: The Circuit of Culture as a Basis for Public Relations Theory," *Journal of Public Relations Research* 17 (May 2005): 91–115.

Drobis, David R. "The New Global Imperative for Public Relations: Building Confidence to Save Globalization," *Public Relations Strategist* 8 (Spring 2002): 36–38.

Freitag, Alan R. and Ashli Quesinberry Stokes. *Global Public Relations: Spanning Borders, Spanning Cultures.* Boston: Routledge, 2009.

Guth, David. "The Emergence of Public Relations in the Russian Federation," *Public Relations Review* 26 (Summer 2000): 191ff.

Kiousis, Spiro, and Xu Wu. "International Agenda-Building and Agenda-Setting," *The International Communication Gazette* 70 (February 2008): 58–75.

Kobayashi, Sanae. "Characteristics of Japanese Communication," *Communication World* 14 (December 1996-January 1997): 14–16.

Leaper, Norm. "Ahh ... the Pitfalls of International Communication," *Communication World* 13 (June-July 1996): 58ff.

L'Etang, Jacquie. "Public Relations and Diplomacy in a global world: An issue of public communication." *American Behavioral Scientist* 53 (Dec. 2009): 607–626.

Levick, R. "How Cultural Differences Affect Media Management Across Borders," in *Stop the Presses*, 2e, Washington, DC: Watershed Press, 2007.

Molleda, Juan-Carlos, and Candace Quinn. "Cross-National Conflict Shifting: A Global Public Relations Dynamic," *Public Relations Review* 30 (March 2004): 1–9.

Molleda, Juan-Carlos, and Deanna K. W. Pelfrey. "Intercultural Communication: A key aspect of international media preparation," *Public Relations Tactics* 14 (December 2007): 18.

Morley, Michael. *How to Manage Your Global Reputation: A Guide to the Dynamics of International Public Relations.* New York: New York University Press, 1998.

Panol, Zenaida Sarabia. "Philippine Public Relations: An Industry and Practitioner Profile," *Public Relations Review* 26 (Summer 2000): 237ff.

Parkinson, Michael, and Daradirek Ekachai. *International and Intercultural Public Relations: A Campaign Case Approach.* Upper Saddle River, NJ: Allyn & Bacon, 2005.

Reaves, Lynne "One Country, Two Systems: PR in the New Hong Kong," *Public Relations Tactics* 4 (September 1997): 12ff.

Rieff, David. "Their Hearts and Minds?" *New York Times Magazine* 154 (April 9, 2005): 11–12.

Robles, Jennifer De, Carolyn Munckton, and Brian Everett. "Global Perspectives," *Communication World* 22 (September–October 2005): 138ff.

Rugh, William A. *Arab Mass Media Newspapers, Radio, and Television in Arab Politics.* Westport, CT: Praeger, 2004.

Singh, Raveena, and Rosaleen Smyth. "Australian Public Relations Status at the Turn of the 21st Century," *Public Relations Review* 26 (Winter 2000): 387ff.

Sokuvitz, Sydel, and Amiso M George. "Teaching Culture: The Challenges and Opportunities of International Public Relations," *Business Communication Quarterly* 66 (June 2003): 97–113.

"Special Section on China Public Relations" *Public Relations Review* 35(3) (September 2009): 171–334.

Sriramesh, Knshnamurthy, and Dejan Vercic, eds. *The Global Public Relations Handbook: Theory, Research, and Practice*, 2d ed. Mahwah, NJ: Earlbaum, 2009.

Sturaitis, Laura. "What's the Big Idea?" *Public Relations Tactics* 11 (December 2004): 11.

Tang, Lu and Hongmei Li. "Corporate social responsibility communication of Chinese and global corporations in China," *Public Relations Review* 35.3 (September 2009): 199–212.

Taylor, Maureen. "Toward a Public Relations Approach to Nation Building," *Journal of Public Relations Research* 12, no. 2 (2000): 179ff.

Taylor, Maureen, and Michael L Kent. "Challenging Assumptions of International Public Relations: When Government Is the Most Important Public," *Public Relations Review* 25 (Summer 1999): 131ff.

Ting-Toomey, Stella. *Communicating Across Cultures.* New York: Guilford Publications, 1999.

Van Ruler, Betteke. "Communication Management in the Netherlands," *Public Relations Review* 26 (Winter 2000): 403ff.

Wakefield, Robert I. "Theory of International Public Relations, the Internet, and Activism: A Personal Reflection," *Journal of Public Relations Research,* (2008) 20.

Walton, Susan Balcom, and Robert I. Wakefield. "Effective Global Public Relations: Gearing Up for Change" *Public Relations Strategist* 16.4 (Fall 2010): 30.

Wang, Jian. "Managing National Reputation and International Relations in the Global Era: Public Diplomacy Revisited," *Public Relations Review* 32 (June 2006): 91–96.

Wilcox, Dennis L., Philip H. Ault, and Warren K. Agee. "International Public Relations" In *Public Relations Strategies and Tactics,* 9th ed. New York: HarperCollins, 2008.

Wouters, Joyce. *International Public Relations.* New York: AMACOM, 1991.

Zaharna, R.S. *Battles to Bridges: US Strategic Communication and Public Diplomacy after 9/11.* (Palgrave Macmillan, 2010) 240.

———. "Intercultural Communication and International Public Relations: Exploring Parallels," *Communication Quarterly* 48 (Winter 2000) 85–100.

International Public Relations Cases

Case 10-1

Some campaigns tap local cultural values to best resonate with the target audiences. The campaign may also have broad implications for society, such as helping women find a source of income. Exhibit 10-1A is a program flyer, Exhibit 10-1B is a news analysis of the media coverage, and Exhibit 10-1C shows women working on the handbags.

Unilever Turkey's "Garbagelady (Copmadam)" Program

Unilever Turkey with Unite Communications and Hooper Consulting International

OVERVIEW

"One woman's trash is another woman's treasure."

What better result can a Community Relations program have than to focus on community issues that align with social needs? Unilever (UL) did just that: it partnered with a top Turkish university to provide job training for unskilled women in Turkish villages … and furthered its goal to reduce paper waste in its plants. Moreover, the program contributed to UL's sustainability practices.

GarbageLady was the brainchild of an American professor of civil society working at Turkey's Sabanci University, who discovered a fresh way for Turks to experience participatory citizenship through civil involvement. She combined two burning societal issues in Turkey: low employment of women and paper waste disposal—and came up with the idea to make zippered clutch bags. Researching "cool things to make from trash" on the Internet, she discovered a prison in Mexico where such products were being made. She took a sabbatical from her teaching job and traveled to the Mexican prison where she spent five days learning how to braid paper to make the purses. Returning to Istanbul, she targeted her first group of unemployed women in a remote village and taught them how to make the bags. A bright young graduate assistant partnered with her to implement the program. Through a "chance" encounter, UL came into the picture as the provider of materials to make the purses.

And so GarbageLady was born.

RESEARCH

The issues that spurred the Community Relations program were:

- In Turkey, only 1 in 4 women are employed.
- While there is a government requirement that a minimum of 25 percent of trash must be recycled, in actuality the rate barely exceeds 10 percent.

Secondary research was compiled by the project founder and partner with the support of students from Sabanci University, using a myriad of resources via the Internet, university library, government reports largely from the State Planning Committee, industry reports about waste pile up and disposal, and more. Interviews with other professors and academic experts about civil society issues, observed research of the populations attitudes about participatory citizenship and community involvement—all these were instrumental in shaping the program in the following ways:

- A major donor of paper waste would be needed.
- People needed to be motivated to manage waste in a tangible way, as they virtually had no involvement with ecological initiatives or programs.
- Women would welcome job training.
- Small villages were identified to deliver the program.
- Criterion were established to qualify the participating women, i.e., unskilled with no previous compensated work experience.

PLANNING

The overall strategy was to improve relations with targeted communities by providing employment to unskilled women, as well as to save valuable resources for the Republic of Turkey.

UL set out to create the program first by partnering with Sabanci University, KEDV (NGO for women's empowerment) and Boyner (major retailer) under the leadership of the American professor who conceived it. The university provided resources for research, planning, training the women workers, and communications with UL. Boyner provided the sales outlets. UL, for its part, provided the paper resources to manufacture the bags, transportation of these resources to the villages, and public relations support. Ultimately, the program would reinforce UL's image in communities throughout Turkey.

The specific, measurable **objectives** of the program in 2009 were:

- To train a minimum of 50 unskilled women
- To produce no less than 2,500 bags
- To win favor with the communities where the project was conducted
- To elevate UL's reputation via media coverage of the project.

The overall budget covered materials, administrative costs in the communities, shipping of paper waste materials to the villages, payments, and salaries to local employees.

EXECUTION

If people want to change, they will. If they don't want to, it's hard to make them do so. The current interest in the environment is a good thing. The best way to make a contribution in fashion is to promote the idea that a fundamental interest in preserving the environment is itself fashionable. —Giorgio Armani

To launch the Community Relations program, the university founder needed to first identify and recruit the women in the target villages at the grass roots level. Once the first group was assembled, they were trained by two university students to make the bags with unusable paper from UL's plants. The paper was clean and sanitary, but may have had a printing error or been cut in the wrong place, etc.

Study after study about women's entrepreneurship and microcredit programs revealed that they failed because they were not sustainable. That's why it was critical that the women have a direct stake and a sense of ownership of the project. For that reason, a key element of the program was that after the initial launch period, the project transformed itself into a business. After all, the purpose was to enable women to work … and work they did! The sheer volume and logistics required a proper work space, two full-time salaried employees, materials, and more. On top of that, the merchandising of the bags was more efficient when contracts were made with retailers and boutiques.

As the handbags were being sold commercially, they were of course generating revenue that streamed back into the project. This was another reason for the conversion of part of the project into a full-fledged business.

And as the Armani quote above points out, the items had to be fashionable so they would sell. The target markets were largely upscale, trendy, educated young women. Therefore the colors and design of the clutch bags had to be 'cool' and fun so people would buy them. Even the GarbageLady name (the Turkish name is a humorous play on words) and lively logo are a far cry from the staid and sometimes severe names and looks of other women's empowerment initiatives and products.

While there was ample public relations coverage of this unusual and compelling program as it swelled in Turkish communities, a non-traditional tactic was used involving celebrities, a top model, and famous business women (including the female Chairman of Sabanci Holding, who owns the university) to showcase the bags at social, cultural, and business functions.

Word-of-mouth ensued, and GarbageLady found itself fulfilling scores of orders from telephone calls and online sales as a result. Another boost to the program ensued after the American professor was interviewed on CNN International.

EVALUATION

Since its inception, some 250 Turkish women have received job training and have produced some 3,750 bags, recycling more than 8.5 tons of packaging material that have been removed from the garbage. The clutch bags have been sold in 12 of the top boutiques and retailers largely in Istanbul, the most sophisticated city in Turkey that has the market for these products. The program has been so successful, that a group of the women have formed a breakfast club—a remarkable treat since disposable income was not available to them before—and also because it is very unusual for village people to go out for breakfast. Community leaders and other merchants have remarked that GarbageLady has brought life to the neighborhood. They also observe that there is heightened awareness of recycling in the towns and that there is less trash on the streets from wrapper bags. What's next? A line extension, of course. New apparel items and house are in the planning stages.

EXHIBIT 10-1A   Program Flyer

THANK YOU FOR LITTERING

"One person's garbage is another's treasure" but your garbage,
well, we make that into art.

Questioning what is worth saving or not, çöp(m)adam started as an
experimental project in Ayvalık addressing the issues of women's
employment in Turkey and the importance of recycling/re-using
and aims to uitilize waste in a creative, aesthetically and unique way.

çöp(m)adam items are produced from the packaging that would be or
has been thrown away, by women who have never previously earned
a salary. All the produts are one-of-a-kind and signed by its producer.

Claim your own piece, before it goes to trash!

For more information: www.copmadam.com

*çöp(m)adam Project is realized in cooperation with Unilever Turkey and
Sabancı University Civic Involvement Projects.*

SALE POINTS

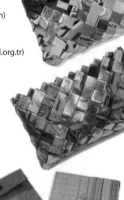

- Building (www.building.com.tr)
- Butik Buka (www.butikbuka.com)
- California Nail Bar (www.californianailbar.com)
- çöp(m)adam Workshop Ayvalık / Balıkesir
- Ece Sükan Vintage Butik (www.ecesukanvintage.com)
- KAMER Diyarbakır Mor Çarşı (www.kamer.org.tr)
- Karınca (www.karincadesign.com)
- PAZ-ART (www.pazart.org)
- Sabancı University Alumni Association (www.sumed.org.tr)
- Sakıp Sabancı Museum(muze.sabanciuniv.edu)

SEASONAL ONLINE SHOPPING WEBSITES

- Bankomarka (www.bankomarka.com)
- Limango (www.limango.com.tr)
- Markafoni (www.markafoni.com)
- Trendyol (www.trendyol.com)

SOON at www.copmadam.com

CONTACT

Tara Hopkins: tara@sabanciuniv.edu
Ayvalık Workshop Phone: 0266 312 13 60
Mobile Phone: 0533 684 46 08
Melih Özsöz: ozsozmelih@hotmail.com
Neşe Aktuğ: nese@sabanciuniv.edu
Ebru Şenel Erim: ebru.senel-erim@unilever.com

Unilever   Sabancı Üniversitesi

Courtesy Unilever Turkey, Unite Communications and Hooper Consulting International

E X H I B I T 10-1B   News Coverage Analysis

OVERALL TABLE FOR MEDIA APPEARANCES

Basic Indicators – Press										
Company Name	No. of News	%	Circulation	%	St x Cm	%	Approximate Advertisement Equivalent ($)	%	Reach	%
Garbage Lady	14	100.00	2,328,729	100.00	388	100.00	29,690	100.00	8,815,369	100.00

Distribution of Basic Indicators by News Impact								
	Absolute Values Distribution				Distribution as Percentages			Net Positive Values
By No. of News	Positive	Neutral	Negative	Total	Positive	Neutral	Negative	
By Circulation	14	0	0	14	100%	0%	0%	14
	Positive	Neutral	Negative	Total	Positive	Neutral	Negative	
By Reach	2,328,729	0	0	2,328,729	100%	0%	0%	2,328,729
	Positive	Neutral	Negative	Total	Positive	Neutral	Negative	
By St x Cm	8,815,369	0	0	8,815,369	100%	0%	0%	8,815,369
	Positive	Neutral	Negative	Total	Positive	Neutral	Negative	
By Advertisement Equivalent $	388	0	0	388	100%	0%	0%	388
	Positive	Neutral	Negative	Total	Positive	Neutral	Negative	
	29,690	0	0	29,690	100%	0%	0%	29,690

Distribution of the Number of News by Publication Content	
Media Group	Garbage Lady
News	9
Economy-Finance-Business	2
Tabloid	1
Shopping-Fashion-Decoration	1
Specific to age and gender groups	1
Total	14

Courtesy Unilever Turkey, Unite Communications and Hooper Consulting International

EXHIBIT 10-1C Campaign Images

Courtesy Unilever Turkey, Unite Communications and Hooper Consulting International

Case 10-2

Here is a creative use of an international "world record" to promote national awareness around an important health issue. The campaign involved high level government support and included many organizational and corporate partners. Notice the powerful visual elements used in the campaign. Exhibit 10-2A is a news release announcing the Guinness World Record and Exhibit 10-2B is a photo of the event.

A Woman's Stand: The Largest Human Pink Ribbon Campaign

Adalid Public Relations

SUMMARY

A Woman's Stand (The Largest Human Pink Ribbon Chain) is a breast cancer awareness campaign under the patronage of Sultan Bin Abdulaziz Foundation and undertaken by Her Royal Highness Princess Reema Bint Bandar Bin Sultan Al Saud and Al Bidayah Center for the Zahra Breast Cancer Association.

The aim of the campaign was to break a Guinness World Record (GWR), in the category of the Largest Human Awareness Ribbon, by organizing the formation of the largest female human pink ribbon chain on October 28, 2010, in Jeddah, Kingdom of Saudi Arabia (KSA). Through this attempt, and numerous side events that happened in conjunction with the Pink Ribbon, the campaign educated the general public on the causes and effects of breast cancer and united the women of Saudi Arabia in a momentous event.

The campaign organizers wanted to demonstrate the strength and determination of Saudi women and prove that through a united front that a difference could be made. The campaign invited women from all backgrounds (ages 12 and up) to participate on October 28 to demonstrate their commitment to each other and to good health.

A Woman's Stand Campaign hoped to attract enough women participants to break this record and secure Saudi Arabia a spot in the Guinness Book of Records.

RESEARCH

The previous Guinness World record for the Largest Human Awareness Ribbon was held by AIDS-Hilfe Frankfurt which was able to reach 3,640 participants on June 29, 2007. Most recently in 2008 in the United Arab Emirates, 1,032 women and their families participated in the formation of a human pink ribbon chain.

PLANNING

As a nationwide awareness campaign on breast cancer in Saudi Arabia, Adalid Public Relations developed and proposed a communications campaign to break the record and win the number one position for Saudi Arabia in the Guinness Book of World Records.

Objectives

1. Build awareness around breast cancer issues in Saudi Arabia.
2. Break the largest Pink Ribbon record made by a human chain in the Guinness Book of World Records.
3. Generate positive media coverage in Saudi Arabia and around the region.
4. Build a reputation for Saudi Arabia as a breast cancer wary nation.

Target Audiences
Media:

Local Saudi and international media from all sectors (TV's, radios, newspapers, magazines, and online newswires).

NGO's:

Sanad Children's cancer support, Women's charitable society, Al Bir Charity Society, Charitable Society for Orphans, The Help Centre, Al Faisaliah Women Charitable Society.

Government Bodies:

Ministries of Education, Health, Information and Labor and Social Affairs.

Educational Institutions:

Female universities, colleges and schools across KSA, with a focus on Jeddah Educational institutions: Effat University, Dar Al Hekmah University, BMC Medical College, CBA, Jeddah Knowledge International School, American School, American Prep, Al Manarat schools, Al Firdaous schools, Dowhat Al Jazeera, Dar Jana, and Al Jazeera Schools.

Oncology and Health Communities:

King Abdul Aziz University Hospital, King Faisal Specialist Hospital and Research Centre, King Fahad Hospital, King Fahad Armed Forces Hospital, SGH, Fakeeh Hospital, and United Doctors Hospital, IMC.

Private Sector and Sponsors:

Food and beverage companies, medical companies, banks, automotive companies, and hyper markets airlines and tourism companies, beauty and cosmetics companies.

EXECUTION

Activities

Pre-Pink Ribbon Formation:

- Building the foundation for a campaign.
- Established ongoing meetings and phone calls with HRH Reema Bint Bandar Bin Sultan, Dr. Modi Batterjee, and Zahra Association to coordinate activities and distribution of work.

  Developed campaign Plans and Materials:

- Drafted backgrounder for the campaign.
- Drafted sponsorship document for the campaign.
- Drafted biographies for HRH Princess Reema and Dr. Modi Batterjee.
- Drafted factsheets A+E, Q&A, and boilerplate documents.
- Drafted event agenda and continued to liaise with Zahra Association to keep agenda updated.

Communications

- Communicated with Guinness World Records to coordinate logistics, record setting requirements, and a timeline.
- Obtained support from Saudi health organizations (Ministry of Health, health NGO's and oncology institutions to include Down Syndrome Charitable Association, Sanad Children Cancer Support Society, and Insan and Disabled Children Association).
- Communicated with and visited educational institutions (universities, colleges, and private schools).
- Developed sponsors (broadcast sponsors, food and beverages sponsors, educational sponsors, VIP's, and well known doctors such as Dr. Muna Baslaim).
- Coordinated with campaign partners (Full Stop Advertising, MEMMS Event Management, Avon, and MBC).

Ongoing Media Relation and Communication Activities Around the Campaign

- Prepared for the launch press conference/round table, and developed media interviews focusing on the Guinness Book Ceremony.
- Worked with Guinness World Records (GWR) on appropriate tactics for our campaign.
- Coordinated with Saudi Ministry of Health, NGO's, and campaign champions.
- Coordinated event timeline with the Ministry of Health.
- Identified potential NGO's for potential support and campaign involvement.

- Worked with the NGO's to identify human ribbon candidates.
- Worked with campaign partners on required support and logistics (i.e. branding, venues, gift items, documenting the formation of the pink ribbon), and approached government agencies in either Riyadh or Jeddah for guidelines and required approvals or processes.
- Approached and commissioned ad agency (Full Stop), event management (MEMMS), photographers & videographers (Rania, Hawazen Ba'ageel), venue (MOE Stadium), and other logistics partners.

Media Relations

Campaign launch press conference:

- Liaised with Zahra Association to secure venue (Al Bidayah Center for Breastfeeding) and logistics for the launch press conference.
- Liaised with Zahra Association to provide catering, media gifts, and set-up for the press conference.
- Prepared/printed/distributed press-kit materials (bio's, backgrounders, factsheets, and Arabic and English press releases for journalists).
- Contacted photographers and briefed them on required photo shoots.
- Drafted a media list and forward to Zahra Association for approval.
- Drafted a media invite/advisory in both Arabic and English.
- Called and invited the media to attend the press conference, and conducted follow up calls.
- Drafted (English & Arabic) Pink Ribbon campaign launch press release entitled "Saudi Women to Form World's Largest 'Pink Ribbon' Human Chain, in Partnership With MBC Group."
- Managed the press conference on July 27—13 news organizations attended.
- Secured and managed a interviews with MBC TV on the ground and with Saudi 1 TV and Saudi Radio by phone.
- Welcomed the media, and introduced the campaign spokesperson (Dr. Modi Batterjee) to the media.
- Provided press-kits to the journalists and media gifts (pink bracelets).

Post news conference support:

- Forwarded a digital copy of the event photographs to the Zahra Association.
- Forwarded press-release to *Al-Watan* newspaper, *Arab News* newspaper, *Al Hayat* newspaper, *Al Riyadh* newspaper, *Okaz* newspaper, *Saudi Gazette* newspaper, *Al Bilad* newspaper, *Al Nadwah* newspaper, *Shams* newspaper, *Al Eqtesadiah* newspaper, *Asharq Al Awsat* newspaper, *Al Madina* newspaper, *Al Jazirah* newspaper, *Al Yaum* newspaper, *Sayidaty* magazine, *Zeina* magazine, *Kolenas* Magazine, *Roa'a* magazine, *Arabian Woman* magazine, *Dazzle* Magazine, *Fawasel* magazine, *Adam Al-Yaum* magazine, *Arabian Man*

magazine, *Laha* magazine, *Cristal* magazine, *Rotana* magazine, *Infinity* magazine, *Adwaa* magazine, *Brand* magazine, *Destination Jeddah* magazine, *Aalam Al-Rajol* magazine, *Layalina* magazine, *Al Jamila* magazine, *Madame Vegro* magazine, *Zahrat Al-Khaleej* magazine, *Al-Yaqza* magazine, and also online newswires.

- Conducted a media follow up to ensure/secure good coverage.
- Conducted a media monitoring on a daily basis and forwarded coverage to Princess Reema and Zahra Association accordingly.
- Coordinated broadcast interviews with key publications (Dr. Modi Batterjee served as the Zahra spokesperson).
  - MBC 1
  - Saudi TV 1
  - Saudi Radio

Post-Conference Communication

Coordinated event support for **Guinness World Record** and GWR participation at the Pink Ribbon event, to include: visas process, secured travel and accommodation for GWR delegates, and ensured compliance with GWR guidelines.

Media Relations:

- Drafted media lists for the Pink Ribbon formation campaign.
- Drafted international media list to invite for the ceremony event (the list to include top ten international and regional media outlets, e.g. CNN, BBC, and NBC).
- Drafted and conducted invites for international media.
- Launched the Pink Ribbon Campaign through organizing a media press conference with spokespeople from the Ministry of Health and Pink Ribbon Campaign spokesperson. The press conference included top dailies, magazines and exclusive TV broadcast MBC, press kits distributed to them (press release A+E, background on the campaign, bios on the spokespeople, photos, and media gifts).
- Pitched for up to three one-to-one media interviews with print and broadcast outlets and conducted two interviews (*Arab News*, *Sayidaty*).
- Drafted a generic article around breast cancer issues in Saudi Arabia.
- Drafted media invites and prepared press kits for the Pink Ribbon formation ceremony.
- Posted print ads on top Saudi dailies (*Al Watan*, *Sayidaty*, and *Arab News*) to attract the required numbers to form the Largest Human Chain Pink Ribbon.
- Built a Facebook page as a means for counting the number of participants/volunteers.

Event Management:

- Researched and proposed best venue (MOE Stadium) to hold the Pink Ribbon ceremony (October 28, 2010).
- Approached proposed outlets and finalized agreement.
- Worked with NGO's, partners, to invite and attract the required female/children through ads, visits, phone calls, and contact with universities and schools, malls, and compounds to form the Largest Pink Ribbon.
- Liaised with advertising partner for 7,000 pink ponchos or Abaya's stitching to be provided on the day of the event for the participants to wear.
- Conducted a volunteer workshop for event management a day before the final event.
- Applied and processed all required governmental papers/approvals.
- Sent SMS shots to more than 200,000 females in Jeddah and Riyadh through Acxiom MENA, leader of the direct marketing industry in the region.

The Largest Pink Ribbon Formation Ceremony (period of 10 days)

- Prepared media lists for the ceremony attendance.
- Drafted media invites for the ceremony.
- Sent media invitations and follow up to secure maximum attendance.
- Followed up with Partners (Ad agency, event management agency, GWR, photographers & videographers, and venue.)
- Conducted final recap meeting with the Campaign's champions (HRH Princess Reema, Dr. Modi, Ghada from Avon, Full Stop Ad agency, and MEMMS event management) for final revision of the ceremony arrangements.
- Drafted and distributed the Largest Pink Ribbon venue announcement press release.

The Largest Pink Ribbon Ceremony

- Managed female/children participants, provided them pink ponchos or pink Abaya's and managed the formation of the pink ribbon.
- Provided needed support for the GWR delegates.
- Managed all partners involved (photography, videography, and event management).
- Secured more than 30 one-to-one interviews (TV's, magazines, and newspapers) on the ceremony ground with the campaign spokespersons and leaders.
- Awarded the Guinness Book of World Record certificate to the campaign owner (HRH Princess Reema and Sultan Bin Abdul Aziz Al Saud Foundation).

Post-Largest Pink Ribbon Event

- Sent digital copy of the event photographs to Zahra Association.
- Distributed post event press release to local, regional, and international publications and online newswires.
- Conducted a media follow up to ensure/secure good coverage.
- Conducted media monitoring on a daily basis and forwarded coverage to Princess Reema and Zahra Association accordingly.

EVALUATION

Achieved tremendous media coverage for Breaking GWR Record event.

- Secured 30 newspapers coverage hits (*Al-Watan* newspaper, *Arab News* newspaper, *Al Hayat* newspaper, *Al Riyadh* newspaper, *Okaz* newspaper, *Saudi Gazette* newspaper, *Al Bilad* newspaper, *Al Nadwah* newspaper, *Shams* newspaper, *Al Eqtesadiah* newspaper, *Asharq Al Awsat* newspaper, *Al Madina* newspaper, *Al Jazirah* newspaper, *Al Yaum* newspaper, and *Gulf News* newspaper).
- Produced coverage in eight magazines such as *Roa'a, Sayidaty,* and *Destination Jeddah.*
- Produced 91 online local and international newswires.
- Secured eight TV & radio stories (MBC, Saudi TV, Al Arabiya TV, Ala'an TV, France 24, Saudi Radio).

Overall, the one-on-one interviews, press releases, and features appeared in all media sectors:

- Total Circulations **4,470,863**
- Total Readerships **659,598,108**
- Total Ad Value *4,029,163* **Million SR**

OUTPUT EVALUATION

Materials Library:

All items from the Pink Ribbon Campaign Foundation (library) were distributed in the press-kits (fact sheet, bios, and approved messages).

Media Relations:

Conducted a quick media training (interviews handling) to make sure that Pink Ribbon Campaign's executives/spokespersons delivered campaign's messages well under pressure. For the press release, the final approval and amendments arrived late and only a couple of hours before the conference. Everything else went well and the release coverage was very good.

Timely approvals:

Approvals were obtained in a timely manner for media lists and the conference, but venue approvals took a long time and caused some lateness for the volunteers training workshop and the event management set up.

Agendas/Timetable:

Zahra Association shared agenda details with Adalid to plan/draft a tentative event plan.

Preparation Meeting:

Campaign's executives & Adalid PR conducted an event meeting to agree on objectives, discuss agenda, and clear roles and responsibilities.

Photography:

For future events, Zahra Association should consider hiring a professional photographer for the press conferences especially when planning to distribute a press release. For the final formation event, photography and videography teams were hired and did a good job.

Event Management:

Volunteer leaders should receive better training in event management for such a big event.

E X H I B I T   10-2A   News Release

We Did It!" Thousands of females stand shoulder to shoulder in Jeddah forming the largest Pink Ribbon in the world

The Attempt to form the biggest human "Pink Ribbon" to raise breast cancer awareness succeeds and has been submitted to Guinness Book of Records for ratification

Jeddah—28 October 2010—Exactly 3,952 women and girls literally tied the pink knot in Jeddah's Ministry of Education stadium and broke a Guinness World Record, in the category of the Largest Human Awareness Ribbon. This pink ribbon beats the previous world record, which was the AIDS-Hilfe ribbon, which consisted of 3,640 participants set in Frankfurt, Germany in 2007.

"I greatly appreciate all those who participated today in forming the Largest Human Awareness Ribbon 'Pink Ribbon' and sharing my vision to eradicate suffering from Breast Cancer due to lack of awareness and early detection of the disease. It was a pleasure to see women from all walks of life, expat and local standing proudly shoulder to shoulder in sending this message out to the rest of the world" stated HRH Princess Reema Bint Bandar Bin Sultan Al Saud, sponsor of 'A Woman's Stand' breast cancer campaign. "We have succeeded magnificently, thanks to the commitment of all who took part today."

Princess Reema added that this event will go down in history not alone as an awareness of breast cancer but how women joined together for a common cause regardless of their color, culture and profession. We women wear many different hats every day; we are mothers, wives, daughters, sisters and friends. Many count on us and we need to take the time to educate ourselves and take care of our health to be there for our loved ones.

This great day signified the enthusiasm of women who came from across the Kingdom to Jeddah and gathered at the education stadium for registration in an attempt to make history. Before the attempt took place, booths dispensing information on breast cancer were available and were busy educating and distributing leaflets to all the attendees.

Preceding the main event, many participated in the Avon Walk for Life—a noncompetitive walk that over years in the whole world has raised millions of dollars and awareness of the prevalence and the curability of breast cancer. Ghada Alsobahi Avon spoke person said "Now it's the time to start Avon walk in Saudi Arabia and join the others 50 countries, and show the whole world that we can!, we are so excited that we helped forming the largest human pink ribbon this year it's a great achievement!

Excitement mounted as the main event got under way and the women, many carrying pink banners, were escorted into a familiar crossover loop that symbolizes the pink ribbon. Eventually the loop was formed and Guinness officials checked the number of participants in the loop. Once confirmed the officials announced that we had achieved our goal. A huge cheer rocked the stadium, women punching the air among scenes of celebration grew around the stadium as a new Saudi world record was accomplished.

The event was significant not simply for the new record and the profile it gives to breast cancer which, contrary to popular belief affects men nearly as much as women. It was possibly the largest gathering at a women only event in the Kingdom and gave an opportunity for Saudi women to work together and help each other.

Dr. Modi Batterjee, campaign spokesperson, volunteering for Zahra Breast Cancer Association and founding member of Al Bidayah Center said, "There are a vast number of women affected by breast cancer in Saudi Arabia. Women are not aware that if breast cancer is detected early enough the cure is effective and a quality of life is attainable. We at the Zahra Association want to educate advice and address any concerns the Saudi population may have regarding this disease."

The private sectors support for the event was instrumental in garnering attention and helping to raise awareness. Partners and sponsors of the event included: Avon, Al Bidayah, MBC Group, Al Watan Newspaper, Sayidaty Magazine, AlHAMA, DK, DKNY, Roch, FAM, Mobily, Almarai, Riyad Bank, Panda, Jeddah Hilton, PEPSICO and Burger King.

-ends-

About the Largest Human Pink Ribbon Campaign "A Woman's Stand":

The Largest Human Pink Ribbon Chain is a breast cancer awareness campaign following the theme of "A Woman's Stand." The campaign is under the patronage of Sultan Bin Abdulaziz Foundation and undertaken by HRH Reema Bint Bandar Bin Sultan Al Saud and Al Bidayah Center (Breastfeeding Resource and Women's Health Awareness Center) for the Zahra Breast Cancer Association. The aim of the campaign is to break a Guinness World Record, in the category of the Largest Human Awareness Ribbon by organizing the formation of the largest female human pink ribbon chain on 28 October 2010 in Jeddah, KSA.

For further information, please contact:

Yahya Hamidaddin
Adalid Public Relations
e-mail: yahya.hamidaddin@adalidpr.com
Tel: +966 2 263 1720 - Ex. 250
Fax: +966 2 263 1730

Yasser Al-Hebsi
Adalid Public Relations
e-mail: Yasser.Alhebsi@adalidpr.com
Tel: +966 2 263 1720 - Ex. 180
Fax: +966 2 263 1730

Courtesy Adalid Public Relations

E X H I B I T 10-2B   Pink Ribbon Event Photo

Courtesy Adalid Public Relations

Case 10-3

Big events offer big rewards for enhancing the reputation of an organization and none is bigger than the summer Olympic Games. Exhibit 10-3A is a news release about the sponsorship for the games.

McDonald's Global 2008 Beijing Olympic Games Sponsorship "Bringing People Together Like Never Before"

McDonald's with GolinHarris

SITUATION ANALYSIS

How can PR effectively leverage a corporate sponsorship for the most anticipated, politicized and sponsor-laden Olympic Games in history? It wouldn't be easy. Media focused on negative issues surrounding the host country, making "feel good" stories harder to get than in any previous Games.

Consider these challenges:

- Competing with other major Olympic sponsors for limited positive media space
- Conveying messages and stories that would engage and resonate with diverse audiences in more than 100 countries
- Navigating International Olympic Committee (IOC) and Beijing Organizing Committee for the Games (BOCOG) restrictions and obstacles, including unprecedented security
- Internally aligning and rallying McDonald's country communicators.

The challenges were met, with many commenting that McDonald's achieved the best media coverage of the 2008 Olympic Games.

RESEARCH

To examine the challenges closer for securing significant, positive media coverage for McDonald's Olympic sponsorship around the world, secondary research and extensive media audits were conducted. The research confirmed the challenges—Olympic coverage focused primarily on China's issues and then on athletes/competitions, not sponsors and their activities. Sponsorship was viewed as old news and seen as commercial—it would take more than a standard media approach to reach media "gold."

PLANNING

The research findings helped to shaped the plan—McDonald's needed a program that was FIRST, that was the ONLY one of its kind that leveraged the BIG-GEST events and athletes to break through the clutter, and that employed the most thorough and aggressive media relations plan to achieve PR objectives:

1. Secure significant positive news coverage worldwide with at least 300 million media impressions and be among the top three most covered sponsors

2. Increase McDonald's involvement on a local level in countries worldwide in the Global PR activation by 25 percent from past years.

   It also helped to define the audiences, which included:

- International media—National, regional, and local media worldwide (print, broadcast, and online) who were mostly uninterested or skeptical of Olympic sponsors—needed to refocus their stories from issues to McDonald's positive sponsorship activation.

- International consumers—Olympic-engaged audiences, including sports/entertainment-minded families with kids and young adults from various cultures and languages with varying perceptions of McDonald's and Olympic Games.

- McDonald's communicators in more than 100 countries—aligning the McDonald's system with breakthrough programs and communication tools and resources for maximum engagement and positive media exposure.

EXECUTION

McDonald's answered the objectives and challenges with a comprehensive strategic plan that packaged the following under an umbrella theme of "Bringing People Together Like Never Before" and utilized a sequenced, well-timed media strategy to execute over a two-year period with a PR budget of $1 million for GolinHarris fee and expenses. The plan included:

- First-ever kids initiative to demonstrate McDonald's ongoing commitment to children's well-being; the McDonald's Champion Kids program gave unique opportunities to children around the world to see the Games firsthand; featured young journalist component where kids shared experiences with hometown media and communities.

- Only alternate reality game (ARG) in partnership with the IOC—"The Lost Ring" became the single largest ARG ever played.

- Legendary Olympians Michael Phelps and Carl Lewis as program ambassadors.

McDonald's and GH trained hard to catapult McDonald's Olympic sponsorship to new heights under the message of "Bringing People Together Like Never Before." McDonald's brought the plan to life through five key time periods:

- One-Year-Out Global Media Event in China to announce new McDonald's Champion Kids program and overall Olympic plans (a first for McDonald's in its 40-year sponsorship history, which generated hundreds of media stories including the coveted CNN International).

- Four-Months-Out Internal Rally of the McDonald's System (making a big splash at McDonald's Worldwide Convention and engaging country communicators to participate in the Olympic sponsorship PR activation).

- One-Month-Out Global Virtual Press Conference—another first for McDonald's, which jumpstarted the media shift from issues-oriented subjects to the company's role as a TOP Sponsor; outlined Olympic activation giving international media exclusive access via a global Webcast with live satellites from three continents; an effective strategy for redirecting media interest and showcasing the programs.

- One-Day-Before Opening Ceremonies Global Media Event—the only media event BOCOG allowed on the Olympic Green; more than 200 international media attended the event, which featured Olympic champion Carl Lewis; the focus was on people, pride and fun and was reported as such worldwide.

- Three-Weeks of Olympic Games Sponsorship PR Activation—McDonald's developed and executed multiple high-energy and news-generating activities that kept the media coming back, including a strategically timed restaurant appearance with Michael Phelps the day after he made Olympic history and broke the Olympic gold medal record, resulting in widespread global coverage.

McDonald's overall strategy allowed the company to start, continue and lead stories before other sponsors and refocus the controversial topics on the positive news, which increased prior to and throughout the Games. "Bringing People Together Like Never Before" involved multiple opportunities and tactics to reach out to media worldwide with three key programs taking the lead:

- McDonald's Olympic Champion Crew—a cornerstone program but for the first time the highest participation of 1,400 McDonald's crew members from 36 countries staffing four new McDonald's Olympic venue restaurants and experiencing China and the Games first-hand; many activities took place to celebrate the crew with Carl Lewis (a former crew member) as spokesperson.

- McDonald's Champion Kids—a brand new program providing a unique opportunity for children and for the world to see the Olympic Games through their eyes; 216 kids from 40 countries were selected to go to Beijing and experience China and the Games (including unprecedented access to the Olympic Village where the athletes live during the Games) and report back to their hometown media; added bonus was securing Michael Phelps as the Global Ambassador.

- The Lost Ring—a first-ever alternate reality game done in partnership with the IOC that connected an online community of 2.7 million participants, spanning 100 countries and 16 languages, who worked together to solve Olympic sport mysteries brought to them by McDonald's; former Olympian Edwin Moses served as a "surprise" gamer.

EVALUATION

The complete sponsorship program surpassed all goals—record number of media impressions reaching all target audiences; sighted as the lead sponsor in coverage; most country participation in McDonald's 40-year history; unprecedented results.

Objective:

Secure media coverage worldwide with a minimum of 300 million media impressions and ensure McDonald's is in the top three of sponsors covered positively in the media.

Result:

Obtained more than double the target—nearly one billion media impressions secured globally; 90 percent being positive (or neutral) in tone.

Breakdown in program impressions:

- Overall Sponsorship: 350+ million
- McDonald's Olympic Champion Crew: 250+ million
- McDonald's Champion Kids: 200+ million
- The Lost Ring: 25+ million

More than 700 print, broadcast and online media stories including coverage in AP, Reuters, CNN International, CNBC, Voice of America, MSNBC, ABC World News Tonight, *USA Today*, *The Wall Street Journal*, *People*, Bloomberg TV, *Business Week*, *Dow Jones*, *Financial Times*, NBC, BBC TV, *The New York Times*, *Chicago Tribune*, *China Daily*, *The Beijing News*, *Guang Ming Daily*, *Economic Observer*, and *The Australian*, among many others around the world.

"For the period July 28 through August 10, McDonald's moved into the lead among the global sponsors in coverage in traditional media sources ..."—Dow Jones Insight 2008 Olympics Media Pulse, August 12

"Coverage of the Games' 12 global sponsors is closing just as it began, with McDonald's, Coca-Cola and Visa leading the way.... coverage of McDonald's was centered on the company's physical presence in Beijing, while Visa and Coca-Cola garnered coverage due to their ads."—Dow Jones Insight 2008 Olympics Media Pulse, August 26

"McDonald's garnered the highest unaided recognition recall above all Olympic sponsors and advertisers in a post-Olympic Games."—Survey by Toronto's Solutions Research Group

In 2008 currencies, was equivalent to an estimated ad value of $9 million USD (U.S.), 9.7 million RMB (China), 920 million KWR (Korea) and 95 million JPY in Japan.

Objective:

Increase McDonald's local country participation worldwide in the Global PR activation by 25 percent from past years.

Result:

Increased McDonald's involvement on a local level in countries worldwide in the PR activation by 85 percent from past years and engaged more than 90 McDonald's countries with breakthrough programs.

E X H I B I T   10-3A   News Release

McDonald's(R) to Sponsor 'Champion' Children From Around the World at Beijing 2008 Olympic Games

Olympian Michael Phelps to Serve as Global Ambassador

OAK BROOK, Ill., Aug. 7 /PRNewswire/—As part of McDonald's ongoing commitment to children, the company will launch its newest Olympic Games program, McDonald's Champion Kids, on Aug. 9, 2007 in Beijing.

   (Photo: http://www.newscom.com/cgi-bin/prnh/20070807/AQTU080LOGO)

   The program will enable up to 300 kids from around the world to travel to the 2008 Olympic Games to share their stories and experiences with their local communities and hometown news outlets. Through this once-in-a-lifetime journey, the children will have the chance to see the Games, meet Olympic athletes, visit cultural sights, and interact with kids from across the globe.

   Six-time Olympic gold medalist Michael Phelps will serve as McDonald's Global Ambassador for the program. Joining Phelps to kick-off the program at a special media event Aug. 9 in Beijing will be International Olympic Committee (IOC) President Jacques Rogge, Executive Vice President of the Beijing Organizing Committee of the Olympic Games (BOCOG) Mr. Wang Wei, People's Republic of China Olympic gold medalist and McDonald's Champion Kids Ambassador in China Guo Jingjing, and other local dignitaries.

   "With the McDonald's Champion Kids program, we are making a significant investment to give hundreds of children the experience of a lifetime," said Mary Dillon, McDonald's Global Chief Marketing Officer. "These kids will reach out to thousands more, connecting with their worldwide peers to communicate the sights and sounds of the Olympic Games and the fascinating culture of China. It's another example of our commitment to the enrichment of children."

Support for the Program

"McDonald's unique Champion Kids program mirrors the passion we have for bringing together youth from around the world, connecting cultures and communities as only the Olympic Movement can," said IOC President Rogge.

"McDonald's is providing a once-in-a-lifetime opportunity for children around the world," said Phelps. "For the kids to experience China and the world's greatest sporting event at one time is simply incredible." McDonald's Olympic Games Activation In addition to the McDonald's Champion Kids program, the company will activate its most comprehensive Olympic Games plan to date, which includes:

– Feeding the World's Athletes—For the seventh consecutive Games, McDonald's will be the Official Restaurant of the Olympic Games. The company is planning to build four restaurants in Beijing. One restaurant will be in the Athlete's Village, where McDonald's will be the only branded restaurant to feed the athletes, giving them a taste of home while in China. The three other McDonald's restaurants will serve spectators, officials and coaches, as well as the 20,000 media expected on site. Customers will find a wide variety of products, including favorites such as the Big Mac(R) sandwich and World Famous Fries(TM), as well as Premium Chicken offerings and Fruit n' Yogurt Parfaits.
– McDonald's Olympic Champion Crew—McDonald's will honor an unprecedented number of restaurant employees by bringing 1,200 best of the best restaurant crew from China and around the world to the Games to experience the fun and excitement of serving the world's best athletes, as well as spectators and media.
– Giving Back—As part of McDonald's Olympic Games tradition to give back to the host city, the company will make a lasting contribution to the host city of Beijing through Ronald McDonald House Charities(R).
– Bringing the Games to Life—McDonald's restaurants around the world will bring the excitement of the Games to life for their customers in a variety of local promotions and activities.

McDonald's Olympic Games History

McDonald's became an Official Sponsor of the Olympic Games in 1976 and has a long-standing commitment to the Olympic Movement. At the 1968 Olympic Winter Games, McDonald's airlifted hamburgers to U.S. athletes competing in Grenoble, France, after they reported being homesick for McDonald's food. Since then, the company has served its menu of choice and variety to millions of athletes, coaches, their families, and fans. The Beijing 2008 Olympic Games mark McDonald's sixth Olympic Games as a Worldwide Partner and seventh as the Official Restaurant of the Olympic Games. McDonald's current sponsorship will continue through the 2012 Games in London.

McDonald's is the leading global foodservice retailer with more than 30,000 local restaurants in 118 countries. Approximately 70 percent of McDonald's restaurants worldwide are owned and operated by independent local men and women. Please visit http://www.mcdonalds.com to learn more about the company.

For free video content from McDonald's, please log on to http://www.thenewsmarket.com/mcdonalds to preview and request video.

CONTACT:

Lisa Howard, McDonald's
630-623-5044 lisa.howard@us.mcd.com

Ben Lincoln, GolinHarris
312-729-4466
blincoln@golinharris.com

McDonald's Olympic Press Kit:
http://www.mcdepk.com/2008OlympicGames

11

Relations with Special Publics

Special publics are defined as those unique or distinctive groups with which an organization needs to communicate. These groups may be minority publics, such as African Americans, Hispanics, or Asian Americans. Practitioners should be aware of the extensive national, geographic, and ethnic subsets that exist within each of these broadly defined minority groups in the United States. For instance, practitioners might mistakenly lump all Hispanics together under the Mexican-American umbrella. For a Hispanic special event, they could employ a mariachi band and serve Mexican dishes. However, such treatment would easily offend Spaniards, Argentines, or Dominicans, all of whose home cultures differ sharply from one another and from that of Mexico, although all share Spanish as a common language. A similar mistake would be to treat Asian Americans as a singular group. Most Asian groups share neither common languages nor common cultural heritages.

When dealing with a minority group with national origins outside the United States, practitioners would be well advised to consult in advance the embassy or consulate of that group's homeland and certainly the group's local leaders as well. In fact, many of the same principles that apply to internal public relations can apply.

In addition to ethnic or national minority publics, practitioners may target for special communications with such groups as women, students, educators, handicapped persons, environmentalists, school-age children, the business community, municipal officials, or community physicians. The list of potential special publics can actually be extended to include all the segments of society.

The fastest growing and most significant of these special groups in the United States is the "senior citizen" segment of the population, a segment expected to double in size by the mid-twenty-first century. Age groupings, such as 50-64 for the "active" seniors, 65-74 for the "less active," and 75-plus for the "elderly," are often used to describe subsegments of the senior citizen audience. These age groupings alone, though, are usually less useful in targeting senior audiences than are their organizational affiliations. Organizations such as AARP (formerly the American Association of Retired Persons), the National Council on the Aging (NCOA), the National Hispanic Council on Aging, the National Council of Senior Citizens, the National Senior Sports Association, and the Gray Panthers have chapter networks and affiliate organizations that can be used to reach their members. Thus, the key to reaching a senior audience may lie in cosponsorship of an event or project with an organization such as AARP or the NCOA.

As with other forms of public relations, the four part ROPE process model is a helpful format for preparing and executing programs that target special publics.

RESEARCH

Research for special programs includes investigation of the client, the reason for the program, and, most important, the distinctive audience to be targeted.

Client Research

Client research for an organization's relations with a special public should focus on the client's role and reputation with the particular audience. How credible is the organization with this public? Have there been significant complaints against it from this public in the past? What are its past and present communication practices toward this audience? What are its major strengths and weaknesses relative to this public? What opportunities exist to enhance its relations with this public?

Opportunity or Problem Research

Should a proactive public relations program be devised for this particular audience? Or has some problem arisen that must be addressed with a reactive program? Why should the organization communicate with this audience at all? Detailed answers to these questions will provide the necessary justification for the outlay of funds required for relations with a given special public.

Audience Research

Obviously, the practitioner should learn as much as possible about a special public. One way to do this is to regard such publics as differentiated communities. In community relations, practitioners address community media, community leaders, and community organizations. These same audience subsets may also be applicable in defining a special public:

> Media utilized by this public
>> Mass
>> Specialized
>> Online and digital or traditional

Leaders of this public

  Public officials

  Professional leaders

  Ethnic leaders

  Neighborhood leaders

  Others

Organizations composing this public

  Civic

  Political

  Service

  Business

  Cultural

  Religious

  Age-based

  Recreational (entertainment and athletic)

  Other

As in community relations, practitioners should develop special contact lists for the appropriate media and for the special public's leaders and organizations. These materials are indispensable in relations with a special public. Remember, some audience segments are more actively engaged in an issue than others.

OBJECTIVES

Programs that target special publics can use both impact and output objectives; and, as in all other types of public relations, the objectives should be specific and quantitative.

Impact Objectives

Impact objectives represent the desired outcomes of informing or modifying the attitudes or behaviors of the special audience. Some examples include:

1. To increase the knowledge of the organization's minority-benefits program among members of this special public (by 50 percent before January 1)

2. To promote more favorable opinion (30 percent) toward the organization on the part of this special public (during the current year)

3. To stimulate greater participation (15 percent) in the organization's programs by this special public (during the summer months)

4. To reduce the incidence of sexually transmitted diseases among senior citizens by 20 percent.

Output Objectives

Output objectives comprise the specific efforts to enhance relations with special publics. For example:

1. To prepare and distribute materials to (30 percent of) the Hispanic community in Washington (during the coming year)

2. To schedule four meetings each year with leaders of the Chinese community in Houston

3. To develop five new projects for African American instructors' use in their classrooms (during the current school year)

PROGRAMMING

Programming for relations with special publics includes planning the theme and messages, action(s) or special event(s), uncontrolled and controlled media, and effective communication principles in the program's execution.

Theme and Messages

Both the theme and messages should reflect the desired relationship between the organization and the targeted special public. They will also be an indicator of past and present relationships that exist between the organization and this public. Cultural, ethnic, and gender values will likely affect the themes and messages used in a campaign so look for messages that will resonate with your public.

Action(s) or Special Event(s)

Actions and special events should concentrate on the major interests of the targeted audience. The most successful actions and special events address the interests, needs, and problems of the particular target group. The special events in the cases in this chapter clearly meet this criterion. For example, if the target audience is very attuned to "family and community," think in terms of family-oriented events.

Uncontrolled and Controlled Media

As mentioned earlier, representatives of both the mass and specialized media aimed at the special audience are an important segment of the audience itself. Uncontrolled media in the form of news releases, photo and video opportunities, feature stories, and/or interviews should be prepared in the language of the designated media; they should be directed to media outlets known to be used by this special public. Cultivate relationships with key bloggers who are reputable with your audience in order to place stories about your campaign.

Controlled media should be prepared with all the cultural, language, ethnic, age, or other demographic specifications of the target public in mind. Obviously, the organization's website will play a crucial role in the program. The website can include a great body of information of interest to the target public. Social media can be used to engage a specific group. For example, campaigns promoting new music may set up a site on MySpace.com in some countries while other campaigns may use Facebook, and send an email or a Twitter feed with a link to a blog and ask people to add their comments. As with other publics, there can be no substitute for personal interaction in the effective execution of programs.

Effective Communication

Principles of effective communication are the same for special audiences as they are for most others. Extra care should be taken, however, in the matter of source credibility, which can be enhanced by the selection of a spokesperson from the same demographic group as the targeted audience.

In addition to source credibility, two-way communication and audience participation should also be given extra emphasis in relations with special publics.

Finally, the use of opinion leaders may be highly significant in relations with special publics, especially when the public is an organized ethnic or demographic group. In sum, all aspects of programming for relations with special publics are similar to those of community relations. The special public, in fact, can often be thought of as a community with its own media, leaders, and organizations.

EVALUATION

The process of evaluating communications aimed at special audiences must take into account the program's objectives. Each one should be measured using previously discussed standards and methods.

Evaluation of special publics cases rely generally on the degree of participation by the target audiences and, in most instances, the amount of publicity generated by the program.

SUMMARY

Research for programs that target special audiences focuses on the credibility of the client with a particular special public, along with the need or justification for the program. The audience itself can be analyzed using the same categories applicable to community relations—media, leaders, and organizations. Special audiences can usually be treated as communities, or subcommunities, in their own right.

Objectives for relations with special publics may be impact or output in nature. Impact objectives express desired outcomes, such as augmenting the public's knowledge or influencing its attitudes or behaviors. Without reference to impact, output objectives consist of practitioner efforts to execute the program.

Programming for special publics often uses the significant events of the public's ethnic or cultural past. Along with this, of course, the programming must also address the problems or potential problems of the special group. Although standard controlled and uncontrolled media are used in this form of public relations, there can be no substitute for two-way communication with such audiences. More than others, they need to know that the organization cares enough about them to include a personal touch.

As with other forms of public relations, the special program's stated objectives must be evaluated appropriately. In general, the level of participation by the targeted group and the publicity generated by the program are used as benchmarks of success.

READINGS ON SPECIAL PUBLICS

Bortree, Denise Sevick. "Exploring Adolescent-Organization Relationships: A Study of Effective Relationship Strategies with Adolescent Volunteers," *Journal of Public Relations Research* 22.1 (2010): 1–25.

Brier, Noah Rubin. "Coming of Age," American Demographics 26 (November 2004) 16–19

Cafasso, Ed. "Millennials in the Workplace: Managing Expectations of PR's Next Generation," *Public Relations Strategist* 13 (Fall 2007): 38–40.

Carlson, Peter. "Wild Generalization X: In Details, a Hilarious Screed on Turning 40 and Not Loving It," *Washington Post* (April 11, 2006): C02.

Chafetz, Paul K., Helen Holmes, Kim Lande, Elizabeth Childress, and Hilda R. Glazer. "Older Adults and the News Media: Utilization, Opinions, and Preferred Reference Terms," *The Gerontologist* 38 (August 1998): 481–499.

Cook, Fred. "It's a Small World After All: Multiculturalism, Authenticity, Connectedness Among Trends to Watch in Next 50 Years," *Public Relations Strategist* 13 (Winter 2007): 30–33.

Ferguson, Robert. *Representing "Race": Ideology, Identity and the Media.* London: Oxford University Press, 1998.

Ford, Rochelle L. "Research Shows Why Race and Ethnicity Matter," *Public Relations Tactics* 13 (March 2006): 6.

Francese, Peter. "Single Family, Condo Style," *American Demographics* 26.8 (October 2004): 47–49.

Frey, William H. "Minority Myth vs. Reality," *American Demographics* 26.8 (October 2004): 33–35.

Gandy, Oscar H. *Communication and Race: A Structural Perspective.* London: Oxford University Press, 1998.

Gardyn, Rebecca. "Educated Consumers," *American Demographics* 24 (November 2002): 18–19.

Gothard, Ann Mane. "Black Newspapers: An Overlooked PR Opportunity," *Public Relations Tactics* 5 (October 1998): 24.

Jackson, Ronald L *African American Communication and Identities* Thousand Oaks, CA: Sage Publications, 2004.

Jandt, Fred E. *Intercultural Communication.* Thousand Oaks, CA: Sage Publications, 2001.

Jones, Mathew, Debra Salmon, and Judy Orme. "Young People's Involvement in a Substance Misuse Communications Campaign," *Drugs: Education, Prevention & Policy* 11 (October 2004): 391–405.

King, Corwin P. "A Diverse Minority Framed by History: Native Americans' Modern Roles and Issues," *Public Relations Strategist* 12 (Summer 2006): 44–45.

Lederman, Linda C. *Beyond These Walls: Readings in Health Communication.* New York: Oxford University Press, 2010.

Liu, Brooke Fisher. "Communicating with Hispanics About Crises: How Counties Produce and Provide Spanish-Language Disaster Information," *Public Relations Review* (September 2007): 330–333.

Lumpkins, Crystal Y., Jiyang Bae, and Glen T. Cameron. "Generating conflict for greater good: Utilizing contingency theory to assess Black and mainstream newspapers as public relations vehicles to promote better health among African Americans," *Public Relations Review* 36.1 (March 2010): Pages 73–77.

Milhouse, Virginia H., Molefi Kete Asante, and Peter O. Nwosu. *Trans-cultural Realities.* Thousand Oaks, CA: Sage Publications, 2001.

Miller, Barbara M. "Community Stakeholders and Marketplace Advocacy: A Model of Advocacy, Agenda Building, and Industry Approval," *Journal of Public Relations Research* 22.1 (2010): 85–112.

Montgomery, Kathryn C. *Generation Digital: Politics, Commerce, and Childhood in the Age of the Internet.* Cambridge, MA: MIT Press, 2007.

Morton, Linda P. "Targeting Hispanic Americans," *Public Relations Quarterly* 47 (Fall 2002): 46–48.

Neuliep, Jim. *Intercultural Communication: A Contextual Approach.* Thousand Oaks, CA: Sage Publications, 2006.

Palen, J. John. *The Suburbs.* New York: McGraw-Hill, 1994.

Pompper, Donnalyn. "'Difference' in Public Relations Research: A Case for Introducing Critical Race Theory," *Journal of Public Relations Research* 17 (2) (2005): 139–169.

Price, Vincent, Lilach Nir, and Joseph N. Cappella. "Framing Public Discussion of Gay Civil Unions," *Public Opinion Quarterly* 69 (Summer 2005): 179–212.

Samovar, Larry A., and Richard E. Porter. *Intercultural Communication.* Belmont, CA: Wadsworth, 2008.

Solloway, Sylvan. "A Growing Influential Audience: Spanish-Language Broadcast Outreach That Works," *Public Relations Tactics* 14 (June 2007): 18.

Somerick, Nancy M. "Strategies for Recognizing Retirees as a Valuable Public Relations Resource," *Public Relations Quarterly* 52.1 (2008): 22–23.

Sweeney, Katie. "The Merger of Faith and Work," *Public Relations Strategist* 13 (Spring 2007): 6–11.

Ting-Toomey, Stella. *Communicating Across Cultures.* New York: Guilford Publications, 1999.

Vahouny, Karen. "Opportunities for Improvement," *Communication World* 21 (May-June 2004): 32–38.

Van Dyke, Mark A., Carmen Haynes and Jennifer Ferguson-Mitchell "Bridging the Divide: A Public Relations Perspective on Intergenerational Communication," *Public Relations Quarterly* 52.4 (2009): 19–23.

Yun Kim, Young. *Becoming Intercultural.* Thousand Oaks, CA: Sage Publications, 2001.

Special Publics Cases

Case 11-1

Special events built around the cultural values of a specific audience may trigger an avalanche of media attention. Exhibit 11-1A is a news release about the Glam Flight and Exhibit 11-1B is a photo taken during the event.

Air New Zealand Pink Flight
Air New Zealand with CRT/Tanaka

SUMMARY

While Air New Zealand is a household name in its native country, off shore, the airline is a small carrier in a saturated market. In order to develop brand awareness and differentiation in North America, Air New Zealand decided to host an event that reflected its diversity-embracing brand culture, established its presence in the high traveling Gay, Lesbian, Bisexual, and Transgender (GLBT) market, and garnered media attention on a national scale. With the support of CRT/tanaka, Air New Zealand launched the first North American gay-themed "Pink Flight" to Sydney, Australia—host of the world's largest Gay and Lesbian Mardi Gras—successfully showcasing its award-winning customer service and unique personality, generating 352 million impressions, and contributing to a 24 percent increase (Y-o-Y) in Air New Zealand's sales in the North American market.

RESEARCH

Although a household name in its native New Zealand, off-shore, Air New Zealand is a small carrier in a saturated airline market. Despite having operated out of the United States for 25 years, with daily flights to New Zealand from Los Angeles, San Francisco, and Vancouver, and additional sectors to Australia and London, Air New Zealand's brand awareness was much lower than its chief competitors, Qantas and United Airlines. In order to develop brand awareness and differentiation in North America, Air New Zealand decided to host an event that would simultaneously garner media attention, and establish its presence within a high-traveling demographic. Research regarding travel habits and spending in the United States revealed that the Gay, Lesbian, Bisexual, and Transgender (GLBT) community spent $40 billion on travel in 2007, with 70 percent of this group owning a passport. This market segment validated the airline's diversity-embracing corporate and brand culture, and served as a foundation for the launch of the first North American gay-themed "Pink Flight" to Sydney, Australia, host of the world's largest Gay and Lesbian Mardi Gras.

PLANNING

Objectives

1. Raise brand awareness about Air New Zealand's unique, kiwi service amongst the GLBT community.
2. Differentiate Air New Zealand's brand from competitors in the United States, with emphasis on the West Coast.
3. Engage Air New Zealand employees worldwide in an event that represents the company's values.

Strategies

1. Create a celebratory event that resonates with the GLBT community.
2. Create a national media relations campaign targeting both GLBT media and mass consumer media.
3. Establish an internal communication campaign to engage/invite employees to participate in the celebratory event.

EXECUTION

Air New Zealand's Pink Flight escorted more than 200 passengers on a chartered flight from San Francisco to Sydney, Australia for the 2008 Gay and Lesbian Mardi Gras. Air New Zealand engaged CRT/tanaka to support the execution of a host of tactics surrounding the Pink Flight, both on-ground and in-air, successfully driving media coverage of the event and increasing brand awareness in the GLBT community.

Secure Notable Celebrity Host

To raise the event's consumer and media profile and extend reach, CRT/tanaka secured Kathy Griffin to be the official hostess—a high-profile comedian that is well-known and well-liked in both the gay community, and among a broader consumer audience. CRT/tanaka was able to engage Griffin for a significantly reduced fee by strategically coordinating with the producers of her Bravo hit show, "Kathy Griffin: My Life on the D-List," and pitching the concept of using her performance on the flight as the focus of an episode. The agency coordinated international filming rights and ground support for the Bravo crew, enabling them to film at the airport, on board the flight, and during the Sydney Mardi Gras parade. CRT/tanaka negotiated all elements of Griffin's Pink Flight performance, arranging for her to wear an Air New Zealand branded t-shirt, announce the final boarding call, scan boarding passes, and perform her live comedy act in air.

Pre-Party and In-Flight Party

All passengers, as well as 75 key community figures, were invited to the pre-flight event at San Francisco International Airport, featuring a DJ, dance floor, live performances from drag queens, and an appearance by hostess Griffin. Pink passengers and partygoers were interviewed by the "pink paparazzi" on a pink carpet and posed for the media, and a party photographer. The plane was also decorated for the event, donning a 70-foot pink boa and 13-inch feather "eyelashes" for enhanced photo opportunities. Once onboard, entertainment included performances from the New Zealand drag queens, live comedy from Griffin, a hot-body contest, and screenings of classic gay-themed films. Passengers received prizes, and a Pink goody bag replete with New Zealand products and other specialty items.

Media Outreach and Coordination at Airport

CRT/tanaka issued a national press release announcing Griffin's involvement, as well as an additional release detailing the success of the flight. CRT/tanaka aggressively pitched the story to GLBT and national media and high-profile GLBT and travel bloggers, with a focus on the West Coast. The agency invited an exclusive number of media onboard, and organized their travel. CRT/tanaka also pitched the Pink Flight pre-party to local San Francisco news stations and newspapers, securing the presence of 12 press outlets for the pre-flight event. CRT/tanaka worked with the airport staff to coordinate all media details on site, which included a media check-in room, security process for non-ticketed journalists, photography and videography on the tarmac, photography, videography and interviews onboard before the flight, and equipment concerns. In addition, a CRT/tanaka representative was on the Pink Flight as a resource for journalists on assignment.

Create Special Media Materials

A unique "Pink" press kit was produced, capturing the event's personality, and providing journalists with information such as food and in-flight entertainment, biographies of the New Zealand drag queens and Griffin, press releases and a fact sheet.

Media Training

At the pre-party, CRT/tanaka scheduled 10 media interviews for Air New Zealand's director of marketing, Jodi Williams. CRT/tanaka drafted key message points and media trained Williams prior to the interviews. CRT/tanaka also briefed Pink Flight crew members on main message points and instructed them to direct any journalistic inquires to the CRT/tanaka representative on board.

Extend Media Coverage

A videographer and photographer were hired for the event in order to extend coverage beyond assigned journalists on the flight. CRT/tanaka released pictures from the flight to a national wire in a multimedia press release. CRT/tanaka negotiated for Bravo to provide a segment for promotional purposes on Air New Zealand's website, and ensured the TV segment gave due credit to the airline for the flight.

The agency also actively engaged the support of bloggers in the GLBT community, communicating up-to-the-minute updates for relay to their respective audiences.

Employee Engagement

To engage employees to participate and promote the flight internally, Air New Zealand invited employees with strong performance records to be considered as crew for the flight. The Pink Flight crew presented a well-rehearsed dance routine at the pre-party and made props to wear during the flight. Event details were regularly communicated to all employees, maintaining involvement, support, and enthusiasm throughout the campaign. Air New Zealand also crowned several employees as 'Pink Flight Ambassadors', driving awareness of the Pink Flight through their involvement with street team promotions in San Francisco.

EVALUATION

Budget

The $200,000 Pink Flight campaign was executed on budget, and the charter of the plane was paid in full through the use of media relations and word-of-mouth tactics to generate ticket sales. Air New Zealand engaged multiple partners to donate items for the flight, including goody bags and alcohol, minimizing the cost of the campaign.

Awareness in the GLBT community

The Pink Flight was enthusiastically received by the GLBT community, both in North America and around the world, generating significant media coverage in GLBT niche outlets, and driving an increase in brand awareness among these consumers.

Differentiation in the market

Air New Zealand's Pink Flight received international attention, successfully showcasing the airline's unique brand personality and support of the GLBT community. The key messages behind the initiative were clearly and effectively conveyed throughout, distinguishing Air New Zealand's uniquely "kiwi" service and point of view. Internally the Pink Flight initiative is attributed with being the largest single contributor to the airline's 24 percent increase in ticket sales in the North American market, comparing sales in 2007 to those of 2008.

Media Results

By the end of 2008, the Pink Flight had generated 352,104,840 total impressions, with a publicity value of $13,006,171.90. In addition to the focus on the flight during an episode of Bravo's "Kathy Griffin: My Life On The D-List," significant media successes include: The Tonight Show With Jay Leno, MSNBC Live, Early Today, Reuters, *San Francisco Chronicle*, *Star Magazine*, CBS News on Logo, MetroSource, *Advocate,* and *Out Traveler.*

E X H I B I T 11-1A   News Release

Air New Zealand's Pink Flight Goes Glam

Airline Escorts Pink Party-ers To Sydney Mardi Gras In Style

EL SEGUNDO, Calif. (Feb. 5, 2009) – From drag queens and pink boas to diamonds and champagne, Air New Zealand knows how to make flying glamorous. Following the success of last year's Air New Zealand Pink Flight to Sydney Mardi Gras, another gay-themed adventure is heading down under. North American travelers can fly from San Francisco or Los Angeles from $978 (USD) roundtrip and Vancouver from $1,078 (CAD) roundtrip including all of the glam experiences of the airline's now-famous Pink party flight, which departs Auckland, New Zealand for Sydney, Australia on March 6, 2009.

While last year's festivities began at the San Francisco International Airport check-in, Air New Zealand is offering North American Pink Flight guests the opportunity to relax and rejuvenate before joining the festivities in New Zealand. Once in Auckland, guests will be escorted to a "Glamour Gate" event—an exclusive pink fliers-only party featuring custom-made chandeliers, a champagne bar, and live music in an ultra-luxurious environment.

Back by popular demand, the iconic drag queen Buckwheat and her girls will host the in-flight party.

"Last year's Pink Flight was a 14-hour, completely scheduled affair," said Jodi Williams, Air New Zealand's director of marketing—the Americas. "This time, we thought we'd blend both the fun and excitement with some relaxation for our guests. We want everyone to enjoy our award-winning service, as well as the party-time frivolity the Pink Flight offers."

"We are always exploring new and creative ways to demonstrate the casual elegance and quirkiness of New Zealand's culture," said Roger Poulton, Air New Zealand's vice president—the Americas. "Air New Zealand reflects the country's diversity-embracing nature and celebrates people from all walks of life. This initiative is one of the many ways we strive to serve our guests, and you can expect many additional kiwi surprises throughout the year."

Air New Zealand's Pink Flight sells out each year. Travelers are encouraged to book now to secure a seat on the infamous flight. To enter a sweepstakes to win tickets or to purchase a ticket, visit http://www.airnewzealand.com/ or http://www.airnewzealand.ca/.

About Air New Zealand

Air New Zealand offers more direct flights to the South Pacific than any other airline, including non-stop flights from San Francisco, Los Angeles, Honolulu and Vancouver to New Zealand, as well as Los Angeles non-stop to the Cook Islands and Samoa. Other popular destinations include Australia, China, Japan and Tonga. In addition to flying non-stop Los Angeles-London, Air New Zealand's route between London and Hong Kong now allows customers to fly round-the-world on one airline. Consistently rated among the world's best international airlines, Air New Zealand's new Inflight Concierge Service provides all passengers with a range of services, from travel advice to assistance with onward bookings. Air New Zealand's most recent accolades include "Best Business Class to Australia, New Zealand and South Pacific" for the third straight year by *Business Traveler Magazine* (USA) "Best Transpacific Airline" at the 26th Airline Industry Awards, "Best Passenger Service" award by *Air Transport World* magazine, and "Best Business Class Red Wine" for the Martinborough Pinot Noir 2005 at the 2007 Cellars in the Sky awards. United Mileage Plus, US Airways Dividend Miles and Air Canada's Aeroplan members earn and redeem mileage on select flights. Flight and vacation essentials can be booked on AirNewZealand.com or by calling 1-800-262-1234 in the USA and 1-800-663-5494 in Canada. Air New Zealand is a member of the Star Alliance network.

Note: The content of all Air New Zealand media releases are accurate at the time of issue, as stated at the top of each release. For updates on any changes, please contact Air New Zealand.

Air New Zealand is proud to be a member of Star Alliance. The Star Alliance network was established in 1997 as the first truly global airline alliance to offer worldwide reach, recognition and seamless service to the international traveller. Its acceptance by the market has been recognised by numerous awards, including the Air Transport World Market Leadership Award, Best Airline Alliance by both *Business Traveler Magazine* and Skytrax. The member airlines are: Adria Airways, Air Canada, Air China, Air New Zealand, ANA, Asiana Airlines, Austrian, Blue1, bmi, Continental Airlines, Croatia Airlines, EGYPTAIR, LOT Polish Airlines, Lufthansa, Scandinavian Airlines, Shanghai Airlines, Singapore Airlines, South African Airways, Spanair, SWISS, TAP Portugal, Turkish Airlines, THAI, United and US Airways. Aegean Airlines, Air India, Brussels Airlines and TAM have been announced as future members. Overall, the Star Alliance network offers 19,500 daily flights to 1,071 airports in 171 countries.

For more information about Air New Zealand visit *www.airnewzealand.com* and for more information about Star Alliance visit *www.staralliance.com*.

###

Courtesy Air New Zealand and CRT/Tanaka

Air New Zealand Flight crew wears the pink boas identified with the "Pink Flights" from San Francisco to the Sidney Mardi Gras.

An Air New Zealand plane sports a pink boa in honor of the "Pink Flights".

Courtesy Air New Zealand and CRT/Tanaka

Case 11-2

Affinity groups have tight knit memberships with their own values and code of conduct. Tapping into those values for a communication effort requires special connections with the audience. Exhibit 11-2A is a program news release, Exhibit 11-2B is a print ad and Exhibit 11-2C shows how the program developed public endorsements.

Changing The Meaning Of "Organ Donor" Among Motorcyclists

Lifeline of Ohio and Fahlgren Mortine Public Relations

SUMMARY

Most Americans support organ donation, in theory. But only 52 percent of Ohioans are registered donors. Lifeline of Ohio and Fahlgren Mortine segmented by affinity audience and appealed to self-interest instead of altruism to turn sentiment into action. In a pilot campaign to turn the term "organ donor" from an insult to a positive in the motorcycle community, 3,000 central and southeast Ohio motorcyclists registered as donors. Each registered donor can potentially save eight lives and improve 50, so registrations the campaign inspired can directly impact 173,942 individuals, not to mention their loved ones.

SITUATION ANALYSIS

While 90 percent of Americans say they support organ donation, only 52 percent of Ohioans are registered donors. This suggests apathy is the primary barrier to building the Ohio Donor Registry. With 18 Americans dying each day waiting for a life-saving transplant, turning sentiment into action is vital. Lifeline of Ohio, the not-for-profit that promotes organ and tissue donation in central and southeast Ohio, partnered with Fahlgren Mortine to overcome apathy and drive action. Fahlgren Mortine proposed a new approach—segmenting by affinity to increase relevance, and appealing to self interest rather than altruism; thus, the "Live On. Ride On." campaign to motorcycle enthusiasts was born.

RESEARCH

- Secondary research showed 95 percent of the population supports donation. (source: 2005 National Survey of Organ and Tissue Donation Attitudes and Behaviors, The Gallup Organization for Division of Transplantation Health Resources and Services Administration) Ohio Bureau of Motor Vehicles (BMV) numbers show 52 percent of Ohioans are registered donors.

- The BMV database also showed how many people hold motorcycle endorsements and are also registered donors, by county. This provided a benchmark to measure against.

- Internet and Mediamark Research (MRI) showed motorcycle enthusiasts defy the "Hells Angels" stereotype. They are more affluent than average— *Cycle World* readers have an average household income of $121,500. Sixty percent are college educated. They have a strong bond and are generous, giving back to the community through charity rides and events.

- Based on input from influencers in the regional motorcycle community (marketing leadership at the two largest motorcycle retailers and the American Motorcyclists Association), the team determined cruisers and sport bikers, the two major categories of motorcycle enthusiasts, would require tailored materials. This outreach also rallied influencers to promote the campaign.

- A cruiser focus group of 12, and sport bike focus group of 13 provided insight into each segment, including most impactful events, communications preferences, and appropriate incentives.

PLANNING

"Organ donor" is a derogatory term among motorcyclists, and the campaign sought to change that and capitalize on the familiarity of the term while increasing donor registrations and creating a pilot for affinity audience outreach. We set the aggressive **goal** of converting five percent of central and southeast Ohio motorcycle enthusiasts to registered organ donors (12,250).

The plan included the following **strategies**:

- Overcome target audience apathy by appealing to people within the context of issues about which they are passionate. (In this pilot, the motorcyclist affinity audience was chosen.)

- Use high-touch interactions to ask people to join the donor registry.

- Use bold graphics and messages to cut through the clutter and grab attention.

Key message/campaign essence (phrasing from in-store display):

I will ride on. Will you? Because I'm an organ recipient, I am able to ride today. Because I'm an organ donor, my spirit could ride on tomorrow. An amazing lady gave me the gift of life through organ donation. Today, I ride with her brother. Tomorrow, someone could ride on because of me. Grab a flier to find out more about the ultimate way to give back. And read the rest of my story at Lifelineofohio.org/LiveOnRideOn. —Tim Jones, heart recipient

The joint Fahlgren Mortine/Lifeline of Ohio team assembled a task force of motorcycle enthusiasts and identified regional motorcycle events to participate in, groups to reach, and stories to tell. Outreach was also planned through motorcycle training programs, which motorcyclists must complete before going to the BMV to get their motorcycle endorsement.

EXECUTION

Execution began with creating custom materials to speak to the audience. These included:

- Cruiser motorcycle patches: "Live On. Ride On. Organ and Tissue Donor" patches were offered to existing donors (confirmed by showing driver's license) or for registering as a donor via a paper form.

- Custom-designed "sport bike" T-shirts: Focus groups showed patches were not applicable in the sport bike world, and that sport bike riders often carried a change of T-shirt, so a custom T-shirt was created and used as the sport bike audience incentive.

- Video and written personal stories: Focused on motorcyclists with a connection to donation, like Tim Jones, a heart recipient who now rides his Harley with his donor's brother. And Tara Newton, whose mother lives on through those she saved after she died tragically in a motorcycle accident. The stories were used in all print and online campaign materials.

- "Live On. Ride On." brochures: Incorporated frequently asked questions that dispel common donation myths, stories of motorcyclists connected to donation, and self-mailing donor registry forms.

- Counter signs with campaign messaging and brochure holders: Carried the message beyond the high-touch interaction of events and into the largest regional retail locations.

- "Live On. Ride On." landing page: All materials pointed to Lifelilineofohio.org/LiveOnRideOn, which shared more information and linked to the online donor registry form and social media presences.

Motorcycle task force members set up a display and staffed 18 events, including the 5th Annual Brandy Winfield Memorial Poker Run, Honda Super Cycle Weekend, and Quaker Steak and Lube Bike Nights. A raffle gave volunteers an easy way to engage in conversation.

Several motorcycle groups were offered materials or a speaker, six of which requested materials and two invited a speaker to address members about donation. A traditional and social media news release announced the campaign's launch in late May 2009, and another told the story of Michael Corea, a liver recipient, sport bike enthusiast, and at 20, a life-saving organ donor.

The team, in partnership with Webbed Marketing, created a "Live On. Ride On." Facebook group and Twitter handle, where personal stories and images were posted and members were updated with event information and news. Lifeline of

Ohio's Board of Directors authorized $70,000 for the campaign. A total of $66,300 was spent, including agency costs, campaign materials, event costs, and raffle prizes.

EVALUATION

Registrations

While it will take four years to gauge the full impact of the campaign because of the renewal cycle for Ohio drivers' licenses, initial goals already have been exceeded. The campaign confirmed the affinity audience approach, which will be used in future campaigns.

- Based on a comparison of BMV records before and after the campaign, 2,999 additional motorcyclists in Lifeline of Ohio's service area are now registered organ donors.

- Motorcycle events that were part of the "Live On. Ride On." campaign generated five times more registrants per hour than the average Lifeline of Ohio event—1.29 versus .27.

- More than 100 paper registrations were collected. The target was 89.

- Each registered donor can potentially save eight lives and improve 50, so registrations the campaign inspired can directly impact 173,942 individuals, not to mention their loved ones.

Grassroots outreach

Motorcyclists wearing campaign badges and T-shirts confirmed that the community had embraced the cause, and other states and regions have expressed interest in replicating the campaign in their areas.

- 2,000 (cruiser) patches and 750 (sport bike) T-shirts were distributed, turning those who wear them into ambassadors for organ and tissue donation.

- In total, 5,429 "Live On. Ride On." brochures, including donor registration forms, were distributed.

Traditional and Social Media Relations

- Print coverage was secured in three regional newspapers and on several blogs and websites. Two social media news releases saw 1,686 full page reads and 502 downloads.

- Traffic from referring sites increased 47 percent during the campaign. Facebook and Twitter were in the top three sites referring traffic to Lifelineofohio.org. Search engine traffic increased 91 percent during the campaign. (Online registrations could not be tracked, as they go through the BMV site.)

- The "Live On. Ride On." page had the longest visit time on Lifelineofohio.org—average 15 minutes.

- During summer 2009, Lifelineofohio.org saw traffic increase 66 percent compared to the previous summer.
- The campaign built an active community of followers—235 Twitter followers and 56 Facebook group members.

EXHIBIT 11-2A   News Release

For Immediate Release

For additional information, please contact:

Rachel Lewis
614.384.7329
rlewis@lifelineofohio.org

May 27, 2009

MOTORCYCLISTS ENCOURAGED TO LIVE ON, RIDE ON AS ORGAN DONORS
Nonprofit partners with enthusiast community to reclaim negative slang phrase

Ask a motorcycle enthusiast what they think of the term "organ donor" and you'll likely get a heated reaction. For years, this slang term has been thrown at bikers by individuals who don't understand or appreciate the passion for biking.

Lifeline of Ohio, the nonprofit organ procurement organization responsible for promoting organ and tissue donation in central and southeastern Ohio, is setting out to change that by reclaiming the phrase and showing the public what an organ donor really is: a hero.

"Motorcyclists should be proud to declare themselves organ donors," said Kent Holloway, CEO of Lifeline of Ohio. "Our goal is to demonstrate the positive impact they can have by registering in the Ohio Donor Registry and let them know they have the opportunity to live on and ride on by donating life."

Lifeline of Ohio is working to connect with motorcycle enthusiasts, a group known for its philanthropic efforts and sense of community. This month, coinciding with Motorcycle Safety Awareness Month, they will launch their "Live On. Ride On." campaign and will reach out over the next several weeks to motorcyclists at events, retail locations, rider training programs, and through social media.

"We chose to launch during Motorcycle Safety Awareness Month because we know the members of this community are safe drivers and we want to show that 'organ donor' shouldn't be a negative term, it's the ultimate gift," said Holloway.

Lifeline of Ohio will kick off its campaign at the 5th Annual Brandy Winfield Memorial Poker Run in Marion, Ohio, on June 6th with a water/information table. The group will also participate in several other events throughout the summer. Event attendees that show they are registered donors, and those who register onsite, will receive their choice of a cruiser-style patch or a sport-bike inspired t-shirt showing support for the cause.

In central Ohio, information displays and brochures will also be available at A.D. Farrow Co. Harley-Davidson locations, Centennial Park Harley-Davidson, and Iron Pony Motorsports Superstore.

Lifeline of Ohio is also spreading the word through outreach to motorcycle groups. Groups interested in learning more about donation can call Rachel Lewis at Lifeline of Ohio (614.384.7329) for materials and to talk about hosting a free speaker who has been touched by donation, like Tim Jones of Cambridge, who is a lifelong motorcyclist and a heart transplant recipient.

Motorcycle enthusiasts can also connect with "Live On. Ride On." online, at www.Lifelineofohio.org/LiveOnRideOn, where they can read stories of motorcyclists who have been touched by donation, see the latest schedule of events, connect through Facebook and Twitter and register to be an organ and tissue donor.

The need for organ and tissue donation is a national crisis, with more than 102,000 Americans waiting for a life-saving transplant. While about 90 percent of the population supports organ donation in theory, only half of Ohioans are registered donors.

—

About Lifeline of Ohio

Lifeline of Ohio (LOOP) is an independent, nonprofit organization whose mission is to promote and coordinate the donation of human organs and tissue for transplantation. Lifeline of Ohio is approved by the Centers for Medicare and Medicaid Services (CMS) of the U.S. Department of Health and Human Services as the designated organ procurement organization (OPO) serving 37 counties in Central and Southeastern Ohio, and Hancock and Wood counties in West Virginia. Lifeline of Ohio provides services to 64 hospitals through its transplant coordinators. LOOP's clinical staff is on call 24 hours a day to coordinate the recovery and transport of tissue and organs for transplant.

Additionally, Lifeline of Ohio offers educational presentations for professional, civic, church, and social organizations, as well as elementary through college level school programs. These programs are offered year-round as a community service and are customized to meet the objectives of the particular audience. Printed materials regarding donation, as well as donor registry information, are also available from Lifeline of Ohio by calling 800.525.5667 or visiting the website at www.lifelineofohio.org.

Courtesy Lifeline of Ohio and Fahlgren Mortine Public Relations

EXHIBIT 11-2B   Print Ad

Courtesy Lifeline of Ohio and Fahlgren Mortine Public Relations

E X H I B I T 11-2C   Public Endorsements

Courtesy Lifeline of Ohio and Fahlgren Mortine Public Relations

Case 11-3

Tackling large issues for the community takes real community engagement by multiple agencies. Exhibit 11-3A is a fact sheet on teen pregnancy prevention and Exhibit 11-3B is the executive summary for a report on the campaign.

United Way of Greater Milwaukee If Truth Be Told Initiative: Addressing Teen Pregnancy, Public Health, and the Cycle of Poverty

United Way of Greater Milwaukee, City of Milwaukee Health Department and Serve

SUMMARY

To address the profound public health crisis caused by teen pregnancy, United Way of Greater Milwaukee convened community leaders to rally for change. More than 2,000 Milwaukee teens have babies each year, ranking the city second in the nation in 2006. The group prioritized increasing public awareness elevating teen pregnancy's far-reaching and deeply-rooted societal consequences, including high rates of violent crime, unemployment, and poverty. To drive its work, the If Truth Be Told Initiative announced an aggressive goal to reduce births to teens 46 percent by 2015. Since 2006, it already achieved a 10 percent drop to the city's lowest rate since 1979.

BACKGROUND

In 2006, Milwaukee ranked second in the nation's 50 largest cities for births to teens. United Way of Greater Milwaukee (UWGM) revealed that teen pregnancy has serious long-term consequences not only for the teen mother and her child, but also for society as a whole. Research showed that it profoundly and negatively affects crime rates, graduation rates, and unemployment. It is closely associated with Milwaukee's high poverty rate—seventh in the nation, and high rate of children living in poverty—fourth in the nation. Taxpayers and businesses bear the long-term financial burden, paying 85 percent of the costs for more than 2,000 babies born to teens in Milwaukee each year—the total annual cost is over $179 million. But the most shocking part about the ranking was that most people didn't flinch. After decades of prevalence, teens having babies had become a social norm.

It was clear that this public health crisis required a unified commitment and comprehensive solutions. As a result, UWGM and the City of Milwaukee Health Department convened community leaders from government, business, education, nonprofits, and the faith community to form a community-driven oversight committee to address the problem. This group prioritized the If Truth Be Told public awareness initiative as the first step toward creating long-term change.

However, UWGM and its partners faced several challenges: teen pregnancy was widely accepted by teens and the community at large, the City's public school system had no universally-implemented comprehensive health and human growth development curriculum, and past and present collaborative efforts had failed. To reach its ultimate goal of reducing Milwaukee's teen birth rate 46 percent by 2015, the initiative had to focus on open, honest, and hard-hitting messages that address the issues contributing to teens having children and engage the community for the long haul.

RESEARCH

UWGM conducted two phases of research. In 2005, extensive studies were conducted to understand how teen pregnancy escalated to and remained at a crisis-level for so long. Fifty-eight teen-serving Milwaukee agencies were reviewed and/or participated in interviews. Listening sessions were held to gather views from agency representatives, concerned parents and citizens, and youth. Statistical data and best practices in prevention were gathered and analyzed. And peripheral issues surrounding teen pregnancy were thoroughly studied. Some of these include: sexual victimization, racial disparity, and unemployment.

The research showed that teens having children correlates to the perpetual cycle of poverty in Milwaukee, with more than 41 percent of children living in that continues to guide the committee's work and provide structure for the Initiative. Secondly, more than 30 focus groups and listening sessions were held with target audiences to test creative concepts. In addition, the oversight committee provides structure for extensive evaluation to ensure consideration of perspectives from diverse audiences.

PLANNING

Objectives

1. Engage a collaborative leadership group to provide structure to address teen pregnancy.

2. Elevate the issue of teen pregnancy to a critical level.

3. Target African-American and Hispanic communities where teen birth rates are highest and sexual relationships between teens and adults are often considered acceptable.

4. Drive implementation of comprehensive sexual health curriculum in Milwaukee Public Schools.

5. Produce measurable results toward overall goal to reduce births to teens 46 percent by 2015.

Strategic Approach

Target four critical audiences with consistent strategic messages.

- Teens: Getting pregnant as a teenager negatively impacts your life.

- Young Adult Males (18-34): Adults having sex with minors is not only wrong but illegal, and statutory rape often has more than one victim—the teen and her resulting child.

- General Community: Teen pregnancy has both economic and societal consequences that radiate into the entire community—it affects everyone in Greater Milwaukee; everyone pays for teen pregnancy through taxes, and everyone has a responsibility to address it.

- Business Community: Teen pregnancy creates a skilled worker shortage and contributes to a poor business climate overall.

EXECUTION

Addressing a public health crisis largely ignored by the community for decades takes hard-hitting, shocking tactics that make people stop in their tracks. Since 2006, the initiative executed more than 25 tactics, leveraging more than 100 stories in print, TV, and radio. The initial phase aimed to increase awareness and get people to stop ignoring the issue. Media outreach included outdoor, indoor, transit, print, radio, TV, collateral, and grassroots efforts like postering and flyering campaigns.

Many of the tactics fooled people into engaging through misdirect campaigns. For example one tactic prompted teens to call for "Extra Cash," but gave them a recorded message with a screaming baby in the background telling teens how having a baby makes their lives a lot harder and doesn't leave a lot of "Extra Cash." As the initiative moved into its second phase in 2007 and 2008, it aimed to change perceptions about teen parenthood and change teen behaviors by connecting them to resources. It also targeted adult males, showing how statutory rape is something ugly and wrong.

Being open and honest about sensitive issues can be controversial at times, as a result lobbying public officials and engaging advocates was often necessary and always successful.

EVALUATION OF SUCCESS

Since its launch in 2006, If Truth Be Told has achieved great successes:

1. Engage a collaborative leadership group to provide structure to address teen pregnancy. In 2006, UWGM convened Milwaukee's community-driven

Teen Pregnancy Prevention Oversight Committee, co-chaired by the city's health commissioner and daily newspaper's publisher. The committee provides structure and leadership for the Initiative's work, utilizing expertise of professionals from across the community by engaging workgroups focused on issues known to contribute to or successfully reduce teen pregnancy. Groups include: Sexual Victimization, Faith-Based Community, Law Enforcement, Collaborative Fund, and Public Awareness.

2. Elevate teen pregnancy and its peripheral issues to a critical level. Teen pregnancy is on the community's front burner. The Milwaukee Journal Sentinel made teen pregnancy a priority in its editorial series "Agenda 08: Growing Metro Milwaukee" and again prioritized teen pregnancy for its "Agenda 09: For a Better Wisconsin." The initiative has secured more than $2.5 million in in-kind media services and placement. The National Campaign to Prevent Teen Pregnancy has recognized Milwaukee's efforts several times— most notably as a model initiative in November 2008. Media relations successes resulted in more than 11.6 million gross impressions in 2008.

3. Target African-American and Hispanic communities where teen birth rates are highest and sexual relationships between teens and adults are often considered acceptable. UWGM established partnerships with African-American and Hispanic community media leaders resulting in placement of print and radio PSAs, as well as editorials and feature articles/stories on sexual victimization and statutory rape and its link to teen pregnancy.

4. Drive implementation of comprehensive sexual health curriculum in Milwaukee Public Schools. Media relations secured editorials, print articles, and television stories elevating the importance of comprehensive sexual health education. The group secured funding for comprehensive sexual health curriculum development and training for all Milwaukee Public Schools (MPS) in 2008. By April 2009, age-appropriate curriculum will be implemented in all fourth- and fifth-grade classes. MPS has committed to implementation in all Kindergarten through 12th-grade classes by the end of 2010.

5. Produce results toward overall goal to reduce births to teens 46 percent by 2015.

In April 2008, the initiative's oversight committee announced a goal to reduce births to teens 46 percent in 17 years—when 4th and 5th graders will be seniors in high school. While work toward the goal continues, achieving a 10 percent drop in one year (2007 over 2006) is clearly impressive. Progress toward the long-term measurable goal keeps the community focused and united against the issue.

Since the Initiative's launch, Milwaukee has dropped to seventh in the nation for births to teens; in November 2008 the City of Milwaukee Health Department announced that Milwaukee's birth rate had dropped 10 percent from 2006 to 2007, to its lowest since 1979. Public health officials attributed the decline to the If Truth Be Told public awareness initiative.

EXHIBIT 11-3A   Fact Sheet on Teen Pregnancy Prevention

Sexual Victimization

FACTS AT A GLANCE

- Juveniles accounted for 73% of Wisconsin sexual assault victims in 2001. [31]
- 42% of sexually active girls younger than 15 reported that their first intercourse was nonconsensual. [32]
- In Wisconsin, 71% of babies born to teen girls are fathered by adult males over 20 years old. In 20% of the cases, the fathers are at least six years older than the mothers. [33]
- 44% of surveyed teens in Wisconsin believed that if a girl had sex with a boy before, it is not sexual assault if he forces her to have sex later. [33]
- 1/2 to 2/3 of teenage mothers are sexually molested prior to their first pregnancy and between 30 and 44% are victims of rape or attempted rape. [34]
- 23% of sexual assault victims become pregnant by their assailants. [35]

One issue that surfaced repeatedly in interviews and listening sessions with those who work directly with teens is that sexual victimization is a major contributor to teen pregnancy. This includes child molestation and other sexual abuse, incest, dating violence and statutory rape.

Research points to a strong connection between sexual victimization and teen pregnancy. A history of sexual abuse has been linked to high-risk behaviors that may account for increased risk of early, unplanned pregnancy, including young age at initiation of sexual intercourse and failure to use contraception. [36]

Below are just a few of the comments made during the listening sessions:

▶ *"We're talking about 12-year-olds who are having sex with 27-year-olds. This is what we're talking about with most of the kids I know and work with. This is rape, and we smooth it over by calling it 'teen pregnancy.'"*

▶ *"This is a topic that's hard to address, but which we NEED to address. We need better training for staff overall, in child abuse, sexual assault, childhood sexual abuse and teen pregnancy. We need to start getting to kids 10 to 12 – when they start thinking about boys or even younger."*

▶ *"Teens are in great need of accurate information about what sexual violence is, because a great many of them grow up with it and believe that this is 'normal sex.' Some are abused by mom's boyfriend or another member of the family or someone they date."*

▶ *"There's a lot of sexual abuse and incest. Those girls just need to know there's someone there they can talk to – even if it's just a school nurse –right away, right after it's happened."*

▶ *"If they're dealing with agencies, they can't tell what happened, because then it has to be reported. So if it's an uncle or a father, they don't say anything.*

▶ *"I know girls who got pregnant because they got raped or because they wanted to join a gang and they had to sleep with the gang leader to get in, and they got pregnant."*

▶ *"The term 'teen pregnancy' dilutes what we're really talking about: molestation, sexual abuse, incest."*

"There is a direct correlation between sexual abuse – which impacts sexual behavior – and pregnancy. I believe that if we can reduce sexual violence, we can reduce teen pregnancy rates."

- MSW therapist working with at-risk youth

Courtesy United Way of Greater Milwaukee

EXHIBIT 11-3B "If Truth Be Told" Final Report

teamwork investment future everyone
family goal drop initiative hope united
hardship youth education resources contraception
strategy unemployment
decision-making
progress **IF TRUTH** birth rate
public health optimistic leadership commitment **BE TOLD...** community prevention health all-hands-on-deck results
passion epidemic teens problem solutions
effort crisis together loss regret reduction success faith
rape coordinated

2006-2011: A 5-YEAR PROGRESS REPORT
ON ENDING MILWAUKEE'S TEEN PREGNANCY CRISIS

United Way
United Way of Greater Milwaukee

Executive Summary

Five years ago, United Way of Greater Milwaukee convened community partners to address the high rate of teen births among 15 to 17 year olds in Milwaukee. In 2008, after two years of progress, these partners teamed up with local public health experts and set a goal to reduce teen births in this age group by 46% over seven years, one of the most ambitious teen pregnancy prevention initiatives in the United States at the time. The partnership was founded on the premise that because teen pregnancy affects everyone, everyone needed to be at the table. Leaders from social service, government, business, public health, philanthropy, faith and education sectors have all been represented on the Teen Pregnancy Prevention Oversight

Committee and its sub-committees. They have provided invaluable guidance and insight for the first five years of this ten-year effort.

According to Sarah Brown, the chief executive officer of the National campaign to Prevent Teen and Unplanned Pregnancy, the efforts in Milwaukee are unique because of the level of partnership, the sustained focus on evidence-based programs, and the numeric goal the initiative set for the community. Setting a goal can have "... a very big impact on people, and it brings a discipline to the system. Milwaukee's goal is aspirational. It helps people concentrate, get motivated and get noticed," according to Brown.

Results of the first five years of this effort are very promising. Although there is still work to be done, there is good reason to be encouraged that the community's hard work led by United Way of Greater Milwaukee has had a major impact. Highlights include:

1. United Way of Greater Milwaukee and partners recorded a four-year decline in teen birth rates in the target group in Milwaukee. From a starting rate of 52 births to teen mothers ages 15 to 17 in 2006, the rate declined to 44.4 births per 1,000 girls in 2009 (15%). These declines occurred even while Milwaukee's poverty level rose. Teen birth rates have traditionally gone up with poverty rates, so this is a significant finding that suggests multiple, positive forces are at work.

2. Thanks in part to implementation of the Healthy Youth Act in 2010, youth in Milwaukee are exposed to more positive messages and are provided with more evidence-based, science-driven health education than ever before. United Way of Greater Milwaukee supported the adoption of the Healthy Youth Act at the state level. At the local level, United Way of Greater Milwaukee helped fund training for nearly 900 teachers in the Human Growth and Development curriculum, a nationally recognized curriculum created by the Wellness and Prevention Office of the Milwaukee Public Schools. The curriculum has helped standardize health education for a district that has a high mobility rate, and the training has been well received by both teachers and administrators. Trained teachers have in turn reached more than 20,000 students in Milwaukee Public Schools.

3. Through its Healthy Girls programs, United Way of Greater Milwaukee gave over 16,000 young people from elementary school through high school access to evidence-based curricula that help them make healthy decisions. Healthy Girls programs provided healthy decision-making education to homeless youth, lesbian, gay, bisexual and transgender youth and other traditionally hard-to-reach, high–risk populations. A study of the effectiveness of these curricula showed that young people who participated were better equipped to prevent teen pregnancy and establish healthier relationships.

4. Media campaigns created by Serve Marketing raised awareness of the issue of teen pregnancy and have elicited inquiries and responses from tens of thousands of teens and adults from across the country. The local media elevated teen pregnancy through sustained coverage, including significant prominence from the *Milwaukee Journal Sentinel* through its editorial focus on the most serious challenges facing southeastern Wisconsin, which included teen pregnancy. In addition, local advertisers and Serve donated more than $4 million in in-kind advertising over the five-year period.

5. United Way of Greater Milwaukee created and distributed thousands of "toolkits" to help parents and children engage in difficult conversations about delaying sexual activity and pregnancy. National data suggests that 46% of teens consider their parents the most important influence when making decisions regarding sex.

Milwaukee youth now have access to greater resources for healthy decision-making than perhaps any time in history, but they also face a number of challenges.

- Milwaukee has become a poorer city than it was five years ago, and young people are over-represented among the ranks of the poor.

- The rate at which young people in Milwaukee graduate from high school is lower than the national average.

- Young people in Milwaukee report being exposed to or involved in violence at high numbers, and many still do not protect themselves from unplanned pregnancy or sexually transmitted infections.

- Many become sexually active very young, and a significant number of young people become sexually involved with much older partners, putting them at risk for a number of adverse health outcomes.

To be successful, the unique partnership formed between United Way of Greater Milwaukee and local leaders across sectors must continue to make teen pregnancy prevention one of its top economic and public health priorities. Co-chair of the Teen Pregnancy Prevention Oversight Committee and president and publisher of the *Milwaukee Journal Sentinel*, Elizabeth Brenner, said, "Milwaukee is hungry for good news, and there is a surplus of smart, committed, savvy people (here)." Fellow co-chair, Commissioner of Health Bevan Baker, said, "We have the resources; we have to focus on the problem."

United Way of Greater Milwaukee and its partners have now had four years of successful decreases in teen birth rates. As Dr. Robert Blum, international teen pregnancy prevention expert said when assisting Baltimore with its strategic plan to reduce teen pregnancy in that city, "Teen pregnancy is a marker for a lot of associated youth problems. Unless and until we have the political, social and moral will to act, we will be condemned in the future to write more plans and continue to wonder why our youth are in trouble. We know why they are in trouble and we know what to do to change it. It is our choice whether or not we will do it."[1]

What Youth Are Saying about Teen Pregnancy

"You need to think before you have sex. Safety first."

"When men have a baby, they don't always want the kid. They don't want to stick around."

"Why is teen pregnancy so high? There is a lack of contraception and people think with their hormones."

"If you get someone pregnant, you won't have time to hang out with your friends. You have to drop out of school to get a job. Both boys and girls drop out."

"Day care at school is a good idea so teen parents can stay in school."

"If you get someone pregnant, your parents will be angry."

"Teen pregnancy overpopulates our city."

Courtesy United Way of Greater Milwaukee

Emergency Public Relations

Chapter 12   Crisis Communication

12

Crisis Communication
reactive + proactive

In preparation for emergencies or crises, the practitioner should be generally aware of the four aspects of the process model, although its use in this form of public relations may be limited given the speed of unfolding events. Practitioners follow a five step cycle in managing a crisis: 1) they manage issues relevant to the organization to prevent a crisis; 2) they prepare to handle a crisis through planning, setting crisis communication policies, training, and preparation; 3) they seek to contain the scope of a crisis to minimize harm to the organization; 4) they help the organization recover from the crisis and rebuild the reputation of the organization; and 5) they analyze the crisis for important lessons that may help prevent future crises from impacting the organization. Thinking strategically about the issue, keeping a focus on the overall values and goals of the organization and remembering the long-term impact of communications are still relevant and important during a crisis.

RESEARCH

Some research will be helpful in reaching a state of readiness for an emergency. The following three types of research used for other forms of public relations are appropriate.

Client Research

Client research should focus on preparing as many "worst-case" scenarios as possible. What can go wrong? How serious is the impact? Is the organization's physical plant vulnerable to fire, explosion, or other crises? Are dangerous equipment and toxic materials located on the premises? How will you respond if the organization's president is indicted for fraud? All division heads in the organization should be asked by the director of public relations to prepare a list of potential trouble spots that could erupt in their respective areas. Whenever possible, corrective action should be taken to neutralize these problems before an emergency can occur or start the preparation to minimize the impact. Research may also examine the client's reputation and handling of past crises.

Opportunity or Problem Research

Emergency public relations is generally reactive in nature. Some practitioners argue that it is impossible to really get ready for all disasters. Emergency planning, however, must be proactive in order to be prepared for a proper reactive response to an emergency. Some problems slowly build due to a series of minor events. Even external issues related to another industry could eventually affect the organization. The public relations staff must monitor trends and detect potential issues to anticipate and prepare for issues that may explode into the public agenda.

Audience Research

The practitioner should make a list of internal and external publics to be immediately notified in case of an emergency. Internal publics would not only include senior leaders in the organization but also other key nodes of people. For example, the "call center" staff may be one of the first groups to be notified so they can anticipate and monitor problems as they surface in calls from consumers. Usually, the entire workforce is notified through existing internal channels of communication such as email or meetings with supervisors. External audiences in emergency crisis should be ranked by order of importance to include law enforcement officials; the families of the injured or dead, notified before the public release of their names; the mass media; government agencies, if appropriate; appropriate social media sites; and trade publications. These internal and external audiences are a suggested starting point. The practitioner needs to be much more specific in creating an emergency contact list designed to notify all concerned parties in a timely fashion and using appropriate communication channels.

OBJECTIVES

Because of the exceptional nature of crises, objectives for this form of public relations cannot be carefully planned. Nonetheless, some general guidelines are applicable:

1. To provide accurate, timely information to all targeted internal and external audiences
2. To demonstrate concern for the safety of lives
3. To safeguard organizational facilities and assets
4. To maintain a positive image of the organization as a good corporate or community citizen.

These guidelines will serve the practitioner well in responding quickly during rapidly evolving events when faced with high uncertainty.

PROGRAMMING

Programming for emergency public relations should focus on timely, accurate, and consistent messages delivered through appropriate (and often multiple) communication channels, and messages should be frequently repeated. The messages should be shorter and more simply supported by evidence than normal public relations messaging strategies. In a crisis, events may easily traumatize and cause panic. People have a harder time listening and absorbing information. It may take repeated exposure to the same message before people understand and act on the information. The message map formula with a "short statement" augmented by a couple of supporting details works best.[1]

To support the necessary flurry of communication needs, don't under-estimate the resources needed to handle the crisis, both in terms of money, time, and people. Crisis plans need trigger points to assess the severity of a crisis so additional communication support can be mobilized as warranted. The additional support may involve people within the organization or even hiring a public relations agency experienced in crisis response. Equally important is training these people and running simulations and exercises to practice for the real thing. The following structural approach is best when handling a major crisis which requires extensive resources.

In a major crisis, communication programming often has two major actions or areas of responsibility: establishing a *public relations crisis headquarters* (PR HQ) and a *media information center* (MIC).

The Public Relations Headquarters

The PR HQ will probably be the regular public relations office itself. If more space is needed, other offices may also be designated as part of the PR HQ. This office will be responsible for notification of all internal and external emergency audiences, for preparation of material for the media and other audiences, and for the establishment of a *public information center* (PIC) to answer inquiries and to control rumors. The director of public relations should likely remain in the PR HQ to supervise these three functions and to coordinate actions with senior leaders in the organization.

Notification, the first function of the PR HQ, will be the top priority of this office as soon as a crisis occurs. The internal and external audiences were discussed above and will be reviewed in Exhibit 12-a, the "Emergency Public Relations Checklist." Names of the injured or dead should be withheld from public release until the next of kin are notified or for 24 hours, whichever comes first.

The second function of the PR HQ will be preparation of materials for the media and the public. As a minimum, a company or organizational backgrounder, fact sheet, biographies of major officers, and their captioned photographs should already be prepared and on the organizational website. Along with assembling these background materials, the public relations staff should immediately begin the task of preparing its first basic news release/statement on the crisis. A good rule of thumb is that this should be ready for release *no more than one hour* after the occurrence of the emergency. The release should include all known facts, such as what happened, how,

E X H I B I T   12-a   Emergency Public Relations Checklist

I.   Public relations emergency headquarters (PR HQ). The PR director acts as
     manager of the crisis communication team and as the primary interface with
     senior leaders in the organization:
     A.   Notification and liaison
          1.   Internal: Coordinate actions and messaging strategy with senior lea-
               ders; and notify other portions of the organization and employees as
               appropriate.
          2.   External: Notify the media; law enforcement officials; government
               agencies; key interest groups; and the next of kin of the injured or
               dead, before public release of names (24-hour rule suggested).
     B.   Preparation of materials for media
          1.   Have company backgrounder, fact sheet, and bios of officers already
               prepared and on the company website. Many organizations prepare a
               "dark website" that is drafted to replace the normal website portal
               during a crisis to better direct viewers to key information.
          2.   Prepare basic news release or release a statement on the crisis as soon
               as possible (one-hour rule suggested).
               a.   Include all known facts—what happened, how, when, where,
                    who, and how many involved—not why (fault) to avoid
                    speculation.
               b.   Be certain all information is accurate; never release unconfirmed
                    information.
               c.   Withhold names of victims until the next of kin are notified
                    (or 24 hours, whichever comes first).
               d.   Clear release with senior management, legal department, and
                    human resources department.
               e.   Issue release immediately to local and national media, specialized
                    publications, employees by email and phone, community leaders,
                    insurance company, pertinent government agencies by fax and
                    email. Be sure to post the release on the company website and
                    provide links from social media sites and Twitter feeds to the
                    release.
          3.   Issue timely statements to media in ongoing crises.
          4.   Use one-voice principle—information only from official organizational
               spokesperson(s).
          5.   Use full-disclosure principle (follow legal restrictions relating to admis-
               sion of responsibility).
     C.   Public information center (PIC)
          1.   Establish and announce a PIC in the PR HQ if appropriate.
          2.   Respond to telephone, social media, and email inquiries with accurate
               information.
          3.   Provide accurate information to counter rumors.
          4.   Hold meetings and dialogue with groups as needed to clarify
               misinformation.
          5.   Coordinate information with the call center.
          6.   Direct company employees to make no unauthorized statements to
               media representatives.
          7.   Monitor and engage online communities (blogs/social networking sites).
          8.   Use one-voice principle—information only from official organizational
               statements.
          9.   Use full-disclosure principle (within legal boundaries).

II.   Media information center (MIC)
  A.   Designate a place for media representatives to gather, if necessary.
  B.   Locate an MIC near the crisis area, but away from the PR HQ. (Media access to a disaster site may require PR escort.)
  C.   Have spokesperson available day or night.
    1.   Use one-voice principle—information only from official organizational statements.
    2.   Use full-disclosure principle (within legal boundaries).

when, where, who, and how many were involved. The question of why may be omitted for two reasons. First, avoid speculation as there is much uncertainty during the initial phases of a crisis. Second, the organization may run the risk of involving itself in litigation through an admission of fault. From a legal standpoint, being "solution oriented" could be different than being "responsible" or "culpable" for damages during the crisis. Therefore, the organization's messages and actions are closely coordinated among the communication team, legal department, and senior management. The release should be cleared as quickly as possible with senior management, the legal department, and possibly the human resources department. The crisis management policies established during the crisis preparation phase and the training of staff will help expedite this process. Then the news release should be issued immediately to local and national media, posted on social media sites, announced via a Twitter feed, and provided to online outlets and specialized publications, employees, community leaders, and pertinent government agencies. In addition to the first basic release, the PR HQ should issue frequent statements to the media in ongoing crises and should coordinate media interviews with the CEO as warranted.

Through all of these emergency public relations procedures, two principles are recommended: a *one-voice* principle and a *full-disclosure* principle. Above all other considerations, the organization should *speak with one voice*. All employees should be briefed to give information to the media or other concerned parties only from official organizational statements, issued by the PR HQ or appropriate senior spokespersons. The full-disclosure principle refers to giving all known information, with the exception of why the emergency occurred if this might involve admission of fault.

The third possible function of the PR HQ is to establish a *PIC*. The responsibilities of the PIC include responding to inquiries with accurate information, providing information to groups to combat rumors, and holding meetings with groups as needed to clarify misinformation. The organization's call center may be part of the PIC process. Again, the one-voice and full-disclosure principles should be observed at all times in its operation.

The Media Information Center

If media representatives will be gathering at the site of an emergency or disaster, the director of public relations should set up an *MIC* at some location near the crisis area but away from the PR HQ. When separated from the PR HQ, the MIC buffers the public relations staff from constant interruptions and allows them to focus on priority tasks without spending all of their time answering media queries. The MIC should, if possible, designate staff people to escort media representatives if there is a hazardous disaster area. Reporters should not be permitted to wander freely through a dangerous zone, although they usually want unrestricted access to everything. The MIC should be a suitable room, preferably where journalists can gather to receive new information about the emergency. A high-credibility spokesperson and several alternates should be designated in advance and, once chosen, a single spokesperson should be on duty as long as necessary at the MIC to interact with the media. Directors of public relations should seldom be designated MIC spokespersons. They should likely remain at the PR HQ to supervise all operations. The spokesperson, however, should be a high-ranking officer in the organization; otherwise, the organization's credibility could suffer. Needless to say, the one-voice and full-disclosure principles should be stringently applied in the operation of the MIC.

Uncontrolled and Controlled Media

In an emergency situation, most of the communication will be uncontrolled in the form of news releases, interviews with organizational officials, dialogues on social media sites and perhaps photographs and b-roll video, although the media representatives will usually take their own photos.

Controlled media will be used sparingly, usually as prepared background material or email, voice mail, or in-house bulletins for employees. The organization's website can become an important resource in emergency public relations. Ongoing news of the crisis, along with a wealth of other information about the organization, can be posted on the website. An organization may elect to post a statement from the CEO on YouTube. After the crisis, the website can be used to clarify the organization's situation and to provide a record of the course of the crisis itself. Some organizations prepare a special website that is "hidden" on the server but can be activated immediately during a crisis. The sites provide additional background material and interactive features to handle exchanges with both the media and the public most affected by the crisis. Engaging the public through social media expands an organization's reach during a crisis. The American Red Cross uses blogs, social media networks (Facebook, MySpace), Twitter, social bookmarking sites (del.icio.us), video-sharing (YouTube) and photo-sharing (Flickr) sites. Your organization should do the same.

Effective Communication

Two-way communication and audience participation may assume greater than usual importance in a crisis. The targeted audiences, especially the media, will want to be involved and interact with the organization and spokesperson as much as possible. Listen to your publics during a crisis; they may have good feedback for you and even good ideas. But, in general, all the previously discussed principles of communication should be observed.

Programming for emergency public relations, then, concentrates on the two major responsibilities of creating a PR HQ and an MIC (see Exhibit 11-a). Beyond that, customary use of uncontrolled and controlled media and principles of effective communication are appropriate.

EVALUATION

The evaluation of emergency public relations will be less precise than for other forms of the discipline. Since emergencies are unplanned, the PR objectives must be, at best, general and nonquantitative guidelines. In a quiet period well after the organization's recovery from the emergency, it will be appropriate to review the general guidelines previously mentioned and informally assess the PR department's degree of success in meeting them. Such a review should also include analyzing media coverage; tracking complaints from consumers, communities (both local and online), employees, and other relevant publics; holding internal meetings on the crisis plan and its implementation; and assessing damage to the organization's image. In a product recall, a company could also review loss of sales and change in market share as indicators on the severity of the crisis. Of course, a formal survey of all participants can also be taken. The results may be used for a variety of purposes, possibly including improvement of emergency public relations procedures.

SUMMARY

Although the ROPE (research, objectives, programming, evaluation) process has limited applicability in emergency public relations, it should not be forgotten or discarded.

Research is useful in preparing for emergencies. Worst-case and most-likely scenarios should be prepared to determine what problems could possibly develop. Although emergency public relations is inherently reactive, planning for such crises should be proactive. Emergency contact lists should be made, including all internal and external individuals, groups, and agencies that are to be notified in a crisis.

Objectives for emergency PR tend to be of an impact nature. They usually concentrate on providing information to important audiences as needed; safeguarding lives, facilities, and assets, and protecting the credibility of the organization.

Programming should still focus on the strategic communication needs of the organization and clear and concise messages that provide timely and accurate information, and clear actions that support crisis recover and image restoration. In a large crisis, the programming likely includes establishing a PR HQ and, if necessary, an MIC. The functions of the emergency headquarters include notification and liaison and preparation of materials for the media. If reporters will be gathering at the site of a disaster or crisis, an MIC should be established near (but usually not on) the site, and an organizational spokesperson should be designated to be on duty to interact with media representatives as long as necessary.

Evaluation for emergency PR is usually less formal than for other types. If objectives have been set before a crisis occurs, each should be appropriately evaluated. If not, the organization should, after the emergency, review its notification functions, its general accessibility and service to the media, and, of course, its media coverage during the event.

ENDNOTE

1. "Creating a Message Map For Risk Communications" (Sep. 27, 2004). *PR News.* 37 (60): 1.

READINGS ON EMERGENCY PUBLIC RELATIONS

Adams, William C. "Responding to the Media During a Crisis: It's What You Say and When You Say It," *Public Relations Quarterly* 45 (spring 2000): 26ff.

Alvey, Robert J. "Creating an Effective Crisis Communication Team," *Public Relations Tactics* 12 (December 2005): 12–13.

Baron, Gerald. "Gulf Spill Communications: Managing the Worst U.S. Environmental Disaster," *Public Relations Strategist* 16.3 (summer 2010): 12.

Benoit, William L. "Image Repair Discourse and Crisis Communication," *Public Relations Review* 23 (Summer 1997): 177–186.

Braud, Gerard. "The Tony Hayward Effect: Examining the Role of the CEO During a Crisis," *Public Relations Strategist* 16.3 (summer 2010): 16.

Briones, Rowena L., Beth Kuch, Brooke Fisher Liu, and Yan Jin. "Keeping up with the digital age: How the American Red Cross uses social media to build relationships," *Public Relations Review* 37.1 (March 2011):37–43.

Brown, Lorra M. "VT Tragedy Teaches Students the True Nature of Public Relations," *Public Relations Tactics* 14 (September 2007): 18–19.

Choi, Yoonhyeung and Ying-Hsuan Lin. "Consumer Responses to Mattel Product Recalls Posted on Online Bulletin Boards: Exploring Two Types of Emotion." *Journal of Public Relations Research* 21.2 (2009): 198–207.

Chong, Mark. "A Crisis of Epidemic Proportions: What Communication Lessons Can Practitioners Learn From The Singapore SARS Crisis?" *Public Relations Quarterly* 51 (spring 2006): 6–11.

Chyi, Hsiang Iris, and Maxwell McCombs. "Media Salience and the Process of Framing: Coverage of the Columbine School Shootings," *Journalism and Mass Communication Quarterly* 81 (spring 2004): 22–25

Cobb, Chris. "The Taco Bell E Coli Outbreak: Calming Public Fears During Food-Borne Illness Scares," *Public Relations Tactics* 14 (February 2007): 11–12.

Coombs, W. Timothy. "An Analytic Framework for Crisis Situations: Better Responses from a Better Understanding of the Situation," *Journal of Public Relations Research* 10(3) (1998): 177ff.

———" Crisis Management and Communications," White Paper published by the Institute for Public Relations (December 2007), accessed January 22, 2008 (NEED DATE), www instituteforpr.org/ipr_info/crisis_management_and_commumcations/.

——— *Ongoing Crisis Communication Planning, Managing, and Responding,* 3d ed. Thousand Oaks, CA: Sage Publications, 2011.

——— and Sherry J. Holladay. "An exploration of the effects of victim visuals on perceptions and reactions to crisis events," *Public Relations Review* 37.2 (June 2011): 115–120.

Dezenhall, Eric and John Weber. *Damage Control*. New York: Penguin Group, 2007.

Doorley, J., and Helio Fred Garcia. "Rumor Has It: Understanding and Managing Rumors," *Public Relations Strategist* 13.3 (summer 2007): 27–31.

Fearn-Banks, Kathleen. *Crisis Communications: A Casebook Approach,* 4th ed. Mahwah, NJ: Erlbaum, 2011.

Hearit, Keith Michael. *Crisis Management, by Apology*. Mahwah, NJ: Erlbaum, 2005.

Holtzhausen, Derina R. and Glen F. Roberts. "An Investigation into the Role of Image Repair Theory in Strategic Conflict Management." *Journal of Public Relations Research* 21.2 (2009): 165–186.

Hyde, Richard C. "In Crisis Management, Getting the Message Right Is Critical," *Public Relations Strategist* 13 (summer 2007): 32–35.

Irving, Christine. "Adding It Up: Public Relations Is at the Forefront of Banks' Recovery," *Public Relations Strategist* 15. 4 (fall 2009): 36.

Jin, Yan and Brooke Fisher Liu. "The Blog-Mediated Crisis Communication Model: Recommendations for Responding to Influential External Blogs," *Journal of Public Relations Research* 22.4 (2010): 429–455.

Jordan-Meier, Jane. *The Four Stages of Highly Effective Crisis Management: How to Manage the Media in the Digital Age*. Boca Raton, FL: CRC Press (2011).

Kenon A. Brown, and Candace L. White. "Organization–Public Relationships and Crisis Response Strategies: Impact on Attribution of Responsibility," *Journal of Public Relations Research* 23.1 (2011): 75–92.

Kimmel, Allan J. *Rumors and Rumor Control*. Mahwah, NJ: Erlbaum, 2004.

Levick, Richard, and Larry Smith. *Stop the Presses: The Crisis and Litigation PR Desk Reference*. Washington, DC: Watershed Press, 2007.

Levy, Ronald N. "Your Coming Crisis: How to Triumph," *Public Relations Quarterly* 51 (2006): 26–28.

Loomis, Lynette M. "Managing Emotions: The Missing Steps in Crisis Communications Planning," *Public Relations Tactics* 15 (March 2008): 13.

Lukaszewski, James E "Becoming a Crisis Guru: Why Crisis Management Is as Difficult as Ever," *Public Relations Strategist* 13 (summer 2007): 44–45.

———. "Establishing Individual and Corporate Crisis Communication Standards: The Principles and Protocols," *Public Relations Quarterly* 42 (fall 1997), 7ff.

Millar, Dan P, and Robert L. Heath, eds. *Responding to Crisis*. Mahwah, NJ: Erlbaum, 2004.

Mitroff, Ian, and Gus Anagnos. *Managing Crises Before They Happen: What Every Executive Needs to Know About Crisis Management*. New York: AMACOM, 2005.

Moore, Aaron J. "Roger Clemens and the Dangers of Misreading the Media," *Public Relations Tactics* 15 (May 2008): 27.

Over, Seth, J. Keith Saliba and Franklin Yartey. "More Words, Less Action: A Framing Analysis of FEMA Public Relations Communications During Hurricanes Katrina and Gustav," *Public Relations Journal* 4.2 (2010).

Pedersen, Wes. "I Set Up My Own 'Crisis Monitoring' Operation and Gain a Vital 'Deep Throat' Source in the Process," *Public Relations Quarterly* 52.2 (2008): 22–23.

Pinsdorf, Marion K. *All Crises Are Global: Managing to Escape Chaos*. New York: Fordham University Press, 2004.

Preble, John F. "Integrating the Crisis Management Perspective into the Strategic Management *Process," Journal of Management Studies* 34 (September 1997): 769.

Reber, B.H., V. Murphree, and F. Blevens. "Superhero, Instructor, Optimist: FEMA and the Frames of Disaster in Hurricanes Katrina and Rita," *Journal Of Public Relations Research* 21.3 (2009): 273–294.

Regester, Michael, and Judy Larkin. *Risk Issues and Crisis Management in Public Relations: A Casebook of Best Practices.* London: Kogan Page Publishers (2008).

Ropeik, David, and George Gray. *Risk! A Practical Guide for Deciding What's Really Safe and What's Really Dangerous in the World Around You.* New York: Houghton Mifflin, 2002.

Schock, Nathan. "Handling a Fake Twitter Account," *Public Relations Strategist* 16.3 (Summer 2010): 8.

Schultz, Friederike, Sonja Utz, and Anja Göritz. "Is the medium the message? Perceptions of and reactions to crisis communication via twitter, blogs and traditional media *Public Relations Review* 37.1 (March 2011): 20–27.

Stateman, Alison. "The Tylenol Tampering Crisis as Examined 25 Years Ago," *Public Relations Tactics* 15 (March 2008): 7.

Sweetser, Kaye D., and Emily Metzgar. "Communicating During Crisis: Use of Blogs as a Relationship Management Tool," *Public Relations Review* 33 (September 2007): 340–342.

Thomas, Glen. "Lessons Learned the Hard Way: Stumbling Through to Better Crisis Communications," *Public Relations Tactics* 15 (March 2008): 12.

Ulmer, Robert Ray, Timothy L. Sellnow, and Matthew Wayne Seeger. *Effective Crisis Communication. Moving From Crisis to Opportunity.* Thousand Oaks, CA: Sage, 2007.

Veil, Shan. "Mayhem in the Magic City: Rebuilding Legitimacy in a Communication Tram Wreck," *Public Relations Review* 33 (September 2007): 337–339.

Wigley, Shelley. "Telling your own bad news: Eliot Spitzer and a test of the stealing thunder strategy," *Public Relations Review* 37.1 (March 2011): 50–56.

Crisis Communication Cases

Case 12-1

The worst environmental disaster in U.S. history called for the best in crisis public relations. However, due to the complexity of the response effort and conflicts among decision-makers, it was not to happen. Exhibit 12-1A is the cover of the National Commission on the BP Deepwater Horizon Oil Spill Report, Exhibit 12-1B is a listing of federal agencies involved in the oil spill response, and Exhibit 12-1C is Presidential Executive Order 13543 creating the Oil Spill Commission.

Deepwater Horizon: Offshore Drilling Oil Spill Creates Anxiety Among Key Energy Stakeholders and a Gusher of Conflicting Emergency Public Relations

Napoleon Byars,
Associate Dean for Undergraduate Studies
School of Journalism & Mass Communication
University of North Carolina at Chapel Hill

SUMMARY

Prior to 10 p.m. (CST) April 20, 2010, Deepwater Horizon was not in the common vernacular of average Americans. All that changed when the Transocean offshore drilling platform leased to British Petroleum (BP) exploded killing 11 workers, injuring 16, and forcing 99 others to flee the rig in lifeboats.[1] As events unfolded, the explosion proved to be the signal of a larger emergency.

The platform blast was caused by methane gas that shot up and out the drill column and ignited. The rig exploded in smoke and flames approximately 41 miles off the coast of Louisiana. According to press reports, platform workers were confused about how to react to the emergency. *The National Commission on the BP Deepwater Horizon Oil Spill and Offshore Drilling* report also documented the confusion.

The search and rescue phase of the event was a textbook example of U.S. Coast Guard professionalism. The 72-hour air and sea search covered 5,200 square miles of water. Details of the rescue were updated hourly as Coast Guard officials kept the media informed. Within days all workers were accounted for, or confirmed as missing or dead. Afterwards, emergency responders focused on the threat of an oil leak.[2]

The Deepwater Horizon rig sank on April 22, 2010. Hours later, an oil leak was discovered that would spill into the Gulf of Mexico for more than three months. At its height, the oil slick covered an area the size of Texas and became the largest oil drilling disaster in U.S. history. The volume of oil spilled was approximately 4,900,000 barrels or 206,000,000 gallons. The harmful effects of the spill—both economic and environmental—will likely last far into the future; so will the debate about what could have been done to prevent it.

RESEARCH

The dominant coalition of organizational decision-makers and communicators consisted of former BP Chief Executive Officer Tony Hayward and the straight-talking Coast Guard Admiral Thad Allen, the National Incident Commander for the federal response to the oil spill. The government initially partnered with BP in disseminating information about the emergency. Later, when the flow of oil spilling into the gulf was much worse than BP estimated, the government began distancing itself from BP's information operations.

Key stakeholders in the crisis included BP, the federal government, the Gulf Coast States and news media. From the outset, BP and the government's goal was to stop the flow of oil from the well head and prevent further damage to the environment. As the disaster worsened the list of stakeholders grew to 17 federal agencies (see Exhibit 3). Other stakeholders included the oil industry, investors, environmental groups, Gulf Coast fishing and tourism industries, along with government leaders from Louisiana to the United Kingdom.

PLANNING

Initial emergency planning fell to the Coast Guard, which was responsible for rescue operations. News of the platform explosion was covered by local, national, and global news organizations as well as social media.

As the nature and existent of the oil spill became known, the relationship between the government and BP showed signs of strain, as did the practice of emergency public relations. The solution to effectively stopping the leak took months to achieve. In hindsight, BP's critics and supporters agreed that the company's planning for the disaster could at best be characterized as inadequate.

The 583-page BP emergency-response strategy report prepared in advance of the disaster, and approved by the government, revealed misgivings about what to do to stop a deep sea oil spill were it to happen. Sections of the report appeared not applicable to Deepwater Horizon drilling at all. For example, the report mentioned the need to protect sea lions, sea otters, walruses, and other animals that don't live in the Gulf of Mexico. Absent from the report were procedures to address a deep sea spill such as containment domes, top kill, and junk shots along with a definition of terms for communicators. Even more disturbing, one source link in the report was to a Japanese shopping website.[3]

The emergency public relations template for government communicators can be found in the training provided by the Federal Emergency Management Agency (FEMA). After the woeful government response to Hurricane Katrina, FEMA instituted a nationwide training program to enhance U.S. emergency management practices. According to FEMA's Web site, the course description for the National Incident Management Systems (NIMS) includes guidelines for communicators practicing emergency public relations and reads as follows:

> NIMS provides a consistent nationwide template to enable all government, private-sector, and nongovernmental organizations to work together during domestic incidents. The public information systems described in NIMS are designed to effectively manage public information at an incident, regardless of the size and complexity of the situation or the number of entities involved in the response.[4]

By nearly all accounts Coast Guard communicators followed NIMS procedures. A Joint Information System (JIS) and Joint Information Center (JIC) stood up to respond to the deluge of information requests by the news media. The JIC helped coordinate, gather, verify, coordinate, and distribute information to the press and other key stakeholders.

EXECUTION

Emergency public relations strategy connected with the Deepwater Horizon oil spill was nothing short of daunting. The scale and complexity of sea and land operations and number of organizations involved was unprecedented. The goals and messages for the government and BP often overlapped. Both sought to communicate that stopping the the leak at the well head and cleaning up the the water and coastline were top priorities. Additionally, both wanted stakeholders to believe the best and brightest minds were working to address the problem.

BP was the expert in deep water drilling and the government had the ability to call on vast resources. However, without viable options to stop the leak, public confidence in the response efforts soon waned. More importantly, the answer to the central question of "Exactly how much oil was leaking into the gulf?" appeared elusive. Early BP estimates pegged the leak at 1,000 barrels of oil per day. However, government estimates put the leak at approximately 5,000 barrels a day. As the emergency continued, oil leak estimates grew to 60,000 to 80,000 barrels.

Complicating matters, BP and government communicators appeared to work at cross purposes at times. Joint press conferences, which hallmarked early cooperation between the government and company officials, were replaced by separate press conferences. As each new approach to stopping the oil leak met with failure, 24/7 news reporting increased the pressure on officials to do something to stop the spill. Eventually, there was a growing perception that the government and BP were on different pages operationally and in their communication efforts.

During a White House press briefing Homeland Security Secretary Janet Napolitano snapped, "They are not our partner, they are not our partner" after a

Coast Guard official commented that BP was a full partner in the overall response.[5] Not to be upstaged, a frustrated U.S. President Barack Obama said during a T.V. interview that he wanted answers "So I know whose ass to kick." Federal officials sought to reassure the public that BP would be held accountable for the spill. BP on the the other hand sought to reassure Gulf Coast communities it was taking full responsibility for cleaning up the oil spill. The *"We will make this right"* public pledge became the centerpiece message of BP's top executives and employees.

Still, BP public relations efforts were not without missteps and gaffes. Tony Hayward's public comments complaining "I'd like my life back" reflected what was perceived as BP's lack of compassion for those most affected by the spill.[6] BP Chairman Carl-Henric Svanberg, after meeting President Obama at the White House commented to reporters "We care about the small people" referring to the residents of the Gulf Coast. Svanberg did not intend to insult local residents, but his words reinforced the old stereotype of oil barons.

As the emergency continued, BP found its footing with a public relations campaign that reached out to communities in the gulf. It put a United States and local face on its outreach by featuring Gulf Coast employees explaining how to file a claim (see Exhibit 4), contact the company or volunteer in the clean-up. The commitment to *"Making this right"* was prominent in each BP communiqué.

Streaming camera footage of the leaking well head was one of the most watched videos on the Internet during the crisis. To counter the video, BP launched a series of commercials and advertisements to communicate multifaceted messages of oil drilling expertise, corporate response to the oil spill and regret for harming the environment. BP also stepped up Web operations to respond to the emergency. Additionally, the company established a BP YouTube Channel and used Facebook and Twitter to help get its message out. The company also purchased search terms relating to the spill so as to direct Web surfers looking for information to its Web site.[7] No stone was left unturned in communicating that BP was committed to stopping the leak and cleaning up the spill.

EVALUATION

Evaluation of the Deepwater Horizon oil spill is well documented in the report by *The National Commission on the BP Deepwater Horizon Oil Spill and Offshore Drilling*. The commission was established on May 21, 2010 by an executive order signed by President Obama. Its mission was to examine the facts and circumstances concerning the root causes of the disaster; develop options for guarding against offshore oil spills drilling and mitigating their impact on the environment; and, submit a report of its findings.[8,9]

Emergency public relations, as practiced by the dominant coalition of decision-makers and communicators continues to be evaluated. Still, there was lots of room for improvement. Too often the government and BP were not on the same page in estimating the volume of the oil leak or what steps to take to stop it. This worked against effective reputation management on both sides. Decision-makers, who also served as lead communicators, frequently were given to emotional statements or gaffes that reinforced the perception of a crisis spinning out of control. On a positive note, the U.S. Coast Guard's handing of emergency public relations in connection with the search and rescue was exemplary. Finally, BP's *"Make this right"* pledge was backed with a public relations campaign supported by the actions of local BP employees, site managers, and claim representatives.

REFERENCES

1. David Barstow, David Rohde and Stephanie Saul, Deepwater Horizon's Final Hours, *The New York Times*, December 25, 2010.

2. Lieutenant Joseph Klinker, USCG, "Managing the Information Flow: A Case Analysis of the Federal Government's Deepwater Horizon's Crisis Communication Efforts," University of North Carolina Masters Thesis, December 2010.

3. Ian Yarett, "Why Wasn't There a Better Plan?" *Newsweek*, May 28, 2010.

4. Federal Emergency Management Institute, "IS-702.a National Incident Management System (NIMS) Public Information Systems," retrieved February 8, 2011: */training.fema.gov/emiweb/is/is702a.asp*.

5. The White House, *Press Briefing on the BP Oil Spill*, retrieved February 9, 2011: *www.whitehouse.gov/the-press-office/press-briefing-bp-oil-spill-gulf-coast*.

6. Erin McClam and Harry R. Weber, "BP's failures made worse by PR mistakes Oil giant struggles to contain undersea gusher … and its own messaging," *Associated Press*, June 11, 2010.

7. Matthew Shaer, "Gulf oil spill: To control message, BP buys search terms from Google," *The Christian Science Monitor*, June 9, 2010.

8. "Executive Order 13543 of May 21, 2010: National Commission on the BP Deepwater Horizon Oil Spill and Offshore Drilling," retrieved December 18, 2010: edocket.access.gpo.gov/2010/pdf/2010-12805.pdf.

9. National Commission on the BP Deepwater Horizon Oil Spill and Offshore Drilling, "Deepwater: The Gulf Oil Disaster and the Future of Offshore Drilling," retrieved January 18, 2011: *oilspillcommission.gov/final-report*.

EXHIBIT 12-1A Oil Spill Report

National Commission on the
BP DEEPWATER HORIZON OIL SPILL
AND OFFSHORE DRILLING

Search

About   Meetings   Resources   Reports

SHARE

Final Report (Released 01/11/2011)

Full Final Report *(16.76 MB)*

Introduction (Front Matter) *(1.5 MB)*

Part I: The Path to Tragedy *(6.85 MB)*

    Chapter 1 *(2.25 MB)*
    "Everyone involved with the job...was completely satisfied..."
    The Deepwater Horizon, the Macondo Well, and Sudden Death on the Gulf of
    Mexico

    Chapter 2 *(4.02 MB)*
    "Each oil well has its own personality"
    This History of Offshore Oil and Gas in the United States

    Chapter 3 *(1.05 MB)*
    "It was like pulling teeth."
    Oversight--and Oversights--in Regulating Deepwater Energy Exploration and
    Production in the Gulf of Mexico

Part II: Explosion and Aftermath *(15.01 MB)*
The Cause and Consequences of Disaster

    Chapter 4 *(3.22 MB)*
    "But, who cares, it's done, end of story, [we] will probably be fine and we'll get a
    good cement job."
    The Macondo Well and the Blowout

    Chapter 5 *(3.77 MB)*
    "You're in it now, up to your neck!"
    Response and Containment

    Chapter 6 *(4.92 MB)*
    "The worst environmental disaster America has ever faced"
    Oiling a Rich Environment: Impacts and Assessment

    Chapter 7 *(3.94 MB)*
    "People have plan fatigue . . . they've been planned to death"
    Recovery and Restoration

Part III: Lessons Learned *(6.17 MB)*
Industry, Government, and Energy Policy

    Chapter 8 *(3.49 MB)*
    "Safety is not proprietary"

Chief Counsel's Report

Recommendations for Decision Makers *(7.68 MB)*

Staff Working Papers

Download Press Kit *(2.38 MB)*

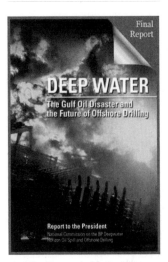

Printed copies of the report can be obtained from The Government
Printing Office, Amazon, and Barnes & Noble.

The first printing of the Commission's Final Report contained the
following typographical errors:

- P. 103, 2nd line in the final paragraph: currently reads "3000
  foot plug"; should read "300 foot plug"
- P. 139, 1st line of the fourth paragraph: "prophesy" should

E X H I B I T 12-1B Federal Agencies Involved in the Oil Spill Response

Federal Agencies Involved with Deepwater Horizon Oil Spill

- United States Coast Guard (USCG), www.uscg.mil
- U.S. Department of Defense (DOD), www.defense.gov
- U.S. Department of Homeland Security (DHS), www.dhs.gov
- U.S. Department of Agriculture (USDA), www.usda.gov
- National Oceanographic and Atmospheric Administration (NOAA), www.noaa.gov
- U.S. Department of the Interior (DOI), www.doi.gov
- U.S. Department of Energy (DOE), www.energy.gov
- U.S. Environmental Protection Agency (EPA), www.epa.gov
- Food and Drug Administration (FDA), www.fda.gov
- U.S. Department of Health and Human Services (DHHS), www.hhs.gov
- U.S. Department of Labor (DOL), www.dol.gov
- National Park Service (NPS), www.nps.gov
- U.S. Fish & Wildlife Service (FWS), www.fws.gov
- U.S. Geological Survey (USGS), www.usgs.gov
- National Institute for Occupational Safety and Health (NIOSH), www.cdc.gov/niosh
- National Institute of Environmental Health Sciences (NIEHS), www.niehs.nih.gov
- U.S. Small Business Administration (SBA), www.sba.gov

EXHIBIT 12-1C   Presidential Executive Order 13543

Presidential Documents

Executive Order 13543 of May 21, 2010

National Commission on the BP Deepwater Horizon Oil Spill and Offshore Drilling

By the authority vested in me as President by the Constitution and the laws of the United States of America, it is hereby ordered as follows:

Section 1. *Establishment.* There is established the National Commission on the BP Deepwater Horizon Oil Spill and Offshore Drilling (the "Commission").

Section 2. *Membership.* (a) The Commission shall be composed of not more than 7 members who shall be appointed by the President. The members shall be drawn from among distinguished individuals, and may include those with experience in or representing the scientific, engineering, and environmental communities, the oil and gas industry, or any other area determined by the President to be of value to the Commission in carrying out its duties.

(b) The President shall designate from among the Commission members two members to serve as Co-Chairs.

Section 3. *Mission.* The Commission shall:

(a) examine the relevant facts and circumstances concerning the root causes of the Deepwater Horizon oil disaster;

(b) develop options for guarding against, and mitigating the impact of, oil spills associated with offshore drilling, taking into consideration the environmental, public health, and economic effects of such options, including options involving:

(1) improvements to Federal laws, regulations, and industry practices applicable to offshore drilling that would ensure effective oversight, monitoring, and response capabilities; protect public health and safety, occupational health and safety, and the environment and natural resources; and address affected communities; and (2) organizational or other reforms of Federal agencies or processes necessary to ensure such improvements are implemented and maintained.

(c) submit a final public report to the President with its findings and options for consideration within 6 months of the date of the Commission's first meeting.

Section 4. *Administration.* (a) The Commission shall hold public hearings and shall request information including relevant documents from Federal, State, and local officials, nongovernmental organizations, private entities, scientific institutions, industry and workforce representatives, communities, and others affected by the Deepwater Horizon oil disaster, as necessary to carry out its mission.

(b) The heads of executive departments and agencies, to the extent permitted by law and consistent with their ongoing activities in response to the oil spill, shall provide the Commission such information and cooperation as it may require for purposes of carrying out its mission.

(c) In carrying out its mission, the Commission shall be informed by, and shall strive to avoid duplicating, the analyses and investigations undertaken by other governmental, nongovernmental, and independent entities.

(d) The Commission shall ensure that it does not interfere with or disrupt any ongoing or anticipated civil or criminal investigation or law enforcement activities or any effort to recover response costs or damages arising out of the Deepwater Horizon explosion, fire, and oil spill. The Commission shall consult with the Department of Justice concerning the Commission's activities to avoid any risk of such interference or disruption.

(e) The Commission shall have a staff, headed by an Executive Director.

(f) The Commission shall terminate 60 days after submitting its final report.

Section 5.*General Provisions.* (a) To the extent permitted by law, and subject to the availability of appropriations, the Secretary of Energy shall provide the Commission with such administrative services, funds, facilities, staff, and other support services as may be necessary to carry out its mission.

(b) Insofar as the Federal Advisory Committee Act, as amended (5 U.S.C. App.) (the "Act"), may apply to the Commission, any functions of the President under that Act, except for those in section 6 of the Act, shall be performed by the Secretary of Energy in accordance with guidelines issued by the Administrator of General Services.

(c) Members of the Commission shall serve without any additional compensation for their work on the Commission, but shall be allowed travel expenses, including per diem in lieu of subsistence, to the extent permitted by law for persons serving intermittently in the Government service (5 U.S.C. 5701–5707).

(d) Nothing in this order shall be construed to impair or otherwise affect:

>   (1) authority granted by law to a department, agency, or the head thereof; or
>   (2) functions of the Director of the Office of Management and Budget relating to budgetary, administrative, or legislative proposals.

(e) This order is not intended to, and does not, create any right or benefit, substantive or procedural, enforceable at law or in equity by any party against the United States, its departments, agencies, or entities, its officers, employees, or agents, or any other person.

THE WHITE HOUSE,
May 21, 2010.
[FR Doc. 2010–12805
Filed 5–25–10; 8:45 am]
Billing code 3195–W0–P

Case 12-2

Many organizations must turn to a public relations agency for additional support when the scope of a crisis exceeds the capabilities of the in-house communication office. Sound strategic crisis communication planning will set in motion the policies to activate outside support when needed.

Crystallizing a Response to a Crisis
Imperial Sugar with Edelman

SITUATION ANALYSIS

On February 7, 2008, nine days after CEO John Sheptor assumed the top position at Imperial Sugar, a massive explosion occurred killing 14 people and injuring 32. Sheptor was conducting his first meeting with employees at the time and watched as first responders and media arrived on the scene to chronicle the company's response, which he knew would have broad implications. The board would have to determine if they would rebuild; investors would have to hold or devalue Imperial's stock; regulators and legislators would react to public sentiments; and employees would take measure of his leadership. Lacking a corporate communication team, Imperial turned to Edelman.

While over 300 media inquiries were logged in three weeks, the public exposure was less important, ultimately, than how the narrative itself was told: Would Imperial be seen as the helpless victim of a disaster or as a company poised to rebuild? Sheptor's ultimate test would be how quickly he could marshal resources to get the company back on track while tending to the emotional needs of employees and the community.

RESEARCH

The Georgia Department of Labor released data making it clear the success of the company's response and recovery went beyond Imperial. For every job inside the plant, seven jobs within the community were dependent upon that employee. If Imperial Sugar failed to rebuild, the community of Port Wentworth would be crippled. The futures of Imperial and the community of Port Wentworth were inextricably tied.

In addition, Edelman's 2008 Trust Barometer found that "people like me" were the most trusted source of information—meaning community members' voices and responses to the tragedy would prove to be equally critical to the company's overall ability to recover.

[9]Courtesy Imperial Sugar and Edelman

On-the-ground primary research was conducted with 27 in-home visits, daily employee meetings, six hospital visits, 13 meetings with elected officials both in Savannah and Atlanta, and coordination with 37 investigative government agencies. These helped to identify immediate needs and community offerings. This quantitative and qualitative research became the basis for Imperial's public engagement program to recover and rebuild.

PLANNING AND EXECUTION

In an immediate crisis, planning and execution occur simultaneously, but are guided with insights from research, which in this case indicated a symbiotic relationship between company and community, a need to build trust through engagement and a need to heal emotional wounds through integrated communications. With no internal communications department at Imperial Sugar, Edelman had to assume communication management of a multi-million dollar corporation. In addition to the incredible emotional challenges posed by the crisis itself, the communication infrastructure at the rural, damaged plant meant sporadic cell phone coverage, no Internet access or working power. The disaster's scale posed very real challenges in a small community, such as limited venue space for the memorial service. The team had to meet tight deadlines for creation and dissemination of materials, and pay particular attention to legal and corporate review due to potential implications of all public statements.

Once engaged, Edelman created a protocol plan that outlined the approval and dissemination process for all written communications. The families of employees who were missing in the still burning plant (many of whom waited days before learning the status of their loved ones) became a primary audience. Employees became a second-tier audience with media and other stakeholders a timely third. This tiered system for sharing information ensured that Imperial Sugar employees and their families were never surprised by news reports, kept rumors to a minimum, and established a working trust.

Edelman worked with Imperial to coordinate key messages and talking points with more than 37 different first responders and local, state, and federal agencies.

While no media relationships existed at the local level prior to the event, regular phone calls, daily briefings, in-depth one-on-one conversations and responsiveness helped build and nurture now long-term positive media relationships. Edelman also helped Imperial handle high-level media inquiries from outlets such as 60 Minutes, the *Los Angeles Times*, Bloomberg, and the *Wall Street Journal*. "A Community Remembers" memorial service was created, managed and conducted to help the Imperial employee family and Port Wentworth community experience closure, which also allowed individual families the dignity of privacy so they could grieve without distraction from the media at visitations and funerals.

EVALUATION

Edelman corrected more than 50 media and wire reports with accurate information within hours of being engaged. Twice-daily press conferences and turn-on-dime responsiveness built a foundation of trust between Imperial and the public and created opportunities to showcase the community's involvement in more than 91.2 million media impressions in six weeks, which captured a company clearly embraced by the community, with headlines like: "Definition of Community" and "They Were Our Friends." The facts behind the headlines were impressive:

- Financial relief efforts totaled more than $1.4 million in a partnership with United Way.

- The Georgia Red Cross collected a record amount of blood, 2,700 units, in just a month's time in Savannah, Augusta, and Port Wentworth.

- Big and small contributions were featured and showcased in local media, including a retiree organizing a "Sugar Ball" relief benefit, a local dressmaker donating dresses to daughters of victims, a local restaurant sponsoring an employee barbeque to improve morale, and a quilting bee campaign, which provided 30 specialized blankets for burn victims.

Positive coverage, including a headline heralding, "Imperial Sugar Rising" only months after the explosion, highlighted the company maintaining full-employment, sponsoring an employee training program and groundbreakings for the new facility. These sentiments were replicated in East Coast investment papers like the *Wall Street Journal* to West Coast human interest stories in the *Los Angeles Times*.

The standard of success in crisis response is how quickly an entity can get back to business. After the public engagement program was executed:

- Imperial's board approved a motion to rebuild.

- The plant restarted production nine months after the explosion, with full employment.

- CEO Sheptor was offered a coveted speaking slot to share best practices at the International Sweetener Colloquium.

- Imperial Sugar's stock stabilized, which while initially paralyzed after the explosion, grew by 38 percent in the months of October and November, while the rest of the market tumbled into a recession—outperforming both the S&P and NASDAQ.

Public relations and public engagement helped Imperial Sugar not only exceed stated communication objectives, but set a course for the company to emerge and reclaim its market status.

Case 12-3

When planning for potential crisis, workplace violence is usually on the list of potential concerns that could have a high impact on an organization. Whether at a school or at a commercial establishment, an episode of violence affects many layers of communities ranging from a large corporation's image to local neighbors. Interviews with the participants provide additional details of a 1997 event that still resonates with many organizations as they prepare to handle a similar crisis.

Trouble Brewing

Richard Stack
Associate Professor, School of Communication
American University

On July 7, 1997, a brutal crime in Washington, D.C.'s upscale Georgetown district shocked the city and stunned a neighborhood unaccustomed to violence. On the evening of July 6, three employees at a Starbucks coffee shop were killed in a botched burglary attempt in the Burleith neighborhood, just north of Georgetown. The triple murder occurred shortly after the store closed at the end of the long Fourth of July weekend. The victims, ages 25, 25, and 18, were found in the coffee shop's back room early the next morning by a shift supervisor.

At the time, public relations firm Brotman, Winter, Fried served as the DC-area representative for Starbucks and BWF executive vice president Kenny Fried was the account executive. After the crime, Fried contacted Dean Torrenga, who was Starbucks' mid-Atlantic regional director. Torrenga was then immediately in touch with Starbucks chairman and chief executive Howard Schultz, who flew from New York City to Washington and spent ten days in the area. Four Starbucks representatives from the company's Seattle headquarters also traveled to Washington the day after the crime since this was the first time something like this happened to the chain. At the time, there were 62 stores in the Washington area, including ten in the city. The Upper Georgetown location opened in 1994.

The following response to the crisis can be viewed in terms of concentric circles, with the first circle dealing with the most immediate connections to the tragedy.

CIRCLE 1: FAMILIES

Schultz personally contacted the family members of the slain employees and offered to take care of anything with which they needed help, including assistance with family matters, such as funeral costs and food. During this time, the Starbucks human resources department worked closely with Dean Torrenga, who also told the families that Starbucks wanted to help in any way possible, in terms of funeral arrangements or anything else the families needed. Madeline Mulcahy, a Washington D.C. district manager at Starbucks, also had day-to-day contact with the family members and was in communication with them for several years after the murder. Also, Schultz attended all three funeral services in Baltimore, Olney, Md., and southern New Jersey. After the Olney, Md., funeral, Schultz went back to the family house to spend time with the victim's loved ones. After the Baltimore funeral, family members addressed the media to discuss how upset they were about the tragedy. The media also covered the New Jersey funeral.

CIRCLE 2: STARBUCKS EMPLOYEES

Schultz immediately met with the surviving employees of the victimized store and assured them that they would remain on payroll. He informed store employees that they could take off whatever time they needed, with pay, and offered counseling that Starbucks arranged. Employees also could transfer to a nearby store if they still wanted to work at the company, since the Georgetown-area location remained closed for seven months. Through internal communications, the company informed Starbucks employees across the country about the incident and kept them updated on the investigation, which extended the idea of "family" to all Starbucks employees. Each employee had a voicemail account and Schultz left messages that everyone in the company received to inform them what the company was doing to help the families and employees. Immediate attention was given to tightening closing protocols at all stores. Security systems also were upgraded.

CIRCLE 3: COMMUNITY OF UPPER GEORGETOWN

Not only did the murder take place in a community unaccustomed to crime, but it also occurred in a high-end retail outlet, which stunned the community and the popular coffee franchise. Schultz wanted to do everything possible to help the families, and that meant cooperating with police. Starbucks offered a $50,000 reward for information that lead to finding the suspect and later added another $50,000. Starbucks organized a nondenominational memorial service at the Georgetown University campus chapel to honor the lives of the deceased employees and bring together the DC-area Starbucks employees. The university gladly offered its facilities for the service. The event was held after the three funerals and drew about 1,000 people. For the Georgetown University service, Dean and Deluca, a café in Georgetown, contacted Starbucks and wanted to help. The company donated food and coffee for the event and its employees served refreshments afterward. Barbara Wallen, gifts manager at the Georgetown Dean and Deluca, said the company strives to give back to the community as part of its mission. "We like to stay involved and connect with our customers," Wallen said. PR firm, Brotman, Winter, Fried assisted Starbucks with event logistics to bring in caterers, florists, and other participants. The firm also contacted a local musician who played piano during the service. Most of these gestures were volunteered freely by individuals and small businesses in the community.

CIRCLE 4: SITE OF THE CRIME

Starbucks remodeled the store, which opened seven months after the crime, to give it a new look and feel. As part of that process, Schultz solicited ideas for an appropriate memorial to honor the three slain employees. He selected an employee in Seattle to create a memorial, which added an artistic and spiritual element to the response. The rectangular sculpture bears the names of the three victims at the base, with three Maplewood panels connected by intertwined blades of grass made of cast aluminum, which symbolizes the playground of youth. Each panel also has white holly to serve as clouds, the symbol of childhood dreams. The final part of the memorial includes small steel boxes with mementos of the victims. Prior to the reopening of the coffee shop, the three victims' family members were invited to the store for a brief ceremony, along with Schultz, who spent time with the families and provided each family member with a key to the boxes if they wanted to fill them with items to memorialize their loved ones. To this day, a local florist in Georgetown brings fresh flowers to adorn the memorial each week.

CIRCLE 5: COMMUNITY OF WASHINGTON D.C.

As part of its response to the crisis, Starbucks decided to donate all future profits from that store to local charities that assist with victims' rights and crime prevention. The company worked with the Community Foundation, which runs charities for organizations. The Community Foundation then managed the foundation and every year, Starbucks provides the foundation with all profits from the store. Brotman, Winter, Fried executive vice president Kenny Fried describes Starbucks' response to the crisis as one that wasn't technical or fancy but instead guided by common decency:

> What happened in that situation was that you had a company that cared and a culture that cared. As a public relations firm, we weren't advising them, really, because Howard [Schultz] reminded everyone involved that Starbucks wanted to help in any way it could and he was always trying to do the right thing. Two years after the crime, Howard wrote a book called *Pour Your Heart Into It* and he dedicated the book to the victims because he was really torn by what happened. Essentially, there wasn't a fancy plan to respond and we weren't trying to get the public behind anything. It was really about the people of Starbucks trying to take a horrible situation and do whatever they could to help—and by doing that, the public reacted in a positive way. It was a lot of common sense.

As far as the relationship with news outlets, BWF helped to manage the media that descended on the Georgetown community and spoke with journalists regularly to give them updates. Because such a crime was unprecedented for Starbucks, as well as highly unusual for the Georgetown community, the story generated hundreds of news reports within a few days. BWF suggested Starbucks should communicate with the media and inform them that the company was in constant contact with the authorities and the families. When the media called to talk to Howard Schultz, he felt that his priority at the time was to focus on the family members and on law enforcement officials and that is where he put his efforts. Schultz finally spoke to the media directly after the Georgetown memorial service. He expressed that he and Starbucks were sending condolences to family members. He explained how the company decided to reopen the store eventually with all of the profits donated to anti-violence and victims rights charities.

Case 12-4

Labor disputes involve mobilizing support from various constituencies while also managing the political jockeying that is inevitable as each constituent group fights to make their plight heard. Exhibit 12-4A is an advertisement placed in a trade publication and Exhibit 12-4B shows some of the visual messaging used during the campaign.

PENCILS DOWN: Making East Coast Writers Voices Heard During the 100-Day Writers Guild Strike

Goldman Communications Group and Writers Guild of America East

SUMMARY

In late 2007, 2,500+ NY-based TV and film writers, members of the Writers Guild of America, East, went on strike for a new contract that compensated them for work being distributed in new media. A comprehensive communications campaign, using new media, non-traditional communications, member outreach, supported by publicity in traditional media, was waged to win public support, pressure media conglomerates to negotiate fairly, build and maintain member solidarity, and, ultimately, win writers a contract that would ensure their future economic survival. The campaign was successful. Writers' voices were heard on the streets, in the media, and at the bargaining table, resulting in a ground-breaking contract that covered new media.

SITUATION ANALYSIS

The Writers Guild of America, East (WGAE) is a labor union representing TV, film, radio, news, and new media writers east of the Mississippi. It has 4,000 members, mostly NY-based, 2,500 of whom write TV or feature films. The Guild struggled to be recognized in the media and industry because TV and film is considered Hollywood-based, even though much originates in NY. TV and film writers

---

[10]Courtesy Goldman Communications Group and Writers Guild of America East

work under the Minimum Basic Agreement (MBA), a contract between the WGA and the Alliance for Motion Picture and Television Producers (AMPTP), made up of 300+ companies with 7 majors, i.e., ABC Disney and Viacom. While there have been strikes in the past, mostly over benefits, 2007 was different. New media was the key issue facing writers and the industry. Shows and movies are no longer confined to TV and film screens; they are streamed online, sold on iTunes, and more. The MBA due to expire October 31st didn't provide compensation for new media, which they knew was the future. It was imperative to get MBA coverage for new media to secure economic survival. In spring 2007, while preparing for MBA negotiations, the Writers Guild also began preparing for a strike, should all other options fail. The WGAE turned to Goldman Communications Group, already on retainer, for communications counsel and implementation leading up to and during the 100-day strike (Nov. 5, 2007–Feb. 13, 2008) which shut down the industry.

RESEARCH

The Guild and Goldman Communications Group analyzed the past bargaining history of the AMPTP, business models and information on the AMPTP companies, and media platforms, finding these key insights:

- Negotiations on new media were always contentious. The AMPTP never agreed to reasonable compensation in the first contract. For example, in the MBA after the invention of VHS tapes, the AMPTP argued it was "new technology without a viable revenue stream," and asked the WGA to defer reasonable compensation until the next contract. The WGA did, but the AMPTP refused to renegotiate that rate in future contracts. The same scenario repeated for DVDs.

- In past strikes, member solidarity was weak partially because Guild messaging did not convey the necessity of a strike to win concessions necessary to all writers. When members crossed picket lines to return to work, the Guild lost leverage at the bargaining table, thus making it difficult to achieve gains in the MBA, and empowering the AMPTP.

- Business information on company Web sites and in annual reports uncovered AMPTP company CEOs routinely touting new media and their own online sites as lucrative revenue streams. (They said the exact opposite to the Guild.)

- They looked at key media that would be integral to any communications outreach plan. They found much of this media relied on AMPTP companies for advertising and/or were owned by AMPTP conglomerates.

- Trade media searches found an industry belief that there would be a joint union action—that writers would not strike until the Screen Actors Guild June 2008 contract expiration. Conversations with members, agents, and reporters showed companies were stockpiling six months of content for this scenario— 150 instead of the normal 50 films were in production, TV shows canceled breaks to shoot continually, and new series were being shot without pilots.

PLANNING

Based upon the research, tactical and communications plans were made, including:

- Writers' best leverage was on their own timetable—October 31, 2007. Waiting longer would let companies stockpile content so there would be no urgency to negotiate. Plans were set to get support of other unions for this strike timing strategy.

- New media would be the primary issue in negotiations and communications. While other issues were "on the table," the new MBA had to include new media compensation. This key message was created: "If You Get Paid, We Get Paid," which was simple, could be understood easily by all audiences, and was catchy for t-shirts, picket signs, and media use.

- Member solidarity was key. Communications had to inform members that their personal, as well as industry survival, depended upon their solidarity and commitment to a strike. All members had to be reached and engaged regularly.

- They would use the companies' own information on new media revenues, which they touted on Wall Street and online, to publicize that new media was viable, and writers deserved a piece of the pie.

- Media strategies would include traditional media, but not rely on it because of the uncertainty of its bias due to its reliance on AMPTP companies for ads and/or ownership. New media, member outreach, non-traditional communications would spread our message. Public support would be leveraged to keep writers engaged and pressure the AMPTP to negotiate.

- They identified our target audiences for communications: members, industry opinion makers (members and leaders of other unions, agents, industry employees, etc.), media, and key stakeholders that would be impacted (i.e., legislators from districts that would lose jobs if production ceased, and Wall Street, which would see stock prices affected).

The **objectives** were to:

- Ensure members understood and believed in a strike's importance and maintained high solidarity to win a good contract
- Position writers as today's typical workforce—like everyone, employees deserving to share in the fruits of their labor—and use this positioning to generate favorable (more than 50 percent) public support for writers
- Create pressure in as many places (a.k.a. target audiences) as possible to pressure companies to negotiate a fair deal.

Key **strategies** were to:

- Leverage the talents and creative abilities of the membership to tell the story to each other and the public
- Leverage industry support to put press on the companies to negotiate.

EXECUTION

A multi-pronged communications strategy was employed leading up to and during the strike.

For **members:**

- Grassroots communications such as in-home meetings (zip code parties) and phone chains provided one-on-one outreach to ensure solidarity and thwart off issues immediately, as well as provide daily communication updates.

- Email blasts and text messages to membership (news, presidential letters) and Web site home page posts about daily pickets ensured everyone was kept up to date and encouraged to stick together.

Other **tactics** included:

- To get the message out that 2,500 NY/WGAE writers were on strike, many picket signs were not the pre-produced "On Strike" signs, but poster boards of the WGAE logo with hand-written messages that writers created onsite. This ensured WGAE branding appeared daily in newspapers and on newscasts, as well as on the streets of New York City.

- Leveraging the talents of comedy/variety writers/members, who wrote pieces about the strike and its core issues that aired on shows such as Saturday Night Live, David Letterman, and The Daily Show leading up to the strike.

- During the strike, these writers were encouraged to set up their own Web sites and also create viral videos for posting on YouTube and Guild Web sites, thereby taking the message directly to the public, bypassing mainstream media.

- Information flow included: publishing advance picket plans/venues; sending Blackberry messages from onsite to media about celebrities/writers at pickets to generate midday updates; daily day-end recaps with photos e-blasted to 300 media around the world, and weekly updates from the WGAE president.

- Special fact sheets on the WGAE and issues pertaining to the contract distributed to media at the pickets.

- Leaflets with key facts and calls to action for the public to pressure AMPTP CEOs were distributed to passersby at every picket.

- Involving the creative and labor communities and showcasing their members (i.e., actors, airline pilots, laborers) at pickets—supporting our objective of writers are like all employees in the workforce.

- Media strategy of total accessibility and transparency. Writers were determined to be the best spokespeople, so all writers were available for interviews. Daily onsite media training and talking points got writers up-to-speed on negotiations. Non-NY reporters got interviews by passing cell phones among writers at pickets. No interview was turned down.

- Taking every opportunity to correct misinformation. Letters to the editor and op-ed pieces were used to correct information or balance negative articles. Comments were also posted on blogs to help spread information.

- Seizing opportunistic moments. When Ellen DeGeneres, who began taping her show after only one day of supporting her striking writers, said she was bringing her show to NY, they immediately issued an "open letter" to Ellen telling her to stay home—she was not wanted in NYC and would be picketed. This resulted in massive coverage, and Ellen canceled her production in NYC—a major coup for writers which enhanced their solidarity.

- Leveraging the "Ellen stance"—asking guests not to cross picket lines and support writers. This led to presidential candidates Hillary Clinton and John Edwards, Michelle Obama and others canceling appearances on The View and other talk shows, thus empowering writers, hurting the AMPTP, and generating tremendous good publicity for writers. Later, it also forced the Democrats to cancel a planned CBS-hosted presidential debate, thus further elevating the writers' position.

- Utilizing special events to generate news coverage continually, including: a Solidarity Day Rally with presidential candidate John Edwards, celebrities, and 1,000 members of NYC's labor community; a photo op timed to the Oscar nominations with Oscar, Emmy and other award winners saying they'd give up their awards for a new contract; and donating 40,000 pencils (raised in the fan-driven "Pencils to Moguls" effort) to the NYC school system, accepted by teachers union president Randi Weingarten. The WGAE also initiated an international day of solidarity, on which writers unions around the world held rallies in their homelands, generating enormous support and overseas press.

For other constituencies:

- They reached Wall Street by picketing and leafleting on Wall Street and having leadership participate in analyst calls. One result: Bear Stearns reported writers were asking little and the companies were losing more by locking them out of work. The report got extensive media play and impacted companies on Wall Street.

- To reach legislators, they lobbied Congressional leaders, met with DC think tanks, and held a mock debate in Congress with Daily Show and Colbert Report writers representing writers and the AMPTP, moderated by Dee Dee Meyers. The debate generated media coverage, buzz in Congress, and strong interest on the Internet.

EVALUATION

The strike and its communications were successful:

- The new MBA includes new media. Writers now receive a percentage of producers' gross of new media revenues.

- 93.6 percent of members voting ratified the contract: exceeding the 51 percent needed and demonstrating they believed in this MBA.

- Member solidarity was strong throughout the 100-day strike and continues. Only a few soap opera writers scabbed. Industry and media touted writers' solidarity as unexpected, amazing, and the reason they won new media in the MBA.

- Press clippings and impressions were not counted. But, media coverage was extensive, reaching international, national, local, print, broadcast, online, trade, blogs, fan clubs, and more. Most recognized NY-based writers, the NY industry, and the WGAE, and said the Writers Guild had "won the PR war" due to the non-traditional tactics used during the strike.

- Public support exceeded expectations. Polls showed writers had a 60+ percent favorable public opinion at all times during the strike—amazing since the strike caused fans' TV shows to disappear and critical to the strike's success and solidarity.

- Organizations lauded the Guild for its communications, i.e., the Sidney Hillman Foundation awarded the Guild for its strike communications; The Center for Communications ran a panel on the strike's successful communications.

EXHIBIT 12-4A   Advertisement

Pencils Down Means
Pencils Down.

"You guys will still break stories, right?" "Your people can still write scripts. I mean, who would know?"

We would.

We would know that doing so undermines the very cause for which we're fighting. We would know that it sends the wrong message to those who honor our picket lines.

We would know that it only serves to prolong a strike.

So, just to be absolutely clear: In the event of a strike, we, the following showrunners, will do no writing and no story breaking — nor will any be asked of our writing staffs — until we get a deal.

Robert Carlock
Tina Fey
(30 Rock)

Warren Bell
(According to Jim)

Tim Doyle
(Aliens in America)

Rich Appel
Mike Barker
Matt Weitzman
(American Dad)

Dee Johnson
(Army Wives)

Steven Levitan
Christopher Lloyd
(Back To You)

Ronald D. Moore
(Battlestar Galactica)

Jason Cahill
(Bionic Woman)

Hart Hanson
Stephen Nathan
(Bones)

Mark Olsen
Will Scheffer
(Big Love)

Greg Berlanti
(Brothers & Sisters, Eli Stone, Dirty Sexy Money)

Matt Nix
(Burn Notice)

Walon Green
(Canterbury's Law)

Marsh McCall
(Carpoolers)

Bill Martin
Mike Schiff
(Cavemen)

James Duff
(The Closer)

Meredith Stiehm
Veena Sud
(Cold Case)

Dennis Rinsler
Marc Warren
(Cory in the House)

Carol Mendelsohn
Naren Shankar
(CSI: Crime Scene Investigation)

Pamela Veasey
(CSI: New York)

Marc Cherry
(Desperate Housewives)

Daniel Cerone
(Dexter)

Matthew Carnahan
Joel Fields
(Dirt)

Josh Reims
Craig Wright
(Dirty Sexy Money)

Marc Guggenheim
(Eli Stone)

John Wells
(ER)

Charlie Craig
Jaime Paglia
Thania St. John
(Eureka)

Ali Leroi
(Everybody Hates Chris)

David A. Goodman
Seth MacFarlane
Chris Sheridan
(Family Guy)

John F. Bowman
(Frank TV)

Jason Katims
(Friday Night Lights)

Anne Kenney
(Greek)

Krista Vernoff
(Grey's Anatomy)

Shonda Rhimes
(Grey's Anatomy, Private Practice)

Steven Peterman
(Hannah Montana)

Tim Kring
(Heroes)

David Shore
(House)

Carter Bays
Craig Thomas
(How I Met Your Mother)

Rob Moelhenney
(It's Always Sunny in Philadelphia)

Carol Barbee
(Jericho)

John Altschuler
Dave Krinsky
(King of the Hill)

Jonathan Lisco
Craig Silverstein
(K-Ville)

Eric Tuchman
(Kyle XY)

Rene Balcer
(Law & Order)

Warren Leight
(Law & Order: Criminal Intent)

Neal Baer
(Law & Order: SVU)

Kathleen Moghee-Anderson
(Lincoln Heights)

Carlton Cuse
Damon Lindelof
(LOST)

Matt Weiner
(Mad Men)

Mark Hudis
(Miss/Guided)

Andy Breckman
(Monk)

Tom Fontana
*(M.O.N.Y.,
The Philanthropist)*

Chip Johanneson
(Moonlight)

Betsy Thomas
(My Boys)

Bobby Bowman
Gregory Garcia
(My Name is Earl)

Kari Lizer
(The New Adventures of Old Christine)

David Manson
(New Amsterdam)

Stacy Traub
(Notes from the Underbelly)

Greg Daniels
(The Office)

Eric Kaplan
(Out of Jimmy's Head)

Marti Noxon
(Private Practice)

Tara Butters
Michele Fazekas
Tom Spezialy
(Reaper)

Dmitry Lipkin
Dawn Prestwich
Nicole Yorkin
(The Riches)

Tom Hertz
(Rules of Engagement)

Donald Todd
(Samantha Who?)

Dan Sterling
(The Sarah Silverman Program)

Ian Biederman
Ed Redlich
(Shark)

Shawn Ryan
(The Shield, The Unit, The Oaks)

James L. Brooks
Matt Groening
Al Jean
(The Simpsons)

Al Gough
Miles Millar
(Smallville)

Josh Friedman
Toni Graphia
John Wirth
(Terminator: The Sarah Conner Chronicles)

Josh Goldsmith
Tim Hobert
Cathy Yuspa
('Til Death)

Joe Medeiros
(The Tonight Show with Jay Leno)

Alan Ball
(True Blood)

Silvio Horta
Marco Pennette
(Ugly Betty)

Peter Murietta
(Wizards of Waverly Place)

R. Scott Gemmill
(Women's Murder Club)

In Solidarity

Steven Bochco
Jim Leonard
Phil Rosenthal
Robin Schiff

You have our word.

Courtesy Goldman Communications Group and Writers Guild of America East

---

E X H I B I T 12-4B Visual Messaging

Pencils Down Means Pencils Down.

"You guys will still break stories, right?"
"Your people can still write scripts, I mean, who would know?"
We would.
We would know that doing so undermines the very cause for which we're fighting. We would know that it sends the wrong message to those who honor our picket lines.

We would know that it only serves to prolong a Strike.
So. just to be absolutely clear: In the event of a strike, we, the following showrunners, will do no writing and no story breaking—nor will any be asked of our writing staffs—until we get a deal.

Writers Guild of America East picket at VIACOM in a hailstorm.

WGAE picket line.

Courtesy Goldman Communications Group and Writers Guild of America East

PART IV

Integrated Marketing Communications

Chapter 13   Integrated Marketing Communications

13

Integrated Marketing Communications

P ublic relations has long been used as a tool for marketing products and services to consumers, but in the past, public relations was segregated or
departmentalized as a function separate from product advertising. Public relations
advertising was strictly defined as advertising used to accomplish public relations
objectives, such as image enhancement, not the sale of products or services.

Since the 1990s, integrated marketing communications (IMC) has become increasingly more popular in promoting the products and services of corporate America,
government social marketing campaigns and nonprofits. IMC simply combines the
operations of traditional public relations with traditional marketing and advertising.
One pioneering definition of IMC is the following:

What is integrated marketing communications? It's a new way of looking at the
whole, where once we only saw parts such as advertising, public relations, sales promotion, purchasing, employee communications, and so forth. It's realigning communications to look at it the way the customer sees it—as a flow of information
from indistinguishable sources. Professional communicators have always been con-
descendingly amused that consumers called everything "advertising" or "PR." Now
they recognize with concern if not chagrin that that's exactly the point—it is all one
thing, at least to the consumer who sees or hears it.[1]

Like the major forms of public relations discussed in this book, IMC can be
clearly understood using the ROPE process.

RESEARCH

Research for IMC may include investigation of the client, the reason for the program, and the publics or "stakeholders" to be targeted.[2]

Client Research

The usual background information needed for other forms of public relations is also necessary in the research phase of IMC: detailed analysis of the client's product or service, its personnel, financial status, and general reputation in its field. A frequently used tool in marketing is the SWOT analysis. SWOT stands for strengths, weaknesses, opportunities, and threats. To begin, the strengths and weaknesses of the client's products or services in the marketplace versus those of the competition should be honestly appraised. With this analysis in hand, the practitioner should assess opportunities or ways by which the client might best increase the market share of its products or services in competitive situations. Finally, an assessment of external threats, or factors that might work against the client, should be made.[3]

Opportunity or Problem Research

The most obvious reason for any marketing program is to sell the client's merchandise, programs, or services. The traditional product-oriented marketing model focuses on the four Ps: product, price, place, and promotion. This process begins with the underlying assumption that a company decides what product to manufacture; then prices it; distributes it in particular places, locations, or outlets; and finally promotes the product in an essentially one-way mode of communication, usually mass media product advertising.[4]

IMC, on the other hand, begins with the assumption that the needs of the consumers and other stakeholders should come first. This, in turn, calls for an audience-centered, transactional model. Instead of simply selling products, IMC attempts to create *relationships* with consumers and other stakeholders. In addition to striving to get consumers to purchase products, IMC strives to get support and loyalty from consumers and other stakeholders. Often called brand loyalty, these enduring relationships are built on good two-way communication and an understanding of underlying values, needs, and motivations, or known by PR practitioners as audience research.

Audience Research

IMC audience research, or stakeholder research, consists of using both nonquantitative and quantitative research methods to learn as much as possible about the groups to be targeted for communication. These stakeholder groups include:

Customers

New customers

Old customers

Potential customers

Employees

    Management

    Nonmanagement

    Sales and marketing staff

    Customer relations departments

    Human resources staff

    Individuals staffing phone call centers

Media

    Mass (broadcast, print, and online)

    Specialized (broadcast, print, and online)

Investors

    Shareowners and potential shareowners

    Financial analysts

    Financial press

Suppliers/vendors

Competitors

Government regulators

Attitudes, behaviors, media habits, psychographic (value-oriented segmentation), and other demographic data about stakeholders are important research information in IMC.

OBJECTIVES

IMC may use both impact and output objectives.

Impact Objectives

Impact objectives may affect stakeholders by informing them or by modifying their attitudes or behaviors. Examples might include the following:

1. To increase (by 20 percent) the stakeholder's knowledge and awareness of the organization's new service (during the next six months)
2. To enhance (by 15 percent) positive attitude formation toward the company's product (during the current year)
3. To increase consumer purchases of the client's product (by 20 percent) during the current year.

Output Objectives

Output objectives for IMC consist of measurable efforts for the client's program:

1. To increase advertising in major metropolitan newspapers by 10 percent during the sale period

2. To place product information on three social media sites during the next three months

3. To schedule five special events for the client's sales campaign during August.

PROGRAMMING

As with the various forms of public relations, IMC may begin with planning the theme and messages. The uniqueness of IMC programming is that it combines the activities of traditional advertising with traditional public relations.

Theme and Messages (consistent, single voice)

Advertising

Print

Broadcast

Radio

TV

Online

Search browsers

Social media sites

Specialty publications

Direct mail

Telemarketing

Point-of-purchase

Specialty advertising

more marketing

Public Relations

Uncontrolled

Print

Broadcast (networks/local/online)

Online social media engagement

Controlled

Print

Audiovisual/video

Interpersonal

Online (websites, to include social media sites, search engine optimization, email, webinars, mobile smart phone application, and blogs)

Action or special events

IMC programming involves a strategic approach. Each public relation component should complement and reinforce marketing efforts. Also, public relations may be more effective with some audiences while direct marketing may work better with other groups. Yet together advertising and public relations form a seamless whole to accomplish essentially marketing goals.

Effective Communication

Since IMC seeks to establish interactive communication between client and stakeholders, the same principles of effective communication apply to it as to public relations. Of special interest to marketing communicators using IMC are the principles of source credibility, two-way communication, and audience participation. IMC is concerned with long-range consumer loyalty, not just the quick, one-shot sale of merchandise. The client's reputation thus becomes a matter of paramount concern. Customer involvement with the client or company is another major hallmark of IMC. Well-established interactive public relations techniques are a decisive advantage in such communication transactions.

EVALUATION

The success of IMC programs should be determined by tracking stated objectives. Impact and output objectives can be measured using the standard tools of public relations programs, as outlined in Chapter 2. The growth of sales or in adoption of new behaviors are also good measures.

SUMMARY

IMC involves a combination of traditional advertising and public relations practices. The ROPE process is a convenient model for this relatively new field, which brings together separated categories of advertising and public relations into a unified communications campaign.

ENDNOTES

1. Don E. Schultz, Stanley I. Tannenbaum, and Robert F. Lauterborn, *Integrated Marketing Communications* (Chicago: NTC Business Books, 1993), p xvii.

2. Stakeholders is the preferred term for IMC audiences. See Thomas L Harris, *Value-Added Public Relations* (Chicago: NTC Business Books, 1998), p. 124, for a concise definition of stakeholders. Also see Tom Duncan and Sandra Monarty, *Driving Brand Value* (New York: McGraw-Hill, 1997), chap. 4, for a more complete discussion of this concept.

3. For discussions of SWOT, see Hams, *Value-Added Public Relations*, p. 235, and Duncan and Monarty, *Driving Brand Value*, pp. 149–152.

4. For a discussion of four-Ps theory, see Schultz, Tannenbaum, and Lauterborn, *Integrated Marketing Communications*, pp. 5 and 12.

READINGS ON INTEGRATED MARKETING
COMMUNICATIONS

Arens, William F., Michael F. Weigold, and Christian Arens. *Contemporary advertising and integrated marketing communications.* Boston: McGraw-Hill Irwin, 2011.

Baidya, Mehir and Bipasha Maity. "Effectiveness of Integrated Marketing Communication," *Journal of Indian Business Research* 2.1 (2010): 23–31.

Blakeman, Robyn. *Integrated Marketing Communication: Creative Strategy from Idea to Implementation.* Lanham, MD: Rowman & Littlefield Publishers, 2007.

Caemmerer, Barbara. "The planning and implementation of integrated marketing communications," *Marketing Intelligence & Planning* 27 (July 2009): 524–538.

Debreceny, Peter, and Lisa Cochrane. "Two Disciplines on the Same Road," *Advertising Age* 75 (November 8, 2004): 28.

Eagle, Lynne, and Philip J. Kitchen. "IMC Brand Communications and Corporate Cultures: Client/Advertising Agency Co-Ordination and Cohesion," *European Journal of Marketing* 34 (May-June 2000): 667ff.

Edmondson, Jan. "Come Together Why Integrated Marketing Works," *Public Relations Tactics* 7 (January 2000): 12.

Gabrielli, Veronica and Bernardo Balboni. "SME practice towards integrated marketing communications," *Marketing Intelligence & Planning* 28.3 (2010): 275–290.

Harris, Thomas L. *Value-Added Public Relations.* Chicago: NTC Business Books, 1998.

Henley, Teri Kline. "Integrated Marketing Communications for Local Nonprofit Organizations: Developing an Integrated Marketing Communications Strategy," *Journal of Nonprofit & Public Sector Marketing* 9 (2001): 141–155.

————. "Integrated Marketing Communications for Local Nonprofit Organizations: Communications Tools and Methods," *Journal of Nonprofit & Public Sector Marketing* 9 (2001): 157–168.

Heslop, Janet. *The American Marketplace: Demographics and Spending Pattern,* 9th ed. Ithaca, NY: New Strategist Publications, 2009.

"How PPv Gives Super Bowl Advertisers More Bang for Their Integrated Marketing Bucks," *PR News* 64 (March 2008).

Hutton, James G. "Defining the Relationship between Public Relations and Marketing: Public Relations' Most Important Challenge," in Heath, Robert L. ed., *Handbook of Public Relations.* Thousand Oaks, CA: Sage, 2004.

Hynes, Aedhmar. "How public relations elevates brand value," *Public Relations Strategist* 15.4 (Fall 2009): 22.

Jones, Susan K. *Creative Strategy in Direct Marketing,* 3d ed Lincolnwood, IL: NTC/Contemporary Publishing, 2005.

Page, Russell. "Michelin Americas Truck Tires with Jackson-Dawson Integrated Marketing Communications," *Public Relations Tactics* 10 (September 2003): 24.

Percy, Larry, *Strategic Integrated Marketing Communications.* Oxford: Butterworth-Hememann, 2008.

Pickton, David, and Amanda Brodenck. *Integrated Marketing Communications,* 2d ed. Englewood Cliffs, NJ: Prentice-Hall, 2005.

Reid, Mike, Sandra Luxton, and Felix Mavondo. "The Relationship Between Integrated Marketing Communication, Market Orientation and Brand Orientation," *Journal of Advertising* 34 (Winter 2005): 11–24.

Ries, Al, and Laura Ries. *The Fall of Advertising and the Rise of PR.* New York: Harper-Collins, 2002.

Schultz, Don E. "Outdated Approach to Planning Needs Revamping," *Marketing News* 36 (November 11, 2002): 6–7.

Sevier, Robert "Solutions for Marketing Strategies," *University Business* 8 (July 2005): 35–41.

Shimp, Terence A. *Advertising, Promotion, and Other Aspects of Integrated Marketing Communications,* 7th ed. Mason, OH: Thomson/South-Western, 2007.

Stevens, Joanna. "Yahoo' PR Events Sing with the Yodel Challenge," *Communication World* 22 (September–October 2005): 40–142.

Swam, William N. "Perceptions of IMC After a Decade of Development: Who's at the Wheel, and How Can We Measure *Success?" Journal of Advertising Research* 44 (March 2004): 46ff.

Taylor, Charles R. "Integrated Marketing Communications in 2010 and Beyond," *International Journal of Advertising* 29.2 (2010): 161–164.

Weiner, Mark, Liney Arnorsdottir, Rainer Lang, and Brian G. Smith. "Isolating the Effects of Media-Based Public Relations on Sales: Optimization through Marketing Mix Modeling." Institute for Public Relations (June 2010).

Werner, Mark. "Marketing PR Revolution," *Communication World* 22 (January–February 2005): 20–25.

"Whatever Happened to Integrated Marketing Communications?" *PR News* 63 (June 2007).

Integrated Marketing Communications Cases

Case 13-1

Generating excitement for a campaign may include mixing a wide variety of community events, media promotions, social media, and marketing. Exhibit 13-1A is letter from the new Maestro, Exhibit 13-1B are promotions for two musical series and Exhibit 13-1C are from the annual report.

The Nashville Symphony Loves Nashville, Starring Our New Maestro

Nashville Symphony

SUMMARY

The Nashville Symphony faced the challenge of sustaining momentum and increasing single-concert ticket sales going into its third season in a new concert hall. Young and enthusiastic, its new energetic Maestro Giancarlo Guerrero was a rising star in the classical music world but still unknown in Nashville. The Symphony teamed up with KVBPR and Locomotion Creative to launch Guerrero as the "face" of the orchestra with a multi-channel communications campaign. The results: a 33 percent increase in classical single-ticket sales; and 12 percent increase in all-season ticket sales. And, Nashville loves its new Maestro.

SITUATION ANALYSIS

2008 marked the start of the Nashville Symphony's third year in the Schermerhorn Symphony Center, traditionally the point at which symphonies moving to new halls see a drop in ticket sales. The Nashville Symphony faced the challenge of sustaining momentum and increasing single-concert ticket sales going into the new season. Giancarlo Guerrero had recently been named the new music director for the Nashville Symphony. He would serve as music director designate in 2008-09, allowing him to fulfill his current contract in Eugene, Ore., and transition to full-time music director for the 2009–10 season.

Young and enthusiastic, Guerrero was a rising star in the classical music world. As the "face" of the orchestra, the Costa Rican-bred conductor gave the Symphony a new, young, and multicultural look. Prior to the 2008-09 season, Guerrero moved his family to Middle Tennessee and was ready to assume leadership of the Nashville Symphony, even though he was travelling to Eugene monthly. The Symphony marketing staff and outside public relations counsel used this opportunity to create a new "star" in Nashville and to launch a single-ticket sales campaign.

RESEARCH

The Symphony relies mostly on national audience research from the League of American Orchestras. However, they recognized they only had one chance to introduce Guerrero to the region. Primary research was conducted on past single-ticket buyers to determine demographic and media habits of the audience.

They found purchasers:

- Were singles, young couples and empty nesters;
- Preferred email and direct mail communications;
- Were likely to visit the website;
- Listened to public radio and watched public TV;
- Read the daily newspaper (print and online); and
- Watched television news.

PLANNING

A targeted, multi-channel communications campaign was planned to leverage Guerrero's persona to drive traffic to the website and sell tickets.

Program Goals

Based on research, goals were to:

- Reach new audiences
- Build awareness
- Sell single-concert tickets

Objectives

- To increase classical single-ticket sales by 26 percent for the 2008–09 season
- To maintain all-season ticket sales for the 2008–09 season

Target Audiences

Based on the research, the target audiences included:

- Past single-ticket buyers;
- Young professionals;

- General business community;
- Nashville's previously untapped, rapidly growing Hispanic community; and
- Adjacent Williamson County.

Strategy

Guerrero's predecessor and the symphony hall's namesake, the late Kenneth Schermerhorn, was an internationally known, traditional conductor who was embraced by classical music lovers throughout the city. Guerrero's style is very different and presented an opportunity to reach new audiences.

The campaign was created to maximize his enthusiasm and reinforce the message that the symphony is a welcoming place for all of Nashville. He embraced the strategy and added his own touches, including sharing his hobbies of dominos and billiards as opportunities for media outreach.

Budget Funding for the Guerrero "launch" came from a symphony patron, who donated $250,000.

EXECUTION

The Symphony marketing team met weekly with KVBPR, its outside PR counsel, to develop a comprehensive campaign in a matter of weeks. KVBPR handled media outreach related to Guerrero, and the internal team focused on concert-related coverage. KVBPR coordinated external speaking opportunities; the internal team conducted events with existing patrons and audiences.

Locomotion Creative worked with both teams to implement the advertising portion of the marketing outreach.

Activities

- Nashville's New Maestro was the theme, with the tagline "I Nashville."
- A TV ad campaign showcased tuxedo-wearing Guerrero "conducting" at local landmarks (traffic in a town square; the fountains at a popular local park; domino players at a Hispanic restaurant) and playing drums in the house band at a famous honky-tonk bar.
- Print ads, mobile billboards, direct mail, Web ads, and Nashville Public Radio and Public TV underwriting complemented the TV ads.
- A viral social media program promoted the creative.
- YouTube posting of spots.
- Links to YouTube from the Nashville Symphony home page.
- E-mail blasts.
- Facebook page and Twitter postings.
- Interactive element on website for fans to post welcome messages.

An aggressive media relations program that included:

- Traditional publicity and blogger outreach about making the commercials;
- Non-performance-related publicity about Guerrero (TV feature on his love of billiards);
- Business coverage about the marketing campaign; and
- Hispanic media outreach about Nashville's new Hispanic celebrity.

A community outreach initiative including:

- Speaking engagements at The Rotary Club of Nashville;
- Receptions and events including Symphony patrons reception ("Grits and Guerrero"), Brentwood Library Foundation event, Conexion Americas and Hispanic Chamber events; and

  A walk-on guest appearance at Shakespeare in the Park.

Challenges

- Guerrero was in the process of moving so his accessibility was sometimes limited.
- The TV spots were shot outdoors in July heat (and he wore a tux).
- A need to be sensitive to the memory of the late Maestro Schermerhorn.

EVALUATION

The campaign far exceeded its objectives of increasing single-ticket sales by 26 percent and maintaining the level of all-season ticket sales.

At this point in the 2008–09 Symphony season, results indicate:

- A 33 percent increase in classical single-ticket sales; and
  A 12 percent increase in season-ticket sales.

  The single ticket on-sale event day resulted in:

- A 59 percent increase in single-ticket sales;
- An 80 percent increase in the sales of specially discounted $15 tickets; and
- A 39 percent increase in season-ticket sales as compared to the 2007–08 kickoff day.

The integrated marketing efforts targeted several new audiences, resulting in:

- A 16 percent increase in new ticket buyers;
- A 25 percent increase in ticket revenue from Williamson County residents; and
- A 19 percent increase in revenue from downtown residents.

Other program successes include:

- In Feb. 2009, with five months left in the season, overall ticket sales totaled $6.8 million, compared to $6.1 million for the entire 2007–08 season.

- A 42 percent increase in ticket sales via the Web.
- A heightened awareness among target audiences, including an ad campaign with more than 7.5 million media impressions, a Facebook fan-base of nearly 1,200 people, and a 17.8 percent increase in unique website visitors.

EXHIBIT 13-1A   Letter from New Maestro

Courtesy Nashville Symphony

EXHIBIT 13-1B   Promotional Brochure

ADAMS AND REESE LLP

JAZZ SERIES

Thanks to the outstanding Adams and Reese Jazz Series, Schermerhorn Symphony Center has become one of the city's premier venues for live jazz music. In the past few years, we've welcomed some of the leading artists in the jazz world, first-class musicians whose appeal transcends generations and styles, and this season promises even more excitement. Whether you love the classic sounds of swing and bebop, or you groove to the offbeat spontaneity of jazz improvisation, the Adams and Reese Jazz Series will delight the senses.

October 9, 2009
AL JARREAU
Nashville Symphony
Matt Catingub, *conductor*

With his stunning, supple voice, Al Jarreau is the rare performer to earn GRAMMY® awards in jazz, R&B and pop. That versatility has kept his swinging style fresh throughout a phenomenally successful career that includes such irresistibly catchy songs as the radio hit "Mornin' " and the theme to the TV show *Moonlighting*.

January 29, 2010
BRANFORD MARSALIS
Concert presented without orchestra

Known for his innovative spirit and broad musical scope, saxophonist Branford Marsalis is part of jazz's most celebrated family. Having appeared as a guest artist with the Nashville Symphony three years ago, he returns this time around to deliver a concert of straight-ahead jazz inspired by the classic tradition of such heroes as Art Blakey and Sonny Rollins.

April 9, 2010
**GUEST ARTIST & PROGRAM
TO BE ANNOUNCED**

NO PRICE INCREASE!
BUY TODAY! Call 615.687.6400
page 24 for more info

*Refer to the flat-floor seating map on page 27.
Artists and repertoire subject to change.*

16 NASHVILLE SYMPHONY 2009/10 SEASON

2009/10 SEASON NASHVILLE SYMPHONY 17

Courtesy Nashville Symphony

EXHIBIT 13-1C   Annual Report

We ♥ Giancarlo Guerrero!

A full year ahead of his official start as the orchestra's seventh Music Director, Giancarlo Guerrero relocated to the Nashville area last summer with his wife, Shirley, and their daughters, Virginia and Claudia. His arrival marked the beginning of a new chapter in the Nashville Symphony's history, while Giancarlo himself represents a new breed of conductor — a serious, committed musician, but also accessible and able to connect with audiences of all ages and backgrounds.

To share our excitement with the community, we launched a series of memorable television advertisements introducing "Our New Maestro." In one spot, a tuxedo-clad Giancarlo could be seen "conducting" the fountains at the Bicentennial Mall, while in another the onetime percussionist could be seen playing drums in the house band at Tootsie's Orchid Lounge. In the months that followed, he was spotted all over town: on billboards and T-shirts, accompanied by the slogan "I ♥ Nashville"; performing a small role at Nashville Shakespeare Festival's annual Shakespeare in the Park; and, of course, on the stage of Laura Turner Concert Hall, where he led the Nashville Symphony with skill and panache.

With his arrival, Giancarlo also helped usher the Nashville Symphony into the digital age: We reached out to new audiences through the use of online social networking tools such as Facebook and Twitter, while Giancarlo himself took part in the Nashville Symphony's first-ever live webcast and answered questions submitted by visitors to our website.

Thanks to Giancarlo and to the musicians of the Nashville Symphony, 2008/09 was a spectacular season at the Schermerhorn — and the coming season promises to be even more thrilling!

Scenes from our award-winning ad campaign. At left: Giancarlo at Tootsie's Orchid Lounge Below, from left to right: on the town square in downtown Franklin, at La Hacienda Taqueria and at Bicentennial Mall State Park

Giancarlo visits with children at Bethlehem Centers of Nashville

A word with Giancarlo

What makes Nashville stand out from all of the other places you've lived?

This is a truly vibrant community; people obviously love living in Nashville, and they are always happy to show hospitality to their new neighbors.

What's your favorite thing about living here?

There's so much to do during every time of the year; my family and I have enjoyed visiting the many parks around town, and we have quite a few favorite restaurants all over the city that we visit regularly.

You've spent a lot of time traveling over the past year. Are there particular things you'd like to do in Nashville once you have more time to enjoy the city?

I want to visit some of the historical sites around Nashville, and I really want to attend more sports and pop concert events. But with all my traveling, I have to say that what I look forward to the most is spending as much time as possible with my family and friends in our home.

What do you love about performing with the Nashville Symphony?

It is a great joy to stand in front of the musicians of the Nashville Symphony; they are not only immensely talented, but very professional and disciplined. It is a privilege to make music with them and be able to host some of the world's most famous guest artists. I also have to mention that we are blessed with an amazing administrative staff and dedicated board of directors.

From this past season, what was your favorite piece of music that you conducted?

Every concert for me was very special, but if I had to pick one, I would choose performances of Mahler's Sixth Symphony in January. This is a piece that I'd been wanting to conduct for quite some time, and because it is such a complex and difficult work, it was a great way to forge a stronger musical bond with the musicians of the Nashville Symphony.

> *Giancarlo has led the Nashville Symphony with skill and panache.*

—— 3 ——

Courtesy Nashville Symphony

Case 13-2

For a national association, a period of crisis around a product recall demands quick communication with association members and rapid actions to protect the interests of the association's product. Exhibit 13-2A is an open letter published in national papers, Exhibit 13-2B is a presentation to members on the campaign initiatives, and Exhibit 13-2C is an ad published to promote the use of peanut products.

National Peanut Board Responds to Recall of More Than 3,000 Products

National Peanut Board with GolinHarris and Lawler Ballard Van Durand 2009 Silver Anvil Award Winner

SUMMARY

The recall of more than 3,000 peanut products struck the peanut industry hard in January 2009. On behalf of America's 10,000 peanut farmers and their families, the National Peanut Board (NPB) responded quickly and efficiently to educate consumers and influencers and restore trust in USA-grown peanuts and peanut products—reversing a downward trend in volume sales and eventually increasing sales over the previous year.

SITUATION

Nine people had died. More than 900 were sickened. Because of recent recalls of beef, spinach and other products, the halls of Washington were abuzz. A full blown panic was brewing and people were throwing away all peanut-related products. Early news reports were largely inaccurate; many continued to be fueled by rumors keeping the story alive for weeks. Eventually, more than 3,000 products were pulled from stores across the nation. Some experts predicted a $1 billion industry loss.

Consumption of all things peanut was dealt a serious blow on Jan. 9, 2009, when the Minnesota Department of Health confirmed that salmonella found in institutional size containers of peanut butter matched the strain that eventually infected people in nearly every state. The product was produced by Peanut Corporation of America (PCA) at its plant in Blakely, Ga., where PCA also made ingredients like granulated peanuts and peanut paste, which it sold to other manufacturers. While PCA produced less than one percent of all peanut butter in the U.S.—and didn't have a single label of its own on the shelf—it quickly became the source of the largest food recall in American history.

Jarred peanut butters sold in grocery and retail stores were not affected—and neither were 99 percent of peanut products. However, because of the daily onslaught of product recalls and non-stop and often inaccurate media reporting, a public panic ensued. Consumers began throwing out peanut butter, a much-loved pantry staple found in the pantries of 90 percent of U.S. homes according to independent consumer research. Grocery stores were discarding unaffected products and restaurants considered pulling anything with peanuts off their menus.

RESEARCH

Information Resources, Inc. (I.R.I.) retail sales scan data showed a 19.42 percent drop in volume sales for jars of peanut butter in January 2009 compared to January 2008. To "get underneath" the sales declines, NPB in mid-February launched the first wave of a proprietary consumer tracking study. The board wanted to know what was driving the sales declines so that we could develop a program that addressed consumer concerns. Second, NPB needed to gauge timing: would consumers already be receptive to messages about peanuts and peanut butter again? The research told NPB among other things:

- There was high awareness: 93 percent believed that peanuts/peanut butter were affected.
- There was a high degree of confusion/misperception: 50 percent believed jarred peanut butter was affected, when in fact no jars of peanut butter contained any PCA ingredients (PCA supplied peanuts/peanut butter as ingredients to companies that made finished products such as nutrition bars, etc.).
- 19 percent reported they stopped eating peanut butter.
- One-third of consumers conducted their own research; the Internet was the top source for information.

PLANNING

Because the crisis originated from a manufacturing facility and not a farm, protocol dictated that the industry's trade organization would take the lead in reacting to media and legislative affairs. At the same time, as the organization representing America's 10,000 peanut farmers, NPB took on the role of driving a "Resumption of Consumption" program once the immediate crisis had passed.

NPB's goal was to reverse the slide in trust, confidence and sales of peanut butter and other peanut products. The board's single-minded objective for the program was to reach Americans directly and indirectly with accurate information about the safety of peanut products. NPB set the following measures for its efforts:

Outputs:

- Engage at least 40,000 consumers in New York directly (and subsequently another 100,000 in additional markets).
- Generate more than 50 million media impressions through the New York events.

Outcomes:

- Drive a reduction in the number of consumers who said they had stopped purchasing, serving and consuming peanut butter.
- Reverse the slide in peanut butter sales.

IMPLEMENTATION
(LABELED EXECUTION IN PROOF)

Beginning in January 2009 and continuing throughout the year, NPB, with agencies GolinHarris and Lawler Ballard Van Durand, aggressively engaged and educated Americans through direct communications, events and traditional and non-traditional media. At the heart of the program, NPB positioned the industry's most credible and authentic spokespeople—peanut farmers and their families—and developed clear, concise messages that focused on the vast majority of products that were never affected.

Key messages were: 1) Major and national store brands of jarred peanut butter are not affected by the recall. 2) America's peanut farmers care and condemn the actions of this single bad-actor manufacturer that caused the outbreak. 3) Visit nationalpeanutboard.org for the latest information, including details on which products were (or were not) affected.

- **Aggressive Traditional and Social Media:** NPB reached out and responded to the media to share the farmers' perspective of the crisis, which generated extensive coverage in The Wall Street Journal, New York Times, CNN Radio, Atlanta Journal-Constitution, and hundreds of newspapers, TV and radio stations and websites from coast to coast reaching tens of millions. NPB moved forward with a new branding campaign, "Peanuts: Energy for the Good Life," through advertising in major consumer, trade and transit media. The board placed a letter from NPB's chairman in USA Today to reassure consumers and let them know farmers care. NPB built a new blog and leveraged social media channels to engage peanut "evangelists" and other influencers (food service executives, school systems, etc.). Employing respected pediatricians, nutritionists, food safety experts and others, the board also worked to ensure that influencers felt confident and safe in recommending peanut products to those with whom they came into contact.

- **"Resumption of Consumption" NYC Event and National Grower Tour:** NPB built a "live" peanut field (with more than 200 plants grown in an Oklahoma greenhouse) in New York's Grand Central Terminal and enlisted more than a dozen manufacturers to hand out free product samples that were unaffected by the recall. A media/blogger chef demonstration and tasting event reached 200+ influencers. NPB also conducted a satellite media tour with Iron Chef Michael Symon and a registered dietitian. The board announced a major donation to the Food Bank for New York City and leveraged that event to reach other food banks that feared distributing peanut butter – one of their most valued staples. Following the successful New York events that showed consumers truly embrace peanut farmers as credible sources of information and reassurance, NPB created a "Grower Tour" with additional stops in Atlanta, Washington, D.C., Minneapolis/St. Paul, Chicago, Nashville, Houston, and Santa Monica.

- **Foodservice Outreach:** With an ongoing foodservice communications and marketing strategy already in place, NPB worked to reach our decision-maker contacts with facts about the recall. The team sent daily email briefings to restaurant chain operators, retailers and manufacturers summarizing the background, facts, NPB's position and highlighted products not affected by the recall.

EVALUATION

- NPB directly reached 50,000 consumers through the Grand Central Terminal exhibit and another 200 million+ through print, broadcast and online media coverage surrounding the program. Subsequent grower city tours collectively reached more than 150,000 consumers.

- According to I.R.I., peanut butter volume sales in 2009 increased every month as compared to the same period in 2008 from the precipitous decline in January. (March, up 5.6 percent over 2008; April, 13.5 percent; May, 24.7 percent; June, 5.1 percent; July, 7.9 percent; August, 18.6 percent; September, 4.8 percent.)

- In the latest wave of the NPB Consumer Study (May 2009), those who said they have stopped eating peanut butter from a jar has dropped 6 points to 13 percent. The percentage of those who have resumed eating peanut butter has increased sharply by 43 points to 70 percent. In a January 2010 article about NPB's response program, PRWeek said, "[NPB's] efforts did more than just restore confidence, they moved the needle."

EXHIBIT 13-2A   Open Letter from Peanut Farmers

National Peanut Board

An Open Letter From America's Peanut Farmers

No one is more deeply disturbed by the recent salmonella crisis than the thousands of USA peanut farmers and their families. For generations, we've worked to deliver the freshest, most wholesome peanuts possible because we value the bond we've built up with you over the years.

Peanuts, peanut butter and peanut products, as much as any food, are part of the American experience, from the familiar PB&J in millions of school lunch boxes to the many innovative uses introduced each year. In fact, it wouldn't be a stretch to say that your confidence in peanuts and peanut butter has helped them become affordable, nutritious staples in the American pantry. But recent events beyond our control have shaken that confidence, and caused many to question the integrity of the peanuts we nurture and grow.

We are all deeply upset by the actions of one isolated company. We may be peanut farmers, but we also are fathers, mothers, sons and daughters—and consumers—just like you. So we understand and share your concerns.

This company's actions also have led to confusion about what is safe to eat. According to the US Food and Drug Administration, "major national brands of jarred peanut butter found in grocery stores have not been among the products recalled," and a vast array of other peanut butters and peanut products are also unaffected.

We want to help answer your questions. Please visit www.nationalpeanutboard.org where you'll find resources and important links to help get the information you need.

America's peanut farmers care. That's why we are in support of efforts to safeguard and protect the growing, manufacturing and distribution of our peanuts. We don't want anyone to ever worry about the safety of peanuts or any food product again.

We will be in New York City at Vanderbilt Hall in Grand Central Terminal on March 4 and 5—to meet and talk with you, answer questions and to share some of the tastes you've always loved. This is one of many events we have coming up throughout the country in the coming months.

We value your trust. We also know it's something we have to earn every day.

Sincerely,

Roger Neitsch

Courtesy National Peanut Board and GolinHarris

E X H I B I T 13-2B   Presentation on the Campaign

TARGETS: Consumers, Food Banks across the nation

Fighting hunger… and getting peanuts back on Food Bank shelves—through donations

America's peanut farmers and our manufacturer partners came together to fight hunger with a major donation to the Food Bank for New York City.

TARGET: Chefs, media, other influencers

Engaging chefs, foodies and writers with peanuts and world cuisines

We stepped up our social media

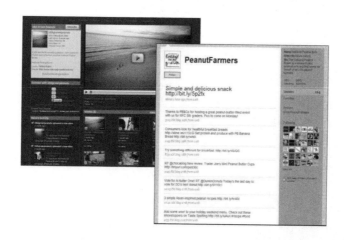

We fast tracked our new peanut blog

Courtesy National Peanut Board and GolinHarris

EXHIBIT 13-2C Campaign Ad

Energy to CARRY ON THE TRADITION. (Plus the THE COOLER AND ALL THAT STUFF.)

EnERgY for the good Life.

www.nationalpeanutboard.org

Courtesy National Peanut Board and GolinHarris

Case 13-3

Tapping into core emotional connections with other people provides a ready way to multiply the impact of a campaign. Birthdays involve so many emotions that a campaign around this theme generates automatic and universal engagement. Using both marketing and public relations strategies can give added clout to the campaign. Exhibit 13-3A is a news release for the campaign.

Creating A World with More Birthdays
American Cancer Society with Brodeur Partners

SUMMARY

The American Cancer Society and Brodeur Partners developed the More Birthdays movement to help deepen understanding of how the Society saves lives in communities nationwide and to unite people passionately committed to creating a world with less cancer and more birthdays. Through the movement, the Society is reinventing itself by simply and positively communicating its progress in saving lives from cancer and engaging new members in the fight. To-date, the effort has shown statistically significant increases in awareness and relevance of the Society's mission and is cultivating a new generation of donors and volunteers for this legacy brand.

SITUATION ANALYSIS

For 96 years, the American Cancer Society (ACS) has played a leading role in the fight against cancer. As a major legacy charity brand, the Society enjoys tremendous brand awareness, trust, and a sterling reputation. Yet, in 2007 the Society began to see a decline in understanding of the value it offers. With understanding down and the Society continuing to "get older," young, fresh competitors were generating public support in more contemporary ways. Now was the time to blow the dust off a 100 year-old brand and help people understand what the Society is all about. The plan? Re-position the most recognized cancer brand to 1) create a greater understanding of what the Society does to save lives from cancer, 2) increase emotional connection and relevance among its key audiences, and 3) create a springboard to engage people around the globe who are passionately committed to creating a world with less cancer.

RESEARCH

The case for a brand refresh was clear. In fall 2007, ACS conducted its biennial Image Study that revealed long-standing positives about the brand, but also concerns. Knowledge about the Society decreased with fewer people reporting they knew "a lot" or even "a little" about the organization. That decline threatened ACS's ability to attract donors and volunteers as the data also showed that greater knowledge translated to greater affinity for the organization. Additionally, competition was gaining visibility and traction among the Society's core constituencies.

This prompted an effort to simplify the way the organization expressed its mission. ACS needed a simple, positive way to share the good work it was doing—a value proposition that communicated the progress being made in the fight against cancer and the ways the Society contributed to that fight. That value proposition was clear: the American Cancer Society saves lives by helping people stay well, get well, by finding cures and by fighting back against cancer. In tests, after exposure to the new value proposition, understanding of what the Society did increased an amazing 47 percent among survey respondents. The challenge would now be translating that value proposition into mass-market-friendly terms and sharing it with the Society's primary audience—women.

The Society turned to its new agency partners, Brodeur Partners and The Martin Agency, for guidance on how to reinvent itself among women 35–64. Understanding the need to break through marketplace clutter and make women take notice, the Society and its agencies adopted a bold campaign theme that was truly unexpected— the Official Sponsor of Birthdays—which honed in on the central message of the Society's new value proposition—the ACS saves lives. Qualitative research confirmed that this theme resonated strongly with the target audience. Extensive primary and secondary research conducted by Brodeur Partners revealed key interests and drivers among the target audience which helped to shape campaign activities.

PLANNING

The notion of "a world with more birthdays" gave the Society and agency partners creative leeway to refresh the brand with a fun and unique program. The extensive research on the target audience—both primary and secondary—quickly helped to focus planning. For example, the research revealed that time constraints are a significant barrier for the audience, so involvement had to be easy and convenient. The team also learned that baking is a key interest, and incorporated this into the plan. Because of the Society's limited marketing resources, well-known, and popular personalities were integrated into the campaign to drive maximum exposure.

The Society also focused on making this program relevant to multicultural audiences, particularly African Americans, since this group is disproportionately affected by cancer. Finally, special attention was paid to the Society's extensive internal audiences—its 6,000 staff around the country and its more than 3 million volunteers—to carry the message as its brand ambassadors. The budget for the More Birthdays public relations brand refresh was $1 million/year.

Target Audience Analysis:

The primary audience for the Society has always been women because they have the greatest impact on health, community service and philanthropic decisions in the home. However, the research showed that to gain market share in today's highly competitive nonprofit category, the campaign would have to 1) target women in new ways and 2) reach a younger demographic to keep the donor and volunteer base fresh and engaged.

Objectives

1. Increase knowledge of what the Society does among women 35–64.
2. Increase emotional connection and personal relevance of the Society among women ages 35–64.
3. Spur engagement through a national movement for a world with less cancer and more birthdays.

Strategies

1. Create an army of brand ambassadors through extensive internal communications.
2. Establish the Society as the Official Sponsor of Birthdays.
3. Empower women to prevent and fight cancer by educating them about the breadth of Society resources.

EXECUTION

The campaign, which consists of internal communications, national advertising, earned media, social media, blogger outreach, multicultural communications, and ongoing e-marketing, launched on April 21, 2009.

The campaign

1. Created an army of ambassadors. ACS generated significant excitement among its volunteers and staff nationwide by conducting an exhaustive series of presentations on the new value proposition and campaign theme, as well as a video series that brought the value proposition and birthdays theme to life leading up to campaign launch. The first video of the series that featured ACS CEO Dr. John Seffrin in a birthday hat created tremendous internal buzz and set a record for the Society's most-viewed internal video ever. An e-learning module, viewed by 3,000 staff members, armed them with messaging they could deliver in local communities.

2. Made engagement easy and convenient. Given the increasing amounts of time women spend online, the team created a vibrant "more birthdays" community through interactive and social media tools to make involvement

fun and easy. This included a new website (www.morebirthdays.com), Facebook presence, Twitter feed and blog (officialbirthdayblog.com) that all allow people to join a global movement for more birthdays. Ongoing email marketing with special offers and promotions keeps the members engaged and the movement growing.

3. Established ACS as a birthday expert. To connect ACS to birthdays, the team created a benchmark birthday survey that gauged attitudes and insights about celebrating birthdays, which successfully generated attention from top national consumer press, including *USA Today* and *Prevention Magazine*. This effort also revealed that African Americans place greater emphasis on birthdays than any other racial group, which the team leveraged with earned media efforts. To reinforce the notion that a healthy lifestyle can help prevent cancer, the team launched a national contest to reinvent the birthday cake with the Culinary Institute of America. The contest (judged on "Ace of Cakes" by celebrity chef Duff Goldman) and the winning cake recipe resonated deeply, with hundreds of downloads from the campaign site and winning rave reviews from *The New York Times*, *Glamour*, and *SELF* among many others.

4. Met women where they really are. Because blogging has become a powerful source of connectivity for women, the team recruited a dozen respected female bloggers for the Society's Blogger Advisory Council, aimed to build awareness and activism around the More Birthdays movement online. The Council has driven hundreds of influential blog posts and educated countless women through its Bloggers for More Birthdays initiative. Earned media also focused on reaching women where they get news—online and from women's magazines including *MORE*, *Parents* and *O, The Oprah Magazine*.

These placements complemented campaign ads which also appeared online and in women's magazines. Presence in African American media as well as at events like the Stellar awards, helped to reach women of color. Engaging celebrities such as the cast of ABC's Private Practice in a "Help Blow Out Cancer" media event helped to draw entertainment media attention to the effort. Finally, the team met women on the ground by deploying the More Birthdays Crew in a series of regional events that wish happy birthday to popular people or organizations, like U.S. President Barack Obama on the White House lawn and Matt Lauer and Meredith Vieira on-air on Today that were then merchandised through social media.

EVALUATION

Spurred by more than 300 million earned media impressions (96 percent directly reflect core messages), billions of social networking impressions, a decorated ad campaign, and a legion of internal brand ambassadors, the More Birthdays campaign has created statistically significant increases in knowledge of the Society's mission and personal relevance as measured by a monthly tracking study (see slides). According to the same study, unaided recall among women associating ACS with the Official Sponsor of Birthdays was 44 percent. African American women have responded strongly to the campaign with eight percent greater knowledge of the Society's mission than the general market.

Our core movement members are 54,000 strong—87 percent of whom are women, predominantly (58 percent) between the ages of 35-64, the campaign's target demo. The movement also counts nearly 32,000 members on Facebook, 93 percent of whom are female (45 percent in target demo). A long-term effort, the campaign continues to evolve and grow to build a strong movement for less cancer and more birthdays.

E X H I B I T 13-3A   News Release

American Cancer Society Unveils the Ultimate Online Birthday Destination: morebirthdays.com

Redesigned site features breakthrough group e-card technology, celebrity entertainer phone calls, great gifts, and birthday scheduling tools—all to help fight cancer

ATLANTA – November 29, 2010 – The American Cancer Society, the official sponsor of birthdays, today announced exciting new details of its recently redesigned morebirthdays.com website—the **ultimate online birthday destination**. The new morebirthdays.com features groundbreaking technology and birthday merchandise that make wishing loved ones a "happy birthday" and contributing to the fight against cancer, fun, easy and convenient.

Since September, more than two dozen leading entertainers and artists, including Rihanna, Keith Urban, Lady Antebellum, Justin Bieber, Usher, Eric Carle and Masha D'Yans, have come together to generously donate their talent to support the More Birthdays movement and help the Society create a world with less cancer and more birthdays. The art and "Happy Birthday" music videos have been turned into a variety of birthday products and resources, making morebirthdays.com a one-stop destination for all your birthday needs.

Every custom-created piece of art featured has its roots in an inspirational fact about the role the American Cancer Society plays in fighting the disease, including: the American Cancer Society is the largest private funder of cancer research in the U.S.; nearly 70 percent of America is now covered by smoke-free laws in public spaces; and the American Cancer Society has fought to provide millions of cervical and breast cancer screenings to women who could not afford them. Recently launched birthday resources include:

- **Celebrity Phone Calls**—Want to send your daughter a phone call from Justin Bieber singing her "Happy Birthday?" Visit the new morebirthdays.com and select from a number of music videos, enter a personal message, and then schedule the phone call to be sent on any future date and time for up to one year. Check-out this how-to video from blogger Julie Pippert of Using My Words on why she finds the birthday phone calls to be a great way to send birthday greetings to her loved ones: morebirthdays.com/birthdaydestination.

- **Group Birthday E-Card**—Debuting this week on morebirthdays.com are unique multi-media interactive group e-cards. These enable co-workers, or a group of friends and family who are spread out across the globe, to join together to send a birthday wish to someone special. Each contributor to the group e-card can choose from the wide variety of art and music featured in the birthday gallery, add a personal message, video, or photo, and the final multi-media collection of wishes is sent along to the recipient. As with the musician phone calls, the group e-cards can be created and scheduled for delivery anytime in 2010 or 2011, allowing busy people to never forget a loved one's big day. Check out the new group e-card how-to video launching today featuring Tech Savvy Mama's Leticia Barr at morebirthdays.com/birthdaydestination.

  - The group e-cards and musician phone calls are both free to send, or a user can make a minimum $5 donation to the American Cancer Society. By making a donation, a user turns a birthday wish into a meaningful gift that helps the American Cancer Society save lives.

- **Birthday Dance**—A fun twist on a birthday e-card is the birthday dance. Users upload a photo of their friend or family member to place on the body of an animated dancer. The user then selects from options including the breakdance, moonwalk or disco, adds fun props, and the dance is created. The dance can then be sent by e-mail to the birthday celebrant.

- **Birthday and Holiday Gifts**—For gift seekers, the inspirational art from the campaign that has been inspired by the American Cancer Society's lifesaving work has been turned into prints and limited edition posters. And, for anyone looking to make every gift a gift that gives back, gift wrap featuring the artwork is also available for purchase. Each item purchased or donation made will help the American Cancer Society raise money and save more lives to create a world with less cancer and more birthdays. Also, 100 percent of the proceeds from the sale of items go directly to the American Cancer Society, which helps people stay well, get well, find cures and fight back against cancer.

By sharing the art and music featured on morebirthdays.com, users are helping to spread information about how the American Cancer Society has contributed to progress against cancer. Today and every day, 350 birthdays are being celebrated that would have been otherwise lost to cancer, thanks in part to this progress.

The American Cancer Society invites everyone to visit morebirthdays.com and join these entertainers, artists, and the thousands of supporters who have already joined the movement to create a world with less cancer and more birthdays.

# # #

About the American Cancer Society

The American Cancer Society combines an unyielding passion with nearly a century of experience to save lives and end suffering from cancer. As a global grassroots force of more than three million volunteers, we fight for every birthday threatened by every cancer in every community. We save lives by helping people stay well by preventing cancer or detecting it early; helping people get well by being there for them during and after a cancer diagnosis; by finding cures through investment in groundbreaking discovery; and by fighting back by rallying lawmakers to pass laws to defeat cancer and by rallying communities worldwide to join the fight. As the nation's largest non-governmental investor in cancer research, contributing more than $3.5 billion, we turn what we know about cancer into what we do. As a result, more than 11 million people in America who have had cancer and countless more who have avoided it will be celebrating birthdays this year. To learn more about us or to get help, call us anytime, day or night, at 1-800-227-2345 or visit cancer.org.

Appendix I

Questions for Class Discussion and Case Analysis

The following questions can be used in class discussions of each of the cases in this textbook. Students can gain valuable experience by leading class discussions.

RESEARCH

Does the case give adequate background information about the organization itself? What was the major reason for conducting this program? Was the program proactive or reactive? Which audiences were targeted for communication? Should other audiences have also been targeted? How were research data about each audience obtained? Were the data as complete as necessary? Is there anything unusual about the research phase of this case? What are the research strengths and weaknesses of this case?

OBJECTIVES

Categorize this case's objectives. Which are impact objectives? Specify informational, attitudinal, or behavioral. Which are output objectives? Should they have been more quantitative? Should they have used time frames? Were output objectives used when the ultimate goal was really impact? What is your overall assessment of the objectives used in this case?

PROGRAMMING

Evaluate the theme (if any) used in this case. Is it short, catchy, memorable, to the point? What major message or messages are communicated in this case? Will the messages resonate with the publics identified by your research phase? Evaluate the central actions or special events in this case. Are they truly worthwhile and newsworthy? Are they "pseudoevents"? Was a digital campaign used and appropriate? What emerging communication technology could have been used in the campaign? Evaluate the types of uncontrolled and controlled media that were used. Were any forms of communication omitted that should have been used? Was adequate use made of interpersonal communication? Did the communication achieve a sense of "grassroots involvement" through interpersonal communication, or was there overreliance on mass media publicity placement or impersonal forms of controlled media? Discuss the use of such communication principles as source credibility, salient information, effective nonverbal and verbal cues, two-way communication, opinion leaders, group influence, selective exposure, and audience participation. How effectively were these principles used? Explain.

EVALUATION

Was each of the case's objectives separately evaluated? Describe the evaluative methods used. How appropriate and effective were these methods? Did the program achieve its stated objectives? Was there a real link between the case's objectives and its evaluation?

OVERALL JUDGMENTS

As a whole, how effective was this public relations program? What are its major strengths and major weaknesses? Explain. What are the major PR lessons or principles to be learned from this case? What, if anything, would you do differently if you were assigned a public relations problem like this one?

Appendix II

PRSA Member Code of Ethics 2000[1]

PREAMBLE

Public Relations Society of America

Member Code of Ethics 2000

- Professional Values
- Principles of Conduct
- Commitment and Compliance

This Code applies to PRSA members. The Code is designed to be a useful guide for PRSA members as they carry out their ethical responsibilities. This document is designed to anticipate and accommodate, by precedent, ethical challenges that may arise. The scenarios outlined in the Code provision are actual examples of misconduct. More will be added as experience with the Code occurs.

The Public Relations Society of America (PRSA) is committed to ethical practices. The level of public trust PRSA members seek, as we serve the public good, means we have taken on a special obligation to operate ethically.

The value of member reputation depends upon the ethical conduct of everyone affiliated with the Public Relations Society of America. Each of us sets an example for each other—as well as other professionals—by our pursuit of excellence with powerful standards of performance, professionalism, and ethical conduct.

Emphasis on enforcement of the Code has been eliminated. But, the PRSA Board of Directors retains the right to bar from membership or expel from the Society any individual who has been or is sanctioned by a government agency or convicted in a court of law of an action that is in violation of this Code.

---

1. *PRSA Membership Code of Ethics 2000* reprinted with permission from the Public Relations Society of America, New York, NY.

Ethical practice is the most important obligation of a PRSA member. We view the Member Code of Ethics as a model for other professions, organizations, and professionals.

PRSA MEMBER STATEMENT OF PROFESSIONAL VALUES

This statement presents the core values of PRSA members and, more broadly, of the public relations profession. These values provide the foundation for the Member Code of Ethics and set the industry standard for the professional practice of public relations. These values are the fundamental beliefs that guide our behaviors and decision-making process. We believe our professional values are vital to the integrity of the profession as a whole.

Advocacy

- We serve the public interest by acting as responsible advocates for those we represent.
- We provide a voice in the marketplace of ideas, facts, and viewpoints to aid informed public debate.

Honesty

We adhere to the highest standards of accuracy and truth in advancing the interests of those we represent and in communicating with the public.

Expertise

- We acquire and responsibly use specialized knowledge and experience.
- We advance the profession through continued professional development, research, and education.
- We build mutual understanding, credibility, and relationships among a wide array of institutions and audiences.

Independence

- We provide objective counsel to those we represent.
- We are accountable for our actions.

Loyalty

- We are faithful to those we represent, while honoring our obligation to serve the public interest.

Fairness

- We deal fairly with clients, employers, competitors, peers, vendors, the media, and the general public.

- We respect all opinions and support the right of free expression.

PRSA CODE PROVISIONS

Free Flow of Information

Core Principle.   Protecting and advancing the free flow of accurate and truthful information is essential to serving the public interest and contributing to informed decision making in a democratic society.

Intent

- To maintain the integrity of relationships with the media, government officials, and the public.

- To aid informed decision making.

Guidelines

A member shall:

- Preserve the integrity of the process of communication.

- Be honest and accurate in all communications.

- Act promptly to correct erroneous communications for which the practitioner is responsible.

- Preserve the free flow of unprejudiced information when giving or receiving gifts by ensuring that gifts are nominal, legal, and infrequent.

Examples of Improper Conduct Under This Provision

- A member representing a ski manufacturer gives a pair of expensive racing skis to a sports magazine columnist, to influence the columnist to write favorable articles about the product.

- A member entertains a government official beyond legal limits and/or in violation of government reporting requirements.

Competition

Core Principle.   Promoting healthy and fair competition among professionals preserves an ethical climate while fostering a robust business environment.

Intent

- To promote respect and fair competition among public relations professionals.
- To serve the public interest by providing the widest choice of practitioner options.

Guidelines

A member shall:

- Follow ethical hiring practices designed to respect free and open competition without deliberately undermining a competitor.
- Preserve intellectual property rights in the marketplace.

Examples of Improper Conduct Under This Provision

- A member employed by a "client organization" shares helpful information with a counseling firm that is competing with others for the organization's business.
- A member spreads malicious and unfounded rumors about a competitor in order to alienate the competitor's clients and employees in a ploy to recruit people and business.

Disclosure of Information

Core Principle. Open communication fosters informed decision making in a democratic society.

Intent

- To build trust with the public by revealing all information needed for responsible decision making.

Guidelines

A member shall:

- Be honest and accurate in all communications.
- Act promptly to correct erroneous communications for which the member is responsible.
- Investigate the truthfulness and accuracy of information released on behalf of those represented.
- Reveal the sponsors for causes and interests represented.

- Disclose financial interest (such as stock ownership) in a client's organization.
- Avoid deceptive practices.

Examples of Improper Conduct Under This Provision

- Front groups: A member implements "grass roots" campaigns or letter-writing campaigns to legislators on behalf of undisclosed interest groups.
- Lying by omission: A practitioner for a corporation knowingly fails to release financial information, giving a misleading impression of the corporation's performance.
- A member discovers inaccurate information disseminated via a website or media kit and does not correct the information.
- A member deceives the public by employing people to pose as volunteers to speak at public hearings and participate in "grassroots" campaigns.

Safeguarding Confidences

Core Principle. Client trust requires appropriate protection of confidential and private information.

Intent

- To protect the privacy rights of clients, organizations, and individuals by safeguarding confidential information.

Guidelines

A member shall:

- Safeguard the confidences and privacy rights of present, former, and prospective clients and employees.
- Protect privileged, confidential, or insider information gained from a client or organization.
- Immediately advise an appropriate authority if a member discovers that confidential information is being divulged by an employee of a client company or organization.

Examples of Improper Conduct Under This Provision

- A member changes jobs, takes confidential information, and uses that information in the new position to the detriment of the former employer.

- A member intentionally leaks proprietary information to the detriment of some other party.

Conflicts of Interest

Core Principle. Avoiding real, potential, or perceived conflicts of interest builds the trust of clients, employers, and the publics.

Intent

- To earn trust and mutual respect with clients or employers.
- To build trust with the public by avoiding or ending situations that put one's personal or professional interests in conflict with society's interests.

Guidelines

A member shall:

- Act in the best interests of the client or employer, even subordinating the member's personal interests.
- Avoid actions and circumstances that may appear to compromise good business judgment or create a conflict between personal and professional interests.
- Disclose promptly any existing or potential conflict of interest to affected clients or organizations.
- Encourage clients and customers to determine if a conflict exists after notifying all affected parties.

Examples of Improper Conduct Under This Provision

- The member fails to disclose that he or she has a strong financial interest in a client's chief competitor.
- The member represents a "competitor company" or a "conflicting interest" without informing a prospective client.

Enhancing the Profession

Core Principle. Public relations professionals work constantly to strengthen the public's trust in the profession.

Intent

- To build respect and credibility with the public for the profession of public relations.

- To improve, adapt, and expand professional practices.

Guidelines

A member shall:

- Acknowledge that there is an obligation to protect and enhance the profession.
- Keep informed and educated about practices in the profession to ensure ethical conduct.
- Actively pursue personal professional development.
- Decline representation of clients or organizations that urge or require actions contrary to this Code.
- Accurately define what public relations activities can accomplish.
- Counsel subordinates in proper ethical decision making.
- Require that subordinates adhere to the ethical requirements of the Code.
- Report ethical violations, whether committed by PRSA members or not, to the appropriate authority.

Examples of Improper Conduct Under This Provision

- A PRSA member declares publicly that a product the client sells is safe without disclosing evidence to the contrary.
- A member initially assigns some questionable client work to a non-member practitioner to avoid the ethical obligation of PRSA membership.

Index